Richard Theodore Ely

Socialism

An examination of its nature, its strength and its weakness, withsuggestions for social reform

Richard Theodore Ely

Socialism

An examination of its nature, its strength and its weakness, withsuggestions for social reform

ISBN/EAN: 9783337295202

Printed in Europe, USA, Canada, Australia, Japan

Cover: Foto ©Suzi / pixelio.de

More available books at **www.hansebooks.com**

SOCIALISM

AN

EXAMINATION OF ITS NATURE, ITS STRENGTH
AND ITS WEAKNESS, WITH
SUGGESTIONS

FOR

SOCIAL REFORM

BY

RICHARD T. ELY, Ph.D., LL.D.

Professor of Political Economy and Director of the School of Economics,
Political Science, and History in the University of Wisconsin.

FIFTH THOUSAND.

NEW YORK: 46 East 14th Street
THOMAS Y. CROWELL & CO.
BOSTON: 100 Purchase Street
1895

PREFACE.

Dr. Rudolf Meyer, a conservative German author, published a work some twenty years ago entitled "The Struggle of the Fourth Estate for Emancipation." By the "Fourth Estate" he of course meant the wage-earning classes. At that time Dr. Meyer entertained the hope that the acceptance of a program of social reform would be sufficient to save Germany from social democracy. Germany, however, was not ready to go so far as Dr. Meyer recommended, and the growth of social democracy was in no wise impeded. Germany has done much to improve the conditions of the masses, but she has always moved so late that the masses have received the impression that the action was forced by fear, and did not proceed from a real, sincere desire to benefit the less fortunate portions of the community, especially the wage-earning population. Dr. Meyer has just published another book, entitled "Capitalism, *fin de siècle*." Dr. Meyer maintains that it is now too late for Germany to adopt the program of reform which he urged twenty years ago; and he considers it essential that the public authorities should come to at least a temporary agreement with social democracy, and thus work together for the salvation of Germany from impending perils. He apprehends that Germany must make a choice between state socialism and social democracy, and he fears that social democracy may carry the day.

The United States has now the opportunity which Germany had twenty years ago. It is not by any means too late for us to escape the situation in which Germany finds herself. However it may be in Germany, the policy of social reform is still practicable among us; but we must always bear in mind the high ideals which socialism has placed before the masses of the people, and which they have absorbed. Timid, half-way measures will not stem the tide of socialism.

What are the prospects of this reform which can give us the benefits of peaceful and uninterrupted progress? It is not altogether easy — in fact, it is always difficult — to forecast the future. There is probably no country in which more violent, bitter, and even unprincipled extremes may be found. We have, on the one hand, the anarchists of the poor, who aim to arouse bitterness and hatred, and who shrink from no exercise of force, provided they think that thereby they can accomplish their ends. With them, the torch and the dynamite bomb are questions of expediency.

We have, on the other hand, a class of men who advocate the claims of wealth in precisely the same spirit. Every proposal of reform is greeted by them with ridicule and misrepresentation; every advocate of changes, even in accordance with constitutional and legal means, is villified. These fanatics have precisely the same spirit which animates the anarchists. They would not hesitate to use force to maintain existing privileges, and they would rejoice to see anything like a socialistic reconstruction of society prevented, by torturing and putting to violent death the advocates of socialism. It is the old spirit which has ever greeted the reformer who has advocated changes in behalf of the masses with the cry, "Crucify him! crucify him!" Most fortunately, there is, between these two extreme factions, each of them apparently quite small, a large class of fair-minded, well-meaning men and women, who are the hope of the country. America has been called the land of the "almighty dollar," and it has been supposed to be dominated exclusively by a narrow mercantilism; yet one frequently meets, among the business leaders of the country, with a certain broad-mindedness which is as delightful as it is reassuring. Men of this class are men who will favor mutual concessions and a conciliatory policy.

This book has been written in a conservative spirit. It cannot be understood unless the reader bears in mind that its standpoint is that of conservatism. The peaceful progress of society, with the conservation of the results of past historical development, is the author's desire. He will not, however, be surprised to have the charge of radicalism brought against him. We have among us a class of mammon worshippers, whose one test of conservatism, or radicalism, is the attitude which one takes with respect to accumulated wealth. Whatever tends to the preservation of the wealth of the wealthy is called conservatism, and whatever favors anything else, no matter what, they call socialism. A writer's whole nature may be that of a conservative; he may love the old ways; he may to some extent draw his social ideals from a past which he considers, with respect to its feeling about wealth, saner than the present age, and yet, because he would, by social action, endeavor to change certain tendencies, and to conserve the treasures of the past which he feels threatened by new and startling forces, he is still a radical in the eyes of those men whose one and sole test is money.

The socialist, as well as the non-socialist reader of this

book, must clearly understand that the socialism which is described in its pages is not that of any one school. Many a socialist will take up this book and find missing in it that which he considers essential. What the author tries to do, however, is to give what seems to him the true essence of socialism as an industrial system. He has studied carefully the writings of various socialists, and has stripped off from socialism, as frequently presentëd, those accessories which it seems to him are no part of it. He has given that presentation of socialism which seems to him to contain the greatest strength.

The author desires to express his gratitude to many persons who have most kindly given him assistance of one kind and another. Valuable suggestions and important material have been sent him from different countries, and personal friends have read the proofs. Particular acknowledgment must be made to the following: Prof. William A. Scott, the author's colleague in the University of Wisconsin; Mr. Charles Zeublin, of the University of Chicago; Prof. John R. Commons, of the University of Indiana; Sidney Webb, Esq., and Edward R. Pease, Esq., of the Fabian Society; H. W. Lee, Esq., secretary of the Social Democratic Federation of England; Geoffrey Drage, Esq., of London, secretary of the Royal Commission on Labor; Dr. Heinrich Braun, of

x PREFACE.

Berlin, Editor of the *Archiv für sociale Gesetzgebung und Statistik;* Professor Raphaël-Georges Lévy, Baron Pierre de Coubertin, and Theodore Marburg, Esq., all of Paris; Prof. Charles Gide, of Montpellier, France; Dr. Daniel De Leon, and Lucien Sanial, Esq., of New York; Sylvester Baxter, Esq., of Boston; A. G. Fradenburg, Esq., A. M. Simons, Esq., and Paul Tyner, Esq., all advanced students of the author's classes in the University of Wisconsin.

The author must make special mention of two friends who have given him assistance, unusual both with respect to quantity and quality. These are Prof. David Kinley, of the University of Illinois, who has read the manuscript and proofs with great care, and made many helpful suggestions, and Mrs. Helen Frances Bates, a graduate student of the University of Wisconsin, who has rendered him efficient assistance, particularly in the preparation of the bibliography.

UNIVERSITY OF WISCONSIN, MADISON, WIS.
April 25, 1894.

TABLE OF CONTENTS.

	PAGE
PREFACE	v

PART I.—THE NATURE OF SOCIALISM.

CHAPTER
- I. Socialism in a more General Sense Distinguished from Socialism in a Narrower Sense 3
- II. The Elements of Socialism 9
- III. Definitions of Socialism 19
- IV. The Socialistic State 29
- V Some Misapprehensions Concerning the Nature of Socialism 37
- VI. The Origin of Socialism 50
- VII. The Progress of Socialism 56
- VIII. The Evidences of an Alleged Irresistible Current of Socialism 73
- IX. Socialism Contrasted with other Schemes of Industrial Change 85
- X. The Literature of Socialism 96

PART II.—THE STRENGTH OF SOCIALISM.

CHAPTER
- I. Introductory Remarks 113
- II. The Strength of Socialism as a Scheme of Production 116
- III. The Strength of Socialism as a Scheme for the Distribution and Consumption of Wealth 138
- IV. The Moral Strength of Socialism 145
- V. Socialism as a Promoter of Art 157
- VI. Socialism and Present Problems 162
- VII. Services which the Agitation of Socialism has Rendered 166

PART III. — THE WEAKNESS OF SOCIALISM.

CHAPTER PAGE
I. Introductory 175
II. Alleged, but not Valid, Objections to Socialism . . 181
III. Socialism too Optimistic with Respect to the Future, and too Pessimistic with Respect to the Present . 188
IV. The Danger of the Domination of a Single Industrial Principle, and of the Inevitable Concentration of Dissatisfaction under Socialism 197
V. Socialism a Menace to Liberty 206
VI. Objections to Socialism as a Scheme of Production . 215
VII. Objections to Socialism as a Scheme of Distribution and of Consumption 233
VIII. Other Objections to Socialism 244

PART IV. — THE GOLDEN MEAN, OR PRACTICABLE SOCIAL REFORM.

CHAPTER
I. Introductory 253
II. Socialization of Monopoly 262
III. Socialization of Monopoly, Continued: Natural Monopolies and Present Problems 279
IV. The Socialization of other Natural Monopolies, and the Treatment of Artificial Monopolies 292
V. Land Reform 300
VI. Development of the Social side of Private Property . 306
VII. The Desirability of a Field of Private Industry, but a Narrower one, with a Higher Ethical Level than we now have 314
VIII. Other Reforms calculated to lessen the Disadvantages of Private Industry, and Secure some of the Advantages of Socialism 323
IX. Additional Opportunities for Private Efforts . . . 337
X. Political Reforms 344
XI. Conclusion 350

APPENDIX.

		PAGE
I.	THE ERFURT SOCIAL DEMOCRATIC PROGRAM OF OCTOBER, 1891	357
II.	BASIS OF THE FABIAN SOCIETY	363
III.	PROGRAM OF THE SOCIAL DEMOCRATIC FEDERATION (OF ENGLAND)	365
IV.	MANIFESTO OF THE JOINT COMMITTEE OF SOCIALIST BODIES (OF ENGLAND)	368
V.	PLATFORM OF THE SOCIALIST LABOR PARTY OF THE UNITED STATES OF AMERICA	376
VI.	DECLARATION OF PRINCIPLES OF THE NATIONALISTS	380
VII.	DECLARATION OF PRINCIPLES OF THE SOCIETY OF CHRISTIAN SOCIALISTS, ADOPTED IN BOSTON, APRIL 15, 1889	382
VIII.	PLATFORM OF THE CENTRAL LABOR UNION OF CLEVELAND, OHIO	385
IX.	STATISTICS OF SOCIAL DEMOCRACY IN GERMANY (WITH A CHART SHOWING THE VOTES RECEIVED BY THE FOUR LARGEST POLITICAL PARTIES)	387
X.	SOCIALISM IN FRANCE	390
XI.	BIBLIOGRAPHY	399
INDEX		443

PART I.

THE NATURE OF SOCIALISM.

SOCIALISM AND SOCIAL REFORM.

CHAPTER I.

SOCIALISM IN A MORE GENERAL SENSE DISTINGUISHED FROM SOCIALISM IN A NARROWER SENSE.

THE word socialism, which has come into use in the present century, has already acquired a variety of meanings. It seems necessary to any clear thought that we should, first of all, distinguish between socialism in a large but not altogether vague sense, and socialism in a more technical and more precise sense. Socialism in this large sense frequently has reference, in a general way, to the views and aspirations of those who hold that the individual should subordinate himself to society, maintaining that thus alone can the welfare of all be secured. Socialism in this more general sense implies the rejection of the doctrine of selfishness as a sufficient social force and the affirmation of altruism as a principle of social action. Socialism, in this broad sense of the word, means that society is not a mere aggregation of individuals, but a living, growing organism, the laws of which are something different from the laws of individual action. Aristotle was a socialist in this sense of the word, which, it may be remarked, is a true sense of the word; for he maintained that you never could arrive at the whole by a mere addition of the units comprising it, and consequently that the welfare of society could not be secured through exclusive attention to individual claims. The prosperity of the whole, however, he maintained, implied the prosperity of all the individuals which it includes. In other words, this sage of antiquity thought we must proceed in our treatment of social questions from the standpoint of society, and not from that of the individual.

"The state is, by nature," says Aristotle,[1] "clearly prior to the individual and to the family, since the whole is of necessity prior to the part. . . . The proof that the state is a creation of nature, and prior to the individual, is that the individual, when isolated, is not self-sufficing ; and therefore he is like a part in relation to the whole. But he who is unable to live in society, or who has no need because he is sufficient for himself, must be either a beast or a god."

The great thinkers in economics and politics in all ages have been socialists in this general sense of the word, and opposed to them has been a small sect of individualists, who reject the conception of the state as an organism, and believe that the standpoint of the individual is sufficient, both in science and in practice. Two definitions of socialism, as here understood, may be helpful to the reader. The first is taken from an address on Socialism by Dr. Westcott, the present bishop of Durham. It is used to describe, as the author says, not merely a theory of economics, but a theory of life, and is given in the following words : —

"Individualism regards humanity as made up of disconnected or warring atoms. Socialism regards it as an organic whole. . . . The aim of socialism is the fulfilment of service ; the aim of individualism is the attainment of some personal advantage — riches, place, or fame. Socialism seeks such an organization of life as shall secure for every one the most complete development of his

[1] Aristotle's Politics, Book I., 2, §§ 12–14.

powers; individualism seeks primarily the satisfaction of the particular wants of each one, in the hope that the pursuit of private interests will, in the end, secure public welfare."

And further on in the same address Dr. Westcott asserts that "the goal of human endeavor is the common well-being of all alike, sought through conditions which provide for the fullest culture of each man as opposed to the special development of a race or a class, by the sacrifice of others in slavery or serfdom, or necessary subjection;" and he speaks of this as the central idea of socialism. He maintains, however, that "it does not follow that the end can be reached only in one way."

Socialism is then not restricted necessarily to state activity, but it becomes equivalent to affectionate regard for others in society, and the systematic attempt to improve others. It is used as the opposite of individualism, which then means a selfish and inconsiderate exaltation of the individual.

The second definition of socialism to which reference is made, is that given by Prof. Adolph Wagner, the celebrated professor of political economy in the University of Berlin. Defining socialism in a more general sense as the opposite of individualism, he says: —

"It is, therefore, a principle which regulates social and economic life according to the needs of society as a whole, or which makes provision for the satisfaction of those needs, whereas, individualism is a principle which, in social and economic life, places the individual in the foreground, takes the individual as a starting-point, and makes his interests and wishes the rule for society."

The use of the word socialism in the large sense just described is a legitimate one, for it serves to designate a class of thinkers, and to distinguish them from those who hold very different views. Socialism and individualism are two different philosophical systems. The only objection to the use of the word socialism to designate that social philosophy which is contrasted with individualism in the broadest sense, is that socialism has a narrower meaning, to be described presently, which has become prevalent. Thus, if a writer declares, "I am a socialist!" he is more likely to be classed with Karl Marx than with Aristotle.

The word socialism has, however, other general uses which seem to be altogether wanting in any scientific precision of meaning, and which should therefore be rejected. It is employed to designate in such a vague manner a tendency or attitude of mind, that it lacks all metes and bounds. It has, for example, even been used to designate the thoughts and efforts of those who concern themselves with social affairs. Manifestly, in this sense, it would include a large amount of the individualistic as well as the socialistic philosophy. One writer[1] has called socialism the economic philosophy of the suffering classes. Doubtless he himself would not claim for this statement the character of a scientific definition; for socialism is not the only economic philosophy which has been or may be embraced by those spoken of as the suffering classes. We might likewise call anarchy, or voluntary co-operation, or Mr. Henry George's single tax, the economic philosophy of the suffering classes. The radical improvement of the lot of the propertyless majority has been declared to be the material content of socialism. In addition to the objections already urged to the previous statement, it may be said that it is not necessary to view socialism as a class problem, although it must be

[1] Dr. von Scheel.

admitted that it is so viewed by most social democrats in Germany. Socialism may be advocated by an artist from the artistic standpoint, or by a theologian from a religious standpoint. The true aim of the best socialism, it seems to the writer, is that general social amelioration which proposes to sacrifice no class, but to improve and elevate all classes. It does not necessarily mean the abolition of classes, although under any system of socialism other class distinctions would prevail than those which now obtain.

While each honest and careful definition of socialism tells us something, there is a whole class of definitions which must be simply rejected as dishonest.

For example, when one says that socialism is that system which swallows up individual liberty, subordinating entirely the individual to society, it is plain that the so-called definition is no definition, but a condemnation of that which is to be defined. Then there are certain popular and inaccurate ideas which need not occupy our time. There are those who call any general social upheaval and widespread turning things upside down, socialism, although this upheaval manifestly may be as well anti-socialistic as socialistic. Then there are those — and we meet them very commonly — who call whatever they regard as an exaggeration of the social principle, socialism, especially if it takes the form of state activity. Thus, whether the ordinary man calls the government ownership and management of the telegraph socialism or not, will depend upon whether he approves it or not. That kind of governmental activity which is not liked by any particular person is apt to be called by that person socialism. Manifestly we can make no progress in scientific discussion with such vague and unscientific ideas.

The word socialism, as generally employed, has a far narrower meaning than socialism in the broad sense already described. It calls to mind an industrial society which, in its main features, is sufficiently clear and precise. It is not a theory which embraces all departments of social activity, but is confined to the economic department,[1] dealing with others simply as connected with this and influenced by it. This socialism is frequently designated as "scientific socialism." It is with this socialism, which presents a theory of industrial society based upon radical social reconstruction, that the present work deals.

[1] Cf. Prof. Anton Menger's work, Das Recht auf den vollen Arbeitsertrag, p. 2.

CHAPTER II.

THE ELEMENTS OF SOCIALISM.

Socialism, when analyzed, is found to embrace four main elements. The first of these is the common ownership of the material instruments of production. It is not stated precisely how this common ownership is to be brought about, or exactly what form it is to take. Opinions may and do differ about the practical steps which are to be taken to secure the desired end, and also about the nature of the collective organization in which this ownership is to be vested. But no one can be called a socialist in the modern technical sense who does not accept the doctrine of the common ownership of the material instruments of production. The collectivity, that is, society as a whole, is to take the place of individuals and private associations of individuals as owners of land and capital, in order that the advantages of ownership may accrue to the whole, and not merely to a part of the whole. The private receipt of rent and interest in the economic sense then ceases, for rent and interest are the remuneration of ownership.

It is not difficult to understand what this postulate of socialism, namely, the socialization of the material instruments of production, means. It is simply necessary to exercise one's imagination, and to picture to one's self the extension of that which already exists in a comparatively small way. The post-office in the United States is already socialized. It is owned by the people as a whole, and all share in many ways in the advantages of this common ownership. The telegraph in most countries is a part of the post-office, and it is owned by the collectivity. Railways in many countries are public, not private property. Forests are to a considerable extent collective property. All these kinds of wealth are instruments of production; and if that process which has made of these instruments collective property is continued until substantially all the land and all the capital have been socialized, we shall have realized the first demand of socialism.

It is said *substantially* all land and capital, because it is held that it is not necessary that the common ownership should be absolutely all-inclusive. It is a weakness of the extremists to insist on all — inclusiveness in common ownership, which much damages their cause. What is necessary is that the collective ownership should become dominant in such manner as to control all other ownership and confine it within narrow limits. All the great instruments of production, like telegraphs, telephones, railways, forests, arable lands, and large manufacturing plants, must become collective property; but socialism does not imply that it is necessary to restrict individuals in the acquisition of the instruments of production on a small scale, — for example, a wheelbarrow or a cart. Socialism, then, presented in the strongest form, does not proceed so much negatively as constructively. Society is to acquire the instruments of production; but individuals, for the most part, are not to be restrained, except indirectly, by positive social action.

Emphasis has been laid by repetition upon the word *material* as qualification of the instruments of production. This means that man is excluded. For the socialist claims that under socialism man will, for the first time, become free. Man has, in times past, been owned as a slave, and the socialists claim that the wage-earner is even now a wage-slave, and their purpose is to free man.

Attention must be called, also, to the statement that it is the material *instruments of production* which are to be owned in common, and not all wealth. That wealth which is not designed for further production can still remain private property under socialism. This means wealth used for enjoyment rather than for production; for example, the furniture of one's house, family plate, heirlooms of all sorts, pictures, books, clothing, and many other forms of wealth which can easily be enumerated. The ground for the distinction becomes obvious enough on reflection. The design of socialism is the abolition of the private receipt of rent and interest. It desires to abolish private property only in so far as it enables one to gather an income through the toil of others without personal exertions; for that the socialists call levying a tribute upon the labor of others.

The second element in socialism is the common management of production. Not only are the material instruments of production to be owned in common, but they are to be managed by the collectivity, in order that to the people as a whole may accrue all the benefits of management; that is, all those gains of enterprise called profits, as distinguished from interest, and in order that the management may be conducted in accordance with the public need, rather than in accordance with the advantage of private captains of industry. Production is to be carried on to satisfy our wants for material things, and not for the sake of private profits. The distinction is undoubtedly a marked one. Production now ceases when those who manage it are unable to derive profits therefrom. This is a necessity under modern or capitalistic production; but under a socialistic *régime*, production is not stopped so long as wants clamor for satisfaction, and until all wants are satisfied there can, of course, be no real over-production. The distinction between common ownership and common management, that is, management by representatives of the people responsible to the people, is made clear in a moment by one or two simple illustrations. Railways have been sometimes owned by the people in their collective capacity, and operated by a private company. There are those, indeed, who advocate common ownership of all the railways in the United States, with private operation. Land which is owned by the collectivity is frequently cultivated by private individuals. What socialism wants, then, is not merely common ownership, but also a common or collective management.

This common management of production means that the collectivity must furnish work for all who desire it. As the socialistic state assumes the charge of production, leaving only very minor functions to individuals, it rests upon it, of course, to make the industrial society all-inclusive. Indeed, the possibility of socialism once granted, there can be no difficulty about this. Every one is naturally assigned to some function which will make him socially useful; and the problem of the unemployed is inconceivable, as production is no longer conducted for exchange, but for consumption, and the greater the production the more ample will be the means for the satisfaction of all wants. Should it be possible at any moment to produce more than men really desire to consume, it would merely be necessary to shorten the length of the working day. It would not only be true, however, that all could find work, but all would have to work, as, with common ownership, the possibility of income without personal exertion would be cut off. How many could find employment in private service, it is not easy to say. Under socialism, we should expect a social organization of medical attendance and the supply of medicines, which would be simply carrying further tendencies already at work; and yet some might prefer to employ private physicians. Should the members of the socialistic society be willing to give part of their income in return for private medical services, there is no reason why they should be hindered in so doing. Similarly, religious services might be maintained by private contributions, and in the churches there could be large numbers of preachers outside of public employment. Possibly, also, room could be found for remunerative employment, of a private character, of a great many persons in the aggregate, who would concern themselves with the smaller branches of production. Yet, if socialism works as well as it is claimed it will, there would naturally be a preference, altogether apart from any compulsion, for public employment. We see that great public hospitals, at the present time, encroach somewhat on the individual practice of physicians, and that public schools, in many places, drive out private schools, although the law interposes no obstacles in the way of their success.

The third element is the distribution of income by the common authority; that is, the income of society, or the national dividend, as it is frequently called: and it is that part of the wealth produced by society which may be used for enjoyment, after the material instruments of production have been maintained and suitably improved and extended. The common ownership and management of the material instruments of production necessarily results in ownership of the national dividend by the collectivity, in the first instance, just as now those who own and manage industry have the ownership of the products of industry, and from these products satisfy the claims of those who have participated in their production. It remains for the collectivity to distribute all the wealth produced for consumption among all the members of society.

As there is provision of work for all in the public service, so there must be provided an income for all. But this provision of income for all reaches even further than the ranks of the toilers. There must always be in society some who are physically or mentally incapable of toil, and socialism contemplates the provision of an income for these also. The idea of socialism in this respect is that of mutual insurance. We are all insured from our birth against contingencies incapacitating us from earning a livelihood; and provision is made for the satisfaction of our wants, even if we cannot render a personal return.

We are now brought face to face with what we may, perhaps, call the chief purpose of socialism; namely, distributive justice. While socialists have desired to bring about a better industrial organization to increase wealth, and while they even lay emphasis upon the vast additions to the national dividend which, according to them, socialism would bring, it can scarcely be too much to say that almost, if not quite invariably, considerations concerning justice in distribution have given them their initiative.

Yet what is justice in distribution? While all agree that the present distribution is unjust, wide differences of opinion exist as to what is, after all, that justice in distribution which is to be the aim of the new society. A learned jurist, and at the same time an avowed socialist, claims that the socialistic schemes of distribution may be divided into two classes; namely, distribution which aims to satisfy needs, and distribution which aims to accord to each one the full product of his toil. This would hardly seem to be sufficient to cover all socialistic plans of distribution, and perhaps it is better to approach the subject from a somewhat different standpoint. We can distinguish at least four schemes of distributive justice. One is the distribution which aims to secure absolute mechanical equality, that is, equality in quantity and kinds of goods. All must have food, clothing, shelter, education, and, in fact, all good things, so far as this is possible, in like quality and quantity. If distinctions in clothing are made for age and sex, this is the most which can be tolerated.[1] Emphasis is laid upon the equality to be carried out in all details — equality is the aim and end of this sort of distribution. A later idea of distributive justice is that which apportions reward to merit. It has been proposed that society should be organized in hierarchical form, and that in this hierarchically organized industrial society positions should be assigned according to capacity, the highest positions going to the greatest capacity; and that reward should be in proportion to capacity. There could thus be room for quite as many gradations in

[1] This was the view of Baboeuf. See the author's French and German Socialism, where the other views of distribution are also described.

society as at present, but their basis would be personal, and not inherited rank or property.[1] A still later idea of distributive justice is that which assigns the product in proportion to needs, recognizing the inequality of needs, while calling upon each one to render service in proportion to his strength of body and mind. Double strength, then, means double duty, but no greater claim on that account upon the national dividend; for the larger claim upon the national dividend must be based simply upon greater need.[2] The fourth idea of distributive justice, and that which seems now to prevail generally among the more active socialists, is equality of income; not a mechanical equality, but an equality in value.

Each one, according to this idea, is to receive an equal value as his income; but these values may be represented by goods and services the most diverse. There are those who claim that this last distribution accords both with the demand that distribution shall be according to needs, and that it should accord to each one the full product of his toil. For they hold that equal values will enable every one to satisfy all rational needs, and that the services of all who participate in production, according to their strength have substantially equal value. But whatever idea in regard to distributive justice is once adopted, society is to carry it out.

The fourth element in socialism is private property in the larger proportion of income. It thus becomes at once apparent that modern socialism does not propose to abolish private property. Quite the contrary. Socialism maintains that private property is necessary for personal freedom and the full development of our facul-

---

[1] This was the view of the St. Simonians.
[2] Louis Blanc's idea of distributive justice.

ties. The advantages of private property are claimed by the advocates of the existing social order as arguments for its maintenance; but socialism asserts that society, as at present constituted, is unable to secure to each one the private property which he requires. Socialism proposes to extend the institution of private property in such manner as to secure to each individual in society property in an annual income, which shall be, so far as practicable, sufficient to satisfy all rational wants, and to protect all from those attacks upon personal freedom which proceed from the dependence of man upon man. The instruments of production do not exist for their own sake, but for the sake of products for consumption, which again have as their destination man's needs. Now, while private property in the instruments of production is to be reduced to its lowest terms, it is to be extended and strengthened in the products for the sake of which the instruments exist.

Attention must be called to the expression, "the larger proportion of income." Income is derived from the use of property. Even at present the amount of property enjoyed in common is in the aggregate large. Public parks, public galleries, public schools, public highways, are illustrations which readily occur to one. All these institutions yield an income enjoyed freely by all in proportion to needs and capacities; for income as just stated means use or enjoyment. We have at the present time in the United States, in these things, something which may be called true communism. Naturally, under socialism, as the thoughts of men would be more directed to the common welfare, and the inclination of men to enjoy things in common would be greatly strengthened, there would be a very large increase in the number of things enjoyed in common, and thus yielding a common income. Public libraries would unquestionably be greatly increased; and while no sane socialist would propose to prohibit private ownership of libraries, a great increase in public libraries might perhaps diminish the desire to have private libraries. Possibly the same would be true with regard to galleries of art and museums; and it could not fail to be true with respect to grounds for pleasure and recreation. There would be thus a use of more things than at present in common; and thus there would be an absolute increase, and probably also a relative increase, in the common income, and private income would be correspondingly diminished. There is a tendency, even at the present time, to increase very considerably the number and importance of those things that are enjoyed in common; and socialism would simply carry further this tendency and accelerate it. Nevertheless, the greater proportion of the national dividend would, even as at present,.still be private income.

CHAPTER III.

DEFINITIONS OF SOCIALISM.

It is well to give especial attention to definitions in any subject that belongs to moral or political philosophy, because definitions give us the central ideas of their authors. A few significant definitions of socialism, in the narrow sense with which this work is concerned, will be given in the present chapter, in order, on the one hand, that the reader may contrast these definitions with the analysis of socialism given in the preceding chapter; and on the other, that he may, by comparison, see the points most significant in the program of socialism as they present themselves to the minds of different persons.

First of all, the results of the analysis of socialism may be brought together in a definition which would read somewhat as follows : *Socialism is that contemplated system of industrial society which proposes the abolition of private property in the great material instruments of production, and the substitution therefor of collective property; and advocates the collective management of production, together with the distribution of social income by society, and private property in the larger proportion of this social income.*

Two of the most noteworthy writers on socialism who are not themselves socialists are Dr. Schäffle, whose works, " The Quintessence of Socialism" and " The Impossibility of Social Democracy," have attracted so much attention, and Professor Adolph Wagner, who has so successfully attempted the utilization of the results of socialistic thought, without the acceptance of anything like its entire program. Both these writers have given definitions of socialism which well deserve attention. That of Dr. Schäffle is given in a description of the real aim of socialism, and reads as follows: —

"To replace the system of private capital (that is, the speculative method of production, regulated on behalf of society only by the free competition of private enterprises), by a system of collective capital, that is by a method of production which would introduce a unified (social or 'collective') organization of national income on the basis of collective or common ownership of the means of production by all the members of the society. This collective method of production would remove the present competitive system, by placing under official administration such departments of production as can be managed collectively (socially or co-operatively), as well as the distribution among all of the common products of all, according to the amount and social utility of the productive labor of each."

The contrast carried through this definition between socialism and the present social order should be particularly noticed. The definition is complicated, but when it is analyzed it will be found to contain the elements described in the preceding chapter. Perhaps it is defective in the statement that socialism proposes to place under official administration such departments of production as can be managed collectively, without stating directly that socialism maintains the possibility of a collective management substantially of all production. The definition may also be considered faulty because it carries with it one particular idea of distributive justice; namely, distribution according to services, and, as we have already seen, this is not the only idea of distributive justice known to socialism.

Professor Wagner gives the following definition of socialism in the narrower or more special sense: —

"Extreme socialism, or the modern scientific, economic socialism, is a system of economic legal order opposed to the present order. Socialism demands that the material means of production, that is, land and capital, should not be, as at present, mostly the private property of single private members of the social body, but should be the collective property of society itself; that, consequently, private undertakings designed to secure profit should not stand on one side, and wage-earners, paid according to the conditions of the labor-contract, on the other, these various undertakings and wage-earners competing with one another; that production should not be conducted by individual capitalistic managers according to their individual estimate of demand, which means, on the whole, an unregulated production dependent upon the course of speculation and the influences of chance, and that the distribution of the product should take place according to the accidents of the law of supply and demand. Socialism requires, on the contrary, that production should take place according to plans based upon the carefully ascertained demand of the consumers, and that it should be duly regulated by public authority; that it should be carried on in a co-operative manner, or in state and municipal institutions, etc., and that the product should be divided among the producers in a juster manner than at present, when the distribution is effected by means of the law of demand and supply."

This definition adds something to our previously ascertained ideas of socialism. The first words, "extreme socialism, or modern, scientific economic socialism," are worthy of note. The socialism popularly agitated is pronounced extreme, and is opposed by implication to a more conservative socialism; namely, socialism in the larger, but, after all, truer sense. The second point to which attention is called by this definition, is the scientific character of even this extreme socialism. Modern socialism is by implication contrasted with the more or less fantastic schemes of earlier writers; and it is frankly admitted that socialism, even in the special sense, has been placed upon a scientific basis by thinkers like Rodbertus-Jagetzow, Friedrich Engels, and Karl Marx. The third noteworthy point in the definition under consideration is that which describes socialism as a legal order. The problems involved are largely problems of law. Although it may be going too far to declare that socialism is chiefly, if not exclusively, a question for the jurist,[1] it is undoubtedly true that, like other economic questions, it has not been adequately treated on the side of law. This definition, like the preceding one, carries through it a contrast between socialism and the present industrial order, and brings out some of the weaker points of the latter. The unsystematic, irregular, hap-hazard character of present production is placed over against the social regulation of social production. Under socialism it is proposed, according to this definition, carefully to ascertain the quantities of things of all kinds needed by the members of the social organism, and to produce them regularly in the most scientific manner, as a result of which, it is held, irregularities in production, crises, and industrial stagnation can be avoided. Social control thus replaces chance. It is not stated exactly how products are to be distributed, but it is merely said that the distribution aims to approximate absolute justice more nearly than the present system.

[1] This is claimed by Prof. Anton Menger in his work, "Das Recht auf den vollen Arbeitsertrag."

DEFINITIONS OF SOCIALISM. 23

We now pass over to definitions given by avowed socialists, and it is worth while to devote some attention to several of these. Among those who belong to the socialists there is, perhaps, no one more conservative than Mr. Thomas Kirkup, in whose book, "An Inquiry Into Socialism," the following statement is found:—

> "The essence of socialism is this: it proposes that industry be carried on by associated laborers jointly owning the means of production (land and capital). Whereas industry is at present conducted by private and competing capitalists served by wage labor, it must in the future be carried on by associated labor, with a collective capital, and with a view to an equitable system of distribution" (pp. 11 and 12).

Emphasis is laid on the ownership of the means of production by the collective workers, and Mr. Kirkup elsewhere expressly states that it is a principle which may be partially realized, even on a small scale. While a general system is the aim of socialism, he would not refuse the name of socialism to a co-operative society of workers owning the means of production and carrying on an enterprise on their own account, even under present conditions.

Mr. Bellamy, the founder of the school of socialism called nationalism, declares that "industrial self-government is a very convenient and accurate definition of nationalism." The central thought in socialism, according to Mr. Bellamy, would seem to be democracy in industry. At the present time, while we have democracy in politics, we have in industry a system to which, for the most part, we may properly apply the term despotism. Industry is controlled by the capitalist, and the worker must submit to his commands or quit his service, just as the alternative of obedience to the laws of the Czar is emigration.

The despotic principle in industry, while zealously maintained as desirable by many, is held by socialists to be pernicious; and with Mr. Bellamy they generally declare that political democracy cannot be permanently maintained, unless it is based on economic democracy.

The Nationalists, in their Declaration of Principles, adopted early in their history, did not attempt any formal definition of nationalism; but declared that they wished to substitute a system based on the principle of association for "a system founded on the brute principle of competition."

Perhaps no society of socialists includes in its membership a larger number of highly educated men than the Fabian Society of England. One of its members, Mr. William Clarke, defines a socialist as "one who believes that the necessary instruments of production should be held and organized by the community, instead of by individuals, or groups of individuals, within or outside of the community."[1]

Another Fabian, Mr. Graham Wallas, implies a definition of socialism in his statement that "Socialists work for the owning of the means of production by the community and the means of consumption by individuals."[2]

This society issues a program, in which it is stated that, as it consists of socialists, it aims "at the reorganization of society by the emancipation of land and industrial capital from individual and class ownership, and the vesting of them in the community for the general benefit." It is added that "the society works for the transfer to the community of the administration of such

[1] *Political Science Quarterly*, December, 1888, article "Socialism in English Politics."
[2] Fabian Essays, p. 133.

industrial capital as can conveniently be managed socially." Elsewhere in the writings of the Fabians it is plainly stated that practically *all* industrial capital can conveniently be managed socially.

The Social Democratic Federation of England, a body pursuing, perhaps, methods more popular than those of the Fabian Society, and resembling more closely the social democracy of Germany, states that its object is "The socialization of the means of production, distribution, and exchange, to be controlled by a democratic state in the interests of the entire community, and the complete emancipation of labor from the domination of capitalism and landlordism, with the establishment of social and economic equality between the sexes." A new feature of this statement — which carries with it a definition of socialism — is that it brings out the demand for social and economic equality between the sexes; a demand made by practically all socialistic societies.

A French socialist by the name of Lafargue, a son-in-law of Karl Marx, gives a definition which brings out clearly the thought of the latter, that socialism comes as a result of a natural evolution, and not as the result of man's determination to replace the present social order by a better. He says: "Socialism is not the system of any reformer whatever; it is the doctrine of those who believe that the existing system is on the eve of a fatal economic evolution which will establish collective ownership in the hands of organizations of workers, in place of the individual ownership of capital. Socialism is of the character, therefore, of an historical discovery." [1]

[1] This definition was given in the *New Nation* of March 5, 1892. It appeared originally in the French paper *Le Figaro*, which had offered a prize of one hundred francs for the best definition of socialism. This was one of the six hundred competing definitions.

The claim may, perhaps, be made for the social democratic party of Germany by its friends, that it has developed beyond the stage of definitions. It issues, however, a platform in which is traced the evolution which it is maintained will inevitably issue in socialism, by which is meant social ownership of the means of production, special mention being made of the soil, quarries, mines, raw material, tools, machines, and the means of transportation; and it is stated that production must be carried on by and for society. The doctrine is also brought out in the program that socialism implies of necessity a class struggle, and that the emancipation of the working-class must be achieved by the wage-earners, in opposition to all other classes.

When one understands what socialism means, it cannot be difficult to define the adjective socialistic, which at present is generally used in such an altogether vague and indefinite manner. That line of policy is properly designated "socialistic" which tends to bring about socialism. Manifestly, then, not all government activity can be called socialistic. If the purpose or the spirit of the activity in question is to render the collectivity dominant in the economic sphere, then it must be designated as socialistic; otherwise, not. Those have studied socialism to little purpose who imagine that the socialist approves of all activity of government whatsoever, and that he is ready to indorse any plan which will enlarge the functions of government. As a matter of fact, it is probable that socialists disapprove of nine projects out of ten calculated to enlarge the sphere of government, which are brought forward, nevertheless, by some party or faction. They would disapprove of much of this legislation, because they think it not likely to accomplish the end which its advocates have in view; and a great deal of it receives their condemnation because it reveals a directly anti-socialistic spirit. Much legislation is designed to foster and build up private industry. Naturally, all this is rejected by socialism. Subsidies and grants to private enterprise are anti-socialistic, because their purpose is to bolster up that which socialism disapproves. Bonuses given for the establishment of manufacturing plants are anti-socialistic. It is said that the financial disturbances in the Argentine Republic a few years ago could be traced, in part at least, to government activity. It was stated by a United States consul that "Instead of limiting the government to the doing of the work for which all governments are instituted among men, it is notorious that the late government authorities made use of its credit to promote enterprises which should have been left to individual enterprise; to assist particular schemes which should have remained in the hands of private parties; to float free banks all over the country based on a paper capital, and thus flood the avenues of trade with depreciated banknotes; to loan money or issue cedulas on bond and mortgage." A governmental activity of this sort has been condemned as "socialistic;" but it is nearly all directly contrary to the spirit of socialism. Excessive grants of pensions have also been connected by writers and speakers with the spirit of socialism, whereas, as a matter of fact, the socialists have been strongly opposed to the whole pension system in this country.

There is a governmental activity of a different sort, which is regarded by some as socialistic and by others as anti-socialistic. Whether it is the one or the other must depend on the view which is taken of its probable outcome. Public education is advocated by many because it is thought that it tends to prepare men better for the existing society, and thus to defend society against revolutionary proposals. If one is to take such a view, then one would say that this governmental activity is anti-socialistic. If, however, one takes the view that popular education is designed to awaken a general discontent, which must lead to socialism, or that its purpose is to prepare men for socialism, then one must hold that it is socialistic. It is much to be desired that a more careful use of the word socialistic should take the place of its present loose use.

CHAPTER IV.

THE SOCIALISTIC STATE.

WE cannot understand socialism unless we give careful attention to the attitude which socialists take with respect to the state. It is in respect to this attitude that socialists differ among themselves, perhaps as widely as in regard to any doctrine.

We can conceive of a socialism which would imply simply the present state, enlarged in such a manner that it would include within its functions the production and distribution of wealth. It might be said, however, in general, that no active socialist would approve of this kind of socialism, because socialists do not view the present state altogether with favor. Some socialists desire to change the existing state in minor matters, while others wish to alter it radically, and are inclined to oppose anything likely to strengthen it. The German social democrats take the latter attitude with respect to the state. They, indeed, go so far as to say that they desire the abolition of the state. But it must be borne in mind that they use the word state, as they do " capital," and many other terms, in a technical sense peculiar to themselves. When they say that they desire to abolish the state, they have in mind the state which stands for a class, and which promotes the interests of that class by repressive measures designed to keep down the other classes while they are exploited.

The German social democrats are not only socialists,

they are also democrats, and they live in a state which is anything but democratic. They fear the present state, and they look with little favor, or with positive opposition, upon plans to extend its economic functions. This is what they mean by their opposition to state socialism. State socialism means to correct the wrongs and advance the interests of the masses by economic measures, but does not regard it as necessary to change radically the political constitution of the state. The social democrats of Germany, at their convention in 1892, consequently felt called upon to denounce state socialism as conservative, while declaring that social democracy was a revolutionary force. Their opposition to the state is like their opposition to state socialism. They define the state as "an organized power for the maintenance of the actually existing social relations of property and class domination." The socialistic state to which they look forward — one which will recognize no class interests, but will promote the interests of all equally — is held by them to be something so different that it cannot be properly called a state. Their talk, then, about the abolition of the state implies a doctrine not only with respect to future social organization, but also with respect to the existing state.

The English Fabians and the American socialists do not talk about the abolition of the state; and when a socialist in England or the United States indulges in such talk, it may safely be taken for granted that he stands under foreign, particularly German, influence. This is natural enough, because the political constitution of the state in each of these countries is more democratic, and can be more readily made to serve the interests of the masses without radical political changes.

All active agitators of socialism want a democratic state, because they wish that control of the collectivity over the economic life should be exercised in behalf of the masses. They are all not merely socialists, but democrats, although they do not find it everywhere equally necessary to lay emphasis upon their democracy. Nevertheless, we find all socialists advocating political changes; and it may be said that the country whose political institutions they view with most favor is Switzerland. We may mention two institutions found in Switzerland which meet with almost, if not quite, universal approval; namely, the referendum, compelling, under certain circumstances, the reference of laws to the people for acceptance or rejection; and the initiative, giving to a prescribed number of people the right to propose laws, which must be submitted to the people as a whole for acceptance or rejection. Proportional representation is a third political reform which meets with general favor on the part of socialists. As is well known, this proposes the election of legislators on a general ticket, with such arrangements that parties and factions would have a representation in proportion to the number of votes which they cast. One-tenth of the people could thus, by cumulating their votes, have one representative. The reason why the socialists favor these measures is because they tend to keep government in the hands of the people.

It is for the same reason that all socialists are working for the decentralization of government. They look upon the present state as too highly centralized. They wish to transfer functions from central governments to local political units, in order that the business of the people may be near the people. It is so far from being the truth that they favor centralization, that most of them go to what would ordinarily be called extreme lengths in opposition to centralization, and in advocacy of measures which may build up the local political unit. Local self-government, even of an extreme form, is a watchword among them.

The following two quotations from the Fabian socialists are typical, and indicate a general attitude of socialists in all countries : —

"The division of the country into clearly defined areas, each with its elected authority, is essential to any effective scheme of organization. It is one of the signs of the coming age that, in perfect unconsciousness of the nature of his act, Mr. Ritchie has established the commune. He has divided England into districts ruled by county councils, and has thus created the machinery without which socialism was impracticable." [1]

"At present the state machine has practically broken down under the strain of spreading democracy, the work being mainly local, and the machinery mainly central. Without efficient local machinery the replacing of private enterprise by state enterprise is out of the question." [2]

Still a third socialist speaks of the formation of a definite socialist party as identical with "a party pledged to the communalization of all the means of production and exchange."

The function of a national government in socialism is held to be a federalization of municipalities, and the equalization of their natural advantages, possibly by a system of taxation to yield the funds for general expenses.

When one reflects upon the extreme position in favor

---

[1] Annie Besant, Fabian Essays, pp. 152-3.
[2] G. Bernard Shaw, Fabian Essays, p. 187.

of local self-government, taken very generally by socialists, one cannot help wondering whether adequate provision has been made for those businesses which must be organized on a national scale, like railways and telegraphs. The tendency of socialistic thought, however, it may be said, is one which lays increasing emphasis upon municipalization rather than nationalization of industry. The nationalists in the United States may, perhaps, be regarded as an exception. They speak about the nationalization of industry; and one of their leaders says that, "Nationalism has given American socialism a distinctively national cast, as socialism in France has assumed a distinctively communal cast." At the same time, the special activity of the nationalists has been devoted to measures designed to increase the powers of the local political unit; and the writer, just quoted, adds to his remarks about the national cast of American socialism the statement: "Nationalism has, to a very great extent, promoted the development of interest in enlarged municipal functions, as witness the nationalist agitation for a municipal lighting law in Massachusetts." It would seem, then, that the American socialists known as nationalists, after all, fall in with the general socialistic tendency to favor especially the upbuilding of local self-government.

Equally characteristic of the socialism of to-day is the general desire, on the part of socialists, to reduce the functions of government to a minimum. There is a general agreement among them that there should be as little government as is compatible with their main ends. They all favor whatever government or regulation is necessary to secure the socialistic production and distribution of wealth; and they will indorse all those measures which are held to be necessary to guarantee opportunities to all, for the full development of all their faculties. But beyond this they will not go, and they continually seek to devise plans for the accomplishment of these ends with the least possible exercise of governmental authority.[1] It can safely be said that, outside the educational and economic spheres, they advocate a general *laissez faire*, or non-interference policy. The state church, for example, is not of necessity incompatible with socialism; but, as a matter of fact, socialist parties invariably oppose anything of the kind; and the German social democrats, in their platform, expressly declare religion to be a private matter. Socialists sometimes say what they desire is not a government of men by men, but an administration of things. Some of them hope that what they call administration may take the place altogether of government, by which they evidently mean repressive measures designed to control individuals.

Friedrich Engels, who with Karl Marx was the founder of what is called German scientific socialism, uses these words to bring out this thought: " As soon as there is no longer any social class to be oppressed ; as soon as class domination and individual struggle for existence, caused by past anarchy in production, are removed with all their conflicts and excesses, there will be nothing more to repress which would require a special repressive power, that is to say, a state. The first act in which the state really appears as the representative of society

[1] The French socialist leader, M. Jules Guesde, says that the aims of Socialism have been correctly stated by John Stuart Mill in his autobiography in these words: " The social problem of the future we considered to be, how to unite the greatest individual liberty of action with a common ownership in the raw material of the globe, and an equal participation of all in the benefits of combined labor."

THE SOCIALISTIC STATE.

as a whole, — namely, the seizure of the means of production in the name of society, — is at the same time its last independent act as a state. Interference of the state in social relations gradually becomes superfluous in one department after another, and finally of itself ceases (goes to sleep). The place of government over persons is taken by administration of things and the management of productive processes."[1]

Herr Bebel, in his work, "Woman and Socialism," gives a partial enumeration of the public institutions which he holds will disappear with the introduction of socialism. He mentions ministers, parliaments, standing armies, police, courts, attorneys, taxation; the place of them all being taken by administrative colleges or boards, which are to surround themselves with the best arrangements for production and distribution, for the determination of necessary supplies, and for the introduction and application of the best improvements in art, in education, in the means of communication and transportation, and in the productive processes. He hopes that the former representatives of the state will take their places in the various callings, and help to increase the productive wealth and conveniences of society with their intelligence and their mental and physical powers. To be sure, this is connected with certain moral improvements which he trusts the introduction of socialism will bring with it; and it is not by any means true that all socialists share his optimism in regard to the immediate moral effects of socialism.[2]

---

[1] This statement, peculiar to the German Social Democracy, is taken from Engels's "Die Entwicklung des Sozialismus von der Utopie zur Wissenschaft."

[2] See "Die Frau und Sozialismus," by August Bebel, pp. 312, 314.

There are different views with regard to the selection of those who are to conduct the socialistic state; and the modern socialist is cautious about speaking dogmatically on points of this kind, for he tells us that it is unscientific to attempt to give precise details in regard to future social organization. However, it is held that, whatever the arrangements, they must be thoroughly democratic. There is an inclination to favor the election of headmen, or selectmen, as they may be called, — using an American expression, — by popular vote of the workers. Mr. Bellamy, on the other hand, in his "Looking Backward," describes a different socialistic state, in which the workers have no vote, but are directed by those elected by persons who have served their time in the industrial army.

CHAPTER V.

SOME MISAPPREHENSIONS CONCERNING THE NATURE OF SOCIALISM.

IT will prove helpful, at least to those not accustomed to economic discussions, if brief attention is given to a few current opinions concerning socialism, which are based upon a failure to understand its true nature. One of these opinions most frequently encountered is that socialism proposes to divide up all property equally among all the members of society. This is an assumption upon which rests many a popular refutation of socialism. It is held that if all property should be divided up to-day, to-morrow the old inequalities would reappear. It is furthermore urged that if all wealth were equally divided, the share of one person would not be considerable. Familiar to all is the story of the banker Rothschild, who, when a poor man expressed a longing for communism, took a thaler from his pocket and giving it to the man, told him that was his share of the wealth of a Rothschild. What socialism really proposes is not the division of property, but, as we have already seen, the concentration of productive property, in fact, its complete unification. This is sufficiently apparent to any one who reflects at all upon the preceding chapters. Manifestly the re-appearance of the old inequalities would then be an impossibility, whatever else might happen. In this connection we must also bear in mind that socialism goes down beneath surface phenomena to underlying causes, and that is forgotten by those who urge flimsy objections of the kind mentioned against socialism. They suppose that a division of wealth takes place, and then the production of wealth goes on as at the present time; whereas, nothing could be further from the thoughts of the socialists. Similarly, it is not a question of the wealth which actually exists, but of the wealth which the socialists propose to bring into existence. Socialism, then, does not propose a grand "divide."

A further misapprehension concerning the nature of socialism is that which traces it to the vaporings of wild and unpractical theorists. It is essential to a comprehension of the nature of socialism, to know that it is a system of industrial society which has found advocates among many gifted, learned, and very practical men. The leaders of socialism in the present century have generally been men of extraordinary capacity, placing them far above the ordinary man. One of the earliest English socialists, Robert Owen, was at one time so successful in cotton spinning that he was called "the prince of cotton spinners," and he amassed a large fortune. The three early leaders of the modern German social democracy are Karl Marx, Friedrich Engels, and Ferdinand Lassalle. Karl Marx is recognized by friend and foe as one of the most learned and gifted economic thinkers of the present century; Friedrich Engels is one with whom economic philosophy must deal, and it is said, besides, that he has been more than ordinarily successful in business; while the gifts of Ferdinand Lassalle attracted the attention of all with whom he came in contact, Wilhelm von Humboldt calling him "a miraculous child," and Bismarck declaring in the imperial parliament that he was one of the most gifted and amiable men with whom he had ever associated. Bebel and Liebknecht, the political leaders of the German social democracy of to-day, whatever we may otherwise think of them, have talents and qualifications which enable them to hold their own with the leaders of the other great political parties.

Another prominent German social democrat, a manufacturer, has a fortune which, it is said, places him among the millionnaires of his country.

The English socialists to-day include men who were trained at the great English universities, and who have been successful in whatever they have undertaken. Among the extremists, we may even mention a man like William Morris, who was prominently spoken of for the post of poet laureate when it was made vacant by the death of Tennyson.

Nor can it be denied that those who are giving socialism its shape in Switzerland, France, the United States, and elsewhere, are men who must command our respect on account of their capacities of every sort. Whoever would understand what socialism means to-day, must bear in mind the unquestionable fact that it includes in its ranks men of practical sagacity, as well as native talent and learning.

It follows, quite naturally, from what has been said, that socialism is not a scheme of criminals for theft and robbery. It can, at the present day, scarcely be necessary to dwell on this. It is worth while, however, to call attention to the fact that socialism is not a scheme of social reconstruction which meets with favor on the part of criminals. It is a curious fact, but one well-known by those who have given attention to crime, that the criminal classes are orthodox and conservative in their religious as well as social opinions. An exhaustive treatment of the reasons for this fact — which, naturally, conveys no reproach to orthodoxy of either sort — cannot now be given. The curious reader must consult works on criminal anthropology. Attention may be called, however, to a few characteristics of the criminal. He is a man who is below the average in mental capacity, although he may be shrewd and cunning. He has not that mental alertness and boldness which would lead him to deviate from received opinions. Moreover, he is extremely superstitious, and often hopes to find exculpation in the observance of religious forms, and has even been known to trust to his religion to help him in crime. Prayers for his success in robbery are not infrequent among superstitious and degraded people, and an Italian criminologist, who examined two hundred murderers, found them all religious. Naples is said to be the most religious city in Europe, and yet the most criminal. Sismondi, writing of the Italians of his day, said: "The murderer, still stained with the blood he has just shed, devoutly fasts, even while he is meditating a fresh assassination."[1]

A well-known American wrote an article for a prominent journal during the campaign in which Mr. Henry George was a candidate for the mayoralty of New York City, and attempted to estimate the number of votes which Mr. George might receive. This writer called attention to the fact that there were 20,000 criminals in New York City, and intimated that they would all cast their votes for Mr. George. The author of this book,

[1] See "The Criminal," by Havelock Ellis, pp. 156, 157. London, 1890.

although not an adherent of Mr. George, felt that this was probably an injustice to his followers, and was led to make some inquiries into the political affiliations of criminals. · He formed the conclusion that they would generally be found to be adherents of one of the two older political parties, and that for this reason, in addition to those already mentioned, the criminal is a shortsighted man; and, indeed, short-sightedness may be called so essentially characteristic of crime, that it is not far out of the way to define crime as short-sightedness. The criminal does not look to social reconstruction for which years must pass; but, without thinking so far ahead, he adopts plans which will bring him gain to-day or to-morrow or next day. He adheres to a party which is able to help him at once when he becomes involved in difficulties. He desires what is called in American politics a "pull;" and in consequence of this it is probable that in a given community he will, as a rule, belong to one of the two great political parties, but to that one which has been the stronger in his own city, or more particularly, perhaps, his own ward. In the prosecution of his inquiries, the author wrote a letter to a gentleman who had long worked among the inmates of the Elmira Reformatory, and asked him whether he thought there would be any considerable number of Henry George men, or socialists, or even anarchists, among them, and the reply was, that he thought not. A very interesting confirmation of this opinion has been given in a vote which was taken in the Reformatory, Oct. 24, and 25, 1892, the purpose of which was to allow the inmates to express political preferences for president and vice-president of the United States. The total number of ballots cast was 909, divided as follows: Democratic, 401; Republican, 394; People's

Party, 15; Prohibition, 1; defective, 8. It will be ob served that the People's Party, which approximates most nearly to socialism, received only fifteen votes, while not one socialistic vote was cast.

It has already been mentioned that criminals are inclined to be orthodox in their religious views, so far as they have any. Of course, the religion itself is likely to be a caricature of any true religion; but so far as formal religious doctrines are concerned, the views of criminals harmonize with those which at a given time and place are customarily regarded as orthodox. Socialism proposes not a religious society, but an economic society, and has no direct connection with any peculiar religious doctrines. There will be found among socialists men of all religious views, as there will be among adherents of any other party. Some socialists are extremely conservative in their religious views, while it frequently happens that among the most conservative adherents of the existing social order there will be found persons of what are called liberal, or even loose, religious views. It has been held by some that Christianity has a peculiarly close connection with socialism, and that is true so far as both aim to help the weak and to lift the fallen; but it cannot be said that their means are necessarily identical. If a Christian can be made to believe that socialism will bring the good to the masses of mankind which its adherents claim for it, then he must necessarily accept socialism. But that is only to say that a Christian must be an honest man. The very point at issue is whether or not socialism will bring what it promises. If so, then no man who is upright can refuse to give adherence to it, when once he is convinced that such will be the case, whatever may be his religious doctrines.

Socialism often has to meet the reproach that it is hostile to the family as a social institution, and not infrequently we see the statement that socialism means free love. If we again call to mind the fact that socialism is an economic system, we shall see that it has only an indirect connection with views concerning the family, and we shall not be surprised to learn that among the socialists, as among other people, there are those who hold different views concerning the marriage tie. It is necessary, however, to dwell upon the socialistic position with respect to the family to understand fully its nature. The socialist to-day tells us that the modern industrial system is already destroying the family, and that, if it continues its operations, the family will probably disappear within a century. He claims that modern industrialism is far worse in its action upon the family than was slavery; for the latter only exceptionally separated the members of the family, whereas the arrangements of industrial society to-day regularly and habitually separate husband and wife and children. Our socialist points to the manufacturing towns of New England, which are popularly called "she towns," because they consist of women and children. And with these he brings in contrast the "stag camps" of the West; namely, the logging-camps of the lumber districts, gold and silver mining-camps, and the boarding-tents of the iron ore region. The socialist has strong support for his claim that industrialism is destroying the family, and in industrial centres has already accomplished a good share of its work, so far as homes are concerned. An investigator[1] in the Department of Labor, in an address delivered before the World's Fair Labor Congress at Chicago, entitled. "The Disintegra-

[1] Mr. Ethelbert Stewart.

tion of the Families of the Workingmen," spoke about the effect of modern industry on the family. First of all, he called attention to the fact that divorces are increasing, and marriages decreasing, in industrial centres, and that without any change in the laws. It appears that relatively the number of marriages in Chicago has never since been so great as in 1873, and that the same is true with respect to Philadelphia. On the other hand, it appears that the number of divorces in Pittsburg increased two hundred per cent between 1870 and 1880. It would further appear from investigations that the chief causes for divorce are economic. It is the necessity for the separation of the members of the family, in order that they may gain support. These are the words of the speaker on the occasion referred to: —

"Every one who has gone through the cotton-mill towns of New England and the South has seen house after house locked up, and little faces peering out at the windows. The mother has gone to work in the mill, and left her baby in the house. The father is working somewhere else, probably in another State. I submit that a family is pretty well disintegrated when this is its normal condition — the every-day life of the family. I have walked along rows of factory tenement houses, and found three out of five deserted by father, mother, and all the children big enough to work, while the babies are left to do the best they can." [1]

Herr Paul Göhre has written a noteworthy work, entitled "Three Months a Factory Hand," in which he narrates his experiences in a factory in Saxony, Germany. This Mr. Göhre was a theological student, who desired to see for himself the mode of life of the German workingmen, and to experience their life and to

[1] Mr. Ethelbert Stewart's address, delivered before the World's Fair Labor Congress, Aug. 30, 1893.

learn from familiar every-day conversation with them
their actual views and aspirations. The report which
Mr. Göhre has given in his work is regarded as a re-
markably faithful and impartial picture; and he tells
us, among other things, that the present economic conditions are destroying the family of the wage-earner.
These are his own words: —

"Another fact infinitely significant and ominous, which in
daily intercourse with this class is continually forced on the
attention, is that in consequence of these conditions throughout
wide circles of the industrial population of our great cities, the
traditional form of the family no longer exists. The old organism, based on the consanguinity of parents and children, and
built up exclusively of one kinship, — with the sole exception, in
the higher classes, of more or less closely associated servants, —
has given place to-day, in the ranks of the workingmen, to groups
of people, kindred and stranger, formed upon purely economic
needs of a common lodging and living, and formed, moreover, by
chance. Inclinations of relationship have plainly given way to
economic obligations. The mother has evolved into the household executive, who receives from husband, grown children, and
stranger inmate alike, a fixed sum, with which she contracts to
meet the demands of food, rent, laundry work, and the like; as
to clothing, each relies upon himself.

"It is not the social democrats and their agitation who are responsible for this: precisely these conditions are the result of our
whole industrial system, which makes it impossible for workingmen and their families to share their meals in common; which
compels them to occupy the most ill-arranged and crowded dwellings; and to admit utter strangers, often in rapid succession, to
the most intimate family relations, such as used to be held sacred
for the family itself. Let one but remember the dense packing
of the 'rooms,' that is to say, the family dwelling-places, in
such workingmen's barracks, or the old country houses altered to
their plan; the impossibility of isolating one from the other; the
thinness of the walls in houses so hastily constructed, that they

permit every loudly spoken word to be distinctly heard by the neighbors; the single corridor for the three or four 'rooms' on every story, whose use, as well as that of the water-supply, closets, etc., must be in common. All this leads to a promiscuity of daily intercourse, a publicity of family life, which is appalling to the beholder, and which must inevitably bring about the destruction of domesticity itself. It is absolutely impossible that the children of such families shall not live like brothers and sisters of one blood, when the corridor is their place of common resort, their playground, their opportunity for confidences; that growing lads and girls shall not come into the closest contact with each other; that the men shall not find continual occasion for interchange of ideas, and often of blows; that the women shall not intimately know every nook and corner, every shortcoming, every article of clothing and of household use among their neighbors; nay, more, that the common use of such articles, as, for example, the borrowing and lending of cooking utensils, shall not introduce a distinctly communistic character into the housekeeping of the scantily equipped families. Add to this the confinement and narrowness of the individual quarters, which drive the men out-of-doors in the evening, into the streets and fields when it is possible, or into some neighbor's larger and better room, or the beer saloons and assembly halls. Let one remember, further, how much this congestion is aggravated by the presence of lodgers and strangers, who bring with them their own customs and usages, their different manners, standards, and requirements, which, strange and often enough offensive, they yet express and put in practice as freely as in their own homes. Let one remember that these strangers leave the house with the husband and grown-up children and return with them, and habitually sit around the same table with them until bedtime, reading, smoking, talking, or card-playing. It is a fact that in many families parents and children can be together undisturbed *only* during the night, in the hours of sleep. Even the last chance of a cosey hour together at breakfast and dinner is constantly destroyed by the conditions of labor which I have described, and which make it impossible for father and children to go home for their meals. And even when this can be done, the hour's recess is only just sufficient, in my opinion, to make the double journey — in the nature of things a moderately long one for the workmen of large establishments — and to swallow the food post-haste, without comfort or leisure.

"I shall speak in another place of the effect of this state of things on the morals, characters, and opinions of the wage-earning class. Here I have only to state the bare fact of the complete change in character of the workman's family, and the causes which have brought it about. I repeat that it is, primarily, a product of our present economic conditions. These it is which must bear the heaviest burden of responsibility, and not social democracy, which, in this respect as in others, has but drawn the ultimate conclusions from existing premises, and formulated them into a system. The present evils are the groundwork and opportunity of social democracy, and its doctrine of the ideal future family."

Mr. Göhre adds : —

"We must not be blind to this fact, above all, those of us who represent the avowedly religious section of the community; and, instead of bewailing the obvious decline of the old Christian ideal of the family, and inveighing against social democracy, we ought rather to co-operate in putting an end, definitely and forever, to the economic causes of which the present situation is the inevitable result."[1]

The socialist writer declares, then, that the present social order is the cause of disintegration of the family, and he reproaches it with having destroyed the family, and put nothing better in its place. "This is what you are doing!" he cries to the adherents of the present economic system.[2]

The socialist claims that socialism will again make

[1] See "Three Months a Factory Hand," by Paul Göhre, translated by A. B. Carr, soon to be published by Messrs. Swan Sonnenschein & Co., London.
[2] "Das Erfurter Programm," by Karl Kautsky, chapter iv.

possible ideal love. When the author, some time since, in an article called attention to the fact that socialism did not mean free love, and carried with it no peculiar doctrine concerning the family, he received letters from two excellent young women, both Americans and socialists. One commented upon the passage in this language: —

"Serious and intelligent people surely do not need to be told to-day that socialism has nothing to do with free love or atheism, and would, I should think, resent being told it. Could not you mention the stigma briefly, as a thing of the past and then account for it historically?"

The other, however, wrote as follows: —

"If socialists may speak for socialism, it certainly does entertain the notion that the family of to-day belongs to the economic system of to-day, and that its economic foundation, that is, the economic dependence of the wife upon the husband, passes away with the rest of the economic dependence of one person upon another."

What shall be said in regard to these two contradictory positions? The latter position is that taken by those who adhere to a materialistic conception of history, which traces all social relations to economic conditions, and holds that, as the family has changed in the past, even so it will change in the future, as underlying economic conditions evolve into higher forms. This conception of history is, however, no necessary part of socialism, and no socialist has claimed that there is anything higher than the pure monogamic marriage of man and woman resting upon love. Whatever view we take of the evolution of society, it would not seem to follow of necessity that socialism would, if successful, do anything more than purify and elevate the family. The differences among socialists in regard to the binding character of the marriage tie in the absence of love, or after it has disappeared, are no greater than the differences among other men.

CHAPTER VI.

THE ORIGIN OF SOCIALISM.

MODERN socialism is the natural outcome of modern industrial conditions, and its origin is contemporaneous with the origin of those conditions. We must seek its beginnings in the beginnings of modern industry. We can express this thought differently by saying that modern socialism is the product of the industrial revolution. It has grown with this revolution, becoming international as the industrial revolution has spread over the nations of the world. The peculiarities of socialism are part and parcel of the industrial revolution itself.

The industrial revolution was brought about by the series of inventions following important geographical discoveries. The most important of the inventions which inaugurated the industrial revolution took place about the middle of the eighteenth century, and they may be enumerated as follows: Kay's fly shuttle, invented in 1738, the first of the great inventions to revolutionize the weaving industry in England; Watt's steam engine, invented in 1769, and applied to the manufacture of cotton sixteen years later; John Hargreave's spinning-jenny, patented in 1770; the water frame of Richard Arkwright, the barber's assistant, invented in 1769; Samuel Crompton's mule, invented in 1779; Edward Cartwright's power loom, produced in 1787; and Eli Whitney's cotton-gin, invented in 1793. These inventors may, in a sense, be called the fathers of modern socialism, for without their inventions it could not have come into existence.

The industrial revolution signifies rapid changes in the economic world. Evolution is going on continually, but we speak of changes as revolutionary when they occur with such unusual rapidity that we are not able readily to adjust ourselves to them. What are these changes which have taken place as a result of the great inventions named? We can perhaps best understand these changes, if we look about us and reflect upon those things in the economic world which are new. We have only to go outside our own homes and use our eyes diligently in any great city, to understand what it means when it is said that our present economic world is more different from that of 1776 than the economic world of 1776 was from the economic life of the early Oriental monarchies. Is it even necessary to enumerate these new things? Everyone calls to mind the telegraph, the railway, the telephone, street-cars, electric lights, anthracite coal, petroleum, etc. We may take up the factors in production — land, labor, capital, and enterprise — and trace changes in each one, and we shall find them momentous. Perhaps the changes have been least important with respect to land; yet even in land the changes are not inconsiderable. During this period we have witnessed, first, the contraction of public property in land, and then, more recently, the growth of public property; and, what is more important still, it is within this period that it has become possible to buy and sell land freely like commodities, so that we may almost say that land itself has become a commodity. Slavery and serfdom have been abolished, and labor has been given the right of free settlement and contract. But it is with respect to capital that the most momentous changes have taken place, because it is changes in capital and the management of capital which have carried with them the most significant changes in labor itself. The changes of which we have spoken with respect to labor were necessary to enable capital to do its work; but the chief change was in that force which we call capital. Capital, then, is that which is most significant in the industrial revolution; and Karl Marx showed his insight into what was essential when he called his book on socialism, "Capital," and those are inferior economists who would concentrate attention on land rather than on capital. Capital, taking advantage of the inventions in industry and the improvement of means of communication and transportation brought about by these inventions, was able to extend production and to carry it on on a scale of increasing magnitude. This production upon a vast scale, based upon a far-reaching division of labor, became essentially social production. Armies of men work together in single or allied establishments, each one doing his own small part of a vast whole. Capitalistic production passed out of the shop and entered the factory. The master workman gave place to the captain of industry, and journeymen and apprentices to regiments of wage-earners. Production gradually became more and more socialized, and the process is still going on to-day.

Private property in the instruments of production came, in the meantime, to have a new significance. Formerly private property in the instruments of production meant private property in the tools used by the worker. The master had not a separate and distinct income without direct personal toil; and capital did not separate the industrial workmen into classes. But when production became socialized, private property in the instruments of production meant a great capitalist who no longer toiled at the bench with his workmen, but one who lived in a different quarter of the town, and often did not know them by sight. This private property, in the instruments of production, became the source of a large income altogether separate and distinct from the returns to personal exertion. Now, if we add to all this that there has been going on an extension of political rights, terminating in modern political democracy and increased educational facilities of every sort, all resulting in larger demands on the part of the less favored members of the community, particularly those ordinarily designated as the lower classes, and the growing self-consciousness on their part, as the result of their separation from their employers, have we not given the conditions which must inevitably result in socialistic thought?

We have, as the consequence of the industrial revolution, enormously increased the production of wealth, and that production is social, and not individual. What could more readily suggest itself than the socialization of the instruments of production, to correspond with the socialization of production on the one hand, and political democracy on the other? It was something so obvious that the workers could not help demanding sooner or later that they should have control of industry, as they were acquiring control of politics; and that they should have the advantages resulting from the ownership of the instruments of production which they used, but which advantages they saw now accruing to a distinct class; namely, the capitalist class. "To the workers the tools!" became the rallying cry, which, once uttered, was rapidly taken up, and could not cease to be echoed and re-echoed. The increased production of wealth could not, withal, fail to stimulate desire on the part of those who participated in that production. They could not see why a larger part of the advantages of increased production should not accrue to them. They used tools and machines which frequently multiplied their labor-power a hundred and a thousand fold; but they could not be brought to believe that there was any corresponding improvement in their own condition. It was not necessary to point this out to the toilers, for they could not help feeling it themselves. But when deep thinkers arose and formulated a system of industry which, once introduced, would give to the workers all the results of the increased productivity of labor, they were predisposed to favor this system, and to take up an agitation in favor of the overthrow of the existing system, and the substitution therefor of the new industrial order.

But this is not all. It has been said that socialism grew and developed with the growth and development of the industrial revolution. Early in this century socialists proposed the establisment of small independent communistic societies. Each little village or hamlet was to be voluntarily organized, and to be relatively self-sufficient. The idea was that of a large household of equals working together as brothers and sisters, and producing the things which they needed for their own consumption. As industry became national, and then international, in its scope, solidarity of interests grew likewise. Workingmen's organizations extended from city to city, and from nation to nation, and then to the whole civilized world. Their ideals grew fast, and, wishing to enjoy the fruits of modern inventions and modern industrial processes, their socialism expanded from the village community to the nation, and then to the world. Socialism itself, then, passed through three stages. It was first local, then national, and finally cosmopolitan. The local communistic settlement formed on a voluntary basis cannot enter into the advantages of a modern industry, and, from the standpoint of modern socialism, is held to be an anachronism. Yet another reflection is obvious. Industrial conditions are similar in all parts of the world which have participated in the industrial revolution. These similar conditions must inevitably give rise to similar thought. Socialism is not the only possible conclusion which can be drawn from them, but it is the one which could not fail to be drawn; and the absurdity of the ordinary talk about the importation of socialism from a foreign land becomes apparent.

CHAPTER VII.

THE PROGRESS OF SOCIALISM.

DID we need any justification for the attention which we give to socialism, it could be easily found in the progress which it has been making during the past generation. There existed early in the century a socialism of a utopian type in France, England, and Germany. France, in particular, had a number of thinkers who gained a great reputation at home and abroad, and found followers in many lands. Cabet, Saint-Simon, and Fourier are names which, in this connection, occur to every one who is at all familiar with the history of socialism. They had schemes more or less fantastic, but, withal, not devoid of keen criticism of the existing order, and shrewd proposals for its improvement. England had its Robert Owen, a wealthy manufacturer, who used up a fortune in endeavors to establish communistic villages in England and America. The United States had its wave of Fourieristic socialism, and its Brook Farm and other settlements. Albert Brisbane, Horace Greeley, and George William Curtis, among other distinguished Americans, took part in the movement. About 1860 this early socialism had well-nigh disappeared, or been absorbed by other socialistic movements. The co-operative movement in England, for example, took up the energy which had gone into Robert Owen's socialism, and its only outcome for a time seemed to be the peaceful operations of the co-operative store. Louis Blanc had before this time begun an agitation more national in scope, and proposed to use the power of the state for the transformation of the modern competitive system into socialism. But Louis Blanc and his proposals appeared to be overwhelmed in the disasters of the Revolution of 1848. It was not strange, then, that a French writer about 1865 felt like offering an apology for compliance with a request to furnish an article on socialism for an encyclopædia of political science. Socialism, he said in effect, is something which is now dead and gone; but, after all, it has curious historical interest which may justify the present article. Scarcely was the ink dry on his manuscript, however, before the world began to hear something of a German named Ferdinand Lassalle. Fascinating in manner, admired alike by men and women, fiery and eloquent, he soon began to rally about him the workingmen of Germany. The newspapers said that socialism could not get a foothold in Germany. Socialism was something, it was urged, which might appeal to the restless Frenchman, but could make no headway against the solid common sense and contentment of the educated, but patient, German toiler. Ferdinand Lassalle was undoubtedly drawing his materials in part from the armory of Louis Blanc, and it was natural that socialism should be said to be a foreign importation, and not something which could naturally appeal to Germans. Yet the impossible happened. Ferdinand Lassalle died a romantic death, but his followers revered his memory and took up his work.

In the meantime there had come into Germany an influence proceeding from Karl Marx and Friedrich Engels, then living in London, but native Germans, who had become involved in the revolutionary troubles of 1848, and had been obliged to flee their fatherland. The socialism of Lassalle was more distinctively national in character, while this new influence was more cosmopolitan, and less inclined to operate upon a strictly national basis. Quarrels and dissensions between the factions were a source of satisfaction to the enemies of German socialism, but soon they united, and since then they have worked together. The progress of socialism in Germany has been almost uninterrupted from the beginning, and has been entirely without parallel in such radical social movements. This progress has taken place in spite of opposition of all sorts, both private and public. Laws of Draconian severity passed against the social democracy, and enforced relentlessly, have served only to strengthen and unite the party. The social democrats returned eight members to the parliament of the North German Federation in 1867. At the first election after the formation of the German Empire they returned two members and cast nearly 125,000 votes. The votes increased to nearly 500,000 in 1877, when the number of seats in parliament gained by the party was twelve. Owing to an attempt on the life of the German Emperor, a slight reaction took place in 1878, the party losing some 50,000 votes and three seats in parliament. At the next election the social democrats suffered under the influence of the special laws passed against them, and lost over 100,000 votes, although they gained three seats in parliament, as their votes were so concentrated that they were more effective. From that time until the present, the number of votes cast by the social democrats has increased without interruption, and in 1890 they became numerically the strongest party in the empire, casting nearly 1,500,000 votes. They retained their position as the strongest party in the empire in the elections of 1893, casting nearly 1,800,000 votes, and electing forty-four members of parliament, a far smaller number than proportional representation would give them, as their votes were more scattered than those of the other parties.[1]

Of course this means less than it would in a country like the United States or England, because there are a dozen or more political parties in Germany. Another indication of the growth of social democracy, is the fact that it has gained a foothold among the students of the universities, and that there are formal social democratic organizations in several important German universities. These students held a meeting to discuss their plans for pushing social democracy, in Geneva, Switzerland, in December, 1893.

Next to Germany, England is probably the country where socialism is strongest. It has not made itself felt to a great extent as a separate political party, but has influenced all the parties, and is producing a powerful impression upon the thought and legislation of England. It has participated in local elections, and its candidates have been successful in many instances. London is not only the greatest city in England, but the greatest city in the world; and it is governed by a County Council, the majority of whose members, if not avowed socialists, at any rate act consciously under a pronounced socialist influence. Socialistic thought is a force which to-day is governing London, although, of course, it must be remembered that London alone is so restricted by national

---

[1] See Appendix for full statistics showing the progress of German social democracy. A chart is also added, giving a graphic representation of the advance social democracy has made.

legislation, that it cannot carry out anything like a full socialist program. Yet the drift is unmistakable. Two illustrations will suffice. The London County Council has recently acquired some twenty-one miles of street railways (tramways), and proposes to operate these lines. While the ownership and operation of municipal monopolies does not, of necessity, mean socialism, — while, indeed, an anti-socialist may favor such ownership and operation, — the significant point is that in London the change was brought about by socialist intent, and as part of a socialist program. The second illustration is found in the abolition of the contract system in the construction of artisans' dwellings by the municipality. The municipality has had for some time the power to erect dwellings for artisans, but it had been in the habit of employing contractors in its operations. The abolition of the contract system means a determination on the part of the municipality to organize and carry on the work itself; and this change is also effected because it is in the direction of socialism.

Perhaps equally important has been the changed attitude of the English workingmen. The newspapers of England indulged in talk concerning the relations of English workingmen to socialism, precisely like that found at an earlier date in the German newspapers respecting the relations of German workingmen to socialism. Socialism, it was alleged, was a Continental poison which could not make headway in England. Its workingmen were too prosperous, it was alleged, and, moreover, they were too little inclined to indulge in philosophical speculation to follow the vague and indefinite ideas looking to a remote future prosperity. England, it was claimed, was the classic land of common sense. The English trades unions, once dreaded, now began to receive praise, and were looked upon as bulwarks of conservatism. For some time, indeed, they seemed to merit the praise which was meted out to them; but more and more they have fallen under the influence of socialistic thought, and at the last trades union congress, held at Belfast in September, 1893, a program for political action was adopted which was nothing less than pure socialism. A motion requiring candidates for Parliament receiving financial assistance to pledge themselves " to support the principle of collective ownership and control of all the means of production and distribution," was carried by a large majority. Moreover, an Independent Labor Party was formed in January, 1893; and its object, as stated in the constitution as amended in February, 1894, is "The collective ownership and control of the means of production, distribution, and exchange." Its president is Mr. Kier Hardie, M.P.

Modern socialism has required time to gain a firm foothold in France. Early utopian socialism was practically dead in 1860. During the last decade of Napoleon's reign there was no strong socialistic movement, although the International Workingmen's Association made itself known and felt in France. The uprising of the Paris Commune was only partially socialistic. It was only during the latter part of its history that the socialistic elements began to make themselves prominent. But this uprising was suppressed, and a frightful slaughter of the masses ensued, in which it is said that the larger proportion of the revolutionary population was slain. Socialism did not play any *rôle* in the early history of the republic, and severe laws sought to suppress it. Many conditions, moreover, were unfavorable to the growth of socialism. One of these was the generally unsettled condition of society following upon the revolutionary movement. Troubled times are more favorable to schemes for a violent overthrow of existing institutions than to the development of organized and systematic efforts at a gradual and peaceful reconstruction of society. It may be said in a general way that social tranquillity is favorable to socialism, and a politically unsettled condition is favorable to anarchy. Moreover, for a time, the character of the French masses did not seem to be sufficiently stable and thoughtful to furnish a good soil for socialism. It appeared to be more receptive to the propaganda of revolutionary violence, and to schemes for the overthrow of the existing system and the establishment of a new order in a night. The continued existence of the republic has given France a longer period of domestic peace than she has known since the great revolution of the last century, and the marvellous development of educational institutions in France has furnished a better instructed people as a soil for a social philosophy, which at least requires some considerable intellectual capacity and effort for its comprehension. A group of students began the publication of a socialistic paper in 1876; and Jules Guesde, who at one time had been inclined to favor anarchy, but had become a socialist, founded a "collectivistic" labor party in 1879. Collectivism, it may be remarked in passing, is a designation of socialism which is common in France. Shortly afterward, another convert from anarchy, Dr. Paul Brousse, joined Guesde. It may be said that by 1880 modern socialism had gained a firm foothold in France. The development was slow for a time, and in

1889 the socialists cast only 91,000 votes out of a total of 6,847,000, or 1.30 per cent. Two years later, however, they cast 549,000 out of a total of 6,275,000 votes, that is to say, nearly nine per cent.[1] But it was in 1893 that France was astonished by the success of the socialists in the election for members of the French Assembly. In that year they succeeded in increasing the number of their deputies from fifteen to fifty, becoming thus, as in Germany, a great political party. They have become so strong that they do not seem to have been injured by the tendency to reaction necessarily following upon the explosion of the dynamite bomb thrown among the French deputies by the recently executed anarchist, Vaillant, and the attempts to make the people of France regard the socialists as responsible appear to have been fruitless. This unquestionably means a great deal.

It is also significant that Paris, the second city of the world in size, is, like London, under the government of a socialist municipal council, and that some five or six other French cities are governed by municipal councils, the majority of whose members are either avowed socialists or are socialistically inclined.

The students of France, like those of Germany, seem to be more or less receptive to socialism; for a socialistic society was formed in the student quarter, the well-known Latin Quarter, of Paris in 1891, and it seems to have displayed considerable activity since that time.[2]

An essential feature of the growth of socialism in France is the development of what we may, relatively at least, designate as conservatism. It is probably on this

---

[1] "Der Capitalismus fin de siècle," by Rudolph Meyer, p. 477.
[2] See Appendix for a statement concerning the present condition of socialism in France.

account, as well as on account of greater familiarity with socialist plans, that socialism appears to be less dreaded now than formerly. The author of the report on France issued by the English Royal Commission on Labor describes the change in public opinion in these words: —

"Whatever may have been the meaning originally attached in France to the word socialism, and whatever may be the precise body of doctrine to which it may be applied at the present time, it is certain, as a writer in the *Revue Des deux Mondes* in 1890 pointed out, that it has lost part of the significance of something 'violent and somewhat offensive that it had formerly.' All parties alike in France are agreed as to the fact of the change."[1]

The other European countries require less attention. Modern socialism began to make itself felt in Belgium in 1876, when Dr. César de Paepe, a former anarchist, who had become an adherent of Karl Marx, began an agitation among the workingmen of that country, and established a social democratic party, at first containing two factions, which united in 1879 and formed a political socialistic party, with a program much like that of the German social democracy. Socialism in Belgium has been connected with remarkable co-operative societies which have achieved a rare success, and at the same time have been used as centres of socialistic activity. The two best known of these are the Vooruit of Ghent and the Volkshaus of Brussels. The suffrage has heretofore been so restricted in Belgium that it has been confined to persons of wealth, and the wage-earners have had no chance to make themselves felt in politics. But during the past year the socialists began a tremendous agita-

[1] Royal Commission on Labour's Foreign Reports, vol. vi., France, London, 1893, p. 10.

tion to secure universal suffrage, and developed one of the most remarkable agitations of modern times. They threatened a universal strike, and so alarmed the public authorities that something approximating universal suffrage was established. It remains to be seen what use socialism will make of this new condition of things in Belgium.

Holland has not been so prominent in modern socialism as Belgium; but it has an educated and able leader in Domela-Nieuwenhuis, and of late there seems to have been indications of at least a moderate growth of socialism in Holland. In 1893 the socialists gained control for the first time of the municipal council of a Dutch city, namely Beesterzwaag, in which they have eight out of fifteen municipal councillors.[1]

Of the Scandinavian countries, Denmark and Sweden alone have displayed any considerable socialistic activity, although socialism has made some little progress in Norway, where, however, the backward industrial condition has been unfavorable to its growth. The Danish socialists after various reverses became strong in the eighties, and they have succeeded in gaining a following among the agricultural laborers, as well as among the artisans of the towns. Their principal organ, *Social-Demokraten*, has a large circulation, and, according to the last account accessible to the author, they have four members in the Rigsdag, namely, two each in the Folkething and the Landsthing. Socialism has, during the same period, made considerable, but less, advance in Sweden, where it has a strong central organ, also called *Social-Demokraten*.

Socialism has developed slowly in Austria, where it

[1] See the *Revue Socialiste* for September, 1893.

has had to contend against anarchy; but of late, under the leadership of Dr. Victor Adler, an adherent of Marx, it has become stronger. Although Austrian socialism is still weakened by dissensions and by anarchy, it is claimed that the labor movement in this country is essentially social-democratic. Socialism undoubtedly begins to be felt as a force in Austria, although far weaker than in France, Germany, or England.

Switzerland is politically the most democratic country in the world. It is certainly far more democratic than the United States, and it is a country in which social reform has proceeded more rapidly than in any other country, unless it may possibly be England. Switzerland has been the home also of foreign agitators and socialists from all parts of the world; and yet pure socialism, while it doubtless has its adherents, has never become a very prominent political factor. It seems that social and political reforms which are within the reach of the people have, in the main, absorbed their energy, and diverted into peaceful channels the social current which in other countries has become revolutionary.

The Latin countries generally have furnished a less favorable soil for socialism than the Teutonic countries. The masses have been more ignorant, and, on account of their temperament perhaps, more receptive to a propaganda of anarchistic violence than to socialistic philosophy. It is generally, if not universally, found that where socialism is strong, anarchy is weak; and where anarchy flourishes, socialism languishes. Socialism has, however, at last gained a footing among the agricultural laborers and the artisans of the towns in Italy; and in 1892 a program was drawn up which resembles, in the main, the programs of the other countries mentioned. Of twenty-five socialistic candidates who stood for parliament in this year, four or five were elected; and in the local elections of 1893 several socialist candidates were successful, the party finding support in all parts of the kingdom. The socialist press is reported to be in a flourishing condition, and it includes a scientific review called *La Critica Sociale*.[1]

Socialism has made itself felt in Spain and Portugal, in the former of which countries it gained its first political success in 1891, when five socialists were elected to local legislative bodies in the northern part of the country; four of them being elected to membership in the municipal council of Bilbao. Socialism has, however, in these countries, gained no great strength, although apparently growing in both.

Russia has been the natural home of a propaganda of violent social reconstruction, and this has been the natural outcome of the impossibility of popular agitation and participation in political life. The political despotism of Russia seemed to lend countenance to the idea that what was first of all needed was a violent overthrow of existing institutions. But of late there seems to be in progress a socialistic agitation in Russia which seeks to influence the industrial population of the cities. It is not surprising to be told that the leaders of Russian socialism live in foreign countries.

Socialism is known and is working elsewhere in Europe, but has not become a great force. The countries to which reference is made are those in the southern portion of Europe which are more or less Asiatic in their

[1] Cf. Report of the Royal Labour Commission on the Labour Question in Italy, London, 1893, p. 21.

characteristics, and in which the industrial development has been slow.[1]

What shall be said about socialism in the United States? The earlier socialism was destroyed by our Civil War; but soon after that ceased, foreigners, coming to this country from France and Germany, endeavored to plant the seeds of socialism in our wage-earning population. The socialists of Germany established the Socialistic Labor Party in the seventies, and this continues to the present day. It early entered into political life, and has in recent years been active in several parts of the country, putting up a presidential candidate at the last election. The number of votes cast for the candidates of the Socialistic Labor Party has recently increased considerably, and yet the number is so small as in itself to have no significance. The leaders of the party, however, express themselves as hopeful, and believe that now they have gained a firm foothold, from which they cannot be dislodged. Early adherents were won among the foreign population, but of late they have made more headway among the American-born wage-earning population. They have also exercised more influence than would at first appear, because they have given a socialistic direction to the thought of the labor leaders of the country. Their adherents enter into the labor organizations, and edit labor papers which are not avowedly socialistic, and yet advocate what is essentially socialism. What this party may do in the future is, of course, uncertain; but it cannot be granted that, up to the present moment, they

---

[1] In regard to the present condition of socialism in these countries, see the excellent article on Sozialdemokratie, by Georg Adler, in the *Handwörterbuch der Staatswissenschaften*, edited by Prof. J. Conrad and others.

THE PROGRESS OF SOCIALISM. 69

have exercised a strong influence, likely to have a lasting effect on the country.

Mr. Edward Bellamy wrote "Looking Backward" in 1888. This socialistic work soon attained an enormous circulation, selling for a time at the rate of a thousand copies a day. This was the beginning of the American socialism which has been called nationalism. Nationalist clubs were started in all parts of the country, from Boston to San Francisco. Newspapers in the interest of the agitation sprang up almost daily; and the leaders hoped in a few years to carry everything before them. The movement, as a separate and distinct force, began to grow weaker some two years since, and has seemed to decline almost as rapidly as it rose. Nationalism has, however, exercised a great influence upon American thought, and has not been without effect upon legislation, particularly in Massachusetts, for important laws can be traced to the agitation of the nationalists. They have very generally entered into the Populist movement, not because they accept that in its present form as ideal, but because that movement has seemed to give them the best opportunity for the diffusion of their principles; and there can be no doubt that they have given a socialistic bias to this movement. They have also influenced the labor movement, and, with the Socialistic Labor Party, they have succeeded in producing a strong sentiment in favor of independent political action on the part of wage-earners. Especially noteworthy was the platform for independent political action offered at the meeting of the American Federation of Labor in Chicago in December, 1893. That platform was referred to the bodies represented for consideration, with the understanding that it would come up for action at the next annual meeting of the Federation, which is the largest labor organization in the United States. The president of the American Federation of Labor, Mr. Samuel Gompers, has, in the meantime, expressed the opinion that independent political action was likely to be taken at an early day, and that it would be along the lines of this platform, which reads as follows: —

POLITICAL PROGRAM.

Whereas, The trade unionists of Great Britain have, by the light of experience and the logic of progress, adopted the principle of independent labor politics as an auxiliary to their economic action, and

Whereas, Such action has resulted in the most gratifying success, and

Whereas, Such independent labor politics are based upon the following program, to wit: —

1. Compulsory education.
2. Direct legislation.
3. A legal eight-hour work-day.
4. Sanitary inspection of workshop, mine, and home.
5. Liability of employers for injury to health, body, or life.
6. The abolition of the contract system in all public work.
7. The abolition of the sweating system.
8. The municipal ownership of street cars, and gas and electric plants for public distribution of light, heat, and power.
9. The nationalization of telegraphs, telephones, railroads, and mines.
10. The collective ownership by the people of all means of production and distribution.
11. The principal of the referendum in all legislation.

Therefore, Resolved, That this convention hereby indorses this political action of our British comrades, and

THE PROGRESS OF SOCIALISM. 71

Resolved, That this program and basis of a political labor movement be, and is hereby, submitted for the consideration of the labor organizations of America, with the request that their delegates to the next annual convention of the American Federation of Labor be instructed on this most important subject.

Nationalism has influenced far more considerably than the socialistic labor party the professional classes of the country, and particularly the clergy.

It must be stated, in conclusion, that it is extremely difficult to estimate precisely what strength socialism has in the United States at the present time. The opinions of observers will differ according to their wishes with respect to the growth of socialism. Nevertheless, no thoughtful and impartial person can fail to acknowledge that socialism has, in the United States, become a force which is more likely to increase in strength than to decrease, and one which cannot be ignored, but one with which we must deal.

It is not consistent with the purpose of this book to go into details in regard to socialism in every part of the world, as Australia and Canada. But we may say that socialism is known wherever modern industrial civilization exists. It is one expression of this industrial civilization; not the only one to be sure. It is an interpretation of this industrial civilization which may not be correct, but which was nevertheless inevitable.

Socialists themselves like to compare the growth of socialism to that of Christianity in its early stages. Different as are the two, the comparison is not altogether inappropriate. Both have found their chief strength among the masses, and they have grown with marvellous rapidity, although the growth of socialism, it must be confessed, has been the more rapid. They have both spread from nation to nation, and been international and cosmopolitan in character. They both demand universal dominion, and their progress has not been stopped by persecution. On the contrary, imprisonment and death seem to give new zeal to their adherents. Socialism has become, as well as Christianity, a religion to many, and the devotion which it has awakened is something which nothing short of a religious force is able to arouse. Surely, all these facts not only justify, but demand, that the most careful attention should be given to this new and mighty power which has come into the world.

CHAPTER VIII.

THE EVIDENCES OF AN ALLEGED IRRESISTIBLE CURRENT OF SOCIALISM.

THE various kinds of modern socialism have been divided into two main classes, — ethical systems and a non-ethical system. The ethical systems are those which make prominent the appeal to ethical sentiment. The advocates of these ethical systems of socialism attempt to show that the present order works cruelty and injustice, and that the socialism which they urge men to adopt will establish righteous relations among men, and thus promote human welfare. They think that an exposition of the benefits of socialism, and an appeal to the consciences of men, are the forces which are needed to bring about the new social order. The earlier systems of socialism were, it may be said, mainly ethical in this sense. Exhortation played an important *rôle* in these, for they were urged upon men much as religion is. The non-ethical system is not to be understood as anti-ethical. The expression non-ethical means simply that the ethical element plays no part in the production of anticipated changes. These changes come as the result of natural laws working in society. Man observes these, and he discovers the necessary results of their operation. The most which any individual can do is to work with these social forces, possibly accelerating them somewhat, and rendering the transition from an earlier to a more advanced stage of society a less painful and an easier one than it would otherwise be. This non-ethical socialism is that of which Karl Marx is the founder. It is claimed by his adherents that he has found a law of evolution working in society like that which Darwin found in the natural world; and, in their opinion, the two great intellectual lights of this century are Karl Marx and Charles Darwin. The ethical element plays almost, if not wholly, as subordinate a part in this socialism as in the Darwinian natural science. A materialistic conception goes with this theory of social evolution, and forms an essential part of it. It makes every social advance depend upon the development of the economic sphere. In this extreme form, it makes religion and the family, art and literature, products of the mode of producing, exchanging, and distributing material wealth. This idea of historical evolution was brought forward as early as 1847 by Marx and Engels, in the celebrated "Manifesto of the Communist Party." Engels states the fundamental proposition which forms the nucleus of the Manifesto in the preface to the English edition of 1888 in these words: —

"That proposition is: that in every historical epoch the prevailing mode of economic production and exchange, and the social organization necessarily following from it, form the basis upon which is built up, and from which alone can be explained, the political and intellectual history of that epoch."

In the Manifesto itself we find the following words: —

"Does it require deep intuition to comprehend that man's ideas, views, and conceptions, in one word, man's consciousness, changes with every change in the conditions of his material subsistence, in his social relations, and in his social life? What else does the history of ideas prove than that intellectual production changes its character in proportion as material production is changed?"

It is the development of economic society, then, which is producing the ideas of our time. The ideas are effect and not cause.[1]

When we adopt this materialistic conception of history our socialism becomes entirely a matter of evolution going on in the social world. This socialism is, from its author, often called Marxist socialism, and it is that which is dominant in Germany. At the same time, it must be acknowledged that the German social democrats are not entirely true to this theory of evolutionary socialism. While they give evolution a large place, they do introduce an ethical element, and appeal most earnestly to the wage-earning masses to help forward the socialistic movement. Their action is based upon an assumption of will, free, and not bound wholly, at any rate, by social laws. One of the leaders of the German social democracy, in a recent work giving an excellent succinct summary of the German socialistic philosophy, says that socialism is necessary, because men are men with inclinations and capacity to struggle for the attainment of their desires. The evolution of society is such, he claims, that we must, in the future, either have barbarism or socialism; and, taking men as we find them, we know they will choose socialism, and they will shape their action in accordance with their choice.[2]

The evolution which is inevitably bringing socialism is that which may be briefly described as the development of competing industries into monopolies; and this

---

[1] Cf. this statement in the "Erfurter Programm," by Karl Kautsky: "In the last instance the history of mankind is determined, not by the ideas of men, but by the development of economic society." P. 38.
[2] "Das Erfurter Programm," by Karl Kautsky, pp. 131-145. Der Aufbau des Zukunftsstaates.

development, the socialists maintain, is destined to become practically universal and all-inclusive. The socialists trace the development of industry from the Middle Ages, in which production was carried on in small shops, and the tools were owned by the workers. The private ownership of tools and of land is held to be proper to industry on a small scale. This period of small industries is followed by a period of *manufactures*, distinguished from the present period, called the period of *modern* or *grand industry*. The period of manufactures lasted, it is stated, from the middle of the sixteenth to the last third of the eighteenth century, when the period of grand industry began.[1]

The period of manufactures is characterized by the employment of artisans by a capitalist, who assembles them in one workshop and organizes their industry. There arises in this period the distinct capitalistic and employing class, separated by a wider and wider gulf from the growing wage-earning, or proletarian class.[2] The development of concentration of production, however, is slow until we enter the period of modern industry, when it begins to move at an accelerating rate of speed, which continually increases, exhibiting finally its true nature in the latter half of the nineteenth century. This development will proceed until we have complete concentration of production, it is claimed by socialists; and the only choice will be between concentration under private and irresponsible, and concentration under public and responsible, management. This concentration of production, finally amounting to unification, demonstrates,

[1] See "The Student's Marx," by Edward Aveling, p. 73.
[2] Proletarian class is now used to designate a class of wage-earners not owning the tools with which they work.

according to the socialistic law of evolution, the possibility of socialism. But this evolution does more than demonstrate the possibility of socialism; it shows its necessity, for along with this growth of concentration in production under private management, the advantages of increasing productivity accrue to a small class, while the lot of the great masses becomes more and more intolerable. There grows up what is called an *industrial reserve army* of unemployed men vainly seeking work. This army naturally depresses wages at all times. Periods of prosperity cannot exhaust it entirely, and thus they do not bring that increase in the rate of wages which would otherwise take place; and periods of depression swell the army to enormous proportions, and render the lot of the masses a more hopeless one than before. Production is carried on vigorously; but this implies a public with purchasing power, if production is to continue. Now, it is precisely characteristic of modern industry that the purchasing power of the masses, relatively at least, declines, and less and less keeps pace with the growth of production. Consequently there must be a *relative overproduction* as well as a *relative over-population*, as seen in the industrial reserve army. Goods pile up until the result is a crisis, and consequent industrial stagnation. Now, as the powers of production increase, crises must become more and more frequent, more and more lasting, until we can scarcely hope to escape from one period of industrial stagnation before we are overtaken by another crisis. This capitalistic law of development, it is held, becomes intolerable, and the change to socialism becomes also easy, because it is simply necessary to change the management of production, and develop it a little further to attain the socialistic state. If we have, for example, a complete monopoly in any line of the business the first change, and the great change, necessary to render this socialistic is to change the manager; "to expropriate the expropriateurs," to use the phrase of Marx. This is easier because the workers have become an army trained and disciplined to act together; and, moreover, an army of men among whom common experiences, common trials, and common sorrows have produced a deeper and deeper feeling of solidarity. The historical development of society is sketched by Friedrich Engels in his work, "The Development of Socialism from Utopia to Science."[1] The most recent and authoritative statement, however, is that which is found in the "Erfurter Programm," the first words of which, "The economic development," are specially significant. It reads as follows:—

"The economic development of industrial society tends inevitably to the ruin of small industries, which are based upon the workman's private ownership of the means of production. It separates him from these means of production, and converts him into a destitute member of the proletariat, whilst a comparatively small number of capitalists and great landowners obtain a monopoly of the means of production.

"Hand in hand with this growing monopoly goes the crushing out of existence of these shattered small industries by industries of colossal growth, the development of the tool into the machine, and a gigantic increase in the productiveness of human labor. But all the advantages of this revolution are monopolized by the capitalists and landowners. To the proletariat, and to the rapidly sinking middle classes, to the small tradesmen of the towns and the peasant proprietors (*Bauern*), it brings an increasing uncertainty of existence, increasing misery, oppression, servitude, degradation, and exploitation (*Ausbeutung*).

[1] An English translation is published in Sonnenschein's Social Science Series. Another translation may be had from the office of the newspaper, *The People*, 184 William Street, New York.

"Ever greater grows the mass of the proletariat, ever vaster the army of the unemployed, ever sharper the contrast between oppressors and oppressed, ever fiercer that war of classes between bourgeoisie and proletariat which divides modern society into two hostile camps, and is the common characteristic of every industrial country. The gulf between the propertied classes and the destitute is widened by the crises arising from capitalist production, which become daily more comprehensive and omnipotent, which make universal uncertainty the normal condition of society, and which furnish a proof that the forces of production have outgrown the existing social order, and that private ownership of the means of production has become incompatible with their full development and their proper application.

"Private ownership of the means of production, formerly the means of securing his product to the producer, has now become the means of expropriating the peasant proprietors, the artisans, and the small tradesmen; and placing the non-producers, the capitalists, and large land-owners in possession of the products of labor. Nothing but the conversion of capitalist private ownership of the means of production — the earth and its fruits, mines and quarries, raw material, tools, machines, means of exchange — into social ownership, and the substitution of socialist production, carried on by and for society in the place of the present production of commodities for exchange, can effect such a revolution that, instead of large industries and the steadily growing capacities of common production being, as hitherto, a source of misery and oppression to the classes whom they have despoiled, they may become a source of the highest well-being, and of the most perfect and comprehensive harmony.

"This social revolution involves the emancipation, not merely of the proletariat, but of the whole human race, which is suffering under existing conditions. But this emancipation can be achieved by the working class alone, because all other classes, despite their mutual strife of interests, take their stand upon the principle of private ownership of the means of production, and have a common interest in maintaining the existing social order.

"The struggle of the working classes against capitalist exploitation must of necessity be a political struggle. The working classes can neither carry on their economic struggle, nor develop their economic organization, without political rights. They cannot effect the transfer of the means of production to the community without first being invested with political power.

"It must be the aim of social democracy to give conscious unanimity to this struggle of the working classes, and to indicate the inevitable goal."

A less extreme position in regard to evolution is taken generally by the English Socialists, especially by the Fabians; and this less extreme position seems, to the author, one which gives socialism in reality a far stronger case. The modern socialist does not think that a plan of social reconstruction can be drawn up out of his own inner consciousness, and then introduced purely by persuasion. He holds that we must observe carefully the tendencies of social evolution, and shape our plans with reference to these. He claims that the evolution of society which is taking place, — chiefly spontaneously, so far as society at large is concerned; that is to say, without any self-conscious effort to bring it about, — is entirely favorable to socialism, and that socialism otherwise could not exist. At the same time, he is not inclined to think that the development in the future must necessarily take one single form, or that it will be satisfactory without self-conscious social effort. He does not adopt the materialist conception of history, but gives room for the play of conscience, and to the conscience he does not hesitate to appeal. The more conservative socialists see many evidences of the break-down of the present social order, showing the necessity of changes, and they observe evidences of a current set in the direction of socialism. Among these evidences may be mentioned, of course, first of all the tendency towards monopoly, as evidenced by combinations, rings, and trusts, and the concentration of wealth of all kinds in a few hands. The growing solidarity of labor, which is becoming national, international, and even cosmopolitan, is adduced as a further evidence. The incompetency of the captains of industry to perform their functions with respect to the continuous production of goods, and their inability to preserve their command over the industrial army, is to them a strong proof that a change must come, and that socialism is the natural outcome of the present system. We are asked to direct our attention to great strikes, like those which have taken place at Buffalo, Chicago, and elsewhere, and to see in these proof positive of the incompetency of the captains of industry, an incompetency for which they as individuals are not necessarily to blame, but an incompetency which arises out of the nature of modern industrial society. It would be held, unquestionably, that something was wrong in an army, if the commanders were not able to preserve order, and to perform the functions which naturally belong to them as leaders who are to conduct the army to victory. Crises and industrial depressions are held by all socialists to be a proof of the break-down of the present industrial system, and an evidence of the need for radical social reconstruction.

Socialists generally attach importance to the moral wretchedness of society, as seen in divorces and embezzlements and defalcations, both in private and public life; because they hold that society at the present day is so constituted that these iniquities are its natural and almost inevitable outcome. Men cannot be honest, we are told, and maintain themselves in the business world. Private business, it is maintained, uses public office for its own ends, and disgraces public life. Competition in business rules the mass of men, and is transferred to competition in expenditures. Everyone desires to make a greater show than his neighbor. This leads to extravagance, this to wild speculation, and this to embezzlement. The end is seen in wide-spread ruin. Families are disrupted in this way among the higher orders, as the needs of industry separate them among the poorer portion of the community. It is claimed by socialists that all this trouble is too deep-seated to be cured by any reform which leaves the present industrial order unchanged in its essential features.

As socialism is expected to come as the result of evolution, to a greater or less extent brought about and guided by the wishes and intelligence of men, it is not anticipated by the modern socialists that it will come all at once. No one expects to go to bed one night under a capitalistic *régime* and to wake up next morning with socialism in full swing. It is held rather that socialism will come piecemeal, although the active and ardent socialists do unquestionably anticipate that large instalments will come in the comparatively near future, and that these will be followed by other large instalments with considerable rapidity. Naturally it is thought that large monopolistic undertakings will be socialized first, and business after business will be absorbed as it becomes monopolistic. It is not, by the most moderate faction, proposed to take over business conducted on a small scale, unless those so conducting it desire to give up their business and enter into the co-operative commonwealth. The small farmer and the artisan working in his own little shop may continue their operations as long as they are able to do so, and desire to do so. At the same time, it is undoubtedly expected that the process of concentration of businesses will be continued and accelerated when something like genuine socialism is well under way. Socialism proposes to carry forward existing industrial tendencies, but to direct the industrial movement in such manner that it may yield the greatest good to the greatest number, and so that the present evils of these tendencies may be altogether avoided, or reduced to an inconsiderable minimum. Consequently it is frankly admitted that the small producer will be less and less able to hold his own against socialistic production. It is urged, however, that even now he is being ruined by the competition of great undertakings, but has no refuge except the lot of the wage-earner, unless he chooses to become a small retail shopkeeper, or the proprietor of a restaurant, to use a German expression for what we would call in the United States a saloon-keeper, having an insignificant hotel attachment, that is to say, maintaining a precarious existence on the fringe of economic society. It is held, on the other hand, that socialism would prove an attractive force, and that the small producers would gradually surrender their businesses and enter some branch of socialist production, so that the expropriation of the small capitalist would take place without the suffering which at present accompanies it.

An interesting question is whether the transformation will take place with or without compensation. The more conservative and sensible socialists desire that it shall be as easy as possible to all concerned, and they do not all deny the possibility of compensation in consumption goods, in values to be used, that is, in consumption, but for which there would be little opportunity to find productive employment, and thus yield income. The Fabian Society of England desires that the change should go forward without payment for capital and land, that is to say, the instruments of production generally, holding that this cannot be required by ethical considerations; but they think that the extinction of private property in land and capital should not be effected without relief to expropriated individuals.[1]

Another interesting question of great importance is whether the changes proposed by socialism are to be accomplished peacefully. It may be said, in general, that socialists earnestly hope that peaceful and legal measures will be sufficient. Some, however, hold that the opponents of socialism, that is to say, in the main, the privileged classes, will rebel against the constituted authorities, when they once clearly perceive that these are exercising their power in behalf of the socialistic state. Yet there are those who hold that socialism is already stealing upon us unawares, and that its approach will be sufficiently gradual and beneficent to meet with more and more favor, and thus anticipate no violence, even from the higher orders of society. Perhaps it can be said, in general, that the English socialists are the least apprehensive that the transformation will be accompanied by anything like civil war.

[1] Appendix II., " Basis of the Fabian Society."

CHAPTER IX.

SOCIALISM CONTRASTED WITH OTHER SCHEMES OF INDUSTRIAL CHANGE.

SOCIALISM in the popular sense is often brought into opposition with what is called state socialism. Reference has already been made to state socialism, and it is not necessary to add many words to what has been said regarding it. State socialism is an expression which originated in Germany, and refers to reforms to be accomplished by the existing state, with a view to the establishment of permanent social peace. State socialism, as viewed in Germany, may mean the absorption of the production and distribution of wealth by the state, or it may mean a further extension of the industrial activity of the state without going so far. But, at any rate, it does not propose radical changes in the state itself. Social democracy, which is, generally speaking, socialism in the popular sense, is socialism plus democracy; but state socialism in Germany is socialism plus monarchy, and is therefore conservative. The social democracy advocates a class struggle to be conducted by the wage-earning class, and to be continued until it is able to abolish all classes. State socialism proposes that a power above the people shall regulate the relations among classes, and establish among them harmony and peace. If state socialism goes so far as to propose that the state should take upon itself the production and distribution of wealth, it contemplates still the existence of higher and lower classes, and would transform the captains of industry into superior civil servants, still guiding and managing production. Social democracy, on the other hand, wants the administration of the economic state to be conducted democratically in such manner that it may confer substantially equal benefits upon all. A leader of German social democracy says that state socialism is a name proper only to those interferences of the state, or extensions of the functions of the state, "which aim to make an end to the class struggle between the bourgeoisie and the proletariat, and to reconcile social classes by means of a strong monarchical political power, which, standing above the classes and independent of them, gives to each one its own. This activity of the power of the state is designed to make it unnecessary, or even impossible, that the proletariat should represent and care for its own interests. The intention is rather that, full of confidence, it should commit its interests to the government."

This same writer says that state socialism presupposes, as an essential characteristic, the existence of a government independent of the masses.[1]

It is difficult, then, to see how, according to the leaders of social democratic thought in Germany, the expression state socialism would have any particular applicability in democratic countries. At the most, the protest against state socialism in these countries can mean that political as well as economic changes are required to bring about the socialistic ideal. It is, however, admitted by all socialists that the present state is not anywhere entirely satisfactory. If it is held that, from the standpoint of

[1] *Die Neue Zeit*, X. Jahrgang, II. Band, s. 706; Karl Kautsky in his article, " Vollmar und der Staatssozialismus."

SOCIALISM WITH OTHER SCHEMES. 87

socialism, there is class government in democratic countries like the United States, as well as in Germany, the question is to be asked, What is the basis of this class government, except private property in the instruments of production, and will it not disappear if private property in the instruments of production is transformed into public property in these instruments? Of course, in Germany, class government has a far broader basis.

Socialism and nationalism are two expressions which require some treatment, because the use of these two terms produces an endless amount of confusion. Nationalism, it may be said, is simply one kind of socialism; and if there is any such thing as a distinctive American socialism, it must be held to be nationalism. Nationalism contemplates, perhaps, fewer changes in the state, — using the word state in its generic sense, — than does social democracy, represented in this country by the socialistic labor party. Nationalism is, in this respect, more conservative. It proposes to use, in the main, the existing political divisions of the country, although Mr. Bellamy contemplates the wiping out of the separate commonwealths as distinct political divisions. This, however, is no necessary part of either the nationalistic or the socialistic program, and it would seem to have been a bad slip on Mr. Bellamy's part, weakening his cause. Nationalism, as it has been presented in this country, is also clear and explicit as to equality in distribution; but this can hardly be put forward as a peculiarity. Perhaps the greatest difference of all, between the socialistic labor party and nationalism, is found in the fact that nationalism does not present socialism as a class movement. The socialistic labor party makes socialism a movement of the wage-earning classes, whereas nationalism appeals to all classes, and hopes to avoid class struggles. Nationalism has found its adherents to some considerable extent among the professional classes, and the spirit and the method with which it has conducted its agitation of socialism distinguish it from the socialistic labor party to a greater extent than differences in final program.[1]

Socialism is often contrasted with Christian socialism, and we frequently hear it said we must either have socialism or Christian socialism. It is to be feared, however, that the expression, Christian socialism con-

[1] A prominent nationalist sends the author the following statement of principles: "Nationalism is logically formulated state socialism. It completes the scheme of democracy by making the plan of political equality practicable through the institution of economic equality. It places political freedom upon its correct basis of economic freedom. It solves the problem of an equitable distribution of the industrial products which, under the capacity of modern mechanical processes, are potentially sufficient to meet the requirements of all mankind, by transferring the ownership of the instrument of production from private hands — which now operate them primarily with reference to personal profit, and only secondarily with reference to public service — to the producers themselves, thus organizing production and distribution as national functions, conducted solely with reference to the public welfare — the instrumentality of the government being what Mr. Bellamy has so aptly declared to be 'the hand of the people.' To attain these ends the nationalist plan is to encourage all tendencies towards augmenting the business efficiency of the community, whether national, state, or municipal. There appears to be no means of equitably apportioning the returns from industrial production among the members of the community — owing to the impossibility of determining the share to which each is entitled — on any basis of merit or effort. An equal division of the products, therefore, appears to be demanded on ethical grounds; and, as under a national organization of industry there would be ample to meet all demands for not only the necessities, but the comforts and the reasonable luxuries of life, there would be no hardship or injustice in such an apportionment. But as this is the ultimate aim, it can only be stated as an ideal, and does not form a feature of any immediate program."

SOCIALISM WITH OTHER SCHEMES.   89

veys no very clear ideas, and is such that it is not easy to define it with any accuracy. Christian socialism means many different things. One thing which it always means is a spirit of brotherly love, which, it is insisted, is an essential part of Christianity. Christian socialism means that we are invariably to make our Christianity something real and vital, and to govern our lives by it seven days in the week, and on the market, as well as in the church building. Christian socialism carries with it a protest against the sham and hypocrisy which play such large parts in the lives of professed Christians. Christian socialism, furthermore, teaches us the doctrine of social solidarity, which signifies that our interests are all intertwined, and that one cannot be truly prosperous while others suffer.[1] What can we say more than this about Christian socialism as a whole? If these characteristics are all we can say of Christian socialism as a whole, is it not something entirely vague and indefinite when we come to its application to economic problems? The vital question, of course, is: How shall we apply these principles of brotherhood to the world's business?

The Christian socialism of the middle of the century in England meant a co-operative commonwealth to be attained through voluntary effort. But Christian socialism sometimes means simply modern socialism plus Christianity, the implication being that Christianity of itself leads to socialism. Of course, whether Christianity does lead to socialism or not must depend upon the view which we take with respect to socialism. As has already been said, the Christian who thinks that social-

[1] " While one man remains base, no man can be altogether great and noble." This utterance of Margaret Fuller is entirely in the spirit of Christian socialism.

ism will bring what its adherents promise must, of course, become a socialist. But the whole question at issue is whether or not socialism is able to keep its promises. Sometimes Christian socialism means socialism with a protest against the•materialism which the Marxists have most unfortunately associated with socialism. It may also have reference to methods of agitation, and mean that only those methods will meet with approval which are compatible with Christian ethics. Christian socialism would thus imply a protest against violent measures. But as socialists have generally renounced anything but peaceful, legal, and constitutional methods, Christian socialism as thus used would not carry with it anything very distinctive. It would seem, perhaps, best to drop the use of the expression Christian socialism as something which leads to confusion rather than to clearness of thought, unless, indeed, accompanying the expression, some clear explanation of it be given.

A few other distinctions require explanation to bring out current misapprehensions, and to render socialistic thought clearer by way of contrast. Socialism is often described as paternalism. Probably no objection to socialism is, in the United States, more frequently heard than that it is paternalism. This is, beyond all doubt, a misapprehension. Most of those who have used the expression paternalism employ it altogether in a loose way, which lacks definite and precise meaning. Paternalism in government is an historical conception which became important in the seventeenth century in England. The controversy between Sir Robert Filmer and the philosopher Locke was one which concerned paternalism in the true sense of the word. It was a controversy regarding the nature of sovereignty, and it did not at all concern the extent of the functions of government. Sir Robert Filmer held that the power of sovereignty was like that of the father of the family, and was in fact derived from Adam, who was the first sovereign as well as father, and that through the patriarchs it descended to kings. Filmer's work was called "Patriarcha, or the Natural Power of Kings." Its character is indicated by the titles of the three chapters into which it is divided. These titles are as follows: Chapter I., That the First Kings were Fathers of Families; Chapter II., It is Unnatural for the People to Govern or to Choose Governors; Chapter III., Positive Laws do not Infringe the Natural and Fatherly Power of Kings.[1] It would seem, then, that those are historically inaccurate who use "paternalism" as if it had reference to the functions of government. They are also illogical when they use the word paternalism to describe the activity of a democratic state, because in a democracy the people themselves exercise power, and the state does not exist as something separate and distinct from them. There has become current, however, a kind of paternalism which meets with much favor on the part of many. It is the paternalism of the rich and powerful.[2]

There are those who look to leaders of wealth and culture to provide for the people many things which the people need. These adherents of paternalism hold that rich men should furnish the people of the United States

[1] Locke's "Essay on Civil Government" was a reply to Patriarcha; the two are printed together in Morley's Universal Library.

[2] An editorial writer in one of the leading weeklies of the United States has expressed himself favorably to the paternalism of the rich, and has given it as his opinion that the American people are willing to tolerate any amount of paternalism of this sort. It is hoped that this is not entirely correct.

with universities, with art galleries, with educational institutions of all sorts, and take the lead in every kind of social activity. The people are not to help themselves through government, but are to wait quietly until it pleases some wealthy person to give them the things which they want. It has also become customary in many parts of the country in all large business undertakings to wait upon the movements of a few leaders of large means; and the masses of the people are, in too many sections of the country, losing that enterprise and initiative which it was claimed characterized the early Americans.

Whatever other accusation we may bring against socialism as actually presented to-day by its active leaders, it is not true that it favors paternalism, either through governments or by the rich. Karl Marx early told the workingmen that they must look to themselves for emancipation, and warned them not to expect or to seek help from other classes. Socialistic agitation has laid extreme emphasis upon self-help, and the wage-earners have been estranged by the social democratic agitation from persons of wealth and social power of other kinds who could render them valuable service in their efforts to improve their conditions.

Socialism and anarchy are often confounded, although they are different enough, and, as a matter of fact, socialists and anarchists are most bitter enemies. Everywhere socialism fights anarchy, and, on the other hand, is antagonized by it. Where the one is strong, the other, as already stated, is likely to languish. Social democracy drove John Most out of Germany, and from early days has exerted itself most vigorously to keep down anything like an anarchistic movement. The weakness of anarchy in Germany is to be attributed more largely to the efforts of the social democracy than to any other force. Anarchists, when discovered, are regularly expelled from the conventions of the social democrats in Germany, and they were expelled from the International Socialistic Convention in Brussels in 1891, and again in Zürich in 1893. So much about the facts of the case.

So far as the anarchistic theory is concerned it may be said that it desires the co-operative commonwealth to be attained by the abolition of all government. It resists authority as the chief evil. It holds that the cooperative commonwealth would spontaneously come into existence, if it were not possible, through government, for one man to exercise authority over another man. This anticipation the socialists look upon as utopian, and they dread above everything the anarchistic agitation against existing governments. The anarchists refrain from participation in government, and seek its overthrow; while the socialists take part in the existing governments, and seek to accomplish their ends by constitutional and legal measures. One moves in one direction and the other in the opposite direction; and it is not strange that the socialistic labor party not long ago published a tract entitled, "Anarchy and Socialism Antagonistic Opposites."[1]

Socialism may be contrasted with voluntary co-operation, especially as presented by the early English Christian Socialists; that is, Ludlow, Hughes, Vansittart Neale, Charles Kingsley, and others. Co-operation, as a scheme of social reconstruction, seeks the co-operative commonwealth; but it hopes to attain this in the main

[1] The Fabian Society has recently published a tract called "The Impossibilities of Anarchism."

without the aid of government, and hopes that using institutions as they exist, by industry and thrift the workers may acquire the instruments of production and organize production themselves, carrying it on at their own risk. It has been hoped that co-operative undertaking would follow co-operative undertaking, until all industry should be absorbed, and the workers should enjoy the benefits resulting from ownership of land and capital, and from the management of business. The ad-adherents of voluntary co-operation, who, it must be acknowledged, are not now very numerous, like the anarchists, do not propose to establish a co-operative commonwealth through government, but through voluntary efforts; but, on the other hand, they do not antagonize existing institutions and governments as hostile to their plans.

Land nationalization, so much discussed, is simply one plank in the platform of the socialists, and socialists only antagonize it when it is presented as something complete and sufficient. The single tax, however, which is the expression used to indicate the plans of Mr. Henry George and his followers, is still farther removed from socialism. What the single tax proposes in itself, as we have already seen, is to tax out of land the value which is due to social effort; to deduct the value of the land itself as distinct from improvements on the land, but to leave the cultivation and other utilization of land to private effort. The recent development of the single taxers in the United States has been in the direction of individualism; but elsewhere, as in Australia and New Zealand, it appears that the single tax has been combined with other measures to which the socialists could give approval, and that it has not in these countries assumed the anti-socialistic cast which it has at present in the United States.

Socialism, finally, must be contrasted with social reform. The two often favor similar measures, and are confounded by loose observers; but the more carefully one looks into them, the greater appears the difference. Socialists themselves have come to see this; but it has not been so generally perceived by the more pronounced opponents of socialism. Social reform has been called by a German writer " Positivism," to indicate its positive constructive nature. It does not hold that an entire social reconstruction is necessary, but believes that much which has been done in the past, and is incorporated in the existing society, is very good; and it proposes the careful development and improvement of existing institutions. Social reform does not find any one panacea for social evils, but holds that remedies are numerous, because society is many-sided and complex. Social reform views with favor what socialists and adherents of the panaceas generally look upon with impatience as mere patchwork. Social reform looks to the church and voluntary associations of men, as well as to the state, for further growth and improvement. Social reform is very generally willing to extend the functions of government, and is not unfrequently willing to go so far as the socialization of monopoly; but it does not see the desirability of the socialization of the entire industrial field. Social reform is conservative, and not revolutionary.

CHAPTER X.

THE LITERATURE OF SOCIALISM.

THE writings of socialists of recognized standing are the primary sources of information concerning socialism. Modern socialism exists nowhere in actual practice, and consequently we cannot study socialism in action. We may observe, on the one hand, certain forces actually at work in society which throw some light on the industrial reconstruction proposed by socialism, and, on the other, we can direct our attention to the agitation of socialists which aims to bring about the realization of their aspirations. While we can derive help in understanding the nature of socialism from existing social tendencies, and from an examination of socialistic agitation, the works written by socialists can alone give us full and complete information at first hand. There are certain men who are acknowledged to be socialist leaders, and there are books which are recognized by socialists as correct expositions of socialism. The spoken utterances of socialists and their writings are decisive concerning modern socialism. The careful student will wish to go to the original sources of information.

The chief writer of modern socialism is unquestionably Karl Marx, and his principal work is "Das Kapital," frequently called "the Bible of socialism." The position which Marx occupies is also illustrated by the statement of a socialist that "socialism is a religion and Marx is its Luther." One volume of Marx's "Kapital" was published before his death, and the second was prepared for publication after his death, from his manuscripts, by his friend, Friedrich Engels; the third volume, likewise prepared by this friend, is expected to appear soon. Karl Marx is regarded, even by many who are not socialists, as one of the greatest thinkers of the century, and few others have influenced the development of economic thought as he has. His work is largely a chain of deductive reasoning, and is difficult reading, but it must be mastered by him who would thoroughly understand what the socialism of to-day is. Marx, unfortunately, attached to socialism certain things which do not belong to it as an industrial system, for he made socialism a philosophy of every department of social life. This is a natural consequence of his materialistic conception of history, to which reference has already been made. Unfortunately his followers in Germany and other countries have not yet been able to emancipate themselves from his materialistic conception of history as a natural evolution determined by economic conditions. Socialism, to the strict Marxist, means a conception of religion, of literature, and of science, as well as of an economic philosophy. It is thus that socialism, in countries like Germany, has raised needless antagonism, because it has seemed to be opposed to Christianity and to many received institutions which have no necessary direct connection with industry. Nevertheless, Marx must be studied carefully, even to understand the socialism of those who reject his materialism and all that goes with it. It is true that in socialism Karl Marx occupies a position like that of Adam Smith in the history of political economy, all going before him in a manner preparing the way for him, and all coming after taking him for a starting-point.

The first volume of "Das Kapital," which is in a measure complete in itself, has been translated into English by Mr. William Moore, a friend of Marx, and by Dr. Edward Aveling, Marx's son-in-law. The translation has been edited by Friedrich Engels, and it may be taken to be a faithful rendering of the original.

Many expositions of Marx's views have been published, but perhaps the two most noteworthy are "The Student's Marx," by Dr. Aveling, and "Karl Marx' Oekonomische Lehren," by Karl Kautsky. It is noteworthy that Dr. Aveling has also prepared a work called "The Student's Darwin," because this is an illustration of the fact that the German socialist assigns a position in social science to Karl Marx like that which Charles Darwin holds in natural science. Dr. Aveling, however, who is a specialist in natural science, does not hesitate to assign a higher position to Marx. The following words are taken from Dr. Aveling's preface :

"Marx was more universal. Darwin was a man given up to biological, or at the most, scientific work in the restricted sense of the word. Marx was, on the other hand, master in the fullest sense, not only of his special subject, but of all branches of science, of seven or eight different languages, of the literature of Europe. He knew and loved all forms of art — poetry and the drama most of all. . . . Another difference between the two men, with the advantage on the side of the economic philosopher, is that he was not only a philosopher, but a man of action. Marx was an active leader of men and of organizations. Thousands of workers of both sexes and of all lands, who may never read a line of his philosophic writings, know him and love him as a practical revolutionist who, more than any other, helped to make the working-class revolt of the nineteenth century, and who as long as he lived took an active and informing part in it." [1]

[1] Pages ix., x.

Friedrich Engels is, next to Marx, the most important man in the history of German social democracy. While he generously ascribed the chief originality in the socialistic philosophy to Marx, it is held by some of his friends that he is the more systematic thinker. Marx and Engels, however, worked together, and it is probably impossible to tell just what each one may owe to the other. The Manifesto of the communist party, issued in 1847, is their joint product and is one of the chief original documents in the history of modern socialism.[1]

The principal works of Engels are: "Lage der arbeitenden Klasse in England, in 1844," published in England in 1845, two years before the Manifesto was issued. This work has been translated by Mrs. Florence Kelley with an appendix written in 1886 and a preface in 1887, and it was published in the latter year.[2] The second is, "Entwickelung des Sozialismus von der Utopie zur Wissenschaft," translated into English and published under the title, "Socialism, Utopian and Scientific."[3] The third is "Ursprung der Familie, des Privateigenthums und des Staates."

August Bebel, one of the two great political leaders of the German social democracy at the present day, has written a work which forms an important part of the literature of German socialism. It is called "Die Frau und der Sozialismus."[4] An early edition of this work

---

[1] An English translation, edited and annotated by Friedrich Engels in 1888, is published by the New York Labor News Co., 64 East Fourth street, New York, and by William Reeves, London, 1888.

[2] New York, John W. Lovell & Co. It has also been published in England by William Reeves, London.

[3] Sonnenschein, London, 1892.   [4] Stuttgart, 1891.

has been translated under the title, "Woman in the Past, Present, and Future."[1]

The works named, if carefully studied, will give one a very correct knowledge of the fundamental principles of German socialism; but one who would understand it fully as it exists to-day would do well to read the clear and concise exposition of the present platform or program of German social democracy by Karl Kautsky. It is called "Das Erfurter Programm."[2]

Die Neue Zeit, a weekly magazine of scientific socialism, will be found helpful to anyone who wishes to go into minute details, and to follow the progress of the movement, especially so far as its theoretical aspects are concerned. *Der Vorwärts* is the chief daily organ of the social democratic party, and gives particular details of the agitation.

A professor in the law school of the University of Vienna, Dr. Anton Menger, has written works which are of importance in modern socialism, especially because they view socialism from the legal standpoint. Attention is called to the two following treatises by Dr. Menger: "Das Recht auf den vollen Arbeitsertrag,"[3] and "Die besitzlosen Volksklassen."[4]

There are two other writers who are of great importance to those who would understand the evolution of socialistic thought in Germany, although their works are not received as authority by the social democratic party. The first is Karl Rodbertus, often called Rodbertus-Jagetzow, a man

[1] Published in New York by John W. Lovell & Co., 1886, and in England by the Modern Press, London, 1885.
[2] Stuttgart, J. H. W. Dietz, 1892.
[3] Second revised edition, Stuttgart, 1891.
[4] Second corrected edition, Tübingen, 1890.

of conservative tendencies, who is regarded as one of the leaders of the state socialists. There can be little doubt, however, that the active socialists of Germany and of other countries have been influenced directly by his writings, the principal one of which is "Zur Beleuchtung der Sozialen Frage," but "Das Kapital" may also be mentioned. The other writer is Ferdinand Lassalle, who, unlike Rodbertus, entered actively into the working-class agitation. Ferdinand Lassalle played an important part in the formation of a working-class party in Germany, but what was peculiar in his thought and his methods has finally been rejected by the social democratic party, which, nevertheless, holds him in honor. A complete collection of his writings has been prepared under the auspices of the party, and edited by one of its leaders, namely, Eduard Bernstein, and published in three volumes in Berlin in 1892, with the title, "Reden und Schriften." This edition is accompanied by notes and an introductory essay upon "Lasalle and His Significance for the Social Democracy." This essay and the notes are especially instructive, because they show the difference between the earlier and the present socialistic thought and agitation in Germany.

French writers seem not to have added much that is essential to the theory of socialism. They may have adapted it better to French conditions and French thought in working it over, but one who is looking for new principles or new measures will scarcely find them in French works. French writers are often inclined to lay special emphasis upon the development of local self-government, but this can scarcely be called a peculiar feature. Among active French socialist authors, we may mention the son-in-law of Marx, Lafargue, who has written a work on "The Evolution of Property," which has been translated into English and into German.[1]

Two French socialist authors of note, recently deceased, are César de Paepe and Benoit Malon, whose most important theoretical work is, perhaps, "Socialisme Intégral." The most important source of information in regard to French socialistic thought is found, however, in the monthly magazine, *La Revue Socialiste*, which has appeared since 1885.

The thought of Marx was early presented to readers in all countries and in all languages by many different authors. Mr. H. M. Hyndman, for example, wrote a work, "The Historical Basis of Socialism in England,"[2] published in 1883; and Laurence Gronlund wrote "The Co-operative Commonwealth," in 1884,[3] in which he professed to present German socialism as it appeared after it had passed through the mind of one who had learned to think and feel as an American. These works appeared before socialism had gained much headway, either in England or in the United States. They have influenced socialism in these two countries, and are still important.

English socialism, as presented by the Fabians in the "Fabian Essays in Socialism,"[4] has become emancipated from the materialistic philosophy of Karl Marx, which, as essentially un-English as well as un-American, could not fail to prove a great obstacle to the growth of socialism among the English-speaking nations. The "Fabian Essays in Socialism" give us a genuine English social-

---

[1] The English edition is published in Sonnenschein's Social Science Series.
[2] Kegan Paul, London, Publisher.   [3] Lee & Shepard, Boston.
[4] Published by the Fabian Society, 276 Strand, London, and by the Humboldt Publishing Co., New York.

THE LITERATURE OF SOCIALISM. 103

ism, practical, straight-forward, divorced from excrescences which have no connection with socialism as an industrial system. The "Fabian Tracts"[1] are also important sources of information concerning English socialistic thought and action. Mr. Sidney Webb's "Socialism in England"[2] belongs to this same school of socialism and must not be overlooked by the careful student. The periodical organ of the Fabians is called *Fabian News*.[3]

The Social Democratic Federation is the only socialistic party in England, besides the Fabians, working on a national scale. Mr. Hyndman is one of its leaders, and, in addition to the work of his already mentioned, there may be added, "The Commercial Crises of the Nineteenth Century."[4] The organ of this party is *Jus-*

[1] Published by the Fabian Society, and can be had either separately or in bound form.

[2] In Sonnenschein's Social Science Series, Second Edition, 1893.

[3] The following quotation from a letter, written by one who is well acquainted with the facts of the case, shows the number of channels through which socialism reaches the English newspaper reading public: "With regard to the three papers, the Chronicle, the Sun, and the Star, copies of which I sent you, I am afraid those individual numbers contained little indication of their collectivism. I will try to send you other copies which contain clearer indications of the lines they adopt. All three are, of course, out-and-out supporters of the Progressive Party in London, and a Progressive is of necessity a practical socialist, since the Program adopted by their party is that set forth in Webb's London Program. Hence we view with considerable satisfaction the appointment of Lord Rosebery as Premier, as he is an undoubted member of the Progressive Party, and, as you will have noticed, has consented to receive an address from the party in a few days at St. James's Hall, when he will make a public declaration on London affairs. The other papers referred to are mostly rather obscure ones, and bring out their socialism in a somewhat indirect fashion. Probably fifty or sixty members of the Fabian Society are editors or journalists of one sort or another, and they let no opportunity slip of working in their ideas."

[4] Sonnenschein's Social Science Series, London.

tice,[1] at present in its eleventh year. The party has also issued a series of social democratic tracts.[2]

The works of T. Kirkup, an English author, deserve mention. They are, "An Inquiry into Socialism"[3] and a "History of Socialism."[4] The significance of these books lies in the fact that they give statements of socialism which seem, to the author of the present work, to be as conservative as socialism possibly can be.

Mr. Bellamy's "Looking Backward" and his organ, *The New Nation*, which has recently ceased to appear, constitute the chief sources of information concerning American nationalism. *The People* is the English organ of the socialistic labor party, and that, with the German socialistic periodical, *Die Volks-Zeitung*, gives full information concerning the movements of that wing of socialism in the United States which is represented by this party.

We have already seen that Christian socialism is something with varied and indefinite meaning; but the literature which is described under that designation is important to the student of socialism, because it reveals the ideas of at least a section of the church with respect to the social questions of the day, and also to socialism itself. Perhaps one of the best works, giving one a tolerably correct picture of that somewhat vague and elusive spirit called Christian socialism, is Miss Katharine Pearson Woods's interesting novel, "Metzerott, Shoemaker."[5] Another American work which is thought by some to give the best statement of Christian socialism in

[1] Published in London by H. Quelch, 37a Clerkenwell Green, E.C.
[2] These can also be obtained from the office of *Justice*.
[3] London, Longmans, Green, & Co., 1887.
[4] London and Edinburgh, Adam and Charles Black, 1892.
[5] T. Y. Crowell & Co., Boston and New York.

its modern applications is, "Socialism from Genesis to Revelation," by the Rev. F. M. Sprague. The Rev. Alfred Barry's "Christianity and Socialism" is also a noteworthy book in this connection.[1] An address on socialism, delivered before the Hull Church Congress in 1892, by the Rev. Dr. B. F. Westcott, Bishop of Durham, should not be overlooked.[2] Most important of all, to those who would keep pace with socialism, is *The Economic Review*, published quarterly at Oxford by the Christian Social Union. Dr. Stewart Headlam's monthly periodical, *The Church Reformer*, is also an exponent of certain Christian socialist tendencies.[3] The organ of Christian socialism in the United States is *The Dawn*, edited by the Rev. W. D. P. Bliss, and published by the editor at Roslindale, Mass.

Protestant German Christian socialism has had two periods of activity. The first centred about the persons of Pastor Rudolph Todt and Court Pastor Adolf Stoecker, and was, to some considerable extent, the product of the former's celebrated work called, " Radical German Socialism and Christian Society" (*Der radikale deutsche Sozialismus und die christliche Gesellschaft*, 1877). Court Pastor Stoecker has given an excellent exposition of his views in his collected "Addresses and Essays."[4] The second period was the product of the awakening due more largely than to any other work, to Paul Göhre's remarkable work, "Three Months a Factory Hand," to which reference has already been made. The centre

[1] Cassell, London, 1890.
[2] Printed as an appendix to Rev. P. W. Sprague's Christian Socialism, and also published separately by W. Reeves, London, 1890.
[3] Published by William Reeves, 185 Fleet St., London, E. C.
[4] Published under the title, "Christlich-Sozial," Bielefeld and Leipsic, Velhagen & Klasing, 1885.

of this new activity is found in the annual gatherings of the Evangelical Social Congress, and the reports of this congress furnish information in regard to what is going forward in Germany along the lines of Christian socialism under Protestant auspices.[1] The monographs issued under the auspices of this Evangelical Christian Congress are also noteworthy.[2]

The Catholics have of late, displayed great activity in the discussion of economic questions, and in this they have been encouraged by Pope Leo XIII., the discussion recently turning largely on his encyclical upon labor. Naturally, this encyclical, as well as other authoritative utterances of the church, are variously interpreted, and the term Christian socialism is often applied to the more radical utterances by Roman Catholics dealing with the labor problem. The two most noteworthy prelates in this connection are the late Bishop von Ketteler of Mainz, and Cardinal Manning, whose activity, however, was practical rather than theoretical. The name of Cardinal Gibbons is also frequently mentioned in this connection,[3] and his remarkable letter upon the Knights of Labor should not be overlooked by one who would familiarize himself with the attitude of the Roman Catholic Church regarding social questions. Probably, however, the work which best deserves attention among all the treatments of social questions from the Roman Catholic standpoint, is still that one on the relation of Christianity to the labor question, written by Bishop von Ketteler, and first published in 1864.[4] The best concise

[1] See Berichte der Evangelisch-Sozialen Kongresse.
[2] Published under the title, Evangelisch-soziale Zeitfragen.
[3] Appendix XI., Bibliography.
[4] Arbeiterfrage und das Christhenthum, 4¹ᵉAuflage mit Einleitung von Windthorst.

and accurate description of Catholic thought and activity in the direction of Christian socialism, is found in an article written by Dr. Andr. Brüll, in the admirable encyclopædia of political science, edited by Professor Conrad and others.[1]

Works written by non-socialists about socialists give us secondary sources of information which are of importance. These works are very numerous, and only a few can be mentioned. Emile de Laveleye's "Socialism of To-day," translated with an addition upon English socialism by Mr. Orpen, is one of the most important works which belong to this class. It is the work of a liberal economist strongly animated by Christian sympathies; but as it was written some ten years ago, it does not give an account of recent movements. Ely's "French and German Socialism" attempts to present impartially the main French and German systems up to the year 1883, when it appeared; and in his "Labor Movement in America," the author has given a descriptive account of socialism in the United States. Graham's "Socialism Old and New," is a recent work, catholic in spirit. Rae's "Contemporary Socialism"[2] is a carefully prepared and scholarly work, but one which takes a more critical attitude than those already mentioned. A work entitled "A Plea for Liberty; An Argument against Socialism and Socialistic Legislation," written by E. S. Robertson, W. Donisthorpe, George Howell, and others, with an introduction by Herbert Spencer, is a work which takes a decidedly more antagonistic spirit with

[1] See "Soziale Reformbestrebungen (Katholisch-Soziale)," in *Handwörterbuch der Staatswissenschaften*, published in Jena, by Gustav Fisher.
[2] Second edition, Sonnenschein & Co., London, 1891.

reference to socialism, and advocates extreme individualism, verging at times on anarchy. Mr. Mallock's books, "Social Equality," "Labour and the Public Welfare," and others, may be mentioned among works taking a position of antagonism to socialism, but which are popular rather than scholarly in character. Sir James Fitzjames Stephens's "Liberty, Equality, and Fraternity" is an able work which takes issue with some of the premises of liberal economics and socialism, especially as found in the writings of John Stuart Mill.

One of the most important earlier treatments of socialism is given by Dr. Rudolf Meyer in his work, "Der Emancipationskampf des vierten Standes."[1] Dr. Meyer wrote this book from the standpoint of an adherent of conservative German politics who took liberal economic views. It is an accurate description of the many phases of socialism, and presents liberal extracts from original documents. It impresses one as the work of a catholic and fair-minded man. Dr. Meyer has, in the present year, published a work in which he gives his impressions based upon subsequent experience. It is entitled "Der Kapitalismus fin de siècle,"[2] and it deserves attention.

The works of Dr. Schäffle, "The Quintessence of Socialism," and "The Impossibility of Social Democracy," both translated into English,[3] are especially worthy of attention. The first of the two attempts to give a correct and colorless statement of the essential ideas of socialism, while the latter criticises severely the social democracy of Germany. It has been found difficult by many to reconcile the one work with the other. Prof.

[1] In 2 vols., Berlin, 1874-5. [2] Vienna and Leipsic, 1894.
[3] Sonnenschein's Social Science Series, London.

Julius Wolf of the University of Zurich, Switzerland. has written a strongly anti-socialistic book which has recently attracted considerable attention. The chief aim of it is to disprove the law of evolution, which is the main feature of the Marxist socialism.[1] While this book was hailed as epoch-making by the newspaper press, specialists have felt called upon to criticise it with unusual severity, as in itself inaccurate, on account of a failure to comprehend socialism, and as inexact in its statistics.

A critique of Marx's socialism, which deserves special attention, is that found in "Die Grundlagen der Karl-Marxschen Kritik," by Georg Adler.[2]

It can scarcely be necessary to add that all economic treatises discuss socialism at greater or less length and more or less fairly. It must be acknowledged, however, that the ordinary political economist has never taken the trouble to master the socialism which he attempts to criticise, and that the criticisms generally found in economic treatises do not go beyond truisms and catchwords, and fail altogether to reach the heart of the subject. There are numerous exceptions, fortunately, and among these exceptions special mention should be made of Dr. Adolph Wagner, who in his "Grundlegung der politischen Oekonomie,"[3] has given an excellent exposition of the fundamental principles at issue in the discussion of socialism.

---

[1] "Sozialismus und kapitalistische Gesellschaftsordnung." Stuttgart, 1892.
[2] Tübingen, 1878.   [3] Third edition, Leipsic, 1892.

PART II.

THE STRENGTH OF SOCIALISM.

PART II.

THE STRENGTH OF SOCIALISM.

CHAPTER I.

INTRODUCTORY REMARKS.

WE have now examined the nature of socialism, and we propose next to look at one side of socialism only, and endeavor to ascertain what good things may be said in its behalf. A consideration of the weakness of socialism will follow; but it seems likely to promote clearness of thought if we separate the one from the other. When it is said that we want to ascertain what strength socialism has, it does not signify a presentation of socialism such as that which an advocate would give. An advocate groups his arguments with reference to the persuasion of those whom he hopes to reach, and he lays particular emphasis upon that which will convince his audience; moreover, he appeals to feeling rather than to intellect, and is inclined to indulge in rhetorical flights. The purpose of the scholar who approaches a subject like socialism with perfect impartiality is quite different. He examines the subject calmly, and seeks to give due weight to all those arguments which an honest and intelligent man must admit in behalf of socialism. He does not endeavor to persuade, but simply to enlighten; and frequently those points which would be most effective in an advocate's plea, he must reject altogether.

The strength of socialism may be considered from two standpoints. One may regard socialism in its influence upon the existing industrial order, and seek to ascertain what beneficial effects it has had, or is likely to have, upon this order, although it may not change it in its fundamental features. It is entirely legitimate to take the position that socialism in itself is not practicable, and yet has strength on account of its criticism of present society, and also on account of suggestions which it offers for reform. It may be held that socialism is a leaven needed at the present moment, although one rejects socialism itself. On the other hand, we may examine the strong features of socialism itself, considered as a system which proposes to supplant the existing social order altogether. Both standpoints must be taken to understand the full strength of socialism.

Undoubtedly one of the strongest features of socialism, considered as a plan for an entirely new industrial society, is its all-inclusiveness. Socialism is a structure of society which takes in all; it leaves no residuum, no "submerged tenth." This all-inclusiveness of socialism appeals strongly to those who have been discouraged by the patchwork and piecemeal character of other social reforms. Take "trades unionism," for example: it has benefited great masses of men, but it always leaves behind a wretched class of unorganized wage-earners; and even should it attain its impossible ideal of complete organization of wage-earners, it would still leave behind the most wretched of all; namely, the dependent and delinquent classes. Take charity organization in all its various forms: it endeavors to minister to the dependent classes, taking them one by one; but it leaves unreached a disheartening number of needy and worthy cases. In fact, those whom one would most like to help are precisely those most generally passed over by charity organization. The same holds true with respect to all private efforts to aid individual cases. Private effort to reach the needy one by one, so resembles pouring water into a sieve, that many turn from it in despair. Socialism follows the method of Aristotle, and proceeds from the whole to the part. Its very structure is such that none are left out, but ample room is found for the cripple as well as for the athlete, for the weak and feeble as well as for the strong and powerful.

CHAPTER II.

THE STRENGTH OF SOCIALISM AS A SCHEME OF PRODUCTION.

WHILE socialism originates in a desire to bring about justice in distribution, it lays great weight on the possibilities of increased production of wealth, which it promises. Socialism reproaches present society, not only with its very unequal distribution of wealth actually produced, but with its small production of wealth. Its adherents claim that but a fractional part of the wealth which could be created is actually produced for the satisfaction of human needs. This is well brought out in a passage in Mr. Bellamy's " Looking Backward," in which Dr. Leete says to Mr. West: —

"I suppose that no reflection would have cut the men of your wealth-worshipping century more keenly than the suggestion that they did not know how to make money. . . . Selfishness was their only science, and, in industrial production, selfishness is suicide."

The first strong point which socialism makes with respect to wealth-creation, is that which provides for the suppression of the wastes of competition. There can be no doubt that this is a valid argument. As socialism proposes the abolition of the present competitive society, it must necessarily do away with the wastes of competition in the abolition of competition. Whether or not it brings evils, as great or greater, in the place of these

THE STRENGTH OF SOCIALISM. 117

wastes, is an entirely different question, which does not concern us at present.

None can say how great the wastes of competition are, but a few illustrations are sufficient to show that they are enormous. Railways in the United States afford the best illustration. The moment we begin reflecting upon wastes in the railway business, we are able to give concrete instances running up into the hundreds of millions of dollars. The railway lines paralleling the New York Central & Hudson River Railway, and the Lake Shore & Michigan Southern, from New York City to Chicago, afford one of the best-known examples of waste in railway construction. These lines were built to compete with the older lines mentioned; but, as is always the case in such instances, the competing lines consolidated. The purpose for which they were built was not accomplished, and the expenditure involved in their construction was a national loss. It has been estimated that these lines cost two hundred millions of dollars, which would be a sum sufficient to construct homes for one million people, if we allow a thousand dollars to a dwelling for a family of five; and this is probably more than the average cost of the houses of the people of the United States, taking city and country together. We see, then, that one single item in our count is a matter of national concern ; but when we have mentioned the waste in construction, we have only made a beginning in the total loss involved in the construction of needless railway lines. The maintenance of the useless lines, and their continued operation, involve perpetual loss. Every station on the parallel line involves waste. Every station-agent is a source of expense, and every needless train run adds to the waste. It is not denied that the parallel railway lines offer some slight accommodation, and therefore service, to the public. The new parallel line will, for example, generally run through a different part of the city, and it is not improbable that the time-table of the new parallel line will be different from that of the older company, so that in this way a variety of trains is offered. At the same time, the expense is mostly waste, because a relatively small additional expenditure on the part of the old company would offer still better accommodations. We have, also, not only to consider the convenience of having stations in the different parts of the city, but the great inconvenience which results from having different stations in the city, the greater risk to travellers on the highway, and the disfigurement of the city, which is always involved in a railway line. Now, what has taken place in the case of the West Shore and the Nickel Plate, between New York and Chicago, has occurred all over the United States; and the total loss must amount to more than a thousand millions of dollars, if we consider only the first cost. If we consider the subsequent expenditure involved, it becomes truly enormous, — a loss like that brought upon a nation by a great war. It is said by a railway manager, that even now it would involve an annual saving of two hundred millions of dollars if the railways of the United States were managed as a unit. If we divide the sum by two, in order that our estimate may be a conservative one, and capitalize it at four per cent, we have a capital loss of two thousand five hundred millions of dollars. It is useless to attempt any precise estimate, but it may not be an extravagant estimate if we claim that the loss due to competition in the railway business in the United States, from the beginning of our railway history up to the present, has been sufficient to furnish all the people of the United States with comfortable dwellings, provided that all the houses now in the United States should be destroyed. Socialism, then, makes a very strong point when it shows that a waste of this kind would be abolished with the abolition of the competitive system.

The experience of England and the United States, the only two great countries which have tried the competitive system in the telegraph business, is most instructive. It is claimed that the capitalization of the telegraphs of the United States, large as it is, does not exceed the amount of capital which has been actually invested, and this estimate would not seem to be an exaggeration, when we bear in mind the fact that, a little over a generation ago, it took a page of an almanac simply to enumerate the companies which existed in this country. The Western Union, which is the principal company, and which has been the concern to swallow the others, is capitalized at $100,000,000. If we leave out of consideration any other company or companies existing at present, and deduct from the $100,000,000 the $20,000,000 which it is estimated would be sufficient to duplicate the plant, we should have a loss of $80,000,000. This, however, is but a fractional part of the total loss, because we must take into account the needless expense involved in operating the plants which have been ultimately absorbed. No one can tell what the total loss is, but certainly $100,000,000 is an underestimate. England tried the competitive system in the telegraph business until about the year 1870, when she became convinced that competition in this line of business, at any rate, was a mistake, and purchased the telegraph, making it a part of the postal system. Now, the capital invested in the telegraph had grown to such enormous proportions, owing to the number of companies which had been engaged in business, and which had all been absorbed at last by one company, that it cost England nearly as much to make the telegraph a part of the post-office as it did all the other countries of Europe put together, because in these the telegraph had been from the beginning a part of the post-office, and the wastes of competition had been avoided.

Gas works offer, in some respects, a better illustration of the wastes of competition even than railways. The loss in the country's industry is not so great, but the business itself is simpler, and the outcome of attempted competition can be the more readily seen. A development which requires decades in railway business, is accomplished in years in the gas business. Rival gas works in a city always consolidate, and monopoly is the inevitable outcome of competition, and loss to the city attempting competition will be equal to the capital wasted in all the unsuccessful attempts which have been made to establish competition in gas supply. While there may be some incidental gains, these will be more than off-set by losses which can be enumerated in dollars and cents. A great deal of disease and death may be traced to a needless tearing up of the streets in cities by rival companies, and disease and death are serious waste.

If we take a single city like Baltimore, and try to ascertain the loss due to the existence of competitive gas companies, we can form in our minds some kind of an idea how enormous the waste during a generation must have been, when we remember that what has happened in Baltimore has happened in nearly all great American cities. There have existed in Baltimore at one time and another, five or six different gas companies; each one has promised the people of Baltimore the alleged benefits of competition, and then, after a gas war, has consolidated with the old company. There is now in Baltimore one company, called "The Consolidated Gas Company," with a capital of $18,000,000, including bonds. Probably it is safe to estimate the difference between the capitalization of this company and what it would cost to duplicate this plant, as waste due to the competitive system. It is said that the plant could be duplicated for less than $5,000,000; but if we deduct $5,000,000 and then $3,000,000 more, so as to make our estimate an extremely conservative one, we still have a waste in this one city of $10,000,000.

The milk business is often adduced by socialists as an example of the waste due to competition. In each city, every company or individual engaged in the milk business supplies people in every part of the city, and the streets of each city are traversed by a large number of milk wagons. The distribution of milk in the city may be contrasted with the distribution of mail. The delivery of the mail is so organized that each mail carrier has a given district assigned to him, and he carries the mail to all persons in his own district. The delivery of milk might be compared to a delivery of letters and newspapers without any system. Let us suppose, in a city like Philadelphia, all the mail, on arrival, was simply put in a heap, and each mail carrier should take up an armful for distribution; it is manifest that it would take very many times the force which it now requires to distribute the mail, because each mail carrier would have to run all over the city, and a dozen mail carriers would traverse each street.

Advertising exists for two purposes: one is to convey information, and the other is to acquire a business, to hold one's business, or to take business away from others. Advertising is like war, and is, indeed, one of the aspects of industrial conflict. The increasing expenses due to advertising may be compared to the increasing expenses due to standing armies in Europe. But a small fractional part of what is paid out for advertising is expenditure for the sake of conveying useful information. The greater part of it is necessitated by the advertising of one's rivals. The grocer A spends a thousand dollars a year in advertising of one sort and another, and his rival, grocer B, spends the same to keep his business. Then grocer A the next year, being what is called an enterprising man, spends fifteen hundred dollars, and grocer B spends two thousand dollars. Let the reader reflect upon the enormous expenditures of rival soap manufacturers, of which no part worthy of mention is employed to convey useful information. To conquer new territory, or to hold its own against the attacks of rivals, each one of several great companies spends enormous amounts, which can scarcely fail to run up into the hundreds of thousands of dollars. We can see an increase in the expenditures for advertising of one sort and another, and the absorption of a considerable talent and ingenuity in the discovery of new and improved ways of advertising, which resemble the growing expense of the armies of France and Germany, and the absorption of talent and enterprise to discover new ways of killing men. Of course it will not be claimed that the economic loss of advertising is anything like the economic loss due to standing armies, and yet it is by no means insignificant. A student[1] who has investigated the subject perhaps as

[1] Mr. P. M. Magnusson.

carefully as any one, and the result of whose labors it is to be hoped will, at a not distant day, be given to the world, estimated the expenses of advertising in this country at five hundred millions of dollars a year, of which five millions would be ample to convey all the useful information given by this advertising. Of course all this expenditure is not total loss; a part of it is saved by those to whom it is paid. What we have to consider from a social standpoint, is capital and labor used up, which leave behind no real utility. If A transfers to B a thousand dollars, society, as a whole, is neither richer nor poorer. That does not represent social waste. But if A spends a whole day in work which accomplishes nothing, or B consumes to no purpose type and paper, we have a real social loss. Economic energy, which might have been so employed as to benefit human beings, has been simply wasted. Now, a part of what is expended for advertising represents simply a transfer of wealth from one section of the community to another; and some may be inclined to hold that the estimate itself of expenditure is a large one. Should we, however, in order to ascertain the social loss, feel obliged to divide the estimate of five hundred millions by five, we would still have a loss of one hundred millions of dollars, which, from the standpoint of society, is by no means insignificant.

The reader can continue for himself illustrations of this kind. Travelling salesmen will readily occur as an illustration of large expenditure, which is, to no inconsiderable extent, waste due to competition. Of course this waste is allied to the waste of advertising.

Socialists call the present production planless, in contrasting production as a whole with the organized system of a single great factory. They propose to substitute for present planlessness of production at large, regular, orderly, systematic production. This is a very strong point in the program of socialism, and the gains resulting therefrom would be many. Not the least important of these would be the limitation of the chance element in production. The chance element is characteristic, either of production on a small scale, or production imperfectly organized. When we have to do with large masses of social phenomena, or with productive forces working on a vast scale, the chance element is reduced to such low terms that it may be almost said to disappear. No better illustration of this general rule can be offered than human mortality. What is more uncertain than death, when we have regard to the death of a single individual? Its uncertainty has been proverbial from time immemorial. No one can tell whether you or I will be alive next year, next month, or even to-morrow, yet uncertainty in regard to life and death disappears when we deal with large numbers of human beings. We can indeed tell how many among ten millions of people will be alive a year from to-day, a month from to-day, or even to-morrow, so great is the regularity with which death occurs among large masses of human beings. This regularity is sufficient to enable us to build upon it one of the largest businesses of modern times; namely, life insurance, which, when intelligently conducted, by no means involves more than an average risk; on the contrary, rather less than average business risk. Thus it is with production. When we consider a single farmer growing wheat in Minnesota, or a planter raising corn in Virginia, the chance element is prominent. Drought may destroy the wheat crop in Minnesota, and flood the corn crop in Virginia. Yet, when we take the country as a whole, the fluctuations due to changes in seasons and other causes are reduced to low terms. If the wheat crop is deficient in one part of the country, it is likely to be abundant elsewhere, and a general average maintained. The same is true with respect to other crops. The larger the scale on which production is organized, the less the risk, because irregularities in one direction or the other are more likely to balance one another. The reader's imagination will enable him to supply illustrations without limit.

When the chance element visits one adversely time after time, human energy suffers impairment, and at times becomes almost paralyzed. Every one has seen numerous illustrations of the frequent effect of repeated but undeserved misfortune.

The present planlessness of production may be viewed from still another standpoint. At the present time the wheat grower produces for an uncertain, capricious market, and his destiny is only to an inconsiderable extent within his own control. Farmer A observes that the price of wheat has been high for two or three years, and he thinks that wheat is a good crop to raise. He begins to cultivate wheat on a large scale, but he does not know what rival producers are doing or are going to do. Farmer B and Farmer C and thousands of others have made the same observation, and they all begin growing wheat. The result is a large over-production of wheat, and loss to the producers. Farmer A then decides that he will give up wheat and try sheep-raising, because mutton and wool have for some time been high; but thousands of other farmers have at the same time come to this conclusion, and sheep-raising is carried too far.

Mutton and wool fall in price, and again there is loss to individuals, and a loss to society as a whole, because economic energy has not been most advantageously expended. The writer has concrete instances in mind. One of them is grape culture; the farmers along the shore of Lake Erie, in western New York, have observed that it is profitable to grow table grapes; and between Dunkirk in New York and Erie in Pennsylvania, the country is beginning to assume the appearance of a continuous vineyard. Who can tell what the results will be? These growers are able to make only an uncertain estimate of demand, and still more unable are they to estimate the probable supply of grapes throughout the country. Here we have a very large expenditure, continuing through years with uncertain results. Many similar illustrations might be given, if we should turn our attention to manufacturing industries and professional occupations, which afford instances enough of misapplied force, due to a failure to estimate correctly supply and demand.

We may say, indeed, that the producers are playing at hide and seek with supply and demand, and no one can tell what the outcome of the game will be. The socialist makes a strong point when he bids us contrast with this planlessness of production, resulting in large loss and immense human suffering, the regular, orderly, systematic production which he advocates. He proposes to ascertain demand, and organize the forces of production as a unit to meet this demand, but to produce no more than is needed. It can be told in advance, with an approximation to accuracy, how many bushels of wheat will be needed in the United States the coming year; and with a like approximation to accuracy, it may be told how many acres of wheat will supply this need.

THE STRENGTH OF SOCIALISM. 127

Wastes by mistaken undertakings are a necessary feature of the present competitive order of society; but they might be expected to be largely reduced under socialism. This is closely connected with what has preceded, and becomes sufficiently obvious upon reflection. What is more uncertain than the result of a new telegraph company or railway company in the United States? The uncertainty is great on account of the presence of competition. If we turn our attention, however, to a country like Germany, where there is no competition in telegraphing or in the railway industry, because both are government enterprises, we shall find that it is easy to tell in advance very nearly what will be the result of an extension of the telegraph or the railways. It is possible to take into account very nearly all the elements involved in the calculation, both businesses becoming relatively simple the moment the competitive element is removed, although, with this element present, they are extremely complicated. The same holds, although in less degree, with respect to manufactures and mercantile undertakings. It has been claimed that nine-tenths of the men who go into business in the United States fail, and each failure represents a loss of capital and of human energy. Even if, to be on the conservative side in our estimate, we reduce the estimated number of failures by one half, we still have a loss which, in the aggregate, is enormous.

Another claim of socialism is one which, at a time like the present, is peculiarly effective. It is maintained that the wastes from crises and industrial depressions will disappear; and this claim is well founded, because crises and industrial depressions are part and parcel of the competitive system of industry, and would cease to afflict society with the abolition of the competitive system. Perhaps we here touch upon that loss which is chief among all those due to a competitive industrial order, and it may be that a description of the evils incident to crises and industrial depressions is as severe an indictment of present society as can be brought against it. The losses in a single year of industrial crises, and consequent industrial stagnation, amount to hundreds of millions of dollars, and involve untold misery to millions of human beings. Capital is idle; labor is unemployed; the production of wealth ceases; want and even starvation come to thousands; marriages decrease; separations, divorces, and prostitution increase in alarming proportions; and all this happens because the machinery of the industrial system has been thrown out of gear by the operation of some force or another, which, so far as we can judge from experience, is an essential part of the order of competition.

It follows naturally enough from what has preceded, that the waste due to idle labor and idle capital might be expected to cease; production would be carried on for the satisfaction of wants, and so long as wants remained there would be no reason why all labor and all capital should not be employed.

It may fairly be claimed that socialism would promote the full utilization of existing inventions and industrial discoveries. It may not be so clear that socialism would surpass present society in new inventions and industrial discoveries, but there could not well be any opposition to the utilization of those already in existence. On account of the unification and harmony of interests established in society, there would necessarily be a general desire to produce material wealth socially required with the smallest expenditure of economic energy. At the present time, on the other hand, there are important classes in the community who resist the utilization of improved machines and methods. The explanation is, that these classes either actually would suffer, or they think they would suffer, from that which would be a gain to society as a whole. We have, on the one hand, the wage-earners, who often object to new and better machinery and improved processes, because they think the result to them would be either lower wages or entire loss of work; on the other, the opposition of capital to like improvements, involving serious change and outlay, whenever capital has anything like a monopoly.

All are familiar with the destruction of machinery by factory operatives in England early in this century; and while some may entertain exaggerated views of the extent to which wage-earners oppose improvement, there can be no doubt but this opposition is a real force, and that it has to a greater or less degree retarded industrial progress. Undoubtedly, wage-earners have generally been mistaken in the amount of injury which they have anticipated from new inventions and methods; but it is unquestionable that many of them have suffered temporarily, and some of them permanently. One effect of improvement is to render previous skill of no consequence, and to relegate once skilled artisans to the ranks of unskilled labor. Quite likely society may gain, but the individual suffers; and who can help feeling that it is unjust to concentrate the sacrifice of social change upon one, or even upon a few? It has, indeed, been proposed by those not socialists, that an indemnity should be granted to individuals who suffer on account of industrial improvements, in order that the burden involved in a transition from an inferior to a superior industrial process should be divided among society as a whole, and not concentrated upon a few. Manifestly, the difficulties involved in carrying out this idea under our present social system are immense, although the idea itself is a good one. The entire question disappears as a problem under socialism. Let us take the case of a communistic settlement like those which exist in different parts of the United States. Can any ground exist in such a community for opposition to improvement in tools or industrial methods? Let us suppose that some member of the community has gained great skill in performing certain operations by hand, — type-setting, for example, — and that an invention is made in the community by the use of which it is possible for a child easily to perform this operation. Can the one who has acquired the skill object? Scarcely: although his skill is no longer of any use to him, he shares with the rest of the community in the advantages gained by the improvement; whereas, if by a system of socialism his interests were not identical with theirs, they would gain the advantage, and he might suffer loss through a reduction in wages. What would be true in a small communistic settlement, would be true in society at large, under socialism.

It has just been stated that it is not so clear that socialism would lead to new inventions and discoveries, as it is that it would promote the utilization of those already in existence. One exception must be made. It can hardly be questioned that under socialism the inventive powers of men would be stimulated to provide machinery to do disagreeable work, and to render work now disagreeable as agreeable as possible. The inventive power of man now aims to increase the earnings of capital, and not chiefly to render the task of the toiler as light and pleasant as possible. Ocean steamships serve as illustration, and, in so far as they go, as proof. The improvements which have been made within a generation to render an ocean voyage agreeable to first-class travellers are remarkable. The ingenuity which has been expended in this direction is admirable, and the amount of capital invested in these improvements is very large. What has been done, in the meantime, to render an ocean voyage agreeable to the stokers and ordinary sailors? Very little. The reason is not that improvement is impossible, but that it has not paid. It is true, however, that in proportion as you make men valuable, machinery does disagreeable work.

Now, it is the essence of socialism to insist upon the value of man; and it is evident that this new order could not fail to result in a new class of inventions and discoveries. Even now we can say that the amount of economic energy expended in lightening menial toil is precisely in proportion to the value which attaches to the ordinary man or woman.

An advertisement (of what is technically called the "before and after" kind) which attracted the author's attention some time since, is significant. It was simply an advertisement of a mop; but as a naturalist can construct from a single bone a likeness of an extinct animal, so a sociologist, sufficiently skilful, could tell us a good deal about the kind of society in which this advertisement appeared. The advertisement gave two pictures; one of an ordinary mop, out of which the water was being wrung by a bedrabbled, sorry-looking maid, and the other of a smiling, comely housewife, who was wringing the dirty water out of the mop by simply turning the handle. This method of extracting the dirty water, without soiling one's hands, was the essential feature of the patented mop. Now, of course, the author knows nothing about the merits of this mop, but he claims that the advertisement itself, of the alleged improvement, signifies a great deal. It is significant that the advertisement appeared in the United States, where women's wages are high, and many women of respectability do their own house work, and not in Germany, where labor is cheap and servants abundant. It is significant that improvements of this kind should be more abundant in the North than in the South. Equally significant is the undoubted fact that the tools used by the slaves in the South were of an inferior kind. The Northern farmer, who hoed his own Indian corn, used a beautifully constructed hoe, weighing a few ounces, and despised the heavy and clumsy tool used by the Southern slave in the field. Equally significant is the fact that, when it was made illegal to send chimney sweeps down chimneys in England, the chimneys were still swept, but by improved tools, and not by boys in the chimneys themselves.[1]

The author spent some time among the Shakers at Mount Lebanon, New York, and was much pleased to see the improvements which had been introduced in the kitchen, rendering kitchen work so agreeable that the sisters preferred it to any other occupation. One thing which he remembers is that the soiled clothes were washed by the aid of water-power. Now, what did all these unusual improvements in the kitchen signify, ex-

[1] This last illustration is given by Mrs. Annie Besant in the Fabian Essays.

cept that the community of interests resulted in the devotion of a larger proportion than usual of the inventive talent and energy of this social group to occupations ordinarily termed menial?

It may further be urged in behalf of socialism, that under socialism all forces will work together for a large product, whereas, at the present time, powerful forces are not infrequently striving for a diminished production of wealth. The reason for the condition of things which exists at the present, becomes obvious when we reflect upon the fact that production is carried on for exchange, and that what the producers want is not abundance of commodities, but large values. The two are by no means identical, for value depends upon limitation of supply. If the supply of commodities could be sufficient to satisfy all wants, then commodities would have no value at all, but would become free like air or water.

Wherever it is practicable, producers, then, must of necessity, in a society like ours, endeavor to check production before diminished value begins to do more than off-set increased quantity. This, also, explains the fact that owners of commodities, for example, fruits, have been known to destroy a share of them in order to keep up value.

Cotton, in the United States, serves as an excellent illustration of the divergence between individual or class interests and general social interests. Naturally, society as a whole wants a large and abundant supply of cotton, which furnishes the raw material of so many useful products, but an important section of the country has been distressed by the abundant yield of cotton. Southern planters have for some time been trying to devise means to diminish the production of cotton. There lie before the author as he writes, clippings and quotations from several newspapers. One of these describes a convention of cotton men, and the heading is "Trying to Wrestle with the Problem of Over-production." The article is a telegraphic despatch dated Memphis, Jan. 8, 1892, and it begins as follows: —

"That the farmers of the South are in earnest in their endeavor to solve the serious problem of over-production of cotton, is evinced by the enthusiastic meeting of delegates to the convention of the Mississippi Valley Cotton Growers' Association, which was called to order in this city this morning."

Another clipping is headed "Cotton Planters: Southern Men advocate a Reduction of the Acreage." A third clipping describes a convention held about a year later at Augusta, Ga. At this convention a "cotton area tax" was suggested. The President of the Boston Chamber of Commerce, in a speech delivered before a notable religious gathering in Washington, referred in these words to the large production of cotton in the South:[1] —

"In 1890 we harvested a cotton crop of over eight million six hundred thousand bales — several hundred thousand bales more than the world could consume. Had the crop of the present year been equally large, it would have been an appalling calamity to the section of our country that devotes so large a portion of its labor and capital to the raising of cotton."

How strange a thing is this bounty of nature! We wish nature to be generous, but not too generous. If nature comes to us with smiling face and outstretched

[1] The Hon. Alden Speare, President of the Boston Chamber of Commerce, Address on Labor and Capital, before the Ecumenical Conference of the Methodist Church in Washington, D.C., as reported in the *Baltimore American*, Oct. 17, 1891.

arms, and pours into our laps her gifts without stint, she impoverishes us, and we hardly know whether to dread the more an excess of niggardliness or an excess of generosity on her part. So full of contradictions is our present economic order, that men must go without coats because too much clothing has been produced, and children must go hungry because the production of grain has been over-abundant. As the socialists have said, with some measure of truth, "In civilization poverty is born of plenty."

As socialism proposes that production should be carried on to satisfy wants directly, the present machinery for exchange of commodities would almost disappear, and trade and commerce, in their existing form, would be practically abolished. The plan of socialism is that products should be gathered into large central stores, and then distributed among the various members of the community according to their claims upon the income of society; in other words, in accordance with their own individual income. It is estimated by Mr. Bellamy that one-eightieth of the population would be sufficient to bring the goods from the producer to the consumer, whereas, he says, that one-eighth of the population is now required for this service. This would then mean a saving of nine-tenths. Whether the saving would be so great as this or not, it is undoubted that socialism, if it could be made to work, would require a far smaller proportion of the population to bring goods from the producer to the consumer than present society.

If we view production of wealth from the standpoint of an employer, we find that socialism is not without its strong features. Surely the employing class cannot find its present relation to the employed altogether agreeable.

It is not pleasant to be engaged in perpetual struggle, and to be viewed with suspicion, and even positive hostility. Many an employer, weary of turmoil, would assuredly welcome a system which promises social peace, although it might effect a reduction in his own income, could he feel convinced that this new system was able to keep its promises in this respect. Working men may say what they please, but the lot of the employer is too frequently anything but an agreeable one, and that he should at times become embittered, when he sees himself perpetually misunderstood, misinterpreted, and antagonized, is not strange. A far stronger plea for socialism, from the standpoint of the employer engaged in production, might be made than one would be inclined to believe at first blush.[1]

The promises which socialism holds out to the em-

---

[1] "In the present stage of human progress, when ideas of equality are daily spreading more widely among the poorer classes, and can no longer be checked by anything short of the entire suppression of printed discussion, and even of freedom of speech, it is not to be expected that the division of the human race into two hereditary classes, employers and employed, can be permanently maintained. The relation is nearly as unsatisfactory to the payer of wages as to the receiver. If the rich regard the poor as, by a kind of natural law, their servants and dependents, the rich in their turn are regarded as a mere prey and pasture for the poor; the subject of demands and expectations wholly indefinite, increasing in extent with every concession made to them. The total absence of regard for justice or fairness in the relations between the two is as marked on the side of the employed as on that of the employers. We look in vain among the working classes in general for the just pride which will choose to give good work for good wages: for the most part, their sole endeavor is to receive as much, and return as little in the shape of service, as possible. It will sooner or later become insupportable to the employing classes to live in close and hourly contact with persons whose interests and feelings are in hostility to them." (John Stuart Mill's "Principles of Political Economy," Book IV. chap. vii. § 4.)

ployed are, indeed, alluring. It proposes that they should constitute a fraternity, govern themselves in industry, and work together for the common good. "No masters, no servants," must have a welcome sound to many, and especially to those who now occupy the subordinate positions.

CHAPTER III.

THE STRENGTH OF SOCIALISM AS A SCHEME FOR THE DISTRIBUTION AND CONSUMPTION OF WEALTH.

ARISTOTLE defended slavery as an institution necessary to social progress, maintaining that, unless there were a class of inferiors who were engaged in the production of material wealth, for the satisfaction of the needs of a superior class, there could be no art, no literature, no statesmanship; in fact, none of those features of a high civilization upon which, ultimately, the general welfare must depend. It is generally admitted that in his day there was a relative truth, at least, in his plea for slavery. One passage in his "Politics" has a prophetic ring. He remarked that if the time should ever come when the plectra of themselves should strike the lyre, and the shuttle should move of itself, then all men might be free; but since his day invention has made many industrial operations well-nigh automatic, and the power of man in production has been increased many-fold. The question suggests itself, cannot the office of slavery, as a foundation of a high and worthy civilization for a few, be performed by modern machinery for all? The larger the production of wealth, the stronger the argument for socialism in distribution. If enough could actually be produced to satisfy all the rational wants of all human beings, many serious objections against socialism as a scheme of distribution would disappear.

It is well known that in certain branches of industry,

the power of man in production has been increased ten, twenty, fifty, one hundred, and sometimes even a thousand-fold. Calico printing, for example, illustrates an increase of capacity which is a hundred-fold; and in the making of books, it would be difficult to say how many thousand-fold has been the increase in human power, if we compare present methods with the days of the copyists, when everything had to be written by hand. When we come to estimates of the total gain in man's productive power, the uncertainty is great and estimates vary widely. A report of the Department of Labor of the United States for 1886, states that the physical power of engines employed in the mechanical industries is over five times that of the men so employed, and that it would require twenty-one millions of men to turn out the product which, as a matter of fact, four millions turn out. Robert Owen claimed that in New Lanark, Scotland, early in this century, the working portion of the population of twenty-five hundred produced as much wealth as, one-half a century before, a population of six hundred thousand could have produced. Another author estimates that the machinery of the civilized world performs a service in production as great as could have been rendered in earlier times by sixty slaves for each family of five. It is probable that both of these latter estimates are far too large, but there can be no question that the socialists make a strong point when they bring forward the increased production of wealth as an argument for the social control of its distribution.

We cannot fail to commend the aim of socialism to substitute an orderly and rational distribution of the social dividend, for that based on a struggle of private interests. This distribution, based upon the struggle of private interests, can satisfy no benevolent person who has intelligence enough to see what it means.

The idea of distribution is the fullest satisfaction of human wants; but at the present time very pressing ones go unsatisfied, while a few persons have such a superfluity that, to their own harm, they can satisfy every whim and caprice. You may find here a young girl who has rare artistic gifts, which, on her own account, as well as on account of society, it is desirable she should be able to develop to the utmost, but by reason of poverty her powers languish, and she is obliged to turn to distasteful work for which she has no capacity; while on another street of the same city you can find a gilded youth, who, in a single night's debauch, will spend enough to his own undoing to give our talented poor girl the best opportunities which money can offer. Instances of this kind fall under our observation every day, and if any way can be discovered to remedy this wrong, it is certainly desirable that it should be known. The effort to mend the evil is indeed commendable.

It is at least conceivable that a distribution of the social income by self-conscious social forces, would be productive of better results, for the nature of distribution would then depend upon the wisdom and integrity with which society performed its functions in this respect. Socialism, in its idea, is unquestionably compatible with a distribution of the national dividend, which would be more productive of well-being than is the distribution which we now witness. Socialism seeks a distribution which avoids the extremes of pauperism and plutocracy. This ideal is that of the Bible, as expressed in Agur's prayer,[1] "Give me neither poverty nor riches;

[1] Prov. xxx. 8, 9.

feed me with food convenient for me: lest I be full, and deny thee, and say, Who is the Lord? or lest I be poor, and steal, and take the name of my God in vain." Socialists have directed special attention to distribution as considered from the standpoint of the wage-earner, but the wish for him is that he should cease to be a wage-earner, and become a partner in production. This is implied in the socialization of the instruments of production; but this common ownership of the instruments of production implies the distribution among the workers of that surplus above wages which is now allotted to rent, interest, and profits, for socialism proposes to lay hold of these shares in distribution and divide them among the producers.

Socialistic distribution has also strength when it is viewed from the standpoint of other classes than the wage-earners. The employer, even if he may receive a smaller share, is free from the harrowing cares and anxieties which now beset him. The fear that he may lose his entire share in the wealth distributed, a fear often realized as large producers annihilate small producers, ceases to torment him, for socialism, as we have already seen, provides an income for all members of society. It is not proposed that the full product of industry, without abatement of any sort, should go to the toiler, because it is desired that a share should be set aside for those who are incapable of themselves engaging in toil, as well as a share for replacement of capital and addition to capital.

When distribution is viewed from the standpoint of those engaged in the learned professions, socialism is not without its attractive features. Those professions are now over-crowded, largely because many, better adapted to mechanical pursuits, endeavor to push up into the learned professions to escape unpleasant conditions attending those occupations for which they are naturally adapted. This might be expected to cease, if agriculture and mechanical pursuits could be rendered more agreeable; and the anxiety of professional men for themselves, and often their still greater anxiety for their children, would no longer perplex them by day and disturb their rest at night.

The strength of socialism as a scheme for the consumption of wealth, is closely connected with what has just been said. The ideal of socialism is private frugality and public luxury, which is almost the exact opposite of current ideals, for these seem to favor boundless luxury on the part of private individuals, with parsimony in public consumption. Even those who come quite up to ordinary ethical standards, do not seem to think that any justification is required for a most lavish expenditure on their own wants, although it include an evening's entertainment which costs ten thousand dollars, or a private mansion which has involved an outlay of half a million. Expenditures on entertainments and private dwellings which cost many times the sum mentioned, do not offend the public conscience of our day. On the other hand, when it comes to school buildings or structures for state universities, library buildings, or art galleries, which minister to the needs of the people as a whole, a legislator who would cut down appropriations to the minimum amount and deprive public buildings of all beauty, is praised and petted as a " watch-dog of the treasury," while a president who uses the veto power freely to defeat appropriations for useful purposes, which have something else in view than the promotion of material interests, is supposed to be animated by a stern sense of duty.

Socialism, fortunately, regards with marked disapprobation, lavishness on the part of private individuals as something ethically unjustifiable, because it diverts a disproportionately large amount of material wealth for the satisfaction of the few, while it favors as commendable all that is best and highest and noblest for public purposes. The most beautifully laid out pleasure grounds, the finest public libraries, grandly housed, magnificent galleries of art, and the noblest architecture, are held by socialism to be none too good for the people; because they find their best use when employed in the public service. Which is the truer ideal of the two? If we survey history, we shall be inclined to entertain little doubt that the periods which meet with our most cordial approbation, are those in which private frugality was commended and large expenditure for public purposes was held to be praiseworthy, while the ages of national decay have been ages in which opposite ideals and the reverse practices have prevailed. In her best days Athens employed a large proportion of all public revenues for art in its various forms, and private life was comparatively simple, but in the time of the decay of Greece, public expenditures declined and private luxury grew apace. The early ages of Rome constitute a period when hard work and simple life were held to honor the citizen, while the best which Rome could afford was thought to be none too good for the state. A high ideal of the state prevailed until the decline of Rome began, and as Rome gradually fell into decay, private expenditure increased until luxury became fairly wanton.

If we hold that it is the purpose of society to offer to all, so far as may be, equal opportunities for the development of all faculties, we cannot fail to acknowledge that the ideal of socialism, with respect to the consumption of wealth, is a noble one.

CHAPTER IV.

THE MORAL STRENGTH OF SOCIALISM.

WHILE a non-ethical system of socialism, based on a materialistic conception of history, has most unfortunately for socialism found favor on the part of a large faction of socialists, socialism has probably found its main strength on its ethical side. The ethical ideals of socialism have attracted to it generous souls and have enlisted in its ranks its best adherents. It is these ethical ideals which have inspired the rank and file of the socialistic army with fiery zeal and religious devotion. It may be said, indeed, that nothing in the present day is so likely to awaken the conscience of the ordinary man or woman, or to increase the sense of individual responsibility, as a thorough course in socialism. The study of socialism has proved the turning-point in thousands of lives, and converted self-seeking men and women into self-sacrificing toilers for the masses.[1] The impar-

[1] The following illustrations are offered of the moral earnestness produced by socialism :

"A young man employed in the Central Post-office at a salary of $650 a year. He has married a very charming and able girl, also a member. They occupy two or three rooms in a suburban house. The young lady has been elected as a guardian of the poor, the only woman among a number of men. Her husband devotes nearly all his spare time, after office hours, to the society's propaganda. He has had a little portable desk and stand made for himself, and at this he speaks at open spaces, on street corners, or wherever he can get an audience. His wife accompanies him and sells literature. Do not suppose that these are a blatant young demagogue and a conventional strong-minded woman. Both are educated, intelligent, of sweet disposition;

tial observer can scarcely claim that the Bible produces so marked an effect upon the daily, habitual life of the average man and the average woman who profess to guide their conduct by it, as socialism does upon its adherents. The strength of socialism in this respect is more like that of early Christianity as described in the New Testament.

The person who takes up socialistic works, having a conscience at all sensitive, will find it quickened and stimulated by passage after passage giving a new view of life, which is based upon the worth of every human being. Quotation after quotation could be given. Mr. Bellamy's "Looking Backward" offers possibility of several; but the following has impressed the author of the present work as one which is especially strong. Edith, the heroine, is shocked to learn that in the

---

but the socialist movement has taken hold of them and given them something they needed, lifted them above the region of what John Morley calls 'greasy domesticity,' and taught them that there is a great suffering world beyond the four walls of home to be helped and worked for. Depend upon it, a movement which can do this has in it some promise of the future.

" Or take the amusing, cynical, remarkable George Bernard Shaw, whose Irish humor and brilliant gifts have partly helped, partly hindered, the society's popularity. This man will rise from an elaborate criticism of last night's opera or Richter concert (he is the musical critic of the *World*), and after a light, purely vegetarian meal, will go down to some far off club in South London, or to some street corner in East London, or to some recognized place of meeting in one of the parks, and will there speak to poor men about their economic position and their political duties. People of this sort, who enjoy books and music and the theatre and good society, do not go down to dreary slums, or even more dreary lecture-rooms, to speak to the poorer class of workingmen, without some strong impelling power; and it is that power, that motive force, upon which I dwell, as showing what is doing in the London of to-day." "The Fabian Society," by William Clarke, in *New England Magazine* for March, 1894.

nineteenth century we permitted people to do things for us which we despised them for doing, and we accepted services which we would have been unwilling to render. Dr. Leete explains to Mr. West the cause of Edith's surprise in these words:—

"'To understand why Edith is surprised, you must know that nowadays it is an axiom of ethics that to accept a service from another which we would be unwilling to return in kind if need be, is like borrowing with the intention of not repaying; while to enforce such a service by taking advantage of the poverty or necessity of a person, would be an outrage like forcible robbery. It is the worst thing about any system which divides men, or allows them to be divided, into classes and castes, that it weakens the sense of a common humanity."

If we go into details somewhat, we find that socialism is strong on its ethical side, because it proposes to make real the brotherhood of man. We have long heard much talk about the brotherhood of man, and we are all aware of the fact that a general belief is expressed in this brotherhood; but when bearing in mind the professed doctrine of brotherhood, we observe the conduct of brother to brother, in our every-day world, we feel like exclaiming, "Words! Words!! Words!!!" It is manifestly a hollow mockery, and, so far as any real service is concerned, most of us would rather be a third cousin to a man by blood relationship, than brother in the general and indefinite sense of the word, even if the brother do call himself a Christian. The conduct of men in their economic relations is anything but brotherly. Socialism may or may not be practicable, but to it the brotherhood of man is something very real. The endeavor of socialism is to carry out the principles of brotherhood in all the relations of life, by introducing a social system, in which the maxim shall obtain, "One for all; all for one." The central idea is that each one should contribute to the common welfare whatever his strength and capacity will permit, and that none shall be permitted to suffer for the lack of anything which he really needs, provided the resources of society are sufficient to satisfy the need.

An adequate provision for the dependent classes is a necessary part of this proposed system of brotherhood. This provision is found, as we have already seen, in the very structure of society itself; for this includes what we might call a mutual insurance system which reaches every one, so that the weak and infirm and other industrially incapable persons have a sure income guaranteed them.

A passage in "Looking Backward" brings out the socialist idea with regard to those who are now the dependent classes as well as anything which could be quoted. Dr. Leete is again explaining the new society to Mr. West, and these words are used:—

"'A solution which leaves an unaccounted-for residuum, is no solution at all; and our solution of the problem of human society, would have been none at all had it left the lame, the sick, and the blind outside with the beasts to fare as they might. Better far to have left the strong and well unprovided for, than these burdened ones, toward whom every heart must yearn, and for whom ease of mind and body should be provided, if for no others. Therefore, it is as I told you this morning, that the title of every man, woman, and child to the means of existence, rests on no basis less plain, broad, and simple, than the fact that they are fellows of one race — members of one human family. The only coin current is the image of God, and that is good for all we have.

"'I think there is no feature of the civilization of your epoch so repugnant to modern ideas as the neglect with which you treated your dependent classes. Even if you had no pity, no feeling of brotherhood, how was it that you did not see that you were robbing the incapable classes of their plain right, and leaving them unprovided for?"

"'I do not quite follow you there,' I said. 'I admit the claims of this class to our pity, but how could they, who produce nothing, claim a share of the product as a right?'

"'How happened it?' was Dr. Leete's reply, 'that your workers were able to produce more than so many savages would have done? Was it not wholly on account of the heritage of the past knowledge and achievements of the race, the machinery of society, thousands of years in contriving, found by you ready made to your hand. How did you get to be possessors of this knowledge and this history, which represent nine parts to one contributed by yourself in the value of your product? You inherited it, did you not? And were not these others, these unfortunate and crippled brothers, whom you cast out, joint inheritors, co-heirs, with you? What did you do with their share? Did you not rob them when you put them off with crusts, who were entitled to sit with the heirs, and did you not add insult to robbery, when you called the crusts charity?'"

It is also a part of this idea of brotherhood, that it contemplates a better future for women and children, providing for their ample support, making marriage a matter of affection and inclination for women, and not a matter of economic necessity, and providing for all children the opportunities for a happy childhood and a full development of all their powers.

It is a natural corollary from the endeavor to make real the brotherhood of man in economic relations, that it proposes the establishment of a harmony of industrial interests. It is thought by socialists, that the production of material goods for use rather than for exchange, will harmonize the interests of the members of industrial society, for then it becomes the interest of all, that there shall be a large and ample production of material goods of the best quality. Let us contrast that with production of things for exchange. When things are produced for exchange, what is wanted is values, and not quantities of commodities, as has been already stated; but value, according to a well-known law, depends upon final utility, or utility of the last thing produced, the result of which is a constant effort to limit production.

Real social riches consist in abundance, but individual interests are always opposed to abundance, in consequence of which we have combinations to diminish production, and corners and rings to forestall the market, resulting in the destruction of cargoes of East Indian spices by the Dutch, and of fish by the English in the Thames, and of fruit by Americans in New York harbor. The arrangement which socialism contemplates is more like that which would hold in a family or among friends. If there is abundance and plenty for all, we rejoice under such circumstances. We say to each one, "Help yourself," and are glad that we are able to do so. This is what happens in the rural districts whenever production is there carried on for use rather than for exchange. The Southern planter, before the war, who produced apples or vegetables for consumption and not for exchange, was glad whenever the yield was large; and it gave him genuine satisfaction to distribute the surplus among his friends and neighbors.

The same law of scarcity which holds for commodities, holds for labor under our present system also. The price of labor is kept up by making it scarce, and to prevent an abundant supply of labor in the branch of industry which they control, is one of the purposes of labor organizations. We thus have, as the result of the law of value, which operates in present society, necessary and universal antagonism of industrial interests. It is not meant to say that absolutely and in every respect, the interests of one man are opposed to the interests of every other man, in present industrial society: no socialist would claim this, but it is maintained successfully that there is necessarily a large amount of antagonism of interests. The point arises in competitive production and distribution, at which interests diverge. The employer and employee, for example, have identical interests up to a certain point, but then their interests become more or less antagonistic. It is a praiseworthy effort to attempt the establishment of a harmony of industrial interests, and the claim that socialism provides a harmonious system of economic life is a strong one.

It becomes clear, from all this, that socialism seeks to establish an environment favorable to the development of moral qualities in human beings; and unless this feature of socialism is carried so far as to make everything, or nearly everything, depend upon environment, it is unquestionably a strong characteristic of socialism. The teaching of modern science, and the outcome of social experience of every kind, lay greater and greater stress upon environment; and recent scientific tendencies make heredity relatively less important, so far as ordinary moral qualities are concerned.[1]

[1] The fact is frequently overlooked that heredity brings a set of circumstances with it, and what really belongs to the circumstances is often attributed to the heredity. A change of circumstances shows whether a greater influence is to be attributed to the circumstances or to the heredity. It has been ascertained that ties of blood and marriage have long connected a large proportion of the criminal and pauper classes in the neighborhood of Indianapolis, Ind. Those thus related have been called "The Tribe of Ishmael." Now the question in regard to this "Tribe of Ishmael" is, which had the greater influence, heredity or circumstances? It is demonstrable, however, in cases of this kind, as well as in the slums of large cities, that a change of surroundings would produce changed results. Almost invariably a

Unquestionably, favorable environment is not enough in itself, but it is often the condition precedent to improvement. Preachers whose traditions have inclined them to lay almost exclusive emphasis upon exhortation and appeal to the individual conscience, have gradually come to see, that for the most wretched and unfortunate classes there is no hope without a change of environment. The testimony of three preachers, of three different religious bodies, is important in this connection. The Rev. Samuel Barnett, for many years rector of St. Jude's Church, and warden of Toynbee Hall, London, tells us in his work, "Practicable Socialism," that in the slums of cities the social reformer must precede, or, at any rate, accompany, the preacher, unless the latter be himself a social reformer. Mr. Barnett is a clergyman of the established Church of England; but a leading Methodist, the Rev. Hugh Price Hughes, gives like testimony, stating that he has had as much experience in evangelistic work as any man in England, and that, in his opinion, it is of no avail to preach to hungry men. General Booth of the Salvation Army tells us plainly, in his "Darkest England," that it was the hopelessness of attempting to save the wretched and outcast population of London, the "submerged tenth," without a change in their environment, which led him to advocate his extensive plans of social reform.

child taken from such environment and placed under a favorable environment becomes a moral citizen, whereas had the old environment continued, the child would probably have become a criminal or a pauper. Such statistics as we have show that more than nine out of ten children are saved by a change in environment. Heredity would seem to have great weight in the case of special talents, as teachers have frequent opportunity to observe; but so far as ordinary moral character is concerned, circumstances would appear to be far more important.

The late Mr. Charles Loring Brace, who, through the Children's Aid Society, of which he was the founder and the soul, was able to save hundreds of thousands of lives, warns us against individualistic religious methods like tract distribution, as of no use in the slums.

After all, this is only a matter of ordinary commonsense, based on ample experience. Every man feels, for his own family, the importance of environment, and he seeks to bring up his own children in a favorable environment. A Christian father of a family, who should leave his own little boys and girls to grow up in the slums of cities, among thieves and prostitutes, is inconceivable. Any father of a family, having the power to take his children out of such environment, and who should not do it, would be considered a monstrosity. After all, the real reason why we hear so much against environment, is because the more fortunate classes desire to shirk the individual responsibility which a true doctrine of environment brings to them. If each individual, regardless of environment, has an equal chance, of course there is little reason why a fortunately situated person should concern himself about the wretched inhabitants of the modern slum, whereas the true doctrine of environment lays a heavy responsibility upon each one who is able in any way to change an unfortunate environment. Socialism in this, as in other respects, helps to tear off the mask of sham and hypocrisy from modern society.

The structure of society, under socialism, would be such as to abolish necessarily the idle classes, and this constitutes a strong feature of socialism. No one, under socialism, can gain a livelihood without personal exertion; and the maxim of St. Paul, "He who will not work, neither shall he eat," would become of universal application.

At the present time, we are making some attempt to abolish idleness on the part of poor people, but we have not seriously attacked the problem of the idle rich. Socialism is strong, then, because it attempts to abolish all idle classes, and idleness is morally pernicious.

Socialists claim that socialism would improve and elevate government, and would raise into prominence a nobler class of men. It may be urged that socialism would improve government, because it would make government a matter of vital concern to all the inhabitants of a country, and would draw into the service of the government all the moral strength and talent of the country. At the present time, on the contrary, government is a matter of such minor concern to large and influential classes, that they neglect it altogether, and very many powerful persons promote their economic interests by the degradation of government. Under socialism, the prosperity of all would depend upon the character of the socialistic administration, and socialism could hope to avail itself of the full mental capacity and moral strength of the community. If socialism could be made to work, it cannot be said that its claim, that it would bring into prominence a nobler class of men, and would produce nobler men, is unfounded. Those who have great fortunes, under our existing system, have such positions of prominence and power that they cannot be ignored. People must do them honor, because they fear to do otherwise. A governor of an American commonwealth was, not long ago, reproved because he would not join in the reception tendered to an industrial magnate whose methods had been such that he could not give them his approbation; for he held that these methods, introduced into the State of which he was governor, would not tend to its development "in the line of public good." His judgment in regard to the moral character of the man was not called in question, but he was criticised because this man, held by many to be guilty even of penitentiary offences, had such power that he could either help or injure the section of the country which he was visiting.

Socialists hold that, under socialism, elevation to positions of importance would be based upon moral qualifications, in part at least. They furthermore urge that the nature of public business is such that it is ennobling. A great leader in private business has his attention concentrated upon himself or upon a few stock-holders, whereas public life enlarges the horizon, and the right thinking person who administers public business, does so with reference to the good of the whole people. It may be justly urged that it is public and not private life which has given us a Washington, a Lincoln.[1] The

---

[1] A critic replies: "It is doubtless true that private service would not give us a Washington or a Lincoln, and it is equally true that public service would not give us a Fulton, a Whitney, a Morse, a Westinghouse, or an Edison."

This is by no means clear to those who know what is going on in the laboratories of the universities in different parts of the world. And it must be remembered that, taking the world as a whole, the greater part of its activity is conducted by those who are in the public service, namely, the professors and their assistants in the State universities. It is safe to say that those men who are named could not have done their work had it not been for the preliminary work carried on in the laboratories of universities. Morse is not the only name to be mentioned in connection with the telegraph. Professor Henry's name also has an honorable record as the inventor of what was essential in the telegraph, and, animated by the spirit which obtains in the public service at the best, he refused to take out a patent. There are, indeed, those who do not recognize the claims of Morse to originality in the practical application of the telegraph; but, of course, it is not necessary for us to enter upon a discussion of this controverted point. It is certain that Morse's work was based upon

heroes of men are those who have served States, and not those who have served private corporations. This shows us why, as John Stuart Mill pointed out, war, and not private business, has heretofore been the chief school of the social virtues. War has an anti-social character, insomuch as it is waged by one society of men against another; but it is carried on to advance the interest of a country, and the soldier feels that he is struggling for his land, and for it he is ready to give up life itself. His occupation cultivates in him generous habits of mind, and a sense of common danger draws him near to his fellow-soldiers.[1]

a great deal of previous activity of a public nature. Public service has given us a Bunsen, a Helmholtz, a Virchow, and many others who quite hold their own with the names mentioned. What reason have we, after all, to say that an Edison would not have given us his best, had he worked in a public laboratory? Those who are familiar with the work going on in the laboratories of universities, know that the entire time and strength of those engaged in these universities is given to their work, and, as a rule, the last thing of which they think is large pecuniary returns. Professor Babcock, in the State University of Wisconsin, invented a milk tester, which, it has been asserted, is worth to the State every year the entire cost of the university; and a professor in the University of Kansas has likewise, it is claimed, made discoveries which are worth, to the State of Kansas, the entire cost of that university. Professor Babcock refused to patent his invention because he did not think it was right for him to do so, as he was in the service of the State.

However, it is not incumbent upon the author of the present work, to show that all our inventions and improvements could result from public life, inasmuch as he endeavors, in the latter part of the book, to demonstrate the importance of a large field for private enterprise.

[1] " Until laborers and employers perform the work of industry in the spirit in which soldiers perform that of an army, industry will never be moralized, and military life will remain, what, in spite of the anti-social character of its direct object, it has hitherto been, the chief school of moral co-operation." — *The Positive Philosophy of Auguste Comte*, by JOHN STUART MILL, New York, 1887, p. 135.

CHAPTER V.

SOCIALISM AS A PROMOTER OF ART.

IT is likely to awaken surprise on the part of those who have not given attention to socialism, to learn that among people of artistic temperament, it meets with much favor. Poets, painters, and authors of talent are much inclined to view socialism with a certain sympathy, and there are many of them who are even outspoken in their adherence to it. John Ruskin advocates something like socialism, although of an aristocratic kind; and William Morris, regarded by many as the worthiest of the English poets to hold the post of Poet Laureate, is not only a socialist, but a rather extreme socialist. Alfred Hayes, prominent among the younger English poets, and Walter Crane, the artist, are members of the Fabian Society.[1] Our own James Russell Lowell at one time said a good word in behalf of socialism, and probably Mr. W. D. Howells would no longer object to being classed among the socialists.

What is the explanation of this fact, which may at first seem a striking and surprising one ? The explanation is found in the unfavorable atmosphere for art and literature which is created by competitive industrialism. Art can thrive only when it is encouraged by a favorable

[1] "The Fabian Society," by William Clarke, in the *New England Magazine* for March, 1894.

social environment.[1] Poverty on the part of the many and wealth on the part of a few, are alike held to be fatal to the highest art or literature. Leisure and moderate comfort on the part of the private citizen, with a grand public life, create the atmosphere in which art thrives. If we look back upon the past, we find that national feeling in its expansive periods has produced a large part of all that is great in art and literature. Three periods may be called to mind : the age of Pericles, when Greek art and literature achieved grand success ; the age of Augustus, which was called the Golden Age ; and the age of Elizabeth in England, which produced Shakespeare. Man achieves great things when in him the national life pulsates, and through him the nation speaks ; but when the national life is mean, man's spirit finds no high plane of thought and expression. Architecture achieved its grandest success in the Middle Ages, when national feeling was becoming powerful, and the age in which this success was attained was not peculiarly a commercial age. It is often said in the United States that when we become richer we shall have a true art; but if what artists tell us is true, what art has to dread in the United States is a plutocracy. The increase of wealth, with present methods of distribution, would seem to be more likely to bring danger with it than promise to art. What is really wanted is more leisure and comfort for the masses, more joy in work, and a genuine revival of true national feeling.

Art is essentially public and not private in its destina-

[1] "The hearing ear is always found close to the speaking tongue, and no genius can long or often utter anything which is not invited or gladly entertained by men around him." — EMERSON: *English Traits*, chap. iv., on Race.

tion, and if it achieves its grandest success, must minister to society, and not to millionaires. This, at any rate, is the socialistic view. One socialistic writer complains that [1] " now a clever workman is kept at tasks prescribed by plutocrats, and must produce baronial sideboards, and the deft-fingered girl hideous artificial flowers." He tells us the gold standards of plutocracy are not art standards, and that an atmosphere is produced by competition, and plutocracy resulting therefrom, in which art cannot thrive; " that competition ties the craftsman hand and foot, but art implies independence." Another socialist, in speaking of the creed of philosophic radicalism in England, which included classical political economy, says that:

" It was essentially a creed of Murdstones and Gradgrinds, and the first revolt came from the artistic side ; the nest of singing birds of the lakes would have none of it."

Mr. William Morris, in an article upon the socialist ideal,[2] makes a plea for socialism from the standpoint of art, and uses these words:

" The great mass of effective art, that which pervades all life, must be the result of the harmonious co-operation of neighbors; and the rich man has no neighbors, nothing but rivals and parasites. . . . When people once more take pleasure in their work, when the pleasure rises to a certain point, the expression of it will become irresistible, and that expression of pleasure is art, whatever form it may take."

Mr. Morris says that we must abolish the privilege of private persons to destroy the beauty of the earth for their private advantage, and he explains that the

[1] See *Church Reformer*, March, 1890.
[2] See *New Review*, January, 1891.

richest man has now license to injure the commonwealth to the full extent of his riches.

One of the most learned English churchmen, Dr. Westcott, now Bishop of Durham, writes on art in the same spirit in his work on the Epistles of St. John. He says of Christian art that:

"It aims not at a solitary, but a common enjoyment; it seeks to make it clear that all to which it is directed has a spiritual value, able to command completest service. . . . If this view of art which has been given is correct, its primary destination is public, not private, and it culminates in worship. Neither a great picture nor a great poem can be for a single possessor; and so it has been at all times, when art has risen to its highest triumphs. . . . When Greek art was greatest, it was consecrated to public use, and one chief danger of modern society is lest the growth of private wealth should lead to the diversion of the highest artistic power from the common service."

One of the best presentations of art, from the socialistic standpoint, is given in an article in the *Christian Union* (now *The Outlook*) for December 17, 1893, and is entitled "Ideal Art for the People."

The following quotation gives the gist of the socialistic thought:[1] —

"The art of the city, in the day when painters, sculptors, and master-singers were in full tide of work and song, did not rest in the genius of the few, but in the mood of the many. The instinct for beauty, and the training which recognized it under all forms, were universal ; for art grows out of a deep, rich soil, and grows

[1] Mr. Wm. Morris gives an extremely interesting presentation of his views concerning art, in an address entitled "Art and Socialism," published by W. Reeves, London, 1884. A Boston architect, Mr. J. Pickering Putnam, treats the subject of architecture in its relations to socialism, under the title of "Architecture under Nationalism," a monograph published by the Nationalist Educational Association, Boston, 1890.

only when such soil is provided for it. It may produce sporadically in an alien atmosphere, but it is never productive of great works, on a great scale, unless it is representative of a wide popular impulse and sympathy, unless it is national or racial. In this country, as in England, art does not really touch our life; it is not yet one of our natural forms of expression: we do not understand its immense importance in a rich and rounded civilization; nor do we realize how much we are losing a homely, every-day content and rest. A real, living art means beauty in dress and habit, joy in the manual industries in the production of things sound and harmonious; it means striving for the ideal in common occupations, and spiritual and intellectual rest and delight in common work.

"We think of art as a luxury, an embellishment, the delicate growth of a fortunate age, and the choice work of a favored few. It is to-day, and in this country, largely the possession of the rich. Nothing could be farther from a true idea of art or a true use of it. Great art is a sturdy, vigorous plant, demanding a rich soil, a broad sky, and free winds; it is never an exotic, to be nourished delicately by a few, and kept from contact with the vulgar world. It is great only when it is so much a part of the world that it is its most inevitable and unforced expression. The Greek tragedies and Shakespeare's plays were part of the intensest popular life of their time."

CHAPTER VI.

SOCIALISM AND PRESENT PROBLEMS.

ONE of the problems of to-day is a simplification of government, and the socialist claims that socialism will solve this problem. A certain force cannot be denied to this argument. Laws are multiplied now without end, and it is extremely difficult to know what is and what is not legal under the complex conditions of modern life. It is also very hard to avoid pernicious legislation, because it requires such incessant watching on the part of well-meaning, intelligent citizens.

Socialism puts forward the claim that it would reduce law-making to a minimum, and would almost abolish courts. If one examines our statute books, one will find that by far the greater portion of legislation concerns private property in the instruments of production, and that litigation also finds its basis in the same institution. Naturally this legislation and this litigation would be abolished with the abolition of the institution upon which it all rests. A comparison of the post-office with our American railways would illustrate this point. The law in regard to the post-office is comparatively concise and simple, and the post-office seldom figures in lawsuits. On the other hand, how endless is the legislation concerning privately owned railways! How complex and complicated is it! How continuously does the private railway figure in lawsuits! The administrative problem under socialism might become more difficult than present public administration, but law would be greatly simplified, and the basis of most litigation before the courts would disappear.

But this is not all; how difficult a problem is taxation! The national Congress and the legislatures of forty-four States and the municipal authorities of hundreds of cities are all struggling with this problem, and the amount of progress which has been accomplished during the past generation is discouragingly small. Unquestionably, our methods of taxation could be vastly improved; but taxation must ever remain a difficult problem. The whole problem, however, practically disappears under socialism. With production socialized it would only be necessary for society to take out of the total product in advance what was needed for public purposes before the distribution among the citizens should be effected.

Still another problem : What of the eight-hour day? The eight-hour day is plainly an ideal, but yet an extremely difficult one to realize under present conditions, look at it as we will. Each man cannot settle it for himself, because in modern production those engaged in the same industrial establishment must, as a rule, work the same length of time; but even those in one industrial establishment cannot decide the problem for themselves, because they are under compulsion which springs from the competition of other industrial establishments in the same country and even in other countries.

The eight-hour day has involved in many a conflict employer and employee; and yet, unfortunately, the employer is well nigh as powerless to effect a change as the employee. Socialism, harmonizing industrial interests, would make the problem a comparatively simple one. The more men produced, the more they would have to enjoy; and it would remain for society to determine on the one hand, how much greater would be the production of wealth resulting from a ten-hour day than from an eight-hour day; and second, whether the additional production was more or less valuable than the additional time.

Compulsory education is another problem which, at best, must occasion difficulties so long as the present competitive system endures. It is a cruel hardship to children not to give them educational advantages; but to do so sometimes deprives a dependent parent, for example, a widowed mother, of what she needs for her support. Doubtless it is better to do this than to allow a child to grow up in ignorance; or, at any rate, it is better to provide in some other way for the mother; but this does not render the problem an easy one. Yet this is only one of the difficulties which an attempt to secure a universal education encounters in actual practice. It is frequently found that the children in the schools in the poorer quarters of the cities have no decent clothing, and that they are often unable to study, because actually hungry. Compulsory education, then, to be really effective, involves in numerous cases the problem of furnishing food and clothing to children as well as schools. Manifestly, if socialism can be made to work at all well, the difficulties of compulsory education simply disappear.

Insurance against the economic contingencies which beset the ordinary man is one of the pressing problems of the day. Germany has elaborated a system under the operation of which some twenty millions of human beings are more or less adequately insured; and the problem is actively discussed in every European country. It is only a matter of time when insurance will become one of the pressing problems of the day in the United States. Yet, whether we adopt the German method, or one of the numerous other methods which have been suggested, the difficulties are immense; while to do nothing will probably be an impossibility at no distant day. The structure of society under socialism is such that it solves the problem.

Private monopoly, with all its difficulties, manifestly disappears under socialism. So we can take up one problem of the day after another, and we shall find that socialism provides a solution for them. We can question whether socialism can be made to work in practice or not; but we cannot well deny that if socialism is practicable, it brings with it the solution of these questions.

CHAPTER VII.

SERVICES WHICH THE AGITATION OF SOCIALISM HAS RENDERED.

THE statement has already been made that we may look at the strength of socialism from two standpoints: First, from the standpoint of a program of complete social reconstruction, and second, from the standpoint of socialistic agitation. We pass now from the first standpoint to the second, and consider the benefits which the agitation of socialism has brought us.

First, we may mention the general awakening of conscience, with respect to social conditions, which it has produced. Probably there never was a time when, generally speaking, the consciences of men were so sensitive with regard to the lot of the poor and unfortunate as at the present day; and this is very largely the direct, and also the indirect, effect of the activity of socialism, for it has promoted the discussion of all economic questions from an ethical standpoint. Even the non-ethical socialism has had this effect, because it has largely lost its non-ethical character when it has been brought under the requirements of practical agitation. What socialism really desires is that the economic life should be entirely subordinate to the other departments of social life. It wishes leisure and opportunity for the cultivation of the higher faculties. Socialism has thus performed an important service in showing what may, at least conceivably, be accomplished by making a struggle for material interests merely a basis of higher things.

Socialism has aided men to picture to themselves an ideal society, and has familiarized them with the idea of social change and progress. This has resulted in a widespread desire to move in the direction of the ideal, and to approximate it as nearly as may be. The result has been that a needed interest in economic questions has been awakened among anti-socialists as well as socialists.

Formerly an excessive emphasis was laid on the individual side of economic life, and this was the outcome of the individualistic philosophy of the latter part of the eighteenth century. Socialism has laid a needed emphasis upon the social side of economic life. When new measures and projects are brought forward, socialism teaches us to look at them from the standpoint of society as a whole, and not from that of individual promoters merely. It is not meant to be said that this was impossible without socialism, but attention is called simply to the undoubted fact that socialism was needed to familiarize us with the point of view which one gets from looking at economic questions from the standpoint of society as a whole. Even up to the present day, we, in the United States, are accustomed to regard projects and measures simply from the standpoint of the immediate interests of a few.

A few men wish a charter for a street railway, or a steam railway, or they desire the privilege of furnishing gas to a city. It is evident that the project will promote the interests of those immediately concerned, and usually they receive what they desire almost without conditions. When, however, enterprises of this sort are viewed from the standpoint of society as a whole, we begin to ask ourselves whether society could not do better than to hand over to private individuals, or corporations, such important services without conditions of any sort. But, as soon as the question is asked, a divergence appears between public and private interests. It is seen, for example, that even with private enterprises it is better to have a limited than an unlimited charter, in order that society may, at some future time, have the right to take hold of the enterprise, and manage it directly, or that it may sell the privilege to persons willing to pay for it its market price. Reflection upon the bearings of such enterprise, when viewed from the standpoint of society, reveals, furthermore, the injustice in society of giving away privileges to a few persons, which have a pecuniary significance, based upon the fact that they yield a surplus over and above the returns to labor and to capital. If socialism had, early in our history, familiarized us with thoughts of this kind, it would have saved to the people of the United States hundreds of millions of dollars. The claim is made, by one long familiar with the finances of New York City, that the value of franchises given away in that city, and thus enriching the few at the expense of the many, would be sufficient to defray all the expenses of the government of New York City. While this does not seem so bad when the matter is viewed simply from the standpoint of the individual, viewed from the standpoint of society, it appears like a wicked robbery of the public, and we see that there is not a working woman in New York City who has not virtually been robbed for the benefit of a favored few; for, had the public interest been guarded, it would be easy to have three-cent street-car fares in New York City or on each fare to have a surplus of two cents to be employed for public purposes, in the benefits of which all would share. If we take up one class of undertakings

BENEFITS OF AGITATION OF SOCIALISM. 169

after another, and view them from the standpoint of socialism, we shall find light thrown upon the public interests. Socialism has thus a high educational value.

But the question is naturally raised by socialism, whether industrial undertakings shall be at all handed over to private individuals or corporations. Socialism claims that society, as a whole, should provide for the satisfaction of economic wants; and while, very generally, this claim has not been admitted with reference to industry as a whole, new light has been thrown upon the industrial functions of government, as one industry after another has been studied from the social standpoint. There are now large classes who will go at least part way with the socialists. As the result of socialism, in part at least, we have a better classification of industrial undertakings, showing us that these undertakings differ among themselves in material respects, and that the advantages of private industry do not hold equally for them all.

The foregoing is only one respect in which socialism has modified, fortunately, the older political economy. It has compelled an examination of the social order itself. Older economists took simply for granted the fundamental features of the existing social order. Private property, freedom of person, free contract, and vested interests were assumed as a mere matter of course. Socialists criticised these institutions, and the result has been a careful, analytical, and historical examination of them. This examination has revealed the fact that they themselves are growths, developing like other institutions, and capable of beneficial modifications. The criticisms of socialism have also led to a re-examination of the doctrines of value and price, with great advantage to political economy, and perhaps there is scarcely any doctrine of economics, which has not, to a greater or less extent, been brought under the influence of socialism, and received beneficial modification.

The agitation of socialism has had a tendency to improve government. What has already been stated has indicated several lines of reform which the agitation of socialism has promoted. The socialistic platforms are, as a rule, divided into two parts, the first of which contains a statement of the ultimate ideal, and the second of which presents immediate demands. Now, many of these immediate demands are such that they have found general favor, and in some instances acceptance.

We may name among them plans to improve and extend local self-government, and to educate the voter; also various measures designed to improve sanitary conditions in factories, to protect the life and health of the wage-earner, and to throw safeguards about women and children; all of which would fall under the general head of factory legislation. Everything designed to purify government, and to protect the ballot, finds support on the part of the socialists. The socialists are now inclined to take the position that what is needed to bring about socialism is not a reaction from excessive misery, but a strong and intelligent wage-earning population. If the reader will consult various socialistic programs given in the Appendix, he will see that there are many "immediate demands" which must receive general approval. But this is not all; socialism conveys to the masses the idea that political questions are far larger than personal questions, and that it is a degradation of government to make political questions centre about the distribution of booty, whether that take the form of fat contracts, or offices, designated in the parlance of the day as "plums" or "snaps."

Socialism makes questions of government something far more than contests of office-holders and office-seekers. Socialism makes government real, live, vital, because it is felt that so much is at stake in politics. Perhaps nothing is more calculated to improve government than a generous leaven of the best kind of socialistic thought.

Proof can be seen in various quarters. When the social democrats gained control of several cities in Saxony, Germany, the excellence of their administration was admitted by all. London, also, offers remarkable proof, for socialism has been largely instrumental in making the administration of London a model for all other cities. Mr. Frederick Harrison, not himself a socialist, says that the London County Council of 1889 "was the most definitely democratic and reforming body of men ever elected in England." He adds, —

"The council has proved itself the most economical municipality which any great city possesses, or, perhaps, ever had, . . . and is, beyond doubt, the purest and most honest. The curse of all great cities is corruption. . . . London has now a municipality which is absolutely free from this taint or even the suspicion of it. . . . The council is the first municipal authority in this metropolis which has shown a steady, earnest, and intelligent desire to raise the condition of the people. . . . No more honest, hard-working, zealous, self-sacrificing body of public servants has ever served a great city. No capital in the world ever had so incorruptible a municipal authority; nor did any have such eminent trained public servants to lead it. It is a pattern to the world for economy, for industry, for earnestness in the cause of the people."

PART III.

THE WEAKNESS OF SOCIALISM.

PART III.

THE WEAKNESS OF SOCIALISM.

CHAPTER I.

INTRODUCTORY.

SOCIALISM is as strong as the strongest presentation which can be made of it. This must be clearly borne in mind by all students of the subject, for in the course of statement and re-statement socialism will be made stronger than any presentation of it which has ever yet been given. No impartial person can deny this, any more than any such person can deny that it has become stronger in its program as time has gone on, and this program has been elaborated and improved.

What, in its nature, is the weakness of socialism? When we examine into this weakness, we must direct our attention to what is essential in socialism, and not to accidental features attached to it by this, that, or the other socialist.

Socialism in England and America can be appreciated in its full strength only when it becomes entirely emancipated from the materialistic conception of history advanced by Karl Marx; for in neither country can socialism meet with favor when it finds its basis in materialism.

Every modern student must admit the great influence of economic conditions, especially of the production, distribution, and exchange of material goods upon the whole of life; but to make everything depend upon economic forces, is shutting one's eyes to other forces, equally great and sometimes greater; and one must be blind to historical and actual phenomena who would make religion merely a product of economic life. Religion is an independent force, often sufficient to modify and even to shape economic institutions. How can it be claimed that our material economy is a cause of religion, when we find religious beliefs so diverse flourishing with like economic conditions? This is not the place to examine the philosophy of materialism; but it can scarcely be called an exaggerated statement to say that it is an antiquated philosophy,—at any rate, in the crude form in which it is presented by Marx's socialism.

Similarly, it is a weakness in one presentation of socialism, which does not touch the essence of socialism, to make it depend upon a precise and accurately defined law of evolution, which is as inflexible as castiron.

Society is not an automaton. That society has some option, some choice, and a conscience to which an appeal can be made, is a fact, if there is any such thing as a fact at all. There is a specious appearance of strength in the claim that the evolution of society is such that things must become worse and worse; wages falling, relatively at least, crises inevitably increasing in frequency and in severity, and the concentration of production going forward, until ultimately we must choose between private or public monopoly in every branch of industry. Such a law of evolution makes socialism turn upon the historical and statistical proof that can be brought forward to substantiate it. We consequently

THE WEAKNESS OF SOCIALISM. 177

have whole volumes of statistics, compiled either to substantiate or to refute socialism, when based upon this law of evolution. So far as these statistics are concerned, it must be said that they are nearly worthless. Each one seems to prove his point, but it is because his statistical presentation is incomplete. Probably there is no sufficient statistical record in existence to enable us either to prove or to disprove the Marxist law of social evolution. But socialism does not depend upon this law. If it could be completely refuted to-morrow, in such manner that every one would have to admit its refutation, socialism would not be weakened thereby, except, perhaps, temporarily.

The real nature of the question at issue is this: Are there general tendencies which are more or less favorable to a socialistic organization of production and distribution? Every one will admit that industrial society must, in the future, be shaped with reference to actual existing social forces, although more than one outcome of these forces is conceivable. Then, if we decide in the affirmative, as we must, that there are certain social, or, speaking more accurately, socio-economic forces, working favorably to socialism, we have to decide whether the socialistic outcome of this social evolution is that which is, on the whole, the more desirable.

A part of this so-called scientific law of social evolution is a doctrine of value, which makes value depend upon labor-time, and finds the profits of capital and the source of new wealth in a surplus value created by labor, and filched from labor by the capitalist. The scientific cast which this law of value seems to give to socialism is merely a superficial appearance. Socialism does not depend upon a law of value; and the refutation of any particular socialistic law of value leaves socialism, as a practical force, as strong as it was before.

The situation is simply this: At the present time the instruments of production are privately owned, and industry is privately managed. This necessitates the existence of rent, interest, and profits. Manifestly, the entire product of industry cannot, under such conditions, go to labor, and there must be idle classes living on rent and interest. Moreover, the capitalist must, under existing conditions, receive, in addition to returns for personal exertions, a return for the ownership of the instruments of production. The vital questions are: Can this be so changed and such an economic organization be brought about that the ownership of the instruments of production will be vested in society as a whole? In the second place, we have to ask the question whether or not this is desirable even if it is practicable. Manifestly, the wage-earner must like to add to his wages the advantages of partial ownership of the instruments of production; and it is only natural that he should desire to participate in the management of production. It is really a great weakness in a presentation of socialism to call rent, interest, and profits, robbery, although they are appropriated by capitalists and other classes than wage-earners. Naturally, the wage-earner cannot be blamed because he desires a reorganization which will compel all capable persons to render useful personal service, and to enable society as a whole to enjoy benefits which now accrue to the few. The Fabian Society in England has been able to exercise an immense influence upon English thought, and a decided influence upon English practice, because it has emancipated itself from a pseudo-scientific presentation of socialism, which was, after all, full of revolting crudities.

It follows naturally from what has been said, that it is not by any means necessary to make socialism a purely working-class movement. The question of socialism is one which concerns all classes of society; and it is by no means evident that wage-earners will obtain greater benefit than any other social class, if socialism can be made to work as well as its adherents claim. What is called an "all-classes socialism" is stronger than a working-class socialism. Socialism has been made largely a working-class movement in Germany, but this has had a most unfortunate effect. Every well-wisher of the United States and England will hope that socialism, in these two countries, may lack the narrowness as well as the bitterness which accompanies it if it becomes a working-class movement. It may be said that in Germany socialism has tended to become more conservative as the socialistic party has become a great power in the land, and that it has lost something of its working-class character to its own great gain. The strength that socialism has, has largely come to it from others than wage-earners. Marx and Lassalle were far enough removed by birth and position and training from the wage-earning class of Germany. Liebknecht and Bebel, as has already been mentioned, are the leaders of German social democracy to-day; and Liebknecht was once a university student, and Bebel a prosperous manufacturer and employer. Robert Owen, the earliest English socialist, was an industrial magnate; and a large proportion of the strength of socialism in England comes from men who have been trained at the English universities. University men also figure prominently in American socialism. Men of such character must be drawn into the socialist movement from conscientious motives, if it is to become powerful. The appeal to self-interest of the masses is proper in its own place, but that is not sufficient. The one who overlooks the capacity in man for self-sacrifice and devotion to others, excludes social facts as real as any which can be mentioned, and, moreover, facts nowhere seen more plainly than in the history of socialism itself.

CHAPTER II.

ALLEGED, BUT NOT VALID, OBJECTIONS TO SOCIALISM.

When we survey the various current arguments against socialism, we are obliged to divide them into two classes. By far the more numerous class of arguments is composed of those which rest upon either misapprehension or wilful misrepresentation. They are not arguments which can be advanced by any one who is at the same time intelligent and ingenuous. Arguments of the second class, however, are arguments which are advanced by those who fully understand what socialism means, and feel that socialism should be treated honestly. They constitute the serious objections to socialism, pointing out the difficulties which stand in the way of its realization. Each writer who is opposed to socialism will have a different view with regard to the weightiest objections to its proposals. But it is the purpose of the author of the present work to present those objections to socialism which seem to him to have most weight.

It may first of all be well to give some little attention to the arguments against socialism which cannot be regarded as valid. Of course, it would require a book much longer than the present work to take up one after the other all these fallacious and misleading arguments; but a few of the more common objections of the kind named will be discussed briefly, by way of illustration.

When we survey the various arguments against socialism in different countries, we cannot fail to be impressed with the fact that that is held to be a valid objection in one country which is not so regarded in another country. An illustration is afforded by free public schools. German writers, and until recently English writers, have regarded the proposal of the socialists to abolish tuition fees as decidedly objectionable. There may be differences of opinion among Americans, but undoubtedly a vast majority of the citizens of the United States give to free schools their cordial indorsement, regard them as one of the bulwarks of the republic, and attack vigorously any one who attempts to undermine them. On the other hand, the idea of public ownership and management of railways is regarded by many Americans as the chief weakness in the program of socialism, while Germans, as a rule, regard such ownership and management as something desirable. They tell us that the test of experience has settled the question for them. These illustrations suggest caution, and a careful survey of the operation of existing institutions in different lands.

The failure of communistic experiments in the United States and elsewhere is often urged as an objection against modern socialism; but, in reality, these experiments, while more or less instructive, throw little light upon the socialism of to-day. Some of them have succeeded; most of them have failed. But had all failed, that would scarcely constitute an argument of weight against proposals like those which we are called upon to consider. The earlier communism of this century represented ideals which find their basis in an earlier stage of industrial development; in so far, at any rate, as this communism attempted to propose something for universal adoption. The communistic village based upon voluntary agreement corresponded to a period of production on a small scale, when each large household group could hope to become economically almost self-sufficient. When production is carried on on a vast national and international scale, the socialism proposed must be national and international. The difficulties in the way of a communistic village are sufficiently apparent when one views them in the light of past experience, or when one examines the methods of production and distribution of the present time. A communistic village must be dependent at the present moment, when production is carried on for exchange, upon outsiders who have no connection with communism, and who are often bitterly opposed to it. Railways and telegraphs may be adduced as simply two important illustrations of many which might be mentioned. The management of these enterprises, privately owned and operated, cannot be expected to conform to the requirements of communistic settlements. Moreover, such settlements would not afford the freedom of movement and the possibilities of organization and reorganization which are required at the present day. When socialism is nationally organized, a man can move about the country to find the place which is most agreeable to him, and for which he is best adapted. Whatever his talents and his acquisitions, they are not lost to the socialistic state because he moves from one city to another. The condition of things is exactly the reverse in a communistic village. It is quite conceivable that the man who is most essential to the life and industries of such a village in the North may find it necessary, on account of his health, to move to Florida, and he thus becomes lost to communism. Moreover, in any communistic village there will very likely fail to be a right assortment of men and women for industrial organization. There may be too many of one kind and too few of another, and it is not possible freely to draw in from the outside world, and to give to the outside world, and still preserve communism.

These are simply a few obvious difficulties in the way of earlier communism, which had reference perhaps as much to the advantages of associated consumption, as to the economies of production on a vast scale: and these difficulties, with others which will occur on reflection, clearly render the earlier communism inadequate. This is conceded as freely by the modern socialist as by anyone. Consequently we find socialists in the United States issuing a pamphlet aiming to discourage any movement in the direction of a communistic village; and the Fabians of England steadily setting their faces against any separate settlements. In a lecture on the Progress of Collectivism, as reported in the *Fabian News* of February, 1894, Mr. Sidney Webb says of the Fabians, that from the beginning they discountenanced proposals to establish utopian communities, and have never seen reason to alter their opinion. Modern socialism does not preach a doctrine of separation, but aims to change the whole structure of modern society.

A socialistic state, under the auspices of the Jesuits, was established in Paraguay in the seventeenth century, and lasted for a hundred years or more, when it fell to pieces, owing to foreign conquest. This failure has been adduced as an argument against modern socialism, but a little reflection will show that it has no bearing on the case; and we can only wonder that this state survived so long, and was ultimately overthrown by a foreign power. The kind of socialism which was established in Paraguay was paternal in the extreme; it lacked the advantages of modern production, and would be altogether abhorrent to the modern socialist. Curiously enough, one writer adduces the remark of a traveller, who visited Paraguay when under the socialistic *régime*, that he saw there many discontented faces, as a serious argument against socialism. One may walk down the street of any great American or English city and discover plenty of discontented faces; but he would be regarded as a strange man who, on this account, would want to overthrow the existing social order.

The allegation is made that under socialism there would be no provision for doing the disagreeable work which is socially necessary. We have already seen, however, that there would be reason to anticipate that if socialism could be made to work at all, far more of the disagreeable work than at present would be performed by machinery. Moreover, much of the work which is now considered unpleasant is so esteemed because of the associations which form no necessary part of it. Hoeing corn is not unpleasant work; on the contrary, it is agreeable work when not continued too many hours a day, say not over eight or ten, and when hoeing corn gives one agreeable companionship. When an educated and cultured man, however, finds that hoeing corn brings him the constant and exclusive companionship of uneducated and degraded men like, for example, the ignorant negroes of the far South, it becomes most intensely disagreeable. It is the associations of work which, so far as nearly all work is concerned, render it agreeable or disagreeable, provided, of course, one is strong and well and is not overtaxed. Should there remain still some work positively disagreeable, it would not seem, after all, unfair that this should be distributed to a certain extent among all the members of the community, rather than heaped upon a few wretched individuals, who thus have to bear disproportionate burdens. It does not seem fair that one class should be made wretched for the sake of the community as a whole, unless it is absolutely necessary, in order that the work of civilization may go forward. It cannot be claimed, however, that there is any social necessity for this concentration of disagreeable work upon a few.

All this reminds one of the argument against socialism so current in Germany, which is called by that tremendous name, "*das allgemeine Stiefelputzenmüssen.*" This means simply that every one must black his own shoes. Will it, after all, interfere with the highest development of culture if each one should black his own shoes? The scholar in Germany rarely, if ever, performs this service for himself; but in America he ordinarily does it, and it would probably be hard to find an American scholar who would say that he found the performance of this task a serious obstacle in the way of the fullest unfolding of all his powers. We are reminded of the question which Abraham Lincoln put to the Englishman who told him that in England no gentleman blacked his own boots. " Whose boots does he black then?"[1]

Another current objection to socialism is that it will not know how to deal with the idle. We have already seen, however, that socialism alone proposes the complete abolition of the idle classes. So far as the idle poor are concerned, we do not hesitate in present society to send them to the penitentiary, or, in the South, to put them

---

[1] For some sensible remarks on this subject see "Die soziale Frage eine sittliche Frage," by Prof. Theobald Ziegler, p. 177.

in the chain gang when they become paupers and tramps. We do not hesitate to apply whatever physical force may be required to make a man work now, if he lacks the means of subsistence, and it cannot be necessary to apply greater compulsion under socialism. Socialists, however, hope that the desire of men to lead idle lives will disappear, or nearly so. The one who looks at this question with cold impartiality will hardly be inclined to share the enthusiastic hopes of the majority of socialists in this respect; but, at the same time, it is instructive to learn that in the communistic settlements idleness has been one of the least difficult factors with which their members have had to contend.

These illustrations of fallacious arguments against socialism serve to throw light, it is hoped, upon the true nature of the problem with which we are confronted, and to clear the ground for those serious objections to socialism which seem to very many to be decisive against its proposals.

CHAPTER III.

SOCIALISM TOO OPTIMISTIC WITH RESPECT TO THE FUTURE, AND TOO PESSIMISTIC WITH RESPECT TO THE PRESENT.

BEFORE we consider special objections to socialism, we will direct our attention to those of the most general character. First of all, certain weaknesses in socialism as ordinarily presented will be noticed, which objections do not, of necessity, adhere to socialism in itself.

If the question is asked, what is necessary to establish socialism, the answer cannot be difficult. It must be shown that socialism, while having its difficulties and its objectionable features, is, on the whole, preferable to the existing social order, both with respect to its characteristics when once introduced, and with respect to its promises for the future. It is conceivable, for example, that although socialism may be better than the present order when first introduced, it may not have in it the same potentiality of further improvement. This brings us to the first valid objection which may be urged against socialism, in its ordinary presentation at least. It is both too optimistic and too pessimistic. It is too optimistic with respect to the future, holding that conditions will be introduced which, on sober examination, seem incompatible with the existence of human beings upon an earth like ours. On the other hand, socialism is too pessimistic, as ordinarily presented, with respect to our present social order. The evils of our present system are vast enough, and every effort to remove them, or to increase the good in the world, deserves cordial approbation. But it may not by any means be affirmed that the present order is without its bright side. If there is a most wretched class, the submerged tenth, there is also a very large class whose needs are fairly well satisfied, and along many lines there has been decided improvement, which is still in progress.

Socialism is too optimistic with respect to the possibilities of wealth creation under socialism. Socialists describe a condition of things in which everyone shall enjoy all those comforts and conveniences which now fall to the lot alone of those whom we regard as wealthy. The possibility of living in a condition of what would now be called luxury is held out to the masses as an inducement to adopt socialism. The necessary limits to the production of wealth found in external nature and in the possibilities of social organization are overlooked. There is no difficulty, to be sure, in regard to the production of cotton or wheat. There is reason to suppose that it is possible to supply all human beings with all that they can need of certain staple articles, although it becomes apparent that this means an immense extension of production, when one reflects upon the millions of human beings whose elementary wants are unsatisfied. There are articles of ordinary consumption which could not, without great difficulty, be so increased that all human beings, even in what are now the civilized parts of the world, could enjoy as much as they would like, or, let us say, equal the consumption of the wealthy at the present time. Meat might be mentioned as one of these articles. The production of meat requires an extensive use of natural resources, and with all the improvements in the means of communication, its retail price seems to rise rather than fall. Should the consumption of meat be very greatly increased it would be attended with more than proportionate increase in the cost, because, either it would be necessary to use more expensive land for raising cattle, or more remote regions would have to be exploited.

The proportion of one's income used in the purchase of those staple articles of production which can be increased very greatly decreases as one's income increases, and it is only a small proportion of the income of the wealthy which is thus employed at the present time. If one examines into the essential conditions of the life of a family which is in marked degree what we call comfortable, not to say luxurious, it will be found that it implies the continuous exertions of several human beings, especially in the way of personal services. Personal services are necessarily limited in amount, and invention cannot increase this amount, although it may, to some extent, lessen the need of these services. Manifestly, not everyone could live in a condition which would imply the personal services of some one else. This means a great deal, and to see how much it means, it is only necessary for those who are familiar with the various parts of the United States to reflect upon the conditions of life in portions of the country where personal services are scarce and high in price. A person of moderate means, coming to the North, or to the far West, from the South, will say life is hard. It is one of the most common expressions used by housewives under such circumstances. When we examine into the conditions, what do we find it is that makes life hard for those who complain, except the scarcity of personal services and the difficulty of securing them? Manifestly, under socialism, servants would be relatively few, or would practically disappear. This may have its bright side, but unquestionably it has also its dark side. It is hoped that household service may be better organized, and things now produced within the home, be produced outside the home. There is a tendency, even now, to carry production outside the home into the factory; but this by no means obviates all the difficulties and objections which would attend such a change. Frugal comfort for all, with large public expenditures, and opportunities for common enjoyment in museums, art galleries, parks, etc., would seem to be the most for which we could hope, even if the plans of the socialists were capable of being reduced to practice.

It is perhaps true that adherents of the existing order are, in a measure, responsible for illusions in regard to the possibilities of wealth creation. We hear it claimed that a single individual has added to the wealth of the country, by his own exertions, one hundred millions of dollars. If it were possible for any human being to add so much to the wealth of the country, or to that of the world at large, the wildest hopes of the socialists with respect to the future might not be ill-founded. When we examine, however, into the processes by which vast wealth is acquired, we find that we cannot admit the claim that it is possible for any human being to add one hundred millions to the store of existing wealth. When such a fortune has been acquired, it means simply that some one has been enabled to appropriate this large amount of wealth. He has established claims which have that value upon present and future production. His methods may have been legitimate and proper, but that does not alter the fact that the fortune is an unearned one, so far as concerns the individual who enjoys it. The process of railway consolidation is responsible for vast fortunes; but this railway consolidation was something which lay in the nature of the enterprises themselves, and certain individuals were in a position to reap the advantages of the natural evolution of railways. The individuals who enjoy these fortunes could not have prevented the consolidation if they had desired to do so. No one need blame them nor find fault with them, as long as they employed proper methods. On the contrary, the blame must then rest upon society, because society made it possible for individuals to appropriate gains which should have gone to society as a whole.

Socialists are too optimistic with respect to the possibilities of change in the near future, or rather let us say in a future so near that we need to concern ourselves with it. We here encounter difficulties in the way of socialism which are largely psychological in nature. Socialism implies a new economic world, with new habits of thought, and new motives. Whereas men have been accustomed to view the everyday work of life from one standpoint, they must learn naturally and spontaneously to look upon it from a different standpoint, if socialism is to work well. This is not merely a question of improvement in human nature, but a question of those psychological habits which would enable men, under radically different social institutions, to appreciate adequately the line of conduct calculated to promote their own interests.

Men are deceived by the rapidity with which political changes have been effected, and with which changes in the modes of production have been brought about. Political forms do not touch in marked degree the everyday life of men. Constitutions come and go, but the ordinary farmer or artisan scarcely appreciates the difference. Yet even political changes often require more time than we are apt to think. Has it not taken a hundred years to establish a republican form of government in France upon a firm basis,—if we grant that even now it has become permanent in France?

Men have to learn to feel themselves republicans. Republican government has to become a part of their habitual consciousness in order to make it secure. The changes in the modes of production have been far more far-reaching, but they have largely been forced upon men by conditions beyond individual control, and even then have not changed, except slowly and gradually, the most fundamental institutions. They have been productive of no change which would correspond to the complete substitution of public industry for private industry.

Some one might hold that, slowly and gradually, as the result of evolution, partly spontaneous and partly socially controlled,[1] we should, at the expiration of a long period, say three hundred years, come to a socialistic state. Such a person, however, would be merely a speculative socialist, and not a practical one. Ordinarily speaking, we can call only those socialists who hold that socialism is near enough so that we ought to shape our action practically with reference to it. So far as the remote future is concerned, the wise man will be very slow to attempt any thing like prediction. We can see forces working in a certain direction at the present time, but we know that

[1] The exact technical term would be socio-teleological, that is change self-consciously guided by society with reference to desired ends.

society, in its development, does not move in a straight line. It seems at one time to move in one direction, and latter in an almost opposite direction; and so it is frequently said that social progress is more like a spiral than a straight line.

Socialism is too pessimistic with respect to the present, because it fails to appreciate adequately the secondary distribution of property brought about by what may be technically called the caritative principle in distribution. The caritative principle is the principle of fraternity, or benevolence. The distribution of property effected by this principle of benevolence is chiefly secondary distribution. After men have acquired property through the primary processes of production and distribution, they frequently distribute it according to quite different methods. A man who enjoys an income of one hundred thousand dollars a year may use a large portion of this income to ameliorate the inequalities and injustices which result from the primary economic processes. He may, for example, educate a poor but promising young person, and give him every opportunity to develop all his talents; and with another part of his surplus income he may relieve the necessities of the aged and infirm.

It is easily possible to exaggerate what may be effected by the caritative principle in society, and the general tendency is to rely too much upon it. At the same time, it is a grievous error to overlook it altogether, or to regard it, as the socialists usually do, as entirely insignificant.

We may similarly object to socialism, that socialists under-estimate the services rendered by the capitalist and the captain of industry in the present society. Our industrial leaders are those who give us our present industrial organization, and their services are necessarily arduous, requiring the exercise of unusual powers. We are not now speaking about the drones who are living upon the past toil of themselves or their ancestors, but about those who are actually employed in industrial leadership. Such men frequently sacrifice themselves, and what is best in life, in their efforts to guide industrial society. They put at stake their wealth, and they plan ceaselessly to utilize the forces of production to the best advantage. Frequently they achieve remarkable success, resulting in a multiplication and cheapening of commodities. Their efforts often result in a better utilization of natural forces, and open up new sources of wealth. We must, on the one hand, not underrate, as the socialists are so much inclined to do, the inherent difficulties in industrial management; and on the other, we make a mistake if we fail to remember the hesitation and timidity which is apt to attend collective action. Capitalists will frequently risk millions of dollars in an undertaking which is so uncertain that one would hesitate to recommend it to the representatives of the collectivity, whether these representatives be the legislators of the present state, or the administrators, so-called, of the socialistic state. The author is not disposed to dwell too much on this weakness in socialism. It is quite possible for society to secure better leaders than those now elected to serve it, and changed circumstances might develop a sufficiently daring public spirit.[1] But those who advocate socialism should do so fully conscious of the services which capitalists render in their personal efforts, and in the risks which they take, and also be well aware of the difficulties accompanying general social action.

[1] Public authority in New Zealand has been more adventurous than private persons in opening up the resources of the country by the extension of railway lines, and by other undertakings.

Socialists are too pessimistic with respect to the present society, because they underestimate the possibilities of developing the social side of private property. Private property has two sides, the individual and the social; but the social side is dominant. Private property is, according to its necessary idea, maintained for social purposes. It exists for the sake of society, and this suggests great possibilities of development, which are still compatible with the existing industrial order. We may keep private property in the instruments of production in the main, and yet introduce serious modifications in the institution itself, to enable it better to subserve social purposes. At the same time, we can extend along certain lines public property, even while allowing private property to remain dominant. An adherent of the existing social order may thus take the position that things have become private property which, according to their nature, should be public property, and that private property in its own sphere includes rights which are no necessary part of it. It was the possibility of developing the social side of private property which led John Stuart Mill, in one part of his "Political Economy," to declare against socialism; for he maintained that we must first know what improvements are compatible with private property, before we decide to abandon the institution itself. He declared frankly, that had he to make his choice between society as it exists to-day and communism, then all the difficulties of communism, great and small, would be but as dust in the balance. But he maintained that this dilemma was not forced upon us, because we had never yet given private property a fair trial.

CHAPTER IV.

THE DANGER OF THE DOMINATION OF A SINGLE INDUSTRIAL PRINCIPLE, AND OF THE INEVITABLE CONCENTRATION OF DISSATISFACTION UNDER SOCIALISM.

WE cannot expect the best results in civilization, unless within it many different principles operate. The claim has been made, indeed, that the domination of a single social principle, as for example the military principle, has caused the downfall of older civilizations, and it has been shown by a thoughtful observer of American life, whose utterances are always fruitful in suggestion, that mercantilism has been the bane of American life heretofore.[1] Mercantilism, as thus used, means the principle of private business. There can be no doubt whatever, that the domination of this principle has caused vast harm to the United States, and that it is even a source of grave danger to our institutions. The custom has been growing of looking at men and measures from the commercial standpoint. Too often everything, including character itself, has been regarded as something which can be estimated in dollars and cents, and the idea that anyone can be actuated by any other than mercantile considerations has been greeted by a large class with scepticism and even mockery. The principle of private business has invaded government, and

[1] Ex-President Andrew D. White, in the address entitled "The Message of the Ninteenth Century to the Twentieth."

office itself has been considered not as a trust but as an article of merchandise. Political contests have been reduced to a struggle for "boodle;" and the suggestion that something higher should dominate practical politics has been scornfully rejected as what is called "Sunday-school politics," while the saying that every man has his price finds believers on every hand.

Socialism, however, proposes to go to an opposite extreme, instead of seeking the golden mean. Socialists want to abolish the principle of private business, to substitute for it the collective industrial principle, and to make that dominate our life to a greater extent than it is now controlled by mercantilism. While the evils might well be expected to be different from those we now experience, it is to be feared that they would by no means be less. The principle of private business has its own place, it would seem, in civilization. There are many persons well fitted to render service to their country in private business because they love bold and daring ventures, and individual initiative is indispensable to the unfolding of their powers. These same men are frequently unfitted, by their very excellence in the field of private business, for public life, which operates quite differently, requiring a careful elaboration of plans and a submission of these plans to boards or councils, which hold men accountable for all that is done, as well as all that is left undone.

Public life, on the other hand, has its charms for many, and requires special preparation if it is to yield its largest results. Many men are better qualified for public life than for private life, as we see from the fact that some have rendered distinguished service to their country in office, who have not succeeded in private industry. Mercantilism in the United States has not made adequate room and provision for those who would gladly give themselves the best possible preparation for usefulness in public office, and has thus deprived the country of great benefits which might have been received. But socialism, while providing amply for the employment of those adapted to public life, would not make provision for the large and numerous class best fitted for private industry.

Far more serious than the objections to socialism which have already been mentioned is the concentration of dissatisfaction which would be inevitable under socialism. Socialism means the unification of production. But even if socialism worked well, there would still be a vast amount of dissatisfaction, more or less well-founded, with the commodities and services furnished to the masses of the community. At the present time the dissatisfaction with material conditions is immense, but it is diffused among a multitude of persons, and thus the burden is borne. We are dissatisfied with the milkman because he uses the pump too freely, but soon our dissatisfaction is diverted into another channel by annoyances in the kitchen. The unsatisfactory service of the cook, however, is presently placed in the shade by exorbitant express charges, and these again are forgotten in the indignation which is experienced when we receive a gas-bill too high by one hundred per cent. Thus it goes throughout life; and one reason why we bear with such extraordinary patience poor services and other abuses in the field of private industry, is because our dissatisfaction is diffused among so many, and no one person or group of persons has to bear the entire load of our indignation. How different it would be under socialism becomes apparent when we reflect upon the present popular attitude with respect to government. Not only do we not appreciate the excellences of government services as we would if they were rendered by private corporations, but we have only a fractional part of the patience with the weaknesses and mistakes of government which we have when we must endure the result of similar weaknesses and mistakes of private individuals or private corporations. A comparison of the services rendered by the post-office and the express companies is quite to the point. The post-office renders better service on the whole for far less money, and it takes much more trouble to accommodate the general public. The efforts and the success of the post-office in tracing addresses and in delivering letters and parcels to the one to whom they are sent are little short of marvellous. The author, when living in Baltimore, has frequently received mail packages sent by mistake to Boston, and when packages and letters have been sent to Baltimore it seemed to make no difference whatever how they were addressed, as they always reached him safely and quickly. Elsewhere he has had similar experience. Everyone who has had experience with the express companies knows that they make little effort to find one, and if they do not at once discover the address of the person to whom a package is sent, they frequently drop a postal card into the post-office with the same address as that given on the package, and the post-office has no difficulty in finding the person not discovered by the express company. The express companies have regular printed forms on postal cards for informing persons that it has not been possible to find them, and then these postal cards are addressed as the express parcels have been. It may not be out of place to give one illustration. Some time since the author had occasion to send a parcel from Madison to Washington, but the parcel was misdirected to a wrong number of the street. The express company sent a postal stating that there was no such number and the parcel could not be delivered. The person to whom the parcel had been sent was notified by a postal card misdirected just as the parcel had been, that the parcel was awaiting him at the express office, and the postal was delivered promptly. So far as speed is concerned, the author may say that for some five years he had occasion frequently to use both the post-office and the express companies, and he never knew an instance in which the post-office parcel did not reach its destination sooner than the express parcel, when both were sent to the same place at the same time.[1] Others who have tried experiments of this kind, or who will reflect upon their experiences, will be able to substantiate what is here said, and yet the facts are far from being generally appreciated. It is supposed that a safety and celerity greater than the facts warrant are furnished by the express company, and the responsibility for loss, which it is generally believed the express companies bear, is frequently rendered illusory by devices too numerous to be mentioned.

Many services rendered by private corporations are such in quality that they would not be tolerated were they public services. Let the reader, when making a journey on a railway, imagine it operated by the govern-

[1] The manuscript of the present work serves as a good illustration. At the request of the publishers it was sent by express to Boston, Mass. It was given to the express agent in Madison, Wis., March 15, and was delivered in Boston five days later; namely, March 20. Had it been sent by mail at the same time, it would have been delivered March 17.

ment, and ask himself what objections would be made to the service, provided its quality should not change at all. When the author made a trip from Baltimore, Md., to Dunkirk, N.Y., *via* Rochester and Buffalo, some time since, it occurred to him that it would not be an altogether bad idea, imitating Mr. Bellamy, to dream that our railways had passed under government ownership, and were controlled by the government; and then to describe the trip as it actually occurred, pointing out the annoyances and inconveniences suffered, and to show how such annoyances and inconveniences would be impossible with a system of free private industry, with its natural desire to please. The line of argument used by so-called orthodox political economists of the present time with regard to private enterprise could be followed. Attention would first be called to the fact that the upper berth in the sleeping-car was lowered, although it was unoccupied; then to the fact that the oil lamps smoked and gave a feeble light, although railways elsewhere had adopted electric lighting or gas, even in the second-class passenger coaches; and further, to the fact, that such a little convenience as a hood to cover the lamps, and to prevent their shining into the eyes of some of the occupants of the upper berths, had not been adopted. It could be shown conclusively that all these abuses could only exist under a system of government ownership. Attention would then be called to the fact that passengers were obliged to wait three-quarters of an hour in Rochester, and five or six hours in Buffalo, where a change was made from the New York Central to the Lake Shore Railway, the Lake Shore train leaving according to schedule time, five minutes before the New York Central train arrived. It could be proved beyond all doubt that under a private system such gross neglect of the convenience of the travelling public could not possibly take place. After a description of the trip, as a dream of experiences under government ownership, the dreamer would wake up and find that it had all actually taken place under private ownership. Then the query would be, "How could it happen?"

Had the classical economist visited Baltimore a few years ago, under the impression that the street-car lines were owned and operated by the city, it is easy to imagine what he would have said. The accommodations for the public, at certain times of the day, were entirely inadequate, and travel was slow, almost beyond comparison. Our economist, under the hypothesis mentioned, would have repeated for us the old phrase: "The government stroke is slow," and the people would have been invited to try active, alert private enterprise. This same person visiting the street in Baltimore called the York Road, would have found it as disgusting a city street, perhaps, as could be found in any city which could with reason boast of a considerable degree of wealth and culture. Looking at the muddy, ill-kept street, poorly paved, full of depressions filled with water, and turning his eyes to the street-car tracks, elevated several inches above the surface, — an unsightly inconvenience, — and observing the general absence of sidewalks, and the poor quality of the walks where they did exist, he would have said: "This is conclusive against municipal enterprise." Careful inquiry would have revealed the fact, however, that all which he beheld was, like the street-car lines, private enterprise; for the York Road was a toll-road, the unsightly and inconvenient car tracks were maintained by a private corporation, and the sidewalks, where they existed, were purely individual enterprises.

These illustrations might be continued indefinitely. It has been necessary to give such illustrations at some length, because they are of great importance in illustrating the fact that any careful observer will notice that we are more impatient with government enterprise than with private industry. We are dealing with psychological phenomena. If we had collective management of industry, the collectivity, or those administering it, would be held responsible for whatever did not suit us; and the psychological result of this concentration of dissatisfaction would be a revolutionary state of mind.

The outcome of socialism, then, it is to be apprehended, would be such an amount of dissatisfaction that one of two things would happen: either socialism would result in a series of revolutions, reducing countries like England and the United States to the condition of the South American republics, and rendering progress impossible; or the dissatisfaction would cause a complete overthrow of socialism, and a return to the discredited social order.

It may be said, in reply, that the higher standard which would be set for government enterprises argues a strength in socialism. This is only true providing that we have a more intelligent and philosophical population than any population which can anywhere be found at present. It is, however, an argument for the extension of government industry along certain well defined lines, as fast as public opinion can be educated in such manner as to appreciate and to support public enterprise.

Closely connected with the weakness of socialism, which has just been discussed, is the objection that the selfishness of designing and unscrupulous men interposes obstacles in the way of progress in the direction of socialism. Such men, even now, utilize unwarranted dissatisfaction with government for their own advantage. They exaggerate any weaknesses or shortcomings of government, and take pains to fan the flames of discontent, if thereby they can get into their possession the business which has heretofore been a public service. The gas-works of Philadelphia furnish an illustration. From time to time men have formed combinations for the purpose of gaining control of these gas-works, in order that they might reap the enormous returns which they would yield to private parties under private management. When the gas in Philadelphia has been poor, the organs of this ring have talked about it, and have told the people that no other city in the country had such poor gas, whereas one who had travelled extensively at all could see that this was an entirely false statement. Every defect in municipal management was exaggerated, every merit was minimized.[1] Not only was the press of the city, at least with few exceptions, operated in behalf of this scheme, but the municipal council was at one time very nearly captured. It required a great effort on the part of the best elements in the city to save to the city this valuable property. Since that time, it is hoped that the public in Philadelphia has been so enlightened, that a further attempt of private parties to secure the gas-works would be unsuccessful. But this illustration shows how slow and difficult progress must be in the direction of the socialization of industry.

[1] It is even claimed that those who wanted to purchase the gas-works used their influence in the council to defeat appropriations needed for the improvement and extension of the gas-plant, thus doing what they could to make the service poor.

CHAPTER V.

SOCIALISM A MENACE TO LIBERTY.

THE danger to liberty, which it is urged socialism would carry with it, is usually mentioned as the chief objection to the proposals of the socialists. The line of argument adopted by those who claim that socialism would be dangerous to liberty is a familiar one, and need not detain us long. We may say that at present there are two spheres of occupation, the public and the private, and that each offers an escape from the other. He who feels that he is restrained or oppressed in the public service may seek relief in private employment, or he may endeavor to establish a business of his own. On the other hand, those who are oppressed in private employment often find a refuge and a larger freedom in the public service. There would, under socialism, be only one considerable sphere of employment, and there is reason to fear that the inability to escape from the public sphere would compel the submission to onerous and tyrannical conditions, imposed by the administrative heads of the business in which one might be engaged. But even this is not all, because it is claimed that private employment, on account of the multiplicity of employers, affords greater protection against oppression than does public service; consequently, that the sphere of occupation offering the chief guaranties would be reduced to insignificant dimensions. We are admonished, furthermore, that parties must always exist. Differences of policy, or personal quarrels, giving rise to political dissensions, would exist under socialism as well as in a competitive society. Would not the dominant party punish opponents? Naturally, it would be impossible to dismiss one from the public service, but one could be oppressed otherwise. It is quite possible to worry and annoy an obnoxious employee, and to favor one whom it is desired to favor, in a thousand and one ways which can be felt, but not formulated and defined in such manner that they can be made the subject of legal proof and formal complaint.

The socialists, however, do not lack for a rejoinder to these current objections, although their reply may not be regarded as a sufficient answer. We must, first of all, notice that socialists have a somewhat different conception of liberty from that which usually obtains. They have their minds fixed upon economic liberty, rather than political liberty. They desire that every man shall have a voice in the control of industry, and not be subjected to rules framed by others. But this is not all. They perceive that the chief restrictions upon freedom of movement at the present time are economic in nature, and in this they are quite correct. Any one who will reflect upon the things which he desires to do, and upon those restrictions which keep him from acting in accordance with his desires, will soon discover that the restrictions upon his movements rarely proceed from government, but generally have their origin in lack of resources. A poor man wishes to spend the winter in Egypt because he has consumption. No statute stands in the way, and yet he is as unable to go as he would be if prohibited by ten thousand legislative enactments. But this is not all. Restrictions proceed from lack of economic resources, and compulsion is connected with our economic necessities. We see men in society coming and going as bidden by others. A few men, comparatively, say to thousands and tens of thousands "go," and they go; "come," and they come. We can witness this in any factory. We have simply to step out of our houses into the streets to find the many obeying the commands of the few. Why do they do so? Are they compelled to do so by statute law? Only in rare cases. Where, then, is the seat of authority? It is found in private property, which, according to its very definition, carries with it the right to exercise control over other men with respect to the objects of private property. Consequently, we hear the socialists using the expression, "wage-slave," — a slavery which they maintain arises out of the nature of the present society. We must have authority if we are to have industrial organization. But what shall be the seat of authority? This brings us at once face to face with one of the critical points in socialism. Will authority be more wisely exercised when it finds its seat in government than when it finds its seat in private property? Or is it perchance a mixed system which affords the greatest guaranties of full and free opportunity for the development of all our faculties?

The socialists have yet something else to urge. They tell us that the ideal freedom in industrial life, which many have sought, is that which belongs to an earlier stage of economic development; namely, the stage of small industries. When production is carried on on a large scale, men must act together. This cannot be otherwise. But socialism proposes that the workers owning the tools of industry shall themselves participate in the enactment of the regulations which they must obey. They also evidently regard the material sphere of existence as merely a means to an end; and they look to the time, free from toil, which they expect socialism will give them, and the resources which they will then enjoy, for the best opportunities of free development and free movement. The main thing with them seems to be liberty outside the economic sphere; and now they claim they do not enjoy this. The position of the socialists in this respect will, perhaps, be made clearer by two quotations taken from writers who very well describe the socialistic position, although, possibly, they are not themselves avowed socialists.

"What is liberty with long hours and low wages? Is it liberty? Can liberty exist with long hours and low wages? What rubbish it is to say that we enjoy liberty, when we work for a bare subsistence, and toil only to keep body and soul together; and at that, only succeed in doing so for a short time. Look at the condition of the masses. What is life or liberty to the majority of them? Life is a burden, and liberty a mere mockery. For the exploiters, it is different; they enjoy life and liberty through big profits." [1]

"The Declaration of Independence yesterday meant self-government; to-day it means self-employment, which is but another name for self-government. . . . Not as an exception, but universally, labor is doing what it does not want to do, and not getting what it wants or what it needs. Laborers want to work eight hours a day; they must work ten, fourteen, eighteen. Crying to their employers, to congress, to legislatures to be rescued, they go down under the murderous couplers and wheels of the railroads faster than if they were in active service in war, marching out of one battle into another. They want to send their children to school; they must send them to the factory. They want their wives to

[1] From the Paterson *Labor Standard*, quoted by the *Carpenter* for November, 1893.

keep house for them; but they, too, must throw some shuttle or guide some wheel. They must work when they are sick; they must stop work at another's will; they must work life out to keep life in. The people have to ask for work, and then do not get it. They have to take less than a fair share of the product; they have to risk life, limb, or health — their own, their wives', their children's — for others' selfishness or whim. They continue, for fear, to lead lives that force them to do to others the cheapening and wrongs of which they complain when done to them." [1]

There are, moreover, not wanting those who claim that the public service, even to-day, is that in which there is found the greater liberty. The workingmen of Belgium, we are told, prefer to work in the government railway shops rather than in those belonging to private railway corporations; and in Germany, we do not see that railway employees have suffered any additional restrictions upon their liberty since the railways passed under public ownership and management. The interferences of private corporations, both with their employees and with others who are obnoxious to them, — in short, their general tryanny and oppression, — are further cited. In all fairness, it should also not be forgotten that those universities which taught the world the value of freedom in learning and in imparting instruction are the German state universities, which are, perhaps, those to-day offering greater guaranties to professors against interferences with their liberty than do any other universities; and they are undoubtedly far ahead, in this respect, of the private foundations in the United States. The impersonal nature of the state itself seems to afford a certain protection. The state does not follow one up relentlessly

[1] From "The Safety of the Future lies in Organized Labor," an address by H. D. Lloyd, before the Thirteenth Annual Convention of the American Federation of Labor.

and persecute one continuously, as private persons sometimes do. The state has a poor memory for offences against itself. It is not entirely insignificant that the presidency of one of the most important State universities in the United States was recently offered to a scholar who had attacked State universities very strongly and made, perhaps, as able an argument as one could against their very right to exist.

There is still a further argument in favor of the position of the socialists, although the socialists themselves have frequently overlooked it. A recent advocate of socialism admits that, under socialism, there would be only one employer. But he was not by any means called upon to make this admission. We have, in the United States, some forty-four commonwealths and many local political units, in addition to the national government. While these local political units would, under socialism, have to act, in the main, according to some common principles, it is not by any means necessary that they should all have one administration. There is no reason why the various units, the nation, the State, and the city, or other local political unit, should not be relatively as free in their administrations as to-day. At the present time, one who is oppressed or wronged in the national civil service may frequently find employment in the service of a commonwealth or of a city. It will happen at times that one party will be in power in the nation, another in the State, and a third in the city; and this cannot fail to offer a measure of protection. German professors, in earlier times, who were oppressed in a university in one German state, frequently found protection and opportunities in a university in another state. And why a multiplicity of states should not still afford a measure of protection under socialism, it is hard to conceive. It is altogether probable that the federal form of government is, on this account, as well as on account of the facilities which it affords for experimentation, that one which is most favorable to socialism. There appears to be no reason why, under socialism, we in the United States should be obliged to abandon any one of our political subdivisions; and it would be a grievous mistake from the socialistic standpoint to denounce the American commonwealth. While some different distribution of powers would be necessitated, it is not clear that the State and the local political unit would not occupy relatively quite as important positions as they do to-day.

The position of the socialists, then, is a far stronger one than is ordinarily supposed, and yet it does not appear to the author of the present work entirely satisfactory. He cannot forget that the world's history is a warning against unchecked and unfettered power. It is true that there would be different political units, affording far better protection than is generally supposed; but even when this is acknowledged, it must not be forgotten what a tremendous power a political faction would have, once it gained control of even a large part of the country. There must be at least some government; and to talk about "administration of things," in the place of "government of persons," does not do away with this necessity. Even if the functions of government should be reduced to the lowest terms compatible with socialism, those in whose hands were centred political and economic control would have tremendous power, however they might be selected or appointed. Nor can we forget the possibilities of combinations between different parties for certain purposes. It would, under socialism, be quite possible for

SOCIALISM A MENACE TO LIBERTY. 213

two or three parties to act together, as sometimes they do now. The frequent assertion that the Democratic and Republican parties have acted together in New York City to control the civil service, seems to be well founded; and it is quite conceivable that two or three parties might act together to promote the interests favorable to a few leaders, and to keep down, if not persecute, obnoxious persons. We have a still better illustration than that afforded by a combination of political parties in a city like New York to control the civil service. The Christian Church and secular governments, in the early centuries of our era, existed as two separate powers. Their spheres seemed to be so entirely different that a person might have supposed that one would afford ample protection against the excesses and abuses of the other; but such was not the case, for now the one and now the other was in the ascendency, and the one in power used the other for purposes of cruel wrong and oppressive tyranny. We must finally bear in mind the most important fact, that restrictions need not necessarily proceed from the base, but that they can also proceed from the conscientious, and that those restrictions upon desirable liberty which find their foundation in conscience, even if it is a perverted conscience, are most dangerous. Those guilty of oppression in the Christian Church were often men who acted conscientiously. They did that which they believed to be right. Let us suppose that in any country the prohibitionists should gain the ascendency. The fact that they are such conscientious people would compel them to use every means in their power to prevent the expression of opinions which they might regard as most dangerous. They could hardly prevent the use of the printing-press, but they might here and there interfere with the right of free and open speech; and, in control of the central government, they might interfere with the circulation of literature to them obnoxious. The reader may say, "But I think this is an excellent argument in favor of socialism, because prohibition is altogether a desirable thing." But, altogether apart from the fact that very many will not agree with him, he should bear in mind that what would be possible with reference to prohibition, would be possible with reference to the free expression and circulation of views on other topics.

CHAPTER VI.

OBJECTIONS TO SOCIALISM AS A SCHEME OF PRODUCTION.

SOCIALISM means a unification of industry. It is based upon the hypothesis that it is possible to organize every branch of industry as a unit. It is, indeed, maintained by adherents of the purely evolutionary theory of socialism, that unification or monopoly in every branch of industry is an inevitable outcome of industrial development. If this is so, we would have only to choose between private and public monopoly, and this would mean that socialism was not merely possible, but inevitable, because there could be no hesitation in regard to our choice if we were obliged to choose between the irresponsible domination of private trusts, and socialism, for the latter signifies equally centralized production, but production under the control of representatives responsible to the people.

We are again brought face to face with one of the most difficult and critical question in the discussion of socialism. We see the work of combination and consolidation going on about us. What will be the outcome? We must not shut our eyes to the fact, and we must admit frankly, that universal private monopoly would only mean the final substitution of public for private control; in other words, again, socialism. When we examine the various industries carefully, we find that it is necessary to classify them, for it is by no means inevitable that the same law of development holds for all. The alleged tendency to monopoly is frankly admitted with reference to a whole class of businesses, which we call natural monopolies. We will return to the discussion of these later; but now attention is called to the fact that they include enterprises like railways, highways, telegraphs, harbors, street-car lines, electric-lighting plants, gas-works, water-works, etc. They also include the exploitation of natural resources so limited in extent that a combination of men can acquire the entire supply. Possibly anthracite coal and petroleum will illustrate this class; perhaps, also, natural gas should be included. As we have admitted the principle of monopoly with respect to these pursuits, we have also admitted that the socialistic plan of production is possible for them. We also observe that collective ownership of all property of the kind mentioned, and the collective management of businesses connected with this property, are possible.

But we witness the existence of trusts outside of this field, especially in manufacturing, and the claim is made that the tendency of manufactures is inevitably towards monopoly. We should always bear in mind, however, the contrast between production on a large scale and monopoly. Production on a very large scale may exist together with the sharpest competition. The question is not whether production will be carried on on a large scale, and whether such production is inevitable, but whether it is possible to organize each prominent branch of manufactures as a single whole. Can every main line of manufacturing industry be brought under unified control? is the same question put in a different form. Socialism affirms that this is possible, and some socialists, as we have seen, affirm not only

SOCIALISM AS A SCHEME OF PRODUCTION. 217

that it is possible, but that it is inevitable. They assert that every business is a natural monopoly, and that the expression itself, "natural monopoly," is as much out of place as would be the expression "natural adults," with reference to human beings. Every human being becomes in time an adult, and so, they say, every business becomes in time a monopoly. Proof is sought in a long list of trusts and combinations which have been more or less successful. When we look into this list of trusts in manufactures, however, we quickly ascertain that few of them have achieved anything like complete monopoly; and if we examine the list of unsuccessful attempts to form trusts, we shall discover that this is longer than the list of partially successful trusts. What we ascertain in reality is a demonstration of the advantages of production on a large scale, and a few attempts to secure a monopoly which have been partially successful, and a far larger number of cases of failure to establish monopoly in manufacturing industries. So far as any historical inductive proof is concerned, we must say that it is, as yet, lacking. The careful thinker will at least demand time for further observation. He will tell us to wait and see what tendencies are revealed by subsequent industrial development. If we turn to deductive proof, however, no convincing arguments have been advanced to support the hypothesis, either that unification of manufactures is, generally speaking, inevitable, or even possible. We must not overlook the immense difficulty of a management so watchful, so alert, so full of resources, so fruitful in initiative and enterprise, that it can permanently secure better results than a number of smaller and competing manufacturers. We may say, furthermore, that the tendencies to form monopolies in manufactures can sometimes be explained by a tariff policy favorable to combinations, or by special favors received at the hands of those conducting railways and other natural monopolies, whose services are indispensable.

Naturally, it would carry us too far, and require too much space, to discuss this question exhaustively. We can claim, however, safely, that the burden of proof rests upon the advocates of the theory of monopoly, and that they have not yet produced the proof, so far as manufactures are concerned. Even if certain great lines of manufacturing should be conducted in accordance with the principles of socialism, there would still remain a large number of manufacturers producing on a comparatively small scale, chiefly for local needs, whose productive operations could not well be unified.

Foreign commerce is of less importance, but yet of vast significance, and it is not easy to see how this could be carried on under socialism. A chief difficulty would be the adjustment of values, and the determination of the extent to which international exchanges should be effected. In the absence of a common organization, including the nations making the exchanges, it would seem necessary to fix values and regulate exchanges in accordance with existing methods; and yet, the basis of existing methods in the present order would be wanting. Then there would be the further danger that a nation still capitalistic would, through foreign commerce, impede, if not upset, the arrangements of the socialistic state.

But, even should the position of the socialists be proved with respect to manufactures and foreign commerce, it would further be necessary to prove it with respect to agriculture. Socialism means that socialistic production and distribution is to dominate our economic life, and should every other pursuit be conducted according to the principles of socialism, and agriculture be left out, we should have something very different from socialism, because a large proportion, and, in many countries, more than half the population, would not be included within the socialistic organization. It can safely be asserted that no plan which is even plausible has been adduced for the organization of agriculture according to the demands of socialism. The tendency to production, even on an increasingly large scale, is so uncertain that it does not seem to have received clear historical and statistical proof. An examination of the results of historical and statistical inquiry leaves us in doubt. The German socialists rely greatly upon more or less correct reports of farming on a large scale which they receive from the United States. They attribute the effectiveness of American agriculture in competition, to the use of improved machinery, and to the introduction of capitalistic methods in American farming. They dwell largely upon the stories told of the so-called bonanza farms. The careful observer in America, however, sees many different tendencies at work. While in parts of the country, especially where a few great staples dominate, agricultural production is in some instances conducted on a very large scale, elsewhere the large farms are divided and subdivided: and practical farmers frequently claim that he who would attain the best results must be careful not to attempt farming on too large a scale. Every one who has had experience of farming in the United States knows that many have found it decidedly to their advantage to sell a part of their land, and to restrict the scale of their operations. At one time, indeed, the feeling in favor of farming on a small scale found expression in the watch-word, "Ten acres enough!" Generally speaking, when, in any part of the country, we find farmers passing over from extensive to intensive agriculture, the tendency seems to be to break up the large farms into smaller farms. An illustration which has fallen under the observation of the author is that of grape culture in western New York. This grape culture took the place of general farming, and especially the production of milk, butter, and cheese, and resulted in a great increase in the number of holdings. Many parts of the country are so varied in the quality of the soil and in situation that production must be carried on on a small scale to secure the best results, because the farmer must know every acre of his land accurately. One field of five acres will be especially well adapted to barley; another field of twenty acres is an excellent meadow; possibly a tract of land including thirty acres is best adapted for pasturage; while a field of five acres at the opposite extremity of the farm, which alone of all the farm has a gravelly soil, is best adapted to small fruits. Facts like these are overlooked by those writers, especially foreign writers, who appear to imagine that the whole of the United States resembles certain portions of the Northwest, where land is found with soil evidently uniform in its situation and qualities, and where the production of one or two staple articles, by extensive agriculture, is advantageous.

Now, if all this is admitted, — and it certainly cannot be maintained that the opposite has been proved, — the socialistic position is untenable with respect to agriculture. Socialists themselves acknowledge that private ownership of the soil is required for the pursuit

SOCIALISM AS A SCHEME OF PRODUCTION. 221

of agriculture on a small scale.[1] The unification of agriculture as a pursuit requires not only careful knowledge of all the land which is under one management, but it implies a unified organization of labor. There must be some central administrative authority, which can have supervision over all the workers, assigning to each one his task, and able to see that he performs it faithfully. Production on a large scale, under a single management, whether this be public or private, implies something like a military organization. We readily see how this can be applied to railways and like pursuits, and to many branches of manufacturing, but it is not clear that it is applicable to agriculture. On the contrary, the difficulties in the way of such an organization of agricultural workers seem to be insurmountable. The successful farmer keeps a constant watch over all his force; they are under his eyes continually, and the geographical extent of agricultural operations limits the possibilities of unified management.

There is, furthermore, reason to fear that socialism does not supply adequate motives for economic activity to men so imperfectly developed as those with whom we must deal. Competition is one of the chief motives, although not the only motive, keeping in operation the wheels of industry at the present time. Competition, in the large sense, means the struggle of individual interests on the basis of the existing social order, which includes, as its fundamental features, private property,

---

[1] This view is expressed by Kautsky in his "Erfurter Programm," and is characteristic of a purely evolutionary socialism. A Fabian socialist raises the question whether we could not have public ownership of land, with private management. Possibly; yet this would give us something quite different from pure socialism.

freedom of person, free contract, and vested interests. Competition means the freedom of an individual acting upon the basis of the existing order, and otherwise within certain legally established limits, to care for his own interests in economic affairs, — to secure the highest price obtainable for the goods and services which he desires to dispose of, and, on the other hand, to procure goods and services at the lowest prices which he can induce any one to accept. Free competition means rivalry and conflict, because manifestly when several persons are seeking the same thing not all can get it. It signifies the attempt of different persons to render the same service or to sell the same kind of commodities to a given person. If one is accepted, the others must be rejected.

Competition has been called brutal, and it is so in many respects. It crushes human beings by the thousand, and continually throws out of the industrial field an immense amount of human rubbish, which is unable to maintain itself in the competitive world. We may take the case of manufacturers competing with one another. Each one tries to sell his products, and often to exclude others from the market. Other things being equal, the larger the sales the larger the gains of the manufacturer. But when several are trying to sell goods to the same person, the one who offers the goods at the lowest price will be the successful person under the system of free competition. The question, then, which confronts the manufacturer is this: How to produce goods at the lowest price, if possible at a lower price than others, and in vast quantities? As the cost of labor is a principal item in the entire cost of the product, the first thing which suggests itself is to reduce wages, then to extend the length of the working day, which

SOCIALISM AS A SCHEME OF PRODUCTION. 223

means procuring a greater amount of labor for the same pay, then to drive labor more remorselessly, and then to replace the labor of grown men by the labor of women and children, who ought not to work away from home at all. These instances might be multiplied indefinitely, and socialists have portrayed them vividly, and deserve praise for forcing them upon our attention.

Another class of evils connected with this rivalry in buying and selling comprises those which find expression in poor quality of workmanship, in the use of inferior materials, in the adulteration of products, all designed to deceive the ultimate purchaser, and make him think that he is getting something different from that which is really offered him. It is not possible, then, to entertain the exaggerated claims often put forward in behalf of competition. The modern competitive system has not existed long, but it has produced much evil. It is not by any means the exclusive force which has brought about the present civilization, and to claim that it has given the modern wage-earner a more desirable material existence than that enjoyed in earlier ages by kings and nobles is an absurdity which it is only possible for those to maintain who entirely fail to appreciate the essential elements in comfortable living on the material side.

It must still further be admitted that progress frequently lies in the suppression of competition, which is the contest for material gain, and the substitution therefor of emulation, which may be regarded as the struggle for approbation. Our law and medical schools, and educational institutions generally, have improved precisely in proportion as they have outgrown the competitive principle. Those medical schools which are still conducted as private institutions designed to secure the highest pecuniary returns to their managers, are inferior institutions, which bring disgrace upon the medical profession in the United States. We call their condition one of degradation. That university which is conducted on the principles of commercial competition is a poor affair indeed. It is in particular unfortunate that the salary of a professor should have any connection with the success of the institution which employs him, if "success" is used in a competitive sense. As the superior schools of the country, however, have improved, a strong spirit of emulation has been increasingly substituted for the competitive principle. Hospitals conducted according to mercantile principles are viewed with suspicion; and if it is known that a hospital in any part of the country is in no sense dependent upon its earnings, and that the physicians care little about these, that hospital unfailingly inspires confidence. The same holds in still higher degree with respect to asylums for the insane. Public management has sins enough to answer for; but it would be hard for public management at its worst to duplicate the abuses and atrocities connected with the care of the insane in England, when it was left to private competitive industry.[1] Literature is mean and contemptible when it falls under the domination of competition; and architecture has achieved its grandest triumphs when competition has been weak in society.

On the other hand, it should be acknowledged freely that competition has led to numberless inventions and improvements in the technical processes of production, and that it has played a very large part in the material progress of the present century. Oppression and degra-

[1] Cf. the description given in Hodder's "Life and Works of the Seventh Earl of Shaftesbury."

dation of labor are not the only means to bring about a reduction in the expenses of production. Improvements which enable the producer to accomplish a given result, with the expenditure of a smaller amount of labor and capital than was previously required, have been frequent, and these improvements signify social as well as individual gain. Now and again it happens that those who attain a brilliant success in industry, even under the pressure of sharp industrial competition, have treated their industrial subordinates well, and have succeeded because they deserved success, having contributed largely to material progress.

Competition likewise affords a stimulus which human nature needs, because competition rewards men for achievement. Competition keeps us alert and active, because we know that we shall be punished by the loss of our industrial position, whatever that may be, if we let others get ahead of us in the race for the material good things of life. Undoubtedly, this struggle to surpass others is not ethically the highest sort of motive; but every one must personally feel the need of some kind of discipline and control, a spur to the putting forth of his best powers. Competition also may be looked at not merely as an attempt to get ahead of somebody else, but as an endeavor to render the highest social service for the smallest return. This is the best aspect of competition, and it must not be overlooked. A and B both want to sell to C a commodity. If A offers his commodity at a lower price than B is willing to take, he has rendered a greater service to C for a given return.

Competition has been supplanted recently in large portions of the industrial field by combination and partial or complete monopoly; and many of the evils from which we suffer are not the result of competition, but of the absence of competition. The objections to trusts and private monopolies are based precisely on the fact of the absence of competition, which places the consumer in their power. If we think that one grocer is asking too high a price for flour or potatoes, we have the opportunity to see if we can do better elsewhere; and the efforts of several really competing persons to sell commodities of the same kind to the same person will keep any one from deriving more than a legitimate profit on capital, and a fair remuneration for labor. Moreover, the danger of loss of opportunity to make at least fair profits and fair wages tends to secure polite and attentive treatment. When, however, we do not like the price charged for gas, and believe that it is exorbitant, our only recourse, usually, is to stop the use of it. It is not merely that, but when we have every reason to believe that we are charged with more gas than we actually consume, we must submit to be robbed because the single gas company will otherwise shut off the supply, and any remedy for the sufferer is too difficult to be practically available. And how unceremonious, brusque, and even impudent are often the agents of private monopolies! If competition is brutal, we must remember that its absence is monopoly, and the experience of history pronounces private monopoly odious.

What has socialism to substitute for competition as a force in production? Upon what can it rely to keep in motion the wheels of industry, and to render progress continuous? It would seem, apart from the necessities of life, which ordinary and indifferent service would give, that socialism must rely, on the one hand, on the greater opportunity for usefulness which superiority would bring with it, and on the other upon honor or social esteem. There can be no doubt that social esteem has been the most powerful motive which has animated the conduct of men in all times. The Greeks, to gain the highest honor in their games, would undergo long and continuous toil, and put forth their best powers, developed to their utmost. Not only did the one who achieved this highest honor receive an immense triumph, but his entire family also shared his glory. Men do not struggle more ardently now for millions of money than the Greeks did for the honors in their games; and, so far as the material content of these honors was concerned, that consisted of a few leaves, — the wreath of wild olive! In every college and university in the land, and indeed in all lands, one may see the force of social esteem, and this social esteem is not won by success in money-making. The atmosphere of universities in this and other lands is a democratic one, and he occupies the first place in the esteem of his fellows who is successful in the pursuit of knowledge. Even in so aristocratic a country as Germany, the careful observer says of the students in the university, "They meet upon terms of fraternal equality. A common devotion to knowledge, without destroying the distinctions of birth and fortune, yet creates above them a higher university, where the most intelligent and laborious take the first place." [1]

Our industrial life, even at the present day, affords no exception to the rule that men are animated by the desire for social esteem. They toil for money because they believe that money brings social esteem with it, and in so far as money ceases to bring social esteem they cease to toil for it. When they have acquired it they part

[1] See Sidney Whitman's "Imperial Germany."

with it to acquire social esteem. We may see a man toiling and moiling for money, sacrificing his own higher faculties, oppressing his employees, and defrauding the public. We say of such a man that he loves money above everything else. But let us watch his career a little longer. He has acquired millions, and has led a mean, contemptible, and even miserly life; but suddenly he purchases a fine mansion and spends a hundred thousand dollars for a grand entertainment. Money flows like water, and it seems, perhaps, that this millionaire is now governed by other motives. Not at all; he sought money because he supposed that with it he could purchase social esteem. Either he had these personal expenditures in view from the start, or he finds that something more than mere possessions is necessary to give him the esteem which he desires. An English manufacturer acquires a great fortune, and then retires from the business which brought him his wealth to live upon a country estate. He voluntarily abandons the opportunity to gain great additional wealth, because he hopes that he will enjoy a higher social position as the owner of large landed estates. The German manufacturer who has, through long self-denial, won a million, parts with a considerable portion of his fortune to marry his daughter to a lieutenant with sixpence a day, because this lieutenant can give his daughter a higher social position, and he may bask in the reflected sunshine of her glory. A familiar illustration is afforded by the servant-girl problem in the United States. American girls prefer other occupations than domestic service, although they yield smaller pecuniary returns, because, rightly or wrongly, they suppose that these other occupations carry with them a higher degree of social esteem; and this supposition is so generally entertained that it produces a marked impression upon the labor market.

Social esteem, then, is an abundantly sufficient motive. We must concede that frankly to the socialists. But we have to ask the question, whether that conduct which is socially beneficial would as a rule meet with social approbation? Those who move among the educated and cultured will be readily inclined, perhaps, to give an affirmative answer. One acquainted only with university life at its best, and judging the whole world by its standards, would not be inclined to entertain serious doubts in regard to the line of conduct which would meet with general social approbation. We must remember, however, that there are many different classes in society, and that each class has its own standards.

The number of men who act in a manner which is disadvantageous to society, is extremely large; and perhaps one can scarcely be deemed guilty of pessimism, if one expresses the opinion that only a minority of men evince any genuine solicitude for the general welfare. Yet each one is animated by the desire for social esteem; but it is the esteem of those about him, the esteem of his own class which governs his conduct. The thief belongs to a class that honors the successful thief; and the daring and successful bank robber, who daily hazards his own life and freely takes the lives of others, is a hero of no small proportions to a very large class. A recent robber, who was shot while carrying out a daring plan of robbery, boasted that he did not want to be outdone by those notorious Missouri robbers, the James brothers. Men of this sort are so honored that accounts of their lives are written, and may be purchased at the bookstalls of many a railway station. The prize-fighter is animated by a desire for social esteem, and his conduct is that which meets with the approbation of a considerable proportion of the entire American community. The most prominent newspapers in the country publish, not columns, but pages, describing the preparations for a prize-fight, and the fight itself, following it with minute account of the subsequent movements of the principal actors in the contest. The achievements of scholars and statesmen, so far as the press of the day is concerned, fade into insignificance when brought into contrast with the encounters of a champion pugilist.

Tax-dodging and many other practices, which are directly anti-social in character, are indulged in freely by those who stand high in the community, and who are not ashamed of their conduct in this respect. They do not, on account of their anti-social practices, lose the esteem of their fellows.

When we call to mind all these facts, and many others which a little reflection will suggest to the reader, can we declare that under socialism we have reason to anticipate that regularly that line of conduct which is socially beneficial would meet with social approbation? If we are obliged to answer the question in the negative, the cause of socialism is at least greatly weakened.

We must examine this question of the motives which impel men to action from the psychological standpoint. We are not merely concerned with what would be in the true interests of men, but with their capacity to appreciate their social interests. We have learned during generations to look at economic questions from the individual standpoint. Will it be easy for us to look at questions concerning our material interests from the social standpoint? We do not now generally appreciate sufficiently the extent to which our material welfare depends upon society. Should we under socialism, when so much more depended upon society, appreciate sufficiently the importance of right social conduct? It is on the social side of man's nature that his development is slowest, and socialism implies a high development of man — and a very high development of man — precisely on this side. A socialist writer himself has spoken of " the individualist blacks of Africa," by which he virtually admits that socialism is inconceivable among a people occupying so low a stage of civilization. But we have thousands and millions of people in the more civilized countries occupying in social development a position not much higher. Most instructive are the lessons which Christianity teaches us. Christianity is a social religion, if it is anything. Its founder, a Jew, called himself not a son of Israel, but a Son of man, to identify himself with humanity. He opposed the religious opinions and religious practices of his day, on the ground that they placed some things above the duty which man owes to his fellows. Many a child thought, and still thinks, that it is more important to give to the church than to care for an aged father and mother. Christ told those who thought that a gift to the church could justify one in neglecting to provide for father and mother, that they made the word of God of no effect. When men came to John the Baptist, Christ's predecessor, inquiring the way of life, he enjoined upon them the observance of social duties; and when men asked Christ what they should do to be saved, he likewise bade them to care for their fellows, telling one inquirer to sell all that he had and give to the poor, and telling another to follow the example of the good Samaritan. The crowning act in Christ's mission manifested the social side of Christianity, — he died for others. Yet while all this is true, it has taken the Christian Church centuries even to approximate the position of Christ with respect to the social nature of religion. Religion has been treated, and is still treated, as an individual question. Individual salvation has been a common and powerful phrase, and it has not been accompanied by its complement, social salvation. We may still go into many a prayer-meeting, and listen to prayer after prayer and address after address, and hear not one word which would indicate that the speaker recognized the existence of any one else in all the universe outside himself and Almighty God. When at last the change begins, people commence to write books entitled "Social Christianity," and "The Philanthropy of God;" but the titles themselves have to many a strange and startling sound.

Many other illustrations of the slow development of man on the social side might be instanced. One is afforded by ethics, which a great writer has declared to be the queen of the social sciences.[1] Ethics has, however, been pursued chiefly as an individual science, and men are only beginning to understand that it is a social science. Must we not, in view of all these facts, reach the conclusion that there are limitations upon social action found in the backward state of development of man's social nature, and that men are still too individualistic in their nature to permit us to hope that for a long time to come they will be able to conform to the requirements of a socialistic state?

CHAPTER VII.

OBJECTIONS TO SOCIALISM AS A SCHEME OF DISTRIBUTION AND OF CONSUMPTION.

WE have already learned that socialists wish to secure justice in distribution, but that they have not been able to agree upon a standard of distributive justice, although they now generally seem disposed to regard equality in distribution as desirable.

Equality is unquestionably the simplest and easiest solution of the problem of distribution under socialism; and it is frequently argued that it meets all the requirements of distributive justice, because it is held that, essentially, one man has rights equal to those which any other enjoys.

Socialism compels us to agree upon a standard of distributive justice which would be generally acceptable, and which would enlist the services of the most gifted and talented members of the community. If we depart from the principle of equality, it is difficult in the extreme to establish any standard in accordance with fixed principles, calculated to settle controversy. Let us suppose we decide to distribute material goods in accordance with merit or service rendered. How shall we decide upon the value of different services when compared with one another? That distribution which may be called ideal is one that leads to the maximum satisfaction of wants, — that is, distribution in accordance with needs. This means equal distribution among equals, but unequal distribution among those who are unequal; and, as a matter of fact, inequalities among men, in capacity and requirements, are immense.

It is desirable to satisfy the most intense wants first, and then those less intense, and so on down the scale. If incomes were distributed equally, there are men whose wants are so limited that they would have more than enough for the satisfaction of every need, while others would be deprived of the means for the satisfaction of genuine and pressing wants. One person has no special intellectual gifts, and can soon acquire all the education which will be beneficial to him, so far, at any rate, as education given in schools is concerned. Another has great gifts which fit him to become a painter, a musician, or an original scholar. It is in the interest of society that the faculties of such a one should be fully developed, and that for their development, the tools, implements, and opportunities, for the exercise of the talent, should be afforded. Yet the education which is required under such circumstances is often expensive, including foreign travel and study, after the school education at home is completed. Such a person can use advantageously a far larger income than the average mechanic or artisan.

But how can we approximate this distribution under socialism? How can we reach agreement in regard to needs? Each one may appreciate his own needs sufficiently, but will he appreciate the needs of others, especially of those who are his natural superiors, and who require ten times as much as he does? Will the ordinary farmer or industrial toiler cheerfully agree to the proposition that some one else needs ten times as much as he does, in order to give equal satisfaction of wants? Unless such is the case, we shall have dissatisfaction and discontent, likely to impair the usefulness of socialism.

SOCIALISM AS A SCHEME OF DISTRIBUTION. 235

And this is not all. While it may be difficult for us to come to an agreement in regard to the differences in the value of services rendered by various members of the community, a little careful observation shows us that the difference, after all, is vast. In many a town, we can find a single individual upon whom the prosperity of the town seems largely to depend. While he lives, the chief enterprises of the place in which he is the leader thrive; but upon his death, mistake after mistake is made in management, and prosperity deserts the town. Everything else remains the same as before, but leadership is absent, and that makes the difference between prosperity and failure. We may take a single industrial establishment and we shall find that, while under one man it thrives, under another it languishes. The question of success is dependent, above everything else, upon right leadership. Now, those who have superior gifts and capacities are generally well aware of their superiority. They know that they render more valuable services than others; and if we take men as they are now, or as they are likely to be for a long time, we have every reason to believe that an assignment of merely equal income would not enlist in socialistic production the most capable members of the community, in such a manner that they would give their best energies to the socialistic state; but unless we could secure from the most talented members of the community willing service, socialism would inevitably prove a serious failure. The poor organization and management of the productive forces of society would lead to far greater waste than that which we experience at the present time. It is much to be feared that men cannot be socialized to that extent that they will generally accept the principle of equal reward for their services, even could it be shown that it were desirable. And it is impossible to show this, for quite the contrary is true.

It is urged that in the family we see what ethical requirements are, and we should blame a father who, at his table, gave the best food to the strong, and inferior food to the feeble, clothed the most capable children in fine clothing, and allowed those who were so unfortunate as to be cripples to go in rags. Such discrimination would shock our consciences. The children of the family may render unequally valuable services, but that cannot justify the inequality in reward; yet this is only a part of the problem of the distribution of income. When it comes to the question of the use of material resources for the development of faculties, we feel that the father is justified in spending far more on the son who has the larger faculties to be developed. If his means are limited, he may keep the feebler son at home, and send the other son away to an academy, college, and university, and finally to travel in foreign lands, spending ten times as much upon him as the other. This is ethically justifiable; but on the other hand, we admit that the son who receives this far larger share of the family income must see to it that he uses these developed faculties for the interest of the weaker brother as well as his own. Otherwise he fails in meeting the requirements of ethics.

Similarly, it is quite proper that various members of society should consume large quantities of economic goods, even when others lack some of the necessities of life, because it is demanded for the sake of the higher interests of society. But those who have been favored must remember that they have been favored, and use all their faculties and resources for the good of society as a whole. Here we draw a line between that consumption of goods which ministers to development in any form, and that consumption which serves simply to gratify vanity, or which merely promotes sensual enjoyment. Luxury stands condemned.

All this brings us to the observation that there is great danger that, under socialism, the true requirements of those engaged in the higher pursuits would be underestimated, and that the importance of those occupations which contribute most to the advancement of civilization would fail to secure adequate appreciation. The extent of natural inequalities, and the differences in the requirements of men, are not understood by the masses of mankind; and it is extremely difficult, if not impossible, to make them understand these inequalities and differences. This being the case, we have every reason to apprehend that, under socialism, there would be inadequate provision by the masses for those who carry forward the most important work; that is to say, those whose products are immaterial, ministering to the higher parts of our nature. If this is so, the result of socialism would be a non-progressive society, and in consequence all would finally suffer, because, under a satisfactory social organization, every class will sooner or later share, to a certain extent, in the advantages resulting from progress in science, art, letters, religion.

Abundant illustrations of this danger are afforded by existing society. It is generally proposed, in fact almost universally proposed, that socialism should be organized as democracy; but it has been the precise weakness of democracy, that it has failed to appreciate the best things, and has been unwilling to grant public money to promote undertakings which do not imply material gain. Democracy has been inclined to raise wages, and for this we must praise it; but it has also been inclined to give low salaries, and for this we must condemn it; because salaries, as distinguished from wages, represent the remuneration for talent and special qualifications. Those who receive the salaries are engaged in occupations which cannot be neglected, if civilization is to continue its progress. We have already cited the course of the London County Council as an illustration of the strength of socialism, but it illustrates also its weakness. Mr. Frederic Harrison, who has praised this council highly, is also obliged to say, "Unfortunately, the zeal of the majority to raise the wages of the laborer has been too often accompanied by an equal zeal to reduce the salaries of the higher professional skill. . . . But it marks the economic zeal of a new public-spirited body, that it listens to John Burns telling it, 'that the man does not live who is worth a salary of five hundred pounds a year.'"[1]

Elsewhere we are told that there are not a score of men in the service of the English municipalities who receive salaries of a thousand pounds a year; and that those representing the new democracy in England are insisting that two hundred and fifty pounds a year shall be the maximum salary for municipal officials, regardless of their qualifications or responsibilities.[2] The United

---

[1] A prominent member of the Fabian Society sends the author the following comment upon the above passage: "May I say that your reference to the London County Council salaries is misleading. It is true that Burns did let slip in the heat of debate the unhappy phrase you quote. But his *action* has been much more sensible. And no one would gather from your statement that the London County Council pays no fewer than forty-seven of its officials over £500 a year, twenty of them getting £1,000 or over — no bad sums according to the English scale."

[2] "Labor Politics in a New Place," by Edward Porritt in the *North American Review*, March, 1894.

SOCIALISM AS A SCHEME OF DISTRIBUTION. 239

States is also, in its entire history, proof and illustration of this tendency in democracy. Our various American governments have always paid wages which have given an upward tendency to the labor market, — wages, in fact, above rather than below those paid by private employers under similar circumstances; but our governments, national, State, and municipal, as a rule, pursue a mean and socially unfortunate policy with respect to salaries; so that a man with high qualifications rarely has an opportunity to serve his country in public office, whether elective or appointive, without making a sacrifice so great that many, who would otherwise confer benefit upon the community in public office, refuse to bear the burden.

At the present time we are not dependent exclusively upon what the democracy will do for us. After we have secured from government all that we can to promote art and letters, and the higher interests of society generally, we can appeal to those who in private industry have won large resources to supply the deficiencies in the public service. Private individuals are also able to take the initiative, by their contributions, to educate the public up to a point where they will do more than they are now doing, to promote the best interests of society. A concrete instance will best illustrate the point. A wealthy woman in Boston, feeling the importance of sewing, cooking, and other industrial features in the public school system, which the educational authorities were unwilling to support, defrayed the expenses out of her own pocket, until the public became educated up to an appreciation of the new features in the public schools, and became willing to support them by taxation.

Similarly, a State university is not now dependent exclusively upon what a legislature will see fit to appropriate for it; but it can appeal to private individuals to supplement public appropriations, to raise salaries if they are inadequate for the best work on the part of the professors, to provide more abundantly books and apparatus, and especially to endow those departments the importance of which is not generally sufficiently appreciated.

Classical philology might be cited as an instance. An American legislature rarely appreciates the importance of classical studies; but a right-minded man of wealth, knowing their value, might give them a firm foundation in a State university by adequate endowment. It would seem, then, that we shall achieve better results if we have the possibility of a co-operation of individual effort with the public effort, than if we rely exclusively upon what the public, as such, is willing to do; for it must be borne in mind that socialism, even if moderate and conservative, would ultimately reduce incomes to such an extent that no one person could do very much out of his own resources to carry forward the work of society.

What we need everywhere in modern society, and especially in the United States, is a natural aristocracy, by which we mean an aristocracy of merit. Provision may conceivably be made for a true aristocracy in the structure of government itself. Such is to some extent the case in countries like England and Germany, although in both countries the so-called aristocracy is largely based upon artificial distinctions, and has no real foundations in superiority of talent or services. Nevertheless, we do find that, on the whole, in these countries, and especially in Germany, those who have control of government show considerable appreciation of the higher goods of life. They know the value of art, of letters, of the highest education, and are well aware of the fact that public expenditure for the encouragement of the higher fruits of civilization yields large return to the tax-payer. The public authorities of Germany know the importance, for example, of investigation in universities, and understand that quality in work means more than quantity. They know also how essential it is to work of the best sort, that professors should enjoy freedom in instruction and research, and also permanent positions with assured income.

This merely offers one illustration of many which might be adduced. Now, the point which we must bear in mind is this: If the structure of government itself does not furnish scope for a true aristocracy, then a place outside the government must be found to give to true aristocracy opportunity to exercise the beneficent influence which belongs to it. And we must not by any means underrate that cultivation of the finer forms and graces of life which is one part of the functions of a true aristocracy. We must only insist that those who have great social opportunities should not use them selfishly, but generously for the public weal.

A wise truth for the guidance of society was offered by Christ in these words, "For unto whomsoever much is given, of him much will be required: and to whom men have committed much, of him they will ask the more."[1]

All this is naturally opposed to a false and most pernicious doctrine of equality. A full recognition of the actual and, indeed, marvellous inequalities among men, in their natural capacities as well as requirements, must tend to mitigate the hardships and injustice which are

[1] St. Luke xii. 48.

apt to accompany actual inequalities. If all men claim that they are naturally equal, then the logical conclusion is that they should be all treated equally. But as a well-known jurist has said: "Nothing can be more unequal than the equal treatment of unequals."[1] The result of a failure to recognize natural inequalities is seen in those judicial decisions which break down beneficent labor legislation on the ground that it interferes with free contract. It is assumed that the feeble, and perhaps half starved, working girl, occupies a position of substantial equality with her powerful millionaire employer, and that she is able to guard her own interests in labor contracts.

The law of population is regarded by many as a fatal objection to socialism. It is generally held that guaranteed incomes, and assured support for one's family as well as one's self, would lead to an excessive growth of population from which all would suffer. At the present time, the very conditions of life impose restrictions upon the growth of population. What, under socialism, would take the place of these conditions, which are often very hard? Experience shows that under favorable circumstances population is capable of doubling itself at least once in twenty-five years; and this would lead to an overpopulation of the world in a very short time, and in a few centuries would fill the world with so many people that there would not be standing-room for any more.

It is easy to say that the increase of population brings new hands and consequently additional productive power,

---

[1] "Man weiss eben heute, dass es keine grössere Ungleichheit gibt, als das Ungleiche gleich zu behandeln." Prof. Anton Menger in "Das bürgerliche Recht und die besitzlosen Volksklassen," Archiv für soziale Gesetzgebung und Statistik, Bd. II. § 20.

but it is only up to a certain point that additional labor power increases production proportionately.

Much may be said about this principle of population, and certain contrary tendencies, which, it is alleged, make the fear of over-population groundless. Certain authors assert that, as men develop intellectually, the rate of population tends to decrease. Others claim that it is the wretched and miserable who add most recklessly to the present population, and that material prosperity, in itself, checks the growth of population. Still others suggest artificial remedies. It is also urged that public opinion would be an adequate restraining force. It must be said that the principle of population has not yet been sufficiently discussed, and that we are still much in the dark in regard to the possibilities which it carries with it, under this or that social system.

Certainly there is more than room on the earth for all who now live upon it; and were society well organized, the population might increase rapidly for some time without disaster. On the other hand, we cannot, in our plans of social reconstruction, safely neglect the dangers and disadvantages of an excessively large population.[1]

[1] Cf. "Die Stellung der Sozialisten zur Malthus'schen Bevölkerungslehre," by Heinrich Soetbeer, and "The Evolution of Sex," by Patrick Geddes and J. Arthur Thomson, chap. xx.

CHAPTER VIII.

OTHER OBJECTIONS TO SOCIALISM

WE have now considered the most serious objections to socialism; and chief among these are the tendencies to revolutionary dissatisfaction which it would be likely to carry with it; the difficulties in the way of the organization of several important factors of production under socialism, notably agriculture; difficulties in the way of determining any standard of distributive justice that would be generally acceptable, and at the same time would enlist the whole-hearted services of the most gifted and talented members of the community; and finally, the danger that the requirements of those persons engaged in higher pursuits would be under-estimated, and the importance of those occupations which contribute most to the advancement of civilization should fail to secure adequate appreciation. These we should call the four main weaknesses of socialism. If socialism could overcome the difficulties which have already been mentioned, perhaps a multitude of others could also be satisfactorily surmounted. Socialists are not, we must confess, altogether wrong in their position that they cannot be expected to solve in advance all the difficult problems of a new society, and that it will be time to meet difficulties when they arise. It is true that if we are persuaded in regard to the main features of socialism, we can make the claim that we can only be required to meet the problems which immediately present themselves, and can adopt as a watchword, "The next thing!" We cannot, however, call ourselves socialists, and take measures to bring about socialism, unless we have reached conviction in regard to the desirability of socialism in its essential features and the possibility of overcoming the chief and fundamental difficulties which stand in the way of this new contemplated social order.

Attention, however, will be briefly called to a few other difficulties and objections of importance. One is the maintenance of an equilibrium between supply and demand. Quite generally socialists have held to the doctrine that value depends upon labor, and is measured by what is called "socially necessary labor-time." This means that the value of an article depends upon the time which it requires the average workman, using modern machinery and industrial methods, to produce it. What is the value of a yard of woollen cloth? We ascertain the number of yards, which, say, ten thousand men can produce, working with due diligence, and using the best appliances and methods. If we divide this number of yards by ten thousand, we shall find the share of the product which must be credited to each man. The value of these yards will be "one day"; for that is the socially necessary time required for their production. This does not hold as a law of value at the present time, for it fails to take account of monopolistic elements found everywhere in production; and it could not hold under socialism, for it would not maintain an equilibrium between supply and demand. The reasons why such a law of value would not be practicable under socialism, any more than at present, are numerous, and only one or two can be mentioned. The articles for consumption find their value in desire, and, we may say, to speak more accurately, unsatisfied desire.[1] We desire the satisfaction of some want as yet unsatisfied, and the intensity of the desire determines what we will give for the article which is able to satisfy the want. Now, the strength of the desire cannot be entirely dependent upon socially necessary labor-time. We may take two kinds of wine: both have required the same quantity of labor for their production; but one has grown on a rare and unusual site, and the other one on a good average piece of land for the production of wine grapes. The bottle of the one has a value, we will say, of five dollars, and the other of one dollar. These differences in value cannot be explained by private property in land, but are due to the natural limitation of land of the best kind for the production of wine. Should socialists in the socialistic state fix the same price upon one which they did upon the other, the supply of the first kind would be immediately exhausted by a general scramble for it, while the second kind would be neglected until the first had been exhausted. Probably many of those receiving the better kind would offer it for sale at a higher valuation, and thus receive that unearned increment which now goes to the land-owner. On account of varieties in soil, other agricultural products serve equally as illustration. The same would hold true with mineral products. Other reasons why a stable equilibrium between demand and supply could not be secured under the operation of the law of value, determined by a socially necessary labor-time, is the capricious and uncertain nature of human wants. It can never be possible to anticipate these with perfect accuracy. If values depended simply upon labor-time, we should have frequently redundant

[1] Cf. Ely's "Outlines of Economics," Part II., chap. i.

OTHER OBJECTIONS TO SOCIALISM. 247

supplies of articles of some kinds, of which it would perhaps be impossible ever to dispose, and frequent deficiencies of other kinds. It would be necessary for socialists to regulate value more in accordance with the laws which actually obtain in society, raising and lowering price in such manner as to keep an equilibrium between supply and demand. This would be likely to result in a surplus above costs of production, corresponding in some degree to present unearned income. This does not suggest an insuperable obstacle if socialism is otherwise practicable, because this surplus could be used for public purposes. It does, however, overthrow a great deal of current socialism, even if it does not attack the essence of socialism.

Ordinarily, there goes with the doctrine of value just described, the proposal to abolish money and substitute therefor labor checks, certifying the amount of labor time. What has been said seems to show that this substitute for money would scarcely be practicable, and it raises the question what could take the place of money? The most natural and easiest method would, perhaps, be to continue our present monetary system, and simply attempt to improve it. The abolition of money is no necessary part of a conservative socialism, and the demand for this abolition may have arisen from a fanatical desire for equality. Of course money would make possible certain inequalities in wealth; but with the great instruments of production socially owned and operated, these would be sufficiently limited to satisfy conservatively inclined socialists

Another difficulty under socialism would be the distribution of labor forces in such manner that production might be developed in harmonious proportions. How shall the men and women of society be allotted to their several spheres? The difficulty is immense. Mr. Bellamy has proposed to equalize various occupations in attractiveness, hoping, thereby, that naturally and spontaneously each one would find his proper place in industrial society. If a certain pursuit is especially disagreeable, and the number offering themselves for the pursuit is insufficient, he holds that the length of the labor day should be shortened, and thus the pursuit be rendered more attractive. Should, however, the number offering themselves for any one occupation be larger than required to satisfy the demand for the services or commodities produced by those engaged in that occupation, he holds that the working day should be lengthened, and thus the occupation rendered less attractive. When we contemplate the various occupations which are necessary, it would hardly seem that equality could in this manner be secured. Could we thus equalize the supply with demand in the learned professions? What extension of the work of university professors would bring down the supply to such an extent that it would equalize the demand for professorships? How could the supply of the highest positions in the socialistic state be equalized with demand, by changing the length of the working day? To ask the question is to answer it. Many occupations now require, and should under any system require, if they are to be carried on satisfactorily, the full strength and time of those who are engaged in them. Moreover, the interests of society demand that there should not be a free selection of occupations, so far as the most influential and desirable positions are concerned, but those should have these positions who are best fitted to fill them. It would seem that it would be necessary to proceed more in accordance with the principles which now govern selection of public servants, where the civil service has attained a condition of excellence; and this means inequalities in reward and selection of men, on the basis of natural talents and acquisitions. It would require a certain amount of compulsion of an economic nature, but very likely a less degree than that which exists in the economic world at present. Look at it as we will, we encounter difficulties.

Finally, we may call attention to certain objections which do not apply to socialism in itself, but which do apply to the ordinary socialistic mode of agitation. While socialistic agitation has had a beneficent influence in drawing the wage-earning classes together, and creating among them a feeling of fraternal solidarity, it has, on the other hand, tended to separate them from other classes in society, depriving them of the help which they could derive from these other classes, and giving them an unwarranted confidence in their capacity for political and industrial leadership. This has been the inevitable outcome of the Marxist socialism, which treats socialism as a class problem, telling the workers that their emancipation must come entirely from their own efforts, and employing the war-cry, " Workmen of all countries, unite!" Socialism will become stronger when it loses its class character and looks for leadership to men of superior intelligence and wide experience.

PART IV.

*THE GOLDEN MEAN, OR PRACTICABLE
SOCIAL REFORM.*

PART IV.

THE GOLDEN MEAN, OR PRACTICABLE SOCIAL REFORM.

CHAPTER I.

INTRODUCTORY.

WE have now traced briefly the nature of socialism. We have examined its strong features, and we have discovered its weaknesses. What is the conclusion thus far reached? It is somewhat like this: Socialism has undoubted strength, especially strength of a negative sort. It points out real defects in our present social order; its indictment of existing institutions is a powerful one. The wastes of the competitive system are so enormous as to be awful; its operations are as cruel as laws of nature. In its onward march it crushes and grinds to powder human existences by the million: its rubbish has magnitude of tremendous proportions, and this rubbish consists of human beings with minds, hearts, and souls, — men, good men often; women, and very frequently, most frequently indeed, innocent women — women with precious gifts which ought to be developed for themselves and others, and little children with all their possibilities.

General Booth, in his work, "Darkest England," speaks of a "submerged tenth;" and this expression, the "submerged tenth," has a rough kind of accuracy. Even if it were a submerged twentieth or fiftieth, it would be horrible. Let the careless and indifferent read this book, and read it chiefly for its faithful pictures, rather than for its remedies. Let Americans, so inclined to boastfulness, remember that just as horrible pictures can be drawn, nay, have been drawn by Mr. Jacob Riis in his work describing New York, "How the Other Half Lives." That, too, is a book to be read and pondered.

Socialism is strong, however, not merely in its indictment of existing institutions, but in its positive program. It has much that is very promising, very attractive. Nevertheless, we find that it carries with it difficulties and grave dangers. We have at present an imperfect social organism. It moves forward, creaking and groaning, and splashes the blood of its victims over us all. Our food, our clothing, our shelter, all our wealth, is covered with stains and clots of blood. Who does not remember Mrs. Browning's " Cry of the Children " ?

> " They look up with their pale and sunken faces;
>   And their look is dread to see,
> For they mind you of their angels in high places,
>   With eyes turned on Deity. —
> ' How long,' they say, ' how long, O cruel nation,
>   Will you stand, to move the world on a child's heart, —
> Stifle down with a mailed heel its palpitation,
>   And tread onward to your throne amid the mart?
> Our blood splashes upward, O gold-heaper,
>   And your purple shows your path;
> But the child's sob in the silence curses deeper
>   Than the strong man in his wrath!'"

But our social organism does move forward. If there is a submerged tenth, there are nine-tenths not submerged, and nine-tenths are more than one-tenth. Let us take care to cling to that which we have achieved. It will not do, in efforts to save the one-tenth, to run serious risk of submerging nine-tenths. Perhaps never, since the days of Christ, taking the world as a whole, did the provision for material wants so nearly approximate a sufficiency for all as at present.

It is a wise warning of John Stuart Mill to beware of reducing all to the level of those now most wretched. But we have accumulated other treasures as a result of the toil and struggle and suffering of countless generations. Progress has been made in the field of morals and religion, and it has cost much. Let us hold fast to this good. Education has made advances, and is more generally diffused than ever before.

We, in the United States, have not, to be sure, kept pace in educational progress with other nations, but we seem once more to be taking a forward movement in this respect. Our higher educational institutions have undoubtedly improved greatly within a generation, and this improvement must before long affect the lower grades of educational institutions.

The light of civilization is gradually becoming brighter, warmer, and its rays are slowly penetrating farther and farther into the darkness.

That wise old sage, Aristotle, said that virtue consisted in avoiding the too much and the too little. Is there not a golden mean between the too little; namely, rigid, obstructive, and revolutionary conservatism, — that conservatism which refuses to recognize defects in the existing social order, and resists obstinately all reform and progress, — and the too much; namely, reckless radicalism, which, in reaching out for improvement, risks the treasures accumulated during so many ages, treasures so painfully gathered together? Can we not, in our industrial life, keep what we have that is valuable, and escape some of the evils which socialism has so vividly depicted? And let us frankly, fully, without equivocation, acknowledge the great services which socialism has, in this as in other respects, rendered society. Can we not carefully, conservatively add to our social order some of the strong features of socialism, and yet keep this social order intact? It seems to the author that this is practicable, and the means for doing this he endeavors to describe as a program of practicable social reform, giving, of course, merely its outlines.

Those who take up social reform at the present day, must remember that they cannot accomplish much that is permanently valuable unless they start with a full knowledge of socialism and its advantages, and attempt to realize these advantages. High ideals for the masses have been established once for all. Some of the things which we must strive to accomplish in social reform may be enumerated as follows: First of all, we must seek a better utilization of productive forces. This implies, negatively, that we should reduce the waste of the competitive system to its lowest possible terms; positively, that we should endeavor to secure a steady production, employing all available capital and labor power; furthermore, the full utilization of inventions and discoveries, by a removal of the friction which often renders improvement so difficult. Positively, this implies, also, that production should be carried on under wholesome conditions.

In the second place, would we secure the advantages of socialism, we must so mend our distribution of wealth that we shall avoid present extremes, and bring about widely diffused comfort, making frugal comfort for all an aim. Distribution must be so shaped, if practicable, that all shall have assured incomes, but that no one who is personally qualified to render service shall enjoy an income without personal exertion. In the third place, there must be abundant public provision of opportunities for the development of our faculties, including educational facilities and the large use of natural resources for purposes of recreation.

One question which meets us at the threshold of our inquiries concerns the possibility of reform. Can we accomplish the ends which we have in view, and will the effort which we put forward to accomplish these ends meet with a return commensurate with the exertion involved? It is frequently urged that all our efforts amount to so little that it is not worth our while to try to improve society. When we look into the efforts to accomplish reform in the past, we cannot find reason for discouragement; quite the contrary. Well-directed effort has accomplished great things; and we are warranted in the belief that a thorough reformation of society, and the reduction of social evils to very low terms, if not a complete abolition, is practicable. The number of those who are submerged, large as it is, is comparatively small, giving, let us say, nine persons to help up one of the fallen; and improvement among the nine-tenths is not difficult.

Some fifty or more years ago the Earl of Shaftesbury began to devote himself not only to the cause of the most wretched, namely, the dependent and delinquent classes, but also, and in particular, to an improvement in the conditions of the wage-earning classes. He continued his work during the remainder of his long life, which terminated some ten years since. He was able, with the help of others whom he rallied about him, to effect improvements which touched beneficially millions of lives. It can scarcely be too much to say that the mass of the English people has been elevated by improvements which he secured chiefly, but not exclusively, by legislation.

The well known English political leader, the Right. Hon. Joseph Chamberlain, M.P., describes the improvement of the last half century in these words: "Pauperism has greatly diminished, and the poor rate is certainly less than half of what it was before the new Poor Law. Crime has diminished in quantity, and has, on the whole, been mitigated in its character. Education has been brought within the reach of every working-man's child and within the means of every parent. Protection has been afforded against excessive toil and overwork; and the observance of proper sanitary conditions for labor has been universally enforced. The laws against combinations have been repealed, trades unions have been legalized, and the workmen are able to meet the employers on more equal terms in the settlement of the rate of wages. The care of the public health has been recognized as a public duty and enforced both upon individuals and the local authorities; the trammels have been removed from industry; the taxes on food and on all the great necessaries of life have been repealed; facilities of travel and intercommunication have been largely extended and developed; opportunities of self improvement and recreation have been afforded to all at the cost of the community." After speaking about the increase of wages, estimated at fifty per cent and more, the reduction in the hours of labor, averaging twenty per cent, the reduction in the price of bread, light, locomotion, the diminution of the death rate, and other improvements, he adds: "An impartial examination of the facts and figures here set forth must lead to the conclusion that there has been a very great improvement in the condition of the people during the period under review, and this improvement has been largely due to the intervention of the state and to what is called socialistic legislation. The acts for the regulation of mines and the inspection of factories and workshops, the Truck Act (preventing the payment of wages in kind), the acts regulating merchant shipping, the Artisans' Dwellings Act, the Allotments Act (enabling local authorities to take land and to provide allotments for laborers), the Education Act, the Poor Law, and the Irish Land Acts, are all of them measures which more or less limit and control individual action." [1]

Karl Marx formulated his social philosophy at the beginning of this period, and he described the condition of things which a passive policy of the state allowed to come into existence. Marx is a social philosopher who describes society when under the *régime* of *laissez faire*.[2] He took the premises of classical political economy and showed the breakdown which must result from the operation of so-called natural laws. That which he and his friend Engels predicted has not taken place, because social efforts have been put forth to guide social evolution. Had things been allowed to take their own course, the condition of the wage-earners would have grown more and more wretched, the concentration of wealth and the centralization of production would have been carried even further,

---

[1] See article "Favorable Aspects of State Socialism," *North American Review*, May, 1891.

[2] He has been called "the philosophic historian of the capitalistic era."

and it is not improbable that the collapse in England would have taken place before this.

A philanthropist in the United States, Mr. Charles Loring Brace, devoted himself to the poor children of New York City, and used chiefly private efforts. It is said that during his life he was able to touch and improve three hundred thousand lives. These examples show how large the returns are which well directed effort secures, and what could be done if men would really concern themselves with the improvement of society. The social resources are more than ample. They are superabundant. It is only necessary that they should be utilized. If one out of ten persons who call themselves Christians should actually guide his conduct by the precepts of Christianity, all reforms of a social nature which can now be suggested would be speedily accomplished.

Perhaps a word in regard to the attitude with which we should approach the question of practicable social reform may not be amiss. We are discussing measures and not men. Those who have made wealth out of practices and institutions condemned, are not by any means to be regarded as necessarily worse than others. We must all live under the social system which exists. A city may make a mistake in preferring private gas-works to municipal gas-works; but so long as private gas-works exist, it is hard to see why any person should be blamed for utilizing private ownership of gas-works for his own advantage. Quite the contrary. The people need gas, and if they do not choose to help themselves, the one who is willing to render them the service is doing something which is praiseworthy. This presupposes, of course, that he uses no improper methods in securing franchises or contracts, and does not attempt by improper means to maintain an excessively high price for gas. It also follows, as a matter of course, that one should not allow his private individual interests to stand in the way of measures calculated to effect improvement. Personal interests should be subordinated. Fortunately, many leaders in the industrial world take this large view. The late Josiah Quincy, author of that charming work, " Figures of the Past," was a railway president, but he himself tells us that he thinks it is not safe to entrust so great a power to any private individual as that which a railway president enjoys. A living railway president has recommended the nationalization of railways; and another well known as a skilful railway manager has criticised with severity American railway methods.

We must furthermore remember that we are not dealing with questions concerning wage-earners alone. We have already stated that the question of socialism can be viewed from the standpoint of different social classes, and that perhaps other social classes have almost equal reason to hope for the coming of socialism, if it brings with it what socialists promise us.

CHAPTER II.

SOCIALIZATION OF MONOPOLY.

SOCIALISM is a theory of monopoly, and we can say, roughly speaking, that it holds good for monopoly. The admission is made that the plan of socialism for the ownership and operation of monopoly by society in its organic capacity is the best which has yet been devised. This plan is socialization, or to use a more current expression, government ownership. It must not be understood by this statement that the ownership and the management by government of businesses which fall under the head of monopoly are devoid of difficulties. On the contrary, we must anticipate serious obstacles to be overcome; but the difficulties and disadvantages of private ownership and management are far greater. The problems of modern civilization are complex at best, and their solution cannot, in the nature of things, be easy.

Monopolies may be divided into two main classes,—natural and artificial; and natural monopolies again may be divided into two sub-classes, namely, First, those businesses which are monopolies by virtue of the qualities inherent in the business itself; and second, those businesses which are monopolies by reason of the fact that the supply of the raw material upon which they are based is so limited in area, that the entire supply can be acquired by a single combination of men.

We will first consider natural monopolies of the first sub-class. These are the natural monopolies ordinarily discussed, and they include the means of communication and transportation, as well as the lighting service by gas or electricity of cities. Railways, water-ways, irrigation works, telegraphs, telephones, are especially important. But street-car lines, whether they are surface lines, subways, or elevated railways, and the means of lighting cities, are scarcely less so. These are all primary businesses in modern society; businesses of every other kind are dependent upon them.

The proof that these pursuits are natural monopolies is twofold; namely, deductive and inductive, or historical. The deductive proof takes account of characteristics of businesses of the kind mentioned, and discovers that businesses with these characteristics must necessarily become monopolies. Their main characteristics are three: They occupy peculiarly desirable spots or lines of land; second, the service or commodity which they supply is furnished in connection with the plant itself; and, in the third place, it is possible to increase the supply of the service or commodity indefinitely, without proportionate increase in cost. Any business which has these qualities tends to become a monopoly by virtue of its inherent qualities, and it must become such in time. The fact that peculiarly desirable spots or lines of land are occupied, gives a business an advantage. If the spots or lines of land are exclusive, of course that establishes a monopoly in itself, but that does not often happen. Street-car lines, however, very often occupy what we may call exclusive lines of land, as in ordinary streets we cannot well have more than two tracks; and so far as the street in question is concerned, the only competition must come from sub-ways or elevated railways. Steam railways sometimes occupy what are practically exclusive lines of land when they go through mountain passes, or when they run between rivers and high mountains very near the rivers. Any competing lines must necessarily be at a great disadvantage, as the cost of excavations would be enormous. The second characteristic is of great importance, because it makes it impossible to bring the commodities or service from a distance for the purpose of competition.

The flour of one city may compete with the flour of another city, but the street-car service of a city must be used in connection with the street-car plant. If telegraph services could be used apart from the plant, we could, in America, order these services from Germany, and get them for less than half of what we now pay for them, but unfortunately they must be used in connection with the plant which furnishes the services.

The third characteristic, however, is one of chief importance, for it includes, by implication, the other two. As the business increases in extent, the cost of the service or commodity decreases, consequently there is always an inducement held out to carry on the business as one undivided whole. If two competing companies are furnishing services or commodities of the kind mentioned, they will gain, and gain greatly, by combination. But gain is the purpose for which business is carried on, and this increased gain is like a powerful magnet; sooner or later, it pulls the competing companies together.

Inductive or historical proof calls attention to actual experience. It is found that sooner or later attempted competition always gives way to combination and consolidation. The gas business furnishes an excellent illustration, because the experience with respect to this is so super-abundant, and because, furthermore, as the geographical area within which the business is conducted is small, the movement towards monopoly has always been comparatively rapid. Competition in the gas business has been attempted in countries with all kinds of political government, and under every circumstance which can be imagined. It has been tried repeatedly with the most solemn promises on the part of those starting rival companies, that competition would be genuine and permanent. But the nature of the business as monopoly has been strong enough to overcome every obstacle, and guaranties have not been worth the paper on which they have been printed. It is probably not too much to say that competition has been tried a thousand times in different countries, and no one can yet point to one single instance of permanently successful competition. It would seem that a thousand experiments should satisfy any one. The telegraph business also furnishes good illustration. Competition in telegraph service was tried many times in England, but always resulted in monopoly; and it has been tried perhaps a hundred times in the United States, but the tendency to monopoly has been too strong. The most serious attempt at competition in recent years was that between the Baltimore and Ohio and the Western Union Telegraph Companies; but when that had apparently the greatest promise of permanence, and when the officers of both companies were assuring the public that nothing was further from their minds than combination, the author of the present work ventured to predict publicly, and to put his prediction into print, that combination was only a matter of time.[1] And so it proved.

The most serious rival of the Western Union Telegraph

[1] *Chatauqua Herald*, August 2 and 3, 1887.

Company, at the present time, is the Postal Telegraph Company; but its absorption, likewise, can only be a matter of time.

Competition of various sorts has been tried with respect to railways. Competition between state owned and operated railways and private railways was expected to produce favorable results in Germany, and has been looked upon with favor elsewhere. The result, however, of attempted competition between the state and private corporations is that one or the other must retire from the field. The greatest confidence has, however, been placed upon the competition of one private corporation with another, but this has likewise proved an illusion. France and England furnish good illustrations. The many companies which once existed in these countries have combined with one another, until now, in each country, a very few companies, acting together, control the railway transportation. America will be held to offer the greatest difficulties in the way of the acceptance of a theory of monopoly in the railway business; but the difficulties only spring from the fact that it is a vast country, in which the railway development is yet far from complete. Combination and consolidation are going forward every day, and it is simply a question of time when monopoly will be secured in the United States, as well as elsewhere. Even now it would require a small book simply to print the names of railway companies which have been absorbed by other companies, and have ceased to exist. Moreover, the points about which agreement is reached in regard to railways are more numerous than is often supposed, and frequently include an understanding that a certain rate of speed shall not be exceeded; as, for example, between Chicago and Minneapolis, and also between New York and Boston. Those who have doubts will only have to wait to see them removed. It is suggestive, by the way, that contests between gas companies, railways, and the like, are called, in popular language, "wars;" as "gas wars," "railway-rate wars." This word indicates a popular feeling that these contests are something different from ordinary competition. A war is not something permanent, but something destructive, which looks forward to termination based on some agreement.[1]

England and America have been inclined to favor private ownership of businesses of the kind mentioned, but in England they are being rapidly socialized; not only are cities acquiring local monopolies, but the telegraph, as already mentioned, has been made a part of the post-office, and there is a strong movement in favor of a nationalization of railways. It is significant that the secretary of the Association of Chambers of Commerce in Great Britain has written a work in favor of government ownership and management of English railways.[2]

When it is said that government ownership is favored, it does not mean government ownership to-day or to-morrow, but government ownership as soon as it can be brought about by constitutional and legal measures. When one considers the immense resources of those who now have the management of monopolistic undertakings, one need not be under the least apprehension that we shall go too fast. If all those who have suffi-

[1] This subject is treated at greater length in the author's works, "Problems of To-day" and "Outlines of Economics," College edition.

[2] "National Railways, an Argument for State Purchase," by James Hole.

cient insight to perceive the advantages of socialization of monopoly put forth their utmost efforts, it will yet take a long time to enlighten the people and to produce the desired action. These undertakings have in their service able lawyers; they control a considerable portion of the press, and with their vast resources are able to impose obstacles towards movement in the direction indicated, which at times appear all but insuperable. It is encouraging to notice, however, that whenever it has been possible to present fairly and fully to the people the issue between private monopoly and socialized monopoly, the decision has generally been in favor of the socialized monopoly, and that by a great majority. Many cities, for example, have given an overwhelming majority in favor of an establishment of a municipal electric light plant, although interested parties have been able to secure almost complete control of the press, and have used every device at their command to secure an adverse vote.

While the results anticipated from the policy advocated are much the same as those advantages of socialism which we have enumerated as some of its strong features, it will be well, from our present standpoint, to call attention briefly to the chief benefits which we may reasonably expect socialization of monopoly to produce. We will first consider those which fall under production.

The socialization of monopoly will lead to better utilization of productive forces. A negative result will be that the wastes of competition will be avoided. Of course, there is a great deal of past waste which cannot now be remedied, and that must be endured as we endure the waste of war, or any other misfortune; but it is still possible to avoid future wastes, and this means an immense saving. If we capitalize the annual saving, we shall ascertain what can be saved, so far as the operation of existing undertakings is concerned; and to find the total gain, we must add the waste which would result from new undertakings, necessitated by the existence of private ownership, which would otherwise be useless. A railway manager, who estimates that it would involve a saving of two hundred millions of dollars a year to operate the railways of the United States as a unit, has already been quoted; and this sum, divided by two in order to make our estimate a safe one, and capitalized at four per cent, gives us, as we have already seen, a gain of two thousand five hundred millions of dollars, which would equal a considerable fractional part of all the wealth in the United States. But this represents a saving in the operation of railways alone; and to find the total social gain, we should have to add the saving which would result from the socialization of all the other monopolies mentioned.[1]

Positive results could also be anticipated, and a few of these may be mentioned. Irregularities in our industrial life have been partially due to the private construction and operation of railways and other plants which fall under the designation of natural monopolies. A period of feverish activity in the field of monopoly is followed by one of prostration, and almost complete stagnation. Government enterprises need not be conducted with such irregularity. Wherever government is stable, a well organized and steadier production is easier and far more natural. It is appropriate to government to weigh plans well, to look ahead, and to carry them out regularly through a long series of years.

[1] Cf. Part II., chap. ii. of the present work.

There is no reason whatever why government plans should not be so executed, for this requires only moderate intelligence and virtue on the part of the masses of the people. But this is not all. Government could so manage industry committed to it, that it would remove some of the disadvantages which result from private undertakings.

It has often been observed that those periods which are unfavorable for private industry, are peculiarly favorable for public undertakings. Whenever there is stagnation in private business, materials are cheap and labor is abundant; while, with unimpaired credit, government can borrow capital at unusually low rates of interest.

Crises could thus be mitigated, idleness diminished, and the productive forces of society more steadily and regularly employed.[1] But even this is not all. Crises have, in the United States at any rate, been aggravated, if not caused, by bad private management of the industries named. Management of the public finances so corrupt as that which has characterized the private railways of the United States, would have produced a revolution long ago. It is partially due to this corruption, and partly, also, to inherent difficulties of private railway management, that at the present time railways, representing some twenty per cent of the railway mileage of the United States, are now in the hands of receivers.[2]

---

[1] The winter time is a trying season for many people. With a large industrial field, government could, to some extent, so plan its operations as to maintain a better equilibrium between economic activity in summer and economic activity in winter.

[2] In the last ten years 309 railway companies, with 74,312 miles of line, or over 42 per cent of the present railway mileage, and with a capitalization of $3,875,000,000, have gone into the hands of receivers. Of this number, 74 roads, with a length of 29,340 miles and a capitali-

Were our railway finances in as good a condition as the finances of the United States government, although in the latter we could now desire an improvement, our industrial situation would be much brighter than it is.

Another advantage which we have mentioned as a strong feature of socialism, is the utilization of existing inventions and industrial improvements. Private monopoly is opposed to improvements, because they involve additional outlay; and, as has already been mentioned, they frequently purchase patents to keep them out of use. This has notoriously been the case with the telegraph; and an economic writer, by no means an ardent advocate of the extension of the functions of government, has recently declared that the telegraph service of the United States is the poorest in the world.[1]

The claim may thus be put forward for the socialization of monopoly, that it would produce a more stable equilibrium in industrial forces than that which we now experience.

The distribution of wealth would also be improved by socialization of monopoly. A general aim, which, as a matter of fact, is observed in industrial reform, and which is altogether praiseworthy, is reduction to its lowest practicable terms of unearned income; and by unearned income we mean income which yields something over and above normal returns to labor, capital, and enterprise. Unearned income must be understood to refer to the individual, for, of course, all unearned income is

zation of $1,781,046,000, became insolvent in 1893; and on December 31, 1893, there were in the hands of receivers 128 roads, with a mileage of 40,279 miles, and with a capitalization of $2,217,656,000, being 23 per cent of the total mileage, and 21 per cent of the total capitalization.

[1] Professor Simon Newcomb, in the Harvard *Quarterly Journal of Economics* for July, 1893.

earned by some one, and the individually "unearned" income is socially earned; that is to say, earned by the exertions of society.

An illustration of unearned income is afforded by real estate, when, without any exertion on the part of the owner, it increases in value. If a city lot is purchased for one thousand dollars and sold for two thousand, the owner having done nothing to improve it, the thousand dollars is unearned income. If gas-works in a city yield an excess over full returns to labor, management, and capital, this surplus is unearned income. The income may be perfectly legitimate so far as the individual is concerned who receives it, because social conditions have been allowed to exist which permit the private receipt of income of this kind; but it is none the less unearned. Now, the very purpose of monopoly is to secure unearned income. Monopoly means that price for services and commodities which will yield the largest net returns. Production stops at that point where a price can be secured which will give the greatest gain, and this price is higher than the competitive price, which leaves no surplus in the sense indicated.

The socialization of monopoly would remove from individual ownership the gains of monopoly. This would tend to avoid those dangerous extremes in private fortunes which have been considered, by political philosophers from the time of Aristotle, to be dangerous, and especially so in a republic. As these gains, heretofore received by private individuals, would, in one way and another, be diffused among the people at large, it would result in a wider enjoyment of moderate comfort.

Estimates concerning the concentration of wealth in the United States and other countries are extremely uncertain; but all estimates agree in one respect, and that

SOCIALIZATION OF MONOPOLY. 273

is in attributing a greater concentration of wealth to the United States than to any other modern country. One estimate is that in England half the wealth is owned by one-thirtieth of the population, and in the United States by one-seventieth; and it must be remembered that England has, until recently, been considered the chief land of concentrated wealth. Another writer estimates that twenty-five thousand people own half the wealth of the United States. The most careful estimate is that made by Mr. George K. Holmes of the United States Census Office, and it is as follows:[1] —

"Twenty per cent of the wealth of the United States is owned by three one-hundredths of one per cent of the population; seventy-one per cent is owned by nine per cent of the families, and twenty-nine per cent of the wealth is all that falls to ninety-one per cent of the population."[2]

Perhaps nothing, however, brings out with greater force the concentration of wealth in the United States during the past generation, than a comparison of a list of rich men of New York published by the New York *Sun*, 1855, with the well-known *Tribune* list of millionaires, published in 1892. The lists may not be, and doubtless are not, entirely accurate, but they are sufficiently so for present purposes.

The New York *Sun* list includes every one who is reputed to be worth one hundred thousand dollars; and very many in the list have no more than that sum, while the millionaires are few and far between. In 1892 there has been such a progress in the concentration of wealth, not only in New York City, but through-

---

[1] See *Political Science Quarterly* for December, 1893.

[2] The diagrams shown on the next page may prove helpful in appreciating the significance of these statistics.

The left hand rectangle represents the total number of families in the United States, divided into classes according to the amount of wealth they possess, as shown in the right hand rectangle.

Families $3/100\%$ Wealth

9 per cent

20% owned by 3/100% of the families

71 per cent owned by nine per cent of the families

91 per cent

29 per cent owned by 91 per cent of the families

out the country, that no one is considered to be worthy of a position among the rich men of the United States who has not at least one million dollars, and many in New York are reputed to have fortunes varying from twenty to two hundred millions of dollars. The total number of millionaires in New York City, according to the New York *Sun* list of 1855, was only twenty-eight, while the total number, according to the *Tribune* list, had, in 1892, reached the enormous aggregate of eleven hundred and three. Now, the *Tribune* list is further instructive, because it gives the businesses in which the millionaires of the country have made their fortunes, the aim being to show that the great wealth of the country cannot be traced to the protective tariff. And it may be remarked, incidentally, that the list is conclusive in this respect. What the list does show is the connection of the concentrated wealth of the country with monopoly of some sort or another, or with the gains of land ownership. Of course, these great fortunes have been partially earned, but very largely they have been individually unearned, and due to the receipt of economic surplus. A conservative estimate traces over three-fourths of the great fortunes of the country to a connection of some kind with economic surplus.[1]

Should the concentrated wealth due to private ownership and management of railways alone be widely diffused, it would produce a marked change in the distribution of wealth in the United States. Of course we cannot undo the past, but we can, in the future, secure management of monopolies favorable to a wide distribution of wealth; and a wise system of regulation and taxation of inheri-

[1] See "Distribution of Wealth," by John R. Commons, chap. vi.

tances, will, in time, tend to break up the mammoth fortunes of the country.

The socialization of monopoly is also calculated to have a favorable influence upon the distribution of wealth, because undertakings of this kind could well be managed in such a manner as to give a great many people an assured income. A wise civil service system would include all those employed in such undertakings, and would in most cases substitute salaries for wages, giving a regular and steady income. This is of the greatest importance, because what the wage-earner wants is not so much larger annual earnings, but a regular receipt of income in the place of the present uncertainty. The wage-earner frequently receives high wages, and then again receives nothing at all; and it requires more wisdom and strength than most of us have to estimate accurately average earnings under such circumstances, and to save up money in a time of plenty for the time of dearth, which will come, no one can tell when.

Furthermore, the abolition or restriction of unearned income would mean personally earned incomes in a larger number of cases; and this change would be beneficial not only to society as a whole, but to those cut off from the receipt of unearned income, which leads to idleness and extravagance, and thus to demoralization.

The socialization of natural monopolies of the kind mentioned, would lead to their utilization for general social purposes, and they would be no longer exploited chiefly for dividends. The question would have to be asked, in what manner can they be so operated that they will yield the largest total social utility, and the answer would decide their management. Let us suppose, for example, the conclusion is reached that a greater decentralization of the population of cities is desired, in order that poor people finding employment in cities may still have homes of their own. It would be possible under government ownership and management, to introduce what is called the "Zone System;" that is to say, the country round about the cities could be divided into three or four different zones, using for each one a radius of a different length. Within the first zone, one rate of fare would be charged for all places. Within the second, a higher fare would be charged, but it would be the same for all places in this second zone. The same would hold true with the third zone, and for any additional number. If it were thought expedient, the fares could be reduced to cost. Not long ago, the system was introduced in Berlin, although it was not developed so far as might be desirable. It should be remembered, however, that, before it was introduced, workingmen's trains were running, on which the fare was only two-thirds of a cent a mile. The zone system has also been introduced into Hungary, and, it is claimed, with very beneficial results.

The Australian railways, owned and operated by the state, are to some extent managed for general social purposes, and the school children are carried free in some parts of Australia, thus helping to scatter the population of cities over larger areas.

Railways can also be so managed under government ownership that they will increase the facilities and ease of travel, thus making it possible for more people to visit different parts of their own country, and even foreign countries. It is altogether desirable that railways should increase enjoyment, and make it easy for people to see the beauties of nature, and thus to cultivate in them an appreciation of these beauties. Macaulay says,

"Of all inventions, the alphabet and printing-press alone excepted, those inventions which abridge space have done most for civilization." If this is true, we must favor an administration of railways, telegraphs, etc., which will place them most fully at the service of the public, making social welfare the chief consideration.

Other monopolies, especially municipal monopolies, could, under municipal ownership and operation, be managed with reference to the greatest good of the greatest number. A special consideration could be shown to those who require help. The working-woman who, in cities, trudges to and from her work because she cannot pay a five cent street-car fare, of which two cents represent economic surplus, could frequently ride instead of walk, if the fare were reduced to three cents.

CHAPTER III.

SOCIALIZATION OF MONOPOLY. (Continued.)

NATURAL MONOPOLIES AND PRESENT PROBLEMS.

THE socialization of natural monopolies is a prerequisite for the solution of the problems of the present time connected with monopoly. So far as the natural monopolies themselves are concerned, it means the abolition of private monopoly. But we have also a class of dependent monopolies — artificial monopolies, which become such on account of their connection with natural monopolies. Businesses which are not monopolies of their own nature frequently become such when they are able to attach themselves firmly to natural monopolies. Railway favoritism has helped to build up many monopolies. Coal mining, for example, has attached itself to railways, and in many instances has become a part of the railway business. Oil refineries have received special concessions from railways, and many manufacturers have been aided by rebates. An illustration of a monopoly secured through the assistance of railways is afforded by the business of transporting passengers and baggage to and from railway stations, and between different railway stations in cities. Companies have been formed for this purpose in all large American cities, and the agents of these companies have the exclusive right of access to passengers on trains and in the railway stations. The result is a monopoly price, and one, in some instances, five times as high as the competitive price. During the past summer, at Chicago, a favored company received fifty cents a passenger for transporting passengers from one station to another, while at the same time a competitive line, whose agents did not have access to the passengers until they left the station, was carrying them between two of the stations for ten cents.

One of the advantages of government ownership of railways in Germany has been found in the equal treatment which all persons have received from the railways. Favoritism has not been shown, and the railways have not assisted in building up artificial monopolies. An article in a prominent German newspaper,[1] not long since, gave expression to a wide-spread opinion, when it stated that Germany had been particularly fortunate in the fact that the railways had been owned and operated by the government during the past fifteen years, because this had prevented that rapid concentration of business which had been witnessed elsewhere, as in France.

The problem of the wage-earner, who is connected with pursuits of the kind under consideration, can be solved by their socialization. These pursuits are primary, and it is indispensable to the continued operation of other industries, that they should not cease to perform their functions. A strike, on the part of their employees, is a very serious matter for the general public; and it has been proposed by some to make such a strike a penal offence. This, however, does not seem just or practicable, unless, at the same time, provision is made for a desirable treatment of the wage-earners. Duties must be reciprocal; and if the general public make special demands of these workers, they must give them guaran-

[1] The *Frankfurter Zeitung*.

ties of fair treatment. Otherwise, to prevent them from striking means to reduce them to a condition of virtual slavery; and it does not amount to anything to give them a theoretical right to strike, and then to keep them from striking in the only way which can possibly be effective; namely, by preconcerted and combined action. The only way out of the dilemma would seem to be government ownership, because, if the workers connected with these enterprises became government employees, they might be guaranteed just treatment, and then punished as soldiers are, if they desert the public service in an emergency. The conditions of the service would necessarily be regulated by public authority; and this public authority would be ultimately the legislative bodies in which the workers would have ample representation. The post-office service in the United States demonstrates how much more easily workers can protect their interests in the public service than they can in the private service of vast corporations.

The farmers have a special interest in the socialization of these monopolies. They are often unable to sell their products at a remunerative price because freight and express charges are so high. Low charges would mean an extension of their markets. Moreover, every increase in the general prosperity must mean a larger demand for agricultural products. What the farmer grows is needed; but the purchasing power of those who need the products is insufficient, and thus mutual wants are not satisfied. Lower passenger rates would also be beneficial to the farmer. Charges for the transportation of passengers, in many ways, enter into the price of goods, and, apart from that, cheaper passenger rates would enable the farmer to enjoy, to a greater extent, the advantages of travel. We have to consider not only the cost of the railway ticket, but also incidental charges connected with travel, as sleeping-car tickets and meals during the journey.

It is claimed also that this reform will be favorable to a desirable development of freedom; for example, free thought and free utterance. Vast corporations are a menace to liberty. They interfere with free thought and free speech and a free vote ten times where government does so once. These corporations even invade the universities, and attempt to muzzle teachers of economics and politics. Not long ago the agent of a gas-ring came to a teacher of political economy in one of the greatest universities in the country, and threatened to "down him," if he did not desist from his agitation of the gas question. This agent professed to be animated by a friendly interest in the teacher, and merely wanted to give him a warning, telling him that his course was injuring the gas business.

It is claimed, furthermore, that this reform will be favorable to the purification of politics. The political corruption of our day in the United States is generally connected with the domination of private corporations of the kind mentioned. The policy, which it is at present attempted to follow, is one of control of private corporations, and the private corporations necessarily attempt to escape this control. The only way to escape control is to enter politics, and this they do. Either an attempt is made to secure the return to the municipal council, State legislature, and Congress, of members favorable to the monopolies, or, after the election, means are taken to influence the representatives of the people. Sometimes the representatives of the people take the initiative and bring in bills which aim to control and regulate corporations of the kind in question, in order that they may be bribed to withdraw or kill their own bills.[1] The result is a vicious circle of corruption, from which we can hardly hope to escape so long as we maintain private ownership of the businesses in question. This corruption takes many forms. Congressmen receive telegraph franks and railway passes; and, during the sessions of State legislatures, the legislators and their friends receive passes in abundance. Long before the expiration of the legislature in a Western State, not long since, a single legislator had received two hundred and sixty passes; and it was estimated that, before the close of the legislature, one legislator would receive a thousand passes. It is commonly said, that, during the sessions of the legislature in that State, "any one can get a pass," and on the trains passes are so abundant that scarcely half a dozen tickets will be taken up on a whole train. What is true of this State is also true of other Western States. The same means are taken to influence public authorities in cities. The author knows one large city, for example, in which the heads of departments receive passes on the street-car lines. But this is by no means all. Sometimes large money bribes are given, although this is rather a crude and old-fashioned method of bribery. Indirect methods are now more commonly taken to punish those who are antagonistic to the interests of private corporations of the kind mentioned, and to reward those who help them in their projects. Even the judiciary does not escape the

---

[1] One makes a grievous mistake who fails to recognize that corporations, and perhaps especially railway corporations, are often wronged. Frequently enough a disposition to plunder them is displayed.

influence of these corporations. Judges receive railway passes, and, unfortunately, have been known to use them. Furthermore, there is reason to believe that these corporations watch, with solicitude, the appointment or election of judges even to the highest courts. Should a judge be appointed who is unfavorable to a corporation, the corporation still has a resource left. The judge may receive an appointment in the service of the corporation as an attorney at a very high salary, and thus be taken from the public service. All this is of the greatest importance in a country like the United States, where our constitutional system gives vast power to the judges.[1]

The policy advocated would also tend to purify politics, because it would give to the mass of men a greater interest in politics, showing the real significance of public affairs. An abler class of men would thus be drawn into political life. A time of expanding and growing national life is a time in which the civil service improves; but a period of restriction in governmental enterprise is one of deterioration in the public service. Enlargement of the public service means its improvement, while the maxim, "The less government the better," means deterioration in the civil service. That which teaches men to esteem the state promotes excellence of administration; but a policy of *laissez faire*, which means a lessened interest in the state, brings with it the degradation of public life.

[1] The following note sent by a correspondent has an important bearing on the question under consideration: —

"A friend of mine here from Colorado tells of a private waterworks company in his town, which appointed as its attorney a lawyer who had been exposing its corrupt methods. That lawyer is silent now!"

The historical proof of the assertion given is ample. Before the French Revolution, the collection of taxes, which requires a large force, was entrusted to private persons, the farmers of the public revenues as they were called. The public life was most corrupt, and it might have been thought folly to intrust to public servants additional functions. Those who proposed to do this might have been told that they should wait until public life was improved. However, when the revolution came, the private collection of taxes was abolished, and a public service substituted therefor, and the civil service was immensely improved. Early in the present century the civil service of Prussia had become a bureaucracy of a bad type, and it was reformed by the great Prussian statesmen, Stein and Hardenberg. The reform was not brought about, however, by the reduction of the functions of the government, but it went on together with an extension of the functions of government. The *renaissance* of the civil service in Prussia was part and parcel of a growing and expanding public life. The period in which the maxim, "To the victors belong the spoils," has prevailed in the United States has been precisely the period in which the maxim, "The less government the better," has been very generally accepted. Even now the spoilsmen in political life are little inclined to favor the extension of the powers of government. The political "boss" is one who likes the motto, *laissez faire.*

Josiah Quincy, to whom reference has already been made, tells us that in 1825 the best men in the country were in Congress. The reason why now so many strong and able men prefer private life is because, relatively, the latter offers so much greater inducements. The policy advocated, by enlarging the sphere of government, would restore the balance. It would give us two spheres of industrial life, the private and the public, and thus render this life richer and fuller.

Many points which will occur to the reader have been neglected in order to avoid expanding the present treatise unduly. The general principles set forth indicate the treatment of special points. A few additional words, however, may not be out of place in regard to one aspect of the socialization of monopoly, to which, it seems to the author, more attention has been given than it merits. The points to which reference is made concerns the votes of those in the civil service. The fear is frequently expressed that all those in the civil service would vote one way, and that if the civil service should be enlarged a party once in power could remain in power indefinitely.

First of all, it may be said that the votes of those who are in the civil service have frequently been held by practical politicians to be of doubtful advantage. When offices are distributed according to the spoils system, there are three or four disappointed men for every officeholder; and quarrels and dissensions are quite likely to outweigh the advantages of the offices.

Second, the plans proposed would increase the civil service of local political units and commonwealths, as well as the national government; and as no one party is always in power in all places, the votes of office-holders of one party would to some considerable extent neutralize the votes of office-holders of another party.

Third, our American experience does not show that the popular will is thwarted by the votes of office-holders. There have been great changes from party to party in federal politics in recent years; and no one can claim that even the most skilful use of offices has, as a matter of fact, ever been able to turn strong popular currents.

Fourth, industrial reform would of necessity bring with it changes in the civil service. No one would maintain that we could have our present civil service should the reforms mentioned in the present work be carried out. As part of a bill for the nationalization of railways, for example, it would be necessary to have a section relating to the organization of the civil service, if the bill should ever become a law; unless, previously, a thorough civil service reform had been accomplished. A bank president, discussing with a friend of the author the socialization of monopolies, said to this friend, whose views coincided with those of the author: "If I thought as you do about the nationalization of railways, I too would be in favor of civil service reform." That is precisely the point. In converting men to the views advocated in the present work, we at the same time convert them to different views from those which are current concerning the proper organization of the civil service.

Fifth, there are many different ways of solving the problem of the votes of the office-holders. The simplest is to deprive office-holders of the suffrage. But this seems like a crude device. It would indeed be strange if, when the American people really attempted to solve the problem, better methods could not be devised. Or are we ready to admit that in this respect we are inferior to other countries, which have had to meet this question, and are in a fair way to solve it?

Another advantage of the policy advocated is that it would simplify legislation immensely, and reduce litigation. Wipe out all the laws in our statute books which are necessitated by private ownership of enterprises of the kind under consideration, and our statute books would begin to look lean indeed! Remove from the courts the cases which are connected in one way or another with monopolistic undertakings, and our judges would have less to do. What is proposed means, then, not more, but fewer, laws; not more, but less, business for the courts.

The test of experience seems to be decisive. The same objections which we now hear against the nationalization of railways in the United States were heard fifteen years ago in Prussia, and the opinion of the people was divided. Now one who travels in Germany, and talks with the people, finds it difficult to discover any one adverse to public ownership and management of the railways. There are some who would like to go back to the old system; but they are few indeed, and they are very generally those who would be apt to derive some private advantage from the change. Professor Cohn of the University of Goettingen voices a general sentiment, when he says that, in Prussia, the question of state ownership and management of railways has been settled by the test of experience. The people of the Australasian colonies are equally clear in regard to the advantages of public ownership and operation of railways. There is considerable enthusiasm in regard to the results of such ownership and operation in New Zealand; and recently the editor of an economic periodical complained because he could not find any one in Australia to write an article adverse to the government ownership and management of railways.

When we turn to the United States, and compare the results of municipal ownership with the results of private ownership of natural monopolies, there can be no doubt which has been the more advantageous to the people as a whole, and which has done the more to promote the excellence of public life. The change from private to public ownership removes a troublesome factor in local politics, and it means, almost invariably, cheaper and better service. For every failure of municipal ownership and management which it would be possible to adduce, twenty failures of private ownership and operation could be named.[1]

The difficulties of payment for these monopolistic undertakings are often mentioned. It must be remembered that public ownership increases their value, because it produces unification in these enterprises, and shuts off the waste of future competition. Frequently public ownership makes it a possibility to unite advantageously several services, and thus effect a saving. Very often a municipal electric lighting plant is connected with the public waterworks, and results in a better utilization of public property, and of the services of those already in the employment of the municipality. The railways which include the larger part of the property of the kind under consideration are generally brought forward as affording the chief illustration of the difficulties of acquisition by the government. The purchase of these practically means the conversion of railway stocks and bonds into government bonds, and while it would add enormously to the public debt, it would add to a still greater extent to the public resources. Besides, it must always be remembered that the change could not be made in a single day.

[1] Many advocates of an exclusive policy of private enterprise, by some strange psychological process, regard one instance of an unsuccessful public work as conclusive, and attach no weight to ten cases of success. On the other hand, the most numerous failures of private undertakings seem to them to carry no argument against private enterprises.

Reformers are often inclined to urge that the payments for railways, telegraphs, etc., should only be sufficient to duplicate the existing plant, and this generally means much less than the selling value of the plant. They make a serious mistake in taking this position. As a matter of policy, this course is not to be recommended, because it needlessly antagonizes such a large proportion of the population of the country. Those who are asked to part with their property at a price less than the market value will feel themselves aggrieved, and will oppose the reform in every way in their power. The plan proposed is also objectionable on the score of justice. The value which property of this kind has in excess of the cost of duplication of the plant is largely due to a public policy which has been approved by a majority, and a vast majority, of the people of the United States. A large capitalization, so far as it exceeds the actual value of the plant, very frequently represents only the waste due to attempted competition, and this attempted competition has been encouraged in every way, directly and indirectly, by the general public. Even when such is not the case, the possibility of an excessively large income, which has brought about the large capitalization, has been due to a considerable extent to failures of the legislature to make proper laws, and of the other public authorities adequately to enforce existing laws. Now, if the property is appraised simply at the cost of duplication of the plant, it would make a portion of the community bear the entire burden of a false public policy, whereas, as the whole of the public is to blame, the burden should be diffused among the people as a whole. If it is necessary to raise large sums to pay off the debt necessitated by the acquisition of enterprises of this kind, it could be done through a wisely devised system of inheritance taxes.

When we consider the difficulties in the way of the socialization of natural monopolies, we must always remember what the alternative is. These difficulties are real, but the difficulties of the present system are even greater. Mention has already been made of many of these difficulties. We cannot expect to have private property well managed, if the managers are obliged to manage it, not as they like, but as somebody else dictates. To interfere at every turn with private management renders illusory the benefits of private ownership of the instruments of production. Moreover, in this attempted minute control, society is likely to be worsted. The special skill is necessarily on the side of those who are to be controlled, because this special skill is acquired by experience in the management of these private industries. The result is that the public authorities wage an unequal contest against private persons, who, in addition, are thereby rendered hostile to the state — a most unfortunate condition of affairs.

CHAPTER IV.

THE SOCIALIZATION OF OTHER NATURAL MONOPOLIES, AND THE TREATMENT OF ARTIFICIAL MONOPOLIES.

NATURAL monoplies of the second class are those which become monopolies because the supply of raw materials, consisting of natural treasures, is so limited that it can all be acquired by a single combination of men. Anthracite coal has been cited as an illustration; other similar cases could be instanced. It is said that it has been possible to purchase practically the entire supply of some raw materials found among barbarous or semi-barbarous peoples; not so much, perhaps, on account of the limitation of the supply, as on account of the fact that it is easy to cheat them, and to buy a great supply at far less than its actual value. Wherever the supply of an article is so limited that it can all be secured by a single combination of men, making monopoly prices possible by limitation of the supply upon the market, the only adequate remedy would seem to be collective ownership — ownership by the nation, commonwealth, or some local political unit.

A distinction must be made between the ownership of agricultural land upon which wealth is produced, and natural treasures which are found ready made, so to speak, mostly beneath the surface of the earth, so that all man has to do is to appropriate them. Private ownership is important with respect to agricultural land, because it encourages production; but the natural treasures of which we speak are found already created, and no social institution can add to their supply. All that can be required is that a sufficient reward should be given to those who appropriate them. This fair return, of course, is all that is needed, even in agriculture; but the distinction is not so easily drawn in that pursuit as it is in the exploitation of the natural treasures of the earth. Even should we grant private ownership in the land, it is an exaggeration of that institution, forming no essential part of the principle of private property, to allow the land-owner to own indefinitely all that is above him, and all that is below him to the centre of the earth. The legal systems of many countries have always regarded the natural treasures below the surface of the earth as public property, and they should be thus regarded everywhere.

So far as barbarous or semi-civilized peoples are concerned, it is difficult to see what they can do until they become more civilized, and form organized governments, unless, indeed, they should receive protection by the civilized nations of the earth.

It does not appear evident at once that the collective management of the property collectively owned is essential. If the anthracite coal mines were owned by the State or by the nation, satisfactory results might, perhaps, be secured by leasing the land, or by allowing individuals or companies to mine coal freely on the payment of a royalty which would absorb any economic surplus above the normal returns to labor and capital.

Artificial monopolies, apart from those which become such on account of their close connection with natural monopolies, whereby they are made to partake of the qualities of the latter, are those businesses which are made so by legislative enactment, or by some act of public authority. These are the monopolies with which our forefathers had to deal; for kings and queens formerly granted exclusive privileges to favored persons, permitting no one else to engage in certain undertakings. These artificial monopolies early became odious, and sovereigns were forced to forego the privilege of granting them. The odium which attached to them is shown by the "bills of rights," like that which forms part of the Maryland constitution, forbidding the creation of any monopolies. Reference was not had, and in the nature of the case could not be had, to the natural monopolies which are now the most important class of monopolies.

The existing artificial monopolies so far as they are created by government are chiefly such as are created by copyrights and patents, and their purpose is the public welfare. The design is to encourage literary production and invention by exclusive privileges strictly limited in point of time. These exclusive privileges appear, on the whole, to promote the public welfare. Where they do otherwise, all that can be desired with respect to them is, perhaps, a clear recognition of the actual principles involved, and certain modifications in the present laws designed to prevent abuses which have grown up, particularly with respect to patents.

Copyrights interfere least of all with industrial freedom, because no two persons can possibly produce the same book, or musical composition, or any other work which is copyrighted. The fact that one person has written a book cannot keep any other person from writing another book on the same subject. There is reason, however, for a limitation of copyrights with respect to the time of their duration. What is wanted is to encourage production, and to give a reward for production, but not to make it possible for persons to live upon the results of the exertions of others. Authors should be granted copyrights, perhaps lasting as long as they live, or during such a period that ordinarily the copyright would cover the lifetime of the author, and possibly also a few additional years in order to provide for the author's family. Perpetual copyrights would, in the case of very valuable works, limit production, and make it possible for the descendants of meritorious men to lead idle and useless lives. Had Shakespeare been granted perpetual copyrights, we might have descendants of his to-day living in the greatest luxury to their own harm, and to the injury of society. Fortunately, we have no dukes and duchesses of Shakespeare's blood ![1]

The author owes much to society, because no literary production is a purely individual effort; but the inventor owes much more. Every invention is simply the capstone of a long line of previous inventions and discoveries. To give too much to the inventor is — to use a different figure — like paying an excessive price to the one who puts the roof on a house, and comparatively little to those who constructed all the rest of the building. The last step which leads to a valuable invention is often unavoidable, and, as a matter of fact, the step is frequently taken by several persons acting independently of each other, so that it is difficult to tell who is really the first inventor. Germany, for example, disputes American claims of originality with respect both to the electric telegraph

[1] Cf. Fabian Essays, "Property under Socialism," by Graham Wallas.

and the telephone, and in America itself, it does not seem to be entirely clear to whom should be attributed the merit of the invention of the telephone. We have, then, to do with a radically different case from that of authorship, because an exclusive right given to one person does interfere with the industrial liberty of others, not permitting others to do that which they would naturally and spontaneously do. It has been proposed by some on this account to abolish the patent system altogether, — and it must be acknowledged that there are other ways of encouraging industrial progress. Able men in the scientific laboratories of the country are continually working to make discoveries and inventions, and they do this without the incitement of any industrial privilege. All that they desire is an assured income, and abundant tools and implements for their scientific work. Emulation supplies the only other motive needed.[1]

It would be far cheaper for the country to spend ten times as much as at present on technical schools and scientific laboratories than to maintain its patent system, if the same results could be reached. The experience of Germany, however, in the absence of an effective patent system, before the formation of the Empire, is not entirely reassuring, because, it is said, it retarded the industrial development of that country. Probably the best results in the United States would be reached by a further development of the American patent system, borrowing some of the features which have been introduced into the patent laws of Germany and England, which are among the best in existence. One American abuse consists in an undue extension, by

[1] Cf. "The Abolition of Patents," Longmans & Co., London, 1869.

various devices, of the time during which a patent practically operates. One way is to make application for a patent, and then not take out the patent for a long time. Still another abuse has recently become apparent through what is called an "interference." Two persons may claim the same invention, and, going to law about it, may delay the issue of the patent for years; and when the patent is granted, it may finally appear that the two different persons have united their interests so that the patent will run for a much longer time than the law contemplated. This, as is well known, is the case with the telephone in the United States. The improvement in regard to which there was a contest, is one which, it is claimed, forms an essential feature of the present system, and it appears, in consequence, not improbable that the telephone patent will last nearly twice as long as the law contemplated. Another abuse consists in the "locking up" of inventions. Exclusive rights to use inventions are purchased by great corporations like a telegraph company, to prevent any one from using the improvements. It is quite practicable, however, following the example of England, to make it compulsory for the owner of an invention to allow others to use it on payment of a royalty. If the payment can be regulated so as to throw open inventions to general use, then many objectionable interferences with industrial freedom can be prevented, and it can also be rendered impracticable to keep inventions out of use. Another improvement which is suggested is that there should be a moderate but progressive tax upon patents during their term of existence, in order that those which are not actually used may no longer continue to exist, making a patent expire upon failure to pay the tax. This is a practice which is followed in many countries, and is commendable. Another abuse can be removed by providing that no patents shall be granted for trifling and insignificant inventions, or such improvements as might readily occur to any one who is engaged in the industry to which they are applicable. An American Commissioner of Patents suggested a further improvement, in the reserved right of the general government to purchase a patent at an appraised valuation, and throw it open to general use.

Certain artificial monopolies of a different sort are those which are called fiscal monopolies in European countries. France has a tobacco monopoly, for example. The manufacture and sale of tobacco is an exclusive privilege, and the purpose is to raise revenue. As this is a fiscal measure, it must be judged largely on financial grounds. It seems, however, in France to yield large returns at comparatively small social sacrifice. Once there was an active agitation for the abolition of these fiscal monopolies; but they have improved in their administration in time; and now they are so generally approved in France, that other countries are proposing to establish similar fiscal monopolies. One writer argues that these fiscal monopolies are a strong argument in favor of socialism, because they have led to the manufacture of pure articles which can be sold at a reasonable price. Indeed, the purity of manufactured tobacco and of the alcoholic beverages under government monopoly, has been urged as an additional reason for the establishment of such monopolies.

Artificial monopolies have also been established to regulate the consumption of articles which are held to be injurious. It is for this reason, that the people of Switzerland have established a government monopoly in

TREATMENT OF ARTIFICIAL MONOPOLIES. 299

distilled spirits,[1] and South Carolina has established a monopoly in the sale of all alcoholic beverages.[2]

A monopoly has, in some instances, been permitted by tariff legislation. The measure needed to prevent monopoly in cases of this kind suggests itself; namely, tariff reform. Careful analysis of monopolistic undertakings will show, however, that the tariff has only a limited influence, and a comparatively small one, — although it cannot be denied that it is a real one, worthy of consideration.

[1] See "State and Federal Government in Switzerland," by J. M. Vincent, chap. xi. Cf. also the "House Report No. 192, on the Norwegian System of Liquor Selling, to the Massachusetts Legislature," 1894, by Dr. H. P. Bowditch and others.

[2] See the article on "The South Carolina Liquor Law," by Governor Tillman, in the *North American Review*, for February, 1894.

CHAPTER V.

LAND REFORM.

LAND is frequently called a natural monopoly, but this hardly seems correct. Monopoly implies management or ownership by one person, or by a combination of persons who can act as a unit. Anything of the kind does not exist with respect either to land ownership, or to the use of the land for agricultural or building purposes. A genuine monopoly in the ownership or exploitation of land, would mean the virtual slavery of all persons not interested in the monopoly. If the farmers of the world could act together as a unit, they could force all others to give everything they might have for food, as the alternative would be starvation. "What will not a man give for his life?" But such a combination is an impossibility, and every attempt to effect a combination, even on a comparatively small scale, with respect to a single staple, like wheat or cotton, has thus far proved a failure. Land has, however, peculiar qualities, on account of the fact that it is strictly limited in supply, and that it varies in desirability with respect to location, and to the fertility of the soil. This enables those who own land of the better class, either in cities or in the country, to gain from it an economic surplus, the well-known unearned increment of land values. Production sometimes suffers on account of the fact that land tends to rise in value with social growth and improvement. Many owners of land keep it out of use, in order that they may grow rich upon the exertions of others, upon whom they not infrequently entail positive harm. There seems to be reason for some change with respect to land tenure, or the method of dealing with land, both from the standpoint of production, and from the standpoint of distribution. Any changes which at present seem desirable, are not radical. Something can be accomplished by the taxation of unused land at its full selling value, and that, in the United States, means simply carrying into effect existing laws. At the present time, land which is held for speculative purposes is almost invariably taxed at a lower value than equally valuable land which is used. A man has to pay, as it were, a fine for putting his land to use, although such use is in the interest of society. Further improvement can be effected, by the exemption of improvements from taxation for a period of years, say three years. This would encourage improvement, because it would give the owner of land, improving it by means of building on it or otherwise, a slight bonus. What is recommended, is a practice which has already been tried in many countries, and that with beneficial results. It cannot therefore be called a radical innovation.

When we consider land reform from the standpoint of distribution, it seems desirable to secure for the general public a larger share than it now enjoys of the unearned increment. The city of Savannah, Ga., offers a suggestion. It has been customary in Savannah for the city to extend its own limits by buying agricultural land by the acre and dividing it into lots which are then sold or leased. If laws were so shaped that all extensions of the cities must be carried out by the cities themselves, a large share of the future unearned increment could be secured. The owners of some of the most valuable land in Savannah pay a ground rent to the city, because this land long ago was leased to those who now occupy it, and was leased at a fixed rental. Unfortunately the city of Savannah has not reserved the right to revise ground rents, and land which has risen greatly in value pays a small rental to the city. Had the city reserved the right to revise the annual rentals every three years, it would now have a large revenue without taxation.

A further change which can be recommended is that no land belonging to the nation, to the States, or to local political units, should hereafter be sold, but should be leased. A step has been taken in this direction in the disposition of school lands in parts of the North-west, where it is provided that they can only be sold at a certain value, at present often far above the market price, and that in the meantime they can be leased. It is easy to provide that the lease shall run for a period of years, and that any one then acquiring the lease shall purchase the improvements at an appraised valuation. If the one who has already enjoyed the lease bids more for it than any one else, he, of course, keeps his improvements, and is obliged to pay simply the additional rental. If another offers more for the lease than he is willing to pay, then one party may appoint one arbitrator, the other a second, and those two may select a third to appraise the improvements. As existing cities are destined to grow much larger, and cities are certain to spring up where there are none now, and some of these, if the reform is carried out, would be located on ground owned by the people in their collective capacity, a far larger share than at present of the unearned increment would accrue to the general public.[1]

[1] Cf. Ely's "Taxation in American States and Cities," Part III., chap. iv.

The larger social aspect of the question is of importance. There will always be a class of tenant farmers, and these will grow in number as the country increases in population. It is impossible, under our present constitutional system, to prevent rack-renting of the worst kind, and we have reason to fear that we shall have the experience of Ireland repeated, or if possible something worse, unless we take measures at an early day to prevent what is known as rack-renting. Large public ownership of land makes it possible to regulate the use of land beneficially for the tenants and the public at large. The state is apt to be a better landlord than the private owner. It is easy for the state to grant long leases, and to make provision for guaranteeing to the cultivator of the land the value of his improvements, and this is all that is required to secure the best cultivation of the land. Cities have also found it advantageous to give allotments of land to laborers, and in the administration of charity such allotments have been found valuable. It is much better to allot a small quantity of land to a laborer, thus enabling him to eke out a small income, than to force him to go to the almshouse, or to give him out-door relief. If we look at the experience of various countries we shall find that public ownership of land is most important in the solution of pressing problems, and in the present uncertainty in regard to the future development of economic institutions, it is only a matter of common prudence for the collectivity to retain whatever land it may now own, and to improve such opportunities as may occur to increase the public landed domain.

The reader will, of course, understand that it is not possible, in a work like the present, to do more than to throw out certain general suggestions. Should the land question be treated in all its details, it would alone require a book as large as the present one.

There are certain minor details of some importance which may be mentioned. The simplification of the transfer of land is desirable, and the so-called Torrens System, which, like so many other improvements, comes from Australia, may be recommended, because it makes the state responsible for the validity of the title, and accomplishes a great social good at comparatively small public expense.

In conclusion, attention may be called to the very instructive experimentation with respect to land ownership and cultivation now going forward in New Zealand. The government of New Zealand is making vigorous efforts to break up large holdings of land, especially of land speculatively held. One means which is designed to accomplish this is a progressive property tax in addition to the ordinary taxes. This progressive tax begins with estates valued at five thousand pounds; and the rate of taxation increases as the value of the estate increases. The rate of progression is not high, but it is sufficient to be effective, and has already broken up some large holdings. If the person taxed objects to the appraised valuation of the land for purposes of taxation, he is asked to value it himself with the understanding that the government may purchase it at his valuation, if this is considered too low. Government land is leased according to two systems. One kind of lease is a lease which gives an option of purchase within ten years. The lessee pays five per cent of the value of the land, which is reassessed once in every three years. This lease may, however, after the expiration of ten years, be changed into a lease in perpetuity, and then the rent paid is equal to four per cent of the appraised valuation. The lessee of all land leased in perpetuity pays four per cent upon the valuation, and the land is reassessed once in every three years. The government of New Zealand has also inaugurated the formation of village settlements to assist in the solution of the labor problem, and to give employment to the unemployed. Land not to exceed one acre is allotted in the villages; and homesteads outside the villages not to exceed one hundred acres are allotted to all who may desire them. These lands are granted on perpetual lease at four per cent on the assessed valuation. Loans are also granted to those taking up land in these village settlements. Government reports give a very favorable account of these village settlements. The government finances of New Zealand are in a flourishing condition; and those familiar with this colony claim that it is the only part of the civilized world where industrial stagnation does not at present obtain. Emigrants in large numbers are going to New Zealand on account of the flourishing condition of the colony.

The single-taxers and other zealous land reformers attribute the prosperity of New Zealand exclusively to the land policy pursued; but the land policy is only one of many social reforms which are now being successfully carried out in New Zealand.[1]

[1] See "Social Experiments in New Zealand," by A. G. Fradenburg, in the *Outlook* for April 7, 1894.

CHAPTER VI.

DEVELOPMENT OF THE SOCIAL SIDE OF PRIVATE PROPERTY.[1]

PRIVATE property is an exclusive right, but never an absolute right. Private property is a growth, changing both with respect to the number of things to which it extends, and with respect to the privileges which it carries with it. Legal codes will be searched in vain for an unlimited right of private property. Should a definition of private property be found which appears to be absolute, limitations will elsewhere be found in the code. These limitations, when carefully examined, all mean one thing; namely, that private property has a social side. But this is not all. An examination of the nature and growth of private property and of its treatment by civilized nations, shows that in case of conflict between the social side and the individual side, the social side is dominant and the individual claims must be yielded. Private property is maintained for social purposes.

We have already seen the desirability of a large extension of public property. But we must not overlook

[1] Again the author must remind his readers that only suggestions can be thrown out. Those who wish to examine his views on this subject more carefully, will find them further elaborated in a series of twelve articles on Private Property, the first of which appeared in the *Record and Guide*, of New York City for March 17, 1894.

the importance of private property, even in the instruments of production. Private property is one of the main incentives to thrift and industry, and thus is beneficial to society as a whole, as well as to the individual. It is also advantageous to society that it should include individuals having more than ordinary strength who may use their superior strength to the advantage of society. This has already been pointed out.

It is important, however, that the social side of private property should receive still further development. Even the protection of private property requires that this further development should take place. This does not mean that private and social rights are to be fused or confused in such a manner that no one can tell where one begins and the other ends. Quite the contrary. What is needed is a clearer definition of rights, both individual and social, than that which now exists.

There are two methods for developing the social side of private property. One is the voluntary method. It is generally recognized as a religious doctrine that private property is a trust. The Christian preacher tells us that private property is a trust, and that we are stewards to administer it in accordance with the will of God. The doctrine of stewardship in this religious sense is one which has never been lost sight of in the Christian church, and one which has been particularly emphasized of late. Unfortunately this doctrine as ordinarily presented is so vague that it does not lead to a great amount of positive action. The general statement is not followed up with an examination of what it implies in detail. Nor is this doctrine brought into connection with other ethical precepts. The church has still a great work to do in the development of the doctrine that private property is a trust. It would take us too far away from the main current of the present book to discuss this subject at length. The reader's attention, however, is directed to the connection which the doctrine of stewardship of wealth has with luxury, which is now so widespread, and in which people who profess Christianity participate so largely.[1] Manifestly, if my property is to be used to benefit society as a whole, and I attach importance to the claims of others like that which I attach to my own claims, I cannot administer my property in any way which ministers to caprice or vanity. Anything which gratifies a love for display, or a desire to outdo others in expenditures, must stand condemned without a moment's hesitation. This, however, it can also be mentioned, does not imply that all should live according to the same scale of expenditure, or that the person who has large means cannot use considerable sums for himself and his family, even while he recognizes the stewardship of wealth. It often happens that one who expends what would seem like an enormous sum from the standpoint of the wage-earner, in developing himself or educating his family, is making a better use of his wealth than he would if he should give it directly to satisfy immediate and even pressing needs of the poor. A strong and cultured man or woman has a greater power for usefulness than has large wealth in itself. The cultivation of the finer forms and graces of life in polite society is also not inconsistent with the stewardship of wealth. Man does not live by bread alone, and it is important for all that gentle and refined manners should become diffused throughout society. All that can be urged is that those who have these exceptional advantages should employ

[1] For treatment of luxury, see Ely's "Outlines of Economics," College edition, pp. 230-234.

them generously, as indeed many do. And in this connection, the precepts of the greatest ethical teacher of all ages should be borne in mind:—

"When thou makest a dinner or a supper, call not thy friends, nor thy brethren, neither thy kinsmen, nor thy rich neighbors; lest they also bid thee again, and a recompense be made thee. But when thou makest a feast, call the poor, the maimed, the lame, the blind." [1]

There are, doubtless, some who, with over-sensitive consciences, or rather consciences not sufficiently guided by intelligence, do not have a sufficient appreciation of their own wants; but these are very few. An attempt on the part of the church to make real the doctrine of stewardship would increase greatly the advantages of private property, and these would show themselves in many other ways than in material gifts and bequests.

The social side of private property may be further developed through public agencies. One of the principal needs is a full and complete recognition of the fact that private property exists for social purposes; for when this is generally understood, it will show itself in a multitude of legislative details, as well as in judicial decisions.

This social theory of private property justifies a regulation of its use; but it must be always borne in mind that if this regulation is carried far, the advantages of private property begin to disappear. When it becomes necessary to regulate private property minutely, we have a clear indication that private property should be replaced by public property. Private property may, however, be regulated in certain general ways, without, at the same time, rendering illusory the advantages of

[1] St. Luke xiv. 12, 13.

the institution. This is particularly the case in cities. There has been too much hesitation, in American cities in particular, about the regulation of the use of land; and many a presumptuous private owner feels that he has a right to injure his neighbor to the full extent of his resources. It is entirely consistent with the institution of private property to exclude stables and offensive manufacturing establishments from certain parts of the city, and to make provisions regarding the width of houses, so that certain streets shall have an ornamental character, etc. Regulations designed to prevent injurious speculation are also consistent with the institution of private property. Taxation, as in New Zealand, may be invoked to bring property into its proper use.

An able follower of St. Simon, early in this century, proposed that inheritances should be abolished altogether, and that property should be distributed in each generation among the persons who could use it to the best social advantage. He desired to maintain private property, but to select anew in each generation the proprietors. The difficulties and disadvantages of such a system become apparent upon careful investigation of the proposition; and it must be said that it has not at all stood the test of time. Other proposals of reform, however, and actual operations of government with respect to inheritances, have not, improbably, grown out of the discussion which followed upon the suggestion of this plan for the redistribution of private property. There is a growing tendency to regulate inheritances, and to tax them in such manner that private property may better subserve the purposes for which it exists. We witness a tendency, even in the United States, to limit the power of disposing of property by last will and testament — a power which is no essential part of private property, as we see in the fact that during the greater part of its history private property has existed in the absence of a power to provide for its disposition by last will and testament. Greater attention is given to the claims of one's family; and the proposition that no one should be allowed to disinherit his children meets with increasing approval. Many countries recognize the rights of children in the property of the father, rights of which the father cannot dispose by gift or by a will. We in America have, as a rule, developed the rights of the wife in the property of her husband as far as any country, but we have not made sufficient provision for the children; although their claims may be considered superior even to those of the wife, as they have no voice in determining their relationship to their parents. What is to be recommended is, that we should follow the practice of the Roman and the German laws, and provide what the Germans call a "duty part" for each child, allowing a parent to dispose of his property by will and testament only in case the claims of the family have been fully satisfied. There would seem to be no reason, however, why the "duty part" of a child should exceed fifty thousand dollars, however great the fortune of a parent. The Illinois Bar Association has indorsed a bill limiting the amount which any one person can inherit to five hundred thousand dollars; and long ago John Stuart Mill favored a limitation of this kind. This is, perhaps, too radical a proposition for consideration at the present moment. The civilized countries of the world are, however, increasingly inclined to favor the taxation of bequests and inheritances, and the tendency is to make the tax doubly progressive — increasing it, on the one hand, as the relationship of the person inheriting the property becomes more distant, and, on the other hand, increasing the rate as the amount of property taxed becomes greater. The tax amounts, in some instances in parts of Switzerland and in some of the Australasian colonies, to twenty per cent in cases of large estates inherited by distant relatives. There is a general feeling, however, that distant relatives should not inherit at all, because they do not constitute a part of the modern family. There seems to be no good reason, whatever, why intestate inheritance should not be limited to persons who are nearly enough related to be able to trace descent from a common great-grandfather.

The wider diffusion of property which proper laws of inheritance would bring about, would prove beneficial to society, both from the standpoint of production and that of distribution. It would render monopoly in many instances more difficult, as a few men of enormous wealth would not be able to acquire a monopoly by the purchase of the sources of production. The result of this wide distribution of property would be that we should have more men living in a degree of ease and comfort favorable to the cultivation of their powers, but not so many Crœsuses. We should also have the further advantage, that a few men would not be separated from their fellows to such an extent as they now are by excessive wealth. Men of moderate means, existing in large numbers all over the country, may prove helpful in the social development of their kind. Men of moderate wealth are also able better than the excessively rich to use their wealth to alleviate distress, because they come in closer contact with their fellow-men. Even if a very rich man were able as easily as a moderately rich man to enter into friendly relations with persons needing assistance, or who could profit by the aid which he extended to them in one way or another, one very rich man could not reach so many people as could ten men of moderate means. Great wealth also tends to concentration in one or two immense cities, while men of moderate fortunes are more likely to be found in every part of the country.

314   SOCIALISM AND SOCIAL REFORM.

CHAPTER VII.

THE DESIRABILITY OF A FIELD OF PRIVATE INDUSTRY, BUT A NARROWER ONE, WITH A HIGHER ETHICAL LEVEL THAN WE NOW HAVE.

COMPETITION is desirable where we can have it in a normal form, as a regular, steady pressure. It is, when properly restricted, upon the whole, a beneficent force; and there seems to be no reason why we should not still have competition in agriculture, manufactures, and commerce. The monopolies which we have already discussed are a new field superimposed upon the old field, with which the founders of this republic had to deal. While those great men desired to abolish special privileges, the plans which they proposed were in the main designed for the field of private competitive industry. The post-office then constituted a collective enterprise, which was in its own nature a monopoly; and this business, at that time something entirely exceptional, was placed under public ownership and management.

Many of the reforms which have been proposed in the previous chapters are calculated to strengthen private industry in its own field. Cheap gas favors many small private businesses; and if electricity reaches the high development which is now anticipated, there is no reason why, under public control, affording light and power at the lowest prices and under like conditions to all, it should not be favorable to a multitude of small industries. The post-office at the present time makes it possible for men to do a business on a comparatively small scale in the country towns, and to find their customers in every part of the country. The author has known a printer in a country town five hundred miles from Brooklyn to do a printing business for men in that city, sending the printed matter by mail to his customers. If to the present post-office we added a parcels' post, it would also be favorable to many private industries.

The question may be asked, however, shall we tolerate the wastes of competitive industries which have already been mentioned, and which are by no means confined to natural monopolies? The milk business, still generally a competitive business, has been instanced as an illustration of waste. While there is waste, however, outside the field of natural monopolies, the greatest wastes are found in that field; and, so far as wastes elsewhere are concerned, it does not seem impracticable to deal with them by other methods. In the olden time the chief illustration of waste was retail trade; but the development of retail trade itself is bringing a better utilization of productive forces. The country shopkeeper and his clerk, idle half the time, are by no means typical retail dealers at the present day. The great city store is as well organized as the factory, and every one employed in it is busy from morning to night. It is desirable, from a broad social standpoint, to bring goods from the producer to the consumer with as small an expenditure of labor and capital as possible. But we are on the way to making great improvements with respect to the forces required to accomplish this service. The further development of the post-office, adding to it the parcels' post, which has already been mentioned, would do still more to weed out needless retail dealers, and to divert their capital and their energies to other pursuits. There is also a possible improvement in the development of co-operation on the part of consumers. This distributive co-operation, as it is called, has already attained great dimensions in England ; and it will grow in the United States and other countries if there is a field for it. The co-operative store does not advertise, and generally avoids many wastes connected with retail shopkeeping. So far as the wastes are concerned, which are a necessary part of the true competitive field of industry, it is more than probable that they are counterbalanced by the gains coming from competition, such as alertness and the free exercise of one's powers by active efforts to meet wants as they arise.

A higher ethical level of private business can only to slight extent be secured by individual action, but it must be largely the work of social action, and still more especially of legislative action. All attempts at reform in the field of private industry will prove useless, unless they are based upon a clear recognition of what we may call the problem of the twentieth man. Private industry is such that, very generally, one man, mean and unscrupulous, is able to coerce nineteen others. The simplest illustration which occurs is the best, and the author thinks of none simpler than that of the barbers in their efforts to close their shops on Sundays. We find the barbers, in their annual conventions, passing resolutions in favor of closing barber shops on Sundays. They seek their freedom through compulsory legislation, paradoxical as it may seem. If there are twenty barbers in a town and Sunday opening is tolerated, it is safe to predict that at least one will open his barber shop on Sunday, although all the others desire them closed, and although even he would rather have his own shop closed with the others, than to have them all open. But this twentieth man will desire to secure an advantage over his fellows, and will keep his shop open, thus drawing, not only the Sunday trade, but also part of the week-day trade which would naturally fall to the others, because a man who goes to a barber shop on Sunday is very likely to go to the same shop on other days. The nineteenth man, not quite so mean and unscrupulous, but withal not a strong man, opens his shop also as soon as a beginning has been made. The eighteenth man follows; then the seventeenth, the sixteenth, and so on, until the pressure becomes too strong, and all the barber shops are open. The conditions then become such that the man who would close his shop on Sunday could no longer gain a livelihood.

Photographic galleries furnish a similar illustration. Not many years ago, when all these galleries were open in New York City, the author heard a photographer say that he would gladly give one hundred dollars to have a law passed closing all the photographic galleries of New York on Sunday. The adulteration of food products serves as additional illustration, as does also the cruel and oppressive treatment of work-people, especially as seen in the employment of young children.

There are certain regulations, designed to raise the ethical plane of private business, which have no special bearing upon any one class in the community. These are regulations of the most general character, like the prohibition of the adulteration of food products, and provision for the inspection of markets. Generally, however, these regulations have special reference to wage-earners, and they are embraced in what is called factory legislation. They are, however, peculiarly important to the public as a whole, because the welfare of society is dependent upon a strong and vigorous wage-earning population, without which the position of a nation cannot be maintained in international competition, and also because many of these regulations, although specially important to the wage-earners, directly and immediately affect society as a whole. Several illustrations will show that such is the case. The establishment of boards of arbitration and conciliation falls under the head of factory legislation, and such boards are most beneficial, as we may see from the experience of England, Belgium, and the United States; especially Massachusetts, which, in all factory legislation, is still the banner State of the Union. It is in the interest of wage-earners that industrial peace should be preserved; but it is also in the interest of society as a whole, as it is materially injured by industrial warfare. Every great strike affects, not only the employers and employees immediately concerned, but also the general public. What is produced in one establishment is raw material for another establishment, which must cease its operations if it no longer receives its supplies. It is desirable in every respect that arbitration and conciliation should be extended; and the Massachusetts board may be recommended as a model to the rest of the Union, although that could, doubtless, be improved in many respects. An important point to be remembered is that private corporations are creatures of the state, and that provision for arbitration and conciliation can be made a condition of incorporation.

Accidents on railways, and in industrial undertakings generally, are mostly avoidable; and other countries, Germany especially, have made great progress in diminishing the number of accidents, which seem to be increasing in the United States, because sufficient social efforts have not been put forward to prevent them. It is well known that railway employees in the United States at times work twenty and more hours in succession, and it is also well known that long hours of work are a prolific cause of accidents. This has been so strongly felt in Prussia, where the railways are owned and operated by the state, that it has been proposed to reduce the hours of railway employees holding responsible positions to eight per day. The telegraph operators already work only that number of hours, except two days in the week. It would be perfectly proper, even from the standpoint of the police powers of the state, to limit the number of hours during which railway employees should be allowed to work. Employers' Liability Acts are also beneficial in reducing accidents, and a good factory system will provide for the fencing in of machinery and other safeguards against accidents. Measures of the kind named would help to prevent pauperism and to maintain a general condition of prosperity. Sanitary inspection, either as something separate and distinct, or as part of the general factory inspection, is a practicable reform of special interest to the wage-earners, but also of interest to society at large; for, altogether apart from humanitarian considerations and from the importance of a sound and vigorous wage-earning population, it is true that disease originating among the poorer and neglected people spreads throughout the whole of society. This sanitary inspection, as well as factory inspection in general, should be well organized, and the penalties for violation of sanitary regulations should be sufficiently severe to induce compliance. Trouble arises when the inspectors are armed with insufficient powers and are inadequately supported; but when once it is seen that the inspection is vigorous and determined, opposition soon ceases.

The abolition of sweat-shops by various regulations like those which have been enacted in Massachusetts [1] and Illinois is a reform of general interest from the sanitary standpoint, as garments made in these sweat-shops carry with them the seeds of disease to all parts of the country. It is also a reform of peculiar interest to the masses of the population. The abolition of the sweat-shops is a difficult measure, requiring strict legislation and vigilant administration. One proposal has been to "ticket" all garments with cards, showing where they were made, and to create an active public prejudice against buying clothing produced under conditions known to be unfavorable to the workers.

The social importance of a rest of one day each week has long been recognized by all who have given attention to it, and has been keenly felt by the wage-earners. The proper way to secure this is to provide that for every worker there shall be each week an uninterrupted period of rest thirty-six hours in duration. This would naturally and spontaneously fall on Sundays, except in cases where Sunday work might be really required. Those

[1] The Massachusetts law against the sweating system begins by defining any tenement or other house in which work is carried on as a "workshop" within the meaning of the factory law. The law provides for proper sanitary measures and proper hours of labor, regulates the employment of women and children, etc. A license must be obtained by each establishment, and this makes further stipulations as to cleanliness and contagious diseases, and provides that no work shall be done in sleeping apartments. Another provision of the law requires that all goods made in tenements shall be so labelled when offered for sale, whether made in the State or not.

who pretend that Sunday work is necessary, when what they really desire is to get more work out of their workpeople, would then have no advantage in working on Sunday, as they would be compelled to give their employees another day of rest in the week. Such a provision would meet the demands of all those who hold that "The Sabbath was made for man, and not man for the Sabbath."

All legislation and social action should have special regard for women and children, — for women, as the mothers of the rising generation and the conservators of the home, and for the children, as those upon whom our future welfare must depend. Compulsory education, real and genuine, as it is in Massachusetts, and not a farce, as it is in most parts of the United States, should be made a part of any factory legislation; and every child should be kept at school until at least fourteen, and under that age no one should be allowed to work in a mercantile or manufacturing establishment. Restrictions should be thrown about the employment of married women, and their employment for a considerable period before and after child-birth should be prohibited under any circumstances. There should also be a restriction of the work-day, as in England, for children and young persons under eighteen, and for women. Such a limitation having a beneficial effect upon the health of the community. It is, furthermore, desirable, in the interest of the wage-earners, to establish a satisfactory normal work-day, for which we may take eight hours as the ideal to be attained at some time in the future. A movement in this direction has begun by lessening the hours of all those employed on public works and in the public service; and labor organizations have followed this up with efforts of their own, by strikes and otherwise, to reduce the length of the work-day, always keeping eight hours before them as an ideal. Now that labor is so divided in factories and elsewhere, and the toil by which one gains a livelihood usually is so dreary and uninspiring, more time outside is needed for the cultivation of one's faculties. The professional man finds in his occupation itself opportunity for growth, and his toil is a delight to him; but the wage-earner needs a shorter working-day, to give him time for those opportunities which the professional man enjoys in his occupation itself. Furthermore, leisure is required for a satisfactory performance of political duties since modern society has become so complex.

Night work should be prohibited for women and persons under eighteen years of age; and, in particular, all work injurious to the female organism should be forbidden to women.

Another reform upon which wage-earners properly insist is the payment of wages in lawful money, and the abolition of the truck stores, which are significantly called "pluck-me-stores." England long ago prohibited payment in kind; but we have lagged behind other countries in our factory legislation.

CHAPTER VIII.

OTHER REFORMS CALCULATED TO LESSEN THE DISADVANTAGES OF PRIVATE INDUSTRY, AND SECURE SOME OF THE ADVANTAGES OF SOCIALISM.

NOTHING can exceed in importance the improvement of education, taking education in the largest sense of the word. Aristotle, over two thousand years ago, perceived the truth which our own Washington uttered so forcefully, that education should be adapted to the conditions of each country, and particularly that in democratic countries education should prepare the young for democratic institutions. "In proportion as the structure of a government gives force to public opinion, it is essential that public opinion should be enlightened." These are the words of Washington. But there never was so much need for education as at the present time, because society never before was so complex, and social problems never before so difficult of solution. We who live in democratic countries call each citizen sovereign, and we should see to it that each citizen has an education befitting a sovereign. If we are wise, we will prepare ourselves as carefully for civil life as Germany trains her sons for war, begrudging no expense, no expenditure of time designed to accomplish our purpose.[1]

[1] Private enterprise has never achieved an organization for a moment to be compared with the German army. What could we not effect were the same energy directed to civil affairs? It would give us, for example, a railway service surpassing anything which the world has yet seen.

Provision of the fullest opportunities for the development of personality requires the co-operation of the individual, of private associations, of the family, of the church, and of the state, for education is physical, mental, moral, and spiritual. Nurseries for children who on account of the necessities of mothers cannot be cared for at home may be mentioned as a beginning of educational institutions, and these should be followed by a universal system of kindergartens, forming an essential part of the public school system. Children, and even young children, should receive special care, for the possibilities of influencing them beneficially are almost boundless. From kindergartens we pass on to common schools, grammar schools, evening continuation schools, high schools, industrial and technical schools of every sort, colleges, and universities. When we begin to examine the schools as affording a preparation for life, we at once appreciate the importance of subjects which have been too much neglected. Cooking is one of these; and this subject, including knowledge of foods, should form an important part in the education of every girl, rich or poor. Well prepared food strengthens and nourishes the body far better than poorly cooked food, and it has been found that intelligent cooking promotes temperance. Systematic instruction in the evil effects of intemperance of every kind cannot well be neglected. Sewing is a subject of extreme importance. Many a woman, working late into the night for a bare pittance, would be able to lead a far more comfortable life did she know how to sew well. Those women whose cases are most pitiable are very generally those who have never been properly trained in any womanly occupation. While we should have special industrial schools, industrial education should form a part of all school training.

Compulsory education up to the fifteenth year is the minimum requirement which meets the conditions of our time, and this should be followed by evening continuation classes for artisans and mechanics ; and upon them also, if practicable, attendance should be compulsory. The first seventeen years of life should be devoted almost entirely to preparation for subsequent life work. The experience of a country like Germany shows that this is practicable, for in that country each child is required to attend school until the completion of the fourteenth year; and at a later period in life three years' military service, far more expensive than the education of civil life, follows for every lad.

Education should be so contrived as to broaden the way to success. Comparatively few can profit by the higher schools, but systems of scholarships and fellowships should offer opportunity for all to carry on general and special studies who have peculiar aptitudes.

But education ought not to end so long as life continues. This is the well-known "Chautauqua idea," and its soundness has been demonstrated by experience. One of the instruments for the promotion of general education on the part of both young and old is the public library, and every community of two thousand inhabitants or more should be provided with one. Massachusetts has almost attained this ideal; and in this respect, as in so many others, this commonwealth sets the example to the rest of the country. One of the important features of the Massachusetts system is a committee to encourage the formation of libraries, which has the power to make a small grant of State funds on condition that the town itself appropriates a certain minimum sum.

New York State has taken a forward step in providing

for the circulation of books belonging to the State library at Albany. Under conditions with which compliance is not difficult, small travelling libraries may be sent to any part of the State; and, by development along this line, even the rural districts may receive the advantages of public libraries.

University extension, which has met with so much favor in England and America, is a desirable agency for popular education, when it is properly conducted.

Farmers' institutes are of a similar nature; and their possibilities are shown by the experience of Wisconsin, in which State they are conducted under the auspices of the State University, and reach some forty or fifty thouand farmers yearly.[1]

The Chautauqua system of education, with its reading courses, correspondence classes, and other features, is also doing a useful work of the same general character.

Helps for physical education and development suggest themselves readily. Ample playgrounds for children, parks for young and old, public baths and gymnasiums accessible to all, are among some of the more important.

Special mention must be made of the church among educational institutions. Experience shows more and more clearly that that education is one-sided and imperfect which neglects the culture of the spiritual side of life. It is a function of the church especially to spiritualize life. All outward reforms and improvements in

---

[1] In this connection, mention should be made of the two names which have a specially honorable record in the history of farmers' institutes; namely, Professor W. A. Henry, Dean of the Agricultural College, and the late Mr. William Henry Morrison, Superintendent of Agricultural Institutes. The latter's recent untimely death was a loss, not only to the farmers of Wisconsin, but to those of the entire country.

external conditions are to be regarded as offering opportunities; and it is the special mission of the church to see that these opportunities are utilized.[1] It must be remembered that all reforms are of no avail in the end unless they touch individual character. The socialists themselves are beginning to see this; and the author not long ago had the pleasure of hearing a socialist close an address with an appeal to his listeners to aim at individual moral improvement, admonishing them that this was needed as much as social improvement, and that the latter was to no inconsiderable extent dependent upon the former.

[1] The seventh Earl of Shaftesbury saw this clearly, and as soon as the working-day had been shortened, he wrote a letter to the Short Time Committee, of which the following is an extract: —

"MY GOOD FRIENDS, —. . . We have won the great object of all our labors; the Ten Hour Bill has become the law of the land; and we may hope, nay, more, we believe, that we shall find in its happy results a full compensation for all our toils.

But with your success have commenced new duties. You are now in possession of those two hours which you have so long and so ardently desired; you must, therefore, turn them to the best account, — to that account which was ever in the minds of your friends and advocates when they appealed to the Legislature on behalf of your rights as immortal beings, as citizens and Christians.

"You will remember the principal motive that stimulated your own activity and the energetic aid of your supporters in Parliament was the use that might be made of this leisure for the moral improvement of the factory people, and especially the female workers, who will now enjoy far better opportunities, both of learning and practising those duties which must be known and discharged, if we would have a comfortable, decent, and happy population.

"You will experience no difficulty, throughout your several districts, in obtaining counsel or assistance on these subjects. The clergy, the various ministers, the medical men, — all who have been so forward and earnest in your cause, — will, I am sure, be really delighted to co-operate with your efforts."

This brings to mind how closely various reforms are connected. A short working-day standing alone may do harm rather than good; on the other hand, public libraries, university extension courses, and like opportunities, cannot produce the best results until the work-day becomes less than ten hours.

Improved dwellings, coupled with sanitary reform, are important from the standpoint of physical education, but ought to be considered chiefly in connection with moral reform and the up-building of the family as a social institution. Those who have given careful thought to the subject, and have examined long and patiently into the workings of tenement houses, tell us that we cannot well exaggerate the moral evils which proceed from them. Voluntary methods to improve the dwellings of the poor have never been very fruitful. Spasmodic efforts have been made now and then, but they have reached only an insignificant minority of those who need better dwellings. Vigorous efforts have been made on the part of preachers and others in New York City to arouse the wealthy to an appreciation of the importance of improved dwellings for the poor, and they have even demonstrated that model tenements yield a moderate but safe return on capital invested. But all the exhortation of a generation has produced less effect than a single sanitary law well administered, or, we may say, even indifferently administered.[1]

The power has been given to English municipalities to tear down unfit tenements and to construct better dwellings; and some use has been made of this power in different cities in England and Scotland. The results have been excellent, and it is to be desired that progress should be made along this line as rapidly as may be without peril to public finance.[2]

[1] Sanitary reform in Berlin, due largely to Professor Virchow, has reduced the mortality in that city forty per cent in thirty years. — *The Outlook*, January 27, 1894.

[2] The State of Ohio, which has gained an enviable position in social reform, has passed a law which enables the city of Cincinnati to order buildings unfit for habitation to be destroyed. When the

The promotion of thrift cannot be too strongly urged, and every means to encourage accumulation and provision for "rainy seasons" should be encouraged. Savings banks readily suggest themselves; but what is needed above everything else is security. Experience has demonstrated that security is of more importance than a high rate of interest. Every time a bank fails it discourages savings. There is no agency for the promotion of thrift which can be compared with the postal savings bank, having back of it the power of the nation. Socialization of railways is of peculiar importance in this connection. The most desirable investment for savings deposited in the post-offices has, in every country where postal savings banks exist, been found to be government bonds. The purchase of the railways would provide a supply of those bonds; and the ultimate outcome would be that large masses of people would, on account of their ownership of bonds, have a special interest in the railway management altogether apart from their interest as citizens. This could scarcely fail to promote good citizenship and excellence of administration.

Building and loan associations which encourage savings, and at the same time lead to the ownership of homes by many who could not otherwise hope to live in a house of their own, have been found helpful, especially where they exist under wise laws which render them safe. The laws and institutions of Massachusetts are, in this respect also, a model to the rest of the United States.

One of the main advantages offered by socialism is an

author was in Cincinnati recently, he had the pleasure of seeing several vacant pieces of land from which the buildings had been removed by order of the city, and he also saw a number of tenements which had been greatly improved through the operation of this law.

assured income, and existing society should do whatever is practicable to connect a like advantage with present institutions. Insurance is one means of accomplishing this end, in part at least; and more and more is there a general appreciation of the importance of an extension of insurance of every kind. Insurance now reaches the professional and better situated classes quite generally, but in England and the United States its benefits have not been extended sufficiently to the masses. What is wanted is, in addition to life insurance, insurance to provide against the ordinary contingencies of life, which constitute disadvantageous features of the present industrial system. Insurance may be made to provide against sickness, invalidism, accidents, and old age. It seems impracticable to extend insurance to all, unless private and voluntary insurance is supplemented by governmental activity. Germany has led the world with respect to insurance; and at the present time there is going forward in that country one of the most remarkable social experiments ever witnessed in the history of the world. Some twenty millions of human beings are insured under the auspices of the imperial government, and the benefits have already proved so great that the social democrats were at one time afraid that this important social reform would prove a serious barrier to their agitation, on account of the contentment produced. While the opinion frequently expressed a few years since that the imperial insurance schemes had taken the bottom out of social democracy appears to be unsubstantiated by subsequent experience, it is not improbable that this social reform may have had an important influence in giving a more conservative tone to social democratic agitation.

New Zealand has established government life insurance; and the greater security which the government is able to afford has won such favor that now more than half of the life insurance business of that colony has fallen to the government insurance department. Insurance is another one of those large subjects which would require an entire book for anything like exhaustive treatment, and simply hints can be thrown out in this place.

Another method of giving at least an assured minimum income to large numbers, in fact, to all who can work, is through provision of employment. The private employment agency is not equal to the test. The evils connected with it are such that it perhaps produces more harm than good; and an agent of the United States Department of Labor, who has observed its workings, has declared that the employment agency is the vilest vulture that ever preyed upon a decaying body. It assists in the reduction of wages by bringing men to places where there is already a superabundant supply of labor, and in every way ministers to greed and lust. The State of Ohio has established public employment bureaus in several large cities, and the claim is made for these that they have produced beneficial results.[1] New Zealand has

[1] The act creating the Ohio Free Public Employment Offices became a law May 6, 1890. Offices were at once established in Cincinnati, Cleveland, Columbus, Dayton, and Toledo. Up to January 1, 1893, these offices had filled 38,352 positions out of 81,464 applications for situations, and 63,564 applications for help. The Labor Commissioner's Report for 1892 says: "In the communities in which the offices are located, many firms depend almost exclusively upon them in securing help, and thousands of employees could testify to their usefulness out of personal experience." For full reports of the working of these bureaus, see the Ohio Labor Bureau Reports for 1890, 1891, and 1892. It must be added that there are careful ob-

also established similar institutions with like beneficial results.

After everything else has been done, there will probably remain those who will have to be frequently employed by public authority. The experience of Teutonic countries shows that it is practicable to guarantee to every one a minimum subsistence; for in these countries it is a well-recognized principle that no one must be allowed to starve to death, and, as a last resort, food, clothing, and shelter must be furnished at public cost.

It is much better that subsistence should be furnished in return for work rather than without work. There is always plenty of work to be done. Care must be taken, however, not to furnish work under such conditions that the normal operations of private industry will thereby be impeded. The right to employment is one which is being more and more urged, and it cannot be indefinitely refused.[1]

The advanced reformers of Switzerland already demand that the right to employment shall be constitutionally guaranteed, and a sufficient number of signatures have been secured to a petition to compel the submission of the proposed amendment to the constitution to popular vote for decision.

servers in Ohio who do not so highly speak of these bureaus, and feel that there are important respects in which they could be improved.

[1] The city of Cincinnati has, in a measure, recognized this right. Citizens raised by voluntary contributions a considerable sum to provide work to those who needed it; and the city itself voted $135,000 to provide work, chiefly on the public parks, intrusting the selection of men to the "Associated Charities," Dr. P. W. Ayres, secretary. It has been found necessary to use only $75,000, and the city has received back a part of this expenditure in the value of the work performed.

It would be necessary, should the right be guaranteed, to provide public work-shops, and possibly public farms, to furnish employment. The example of New Zealand, to which reference has already been made, is most instructive.[1]

The further development of government credit in behalf of the individual is a reform calculated to improve our present industrial society. It is not necessary in this respect to take a radical departure, but simply to develop further institutions, which have been tried and approved by experience in many parts of the world. Public loan establishments, to furnish credit to the masses of the people, on pledge of personal property, have been established in France,[2] Germany, Switzerland, and elsewhere. These institutions protect the masses from the sharks who operate pawn-shops, and give to them the accommodation which ordinary banks furnish to men of larger resources. Private beneficence has made a feeble beginning in this country in this direction, and it is proposed to open loan shops in connection with one or two churches. Experience does not warrant us in anticipating any considerable results from private effort in this direction. New Zealand has, as we have already seen, furnished loans to encourage settlement of villages in the country, and favorable reports reach us in regard to the results achieved. Germany and other countries have also used government credit to some extent in behalf of the farming community,[3] and whatever can be safely and prudently done along this line must re-

[1] Article by A. G. Fradenburg in *The Outlook* for April 7, 1894.
[2] Significantly called *monts-de-piété*.
[3] New York State has been making loans to farmers for a generation and more.

ceive our commendation. Experience shows, however, that we must move very carefully in this direction, or the results will be ruinous. A sensible demand on the part of farmers' organizations would be that Congress should appoint a commission of experts, to investigate thoroughly the use of government credit in various countries and at different times, in behalf of the individual citizen, especially the farmer, and to make a full and complete report, in order that anything which is done should be based upon the lessons to be derived from actual experience.

Careful tariff reform, removing abuses now connected with the tariff, and especially removing anything like favoritism, can be recommended. This, however, is a less important question than many others which do not receive one-tenth part so much attention. In some respects, the tariff question of the United States may be compared with the Irish question in England, inasmuch as it diverts attention from practical improvement, and thus proves an obstacle to progress.

Financial reform, involving a readjustment of taxation in such manner that the burden of taxation shall be more fairly distributed, and that taxation shall involve a minimum of interference with industry, may be mentioned among practicable and desirable reforms.

Monetary reform, to which undue attention has been given by those interested in social reform, is important. What is desired is stability of values. A more ample circulating medium is needed, but every careful student of money feels that money should be international in its character. International bimetalism, which is practicable if adopted by the great nations of the earth, has been urged by many leading economists as the next step in monetary reform. It would not only give a more ample supply of money, but the use of both gold and silver would render international dealings easier, than when some countries use gold, and some silver, and when there is no common measure of value and medium of exchange. Unfortunately, the efforts to bring about an agreement among the nations in favor of international bimetalism have thus far proved anything but encouraging.

One of the requirements of a good monetary system could be secured, either directly by the government or by banking institutions. What is wanted is a flexibility in the monetary supply, so that it may answer the varying needs of an industrial community. The Imperial Bank of Germany has the right to supply money indefinitely, on payment of five per cent tax on its issues which exceed the amount regularly allowed, and this renders possible an expansion of money to answer special needs. The crisis of 1893 would not have proved so disastrous in the United States, if we had had a United States Bank with like power. Various plans have been elaborated for the improvement of our monetary and banking systems in the United States, but thus far it has not been found practicable to agree upon any one system. The more radical parties in the country have not elaborated any plans which have succeeded in gaining adherents among prudent men, even those most inclined to favor social reform.[1]

An extension and development of public property, if carefully carried out, would mean a considerable improvement in present conditions. Many suggestions for an extension of public property have already been offered. The ownership of forests by government is now a gener-

[1] Cf. Kinley's "Independent Treasury," Vol. I. of the Library of Economics and Politics.

ally recognized necessity; and fortunately, even in the United States, we are beginning to move in this direction. Public halls, conveniently located for popular meetings in cities, are demanded by wage-earners, and English cities have begun to comply with the demand to some extent. At present, meetings are frequently held in connection with beer halls and other places, where the consumption of intoxicating beverages is made to pay for the use of accommodations. Schoolhouses can be better utilized than at present. There is no reason why outside of school hours they should not subserve general social purposes, although care must be taken to provide guaranties that the property shall not be injured in any way.

The relation of person to property suggests a class of reforms. At present the aim seems to be to protect property rather than person, whereas person should receive chief protection, and there should be a development of personal rights having pecuniary significance. This applies to employers' liability and to laws designed to secure one in the enjoyment of one's reputation and good name.

Another measure, upon which a vote will be taken in Switzerland presently, is the organization of a medical service with a supply of medicines, as a department of government. The expenses of illness are one of the most serious burdens the poor have to bear; but it is questionable whether it is not better to develop other institutions, like insurance, to meet needs of this kind, and also to improve and extend hospitals and medical dispensaries along lines already approved by experience; and especially whether it is not better to endeavor to prevent illness by sanitary measures.

CHAPTER IX.

ADDITIONAL OPPORTUNITIES FOR PRIVATE EFFORTS.

THE reforms already mentioned have been of such a character that they must be brought about largely, although not exclusively, by public effort. There are many improvements which can be secured by private action. Independent individual attention is required to afford relief and help in cases which do not fall under general rules, and these are many. Social effort, whether of the state or of society, must proceed according to general principles, and its power is thus limited. There are those about us in society continually who can be helped individually, but for whom it would be extremely difficult to provide the assistance needed either by public action or by voluntary social action. We are taking it for granted that public authorities and societies do their full duty; but of course they fall far short of this high standard, and private effort must make up the deficiencies as well as it can. A peculiarly fruitful field for individual effort is found in co-operation with public authorities to secure an excellent administration of laws, and to build up public institutions. The private individual who has gifts as a leader of polite society can also use these gifts to extend the benefits of social culture, and to add a charm where it is too often wanting to social life.

Persons who have large means naturally have peculiar opportunities. They may use these means to assist in developing public schools of all sorts, public libraries, universities, art galleries, and the like. Several philanthropists are inclined to give to the public on condition of public co-operation. Mr. Andrew Carnegie has stated that he did not think it worth while to give to a city a public library unless the people of the city were willing to support it, in part at least, by taxation. Mr. Enoch Pratt required as a condition of his gift of a public library to Baltimore a substantial contribution on the part of the city. Examples of this kind are to be commended, as they encourage self-help and prevent the growth of a bad kind of paternalism, that is, the paternalism of private wealth. Similarly wise philanthropy will often prefer to make gifts to State universities, and thus encourage and develop a spirit of self-help. Art galleries and great schools of art could be advantageously founded by men of wealth, making it a condition that a part of the expenses should be defrayed by taxation.

The question is often raised whether individuals should not help wage-earners by an attempt to exercise control over consumption. It is frequently said that those who have sympathy with workingmen and working-women should not "buy cheap," and should not patronize "bargain counters." This recommendation is not one which can be indorsed. First, if people should cease trying to buy cheap, the result would be a discouragement of improvements. It is commendable to try to offer goods at a low price, and thus bring them within the reach of as many who need them as possible. In the second place, when one patronizes shops where high prices are charged, one has no guaranty whatever that those working for this shop will, on account of high prices, receive better remuneration. The most which could be done in this connection would be to patronize "union" shops,

OPPORTUNITIES FOR PRIVATE EFFORTS. 339

and to purchase "union-made" goods; for the trades unions secure at least a certain minimum of wages, and offer some protection to those who are in them. There has been a decided effort to secure popularity for "union labels." It is not, however, always practicable to buy union goods or to patronize union shops. The protection of the worker must be secured through control of production by factory legislation and the like, rather than through any individual attempt to control consumption.

When private efforts are associated, they can accomplish much more; for it must always be remembered that we are discussing social conditions, and that these are established by social action. Labor organizations have a field, although it is a limited one. All careful thinkers now recognize the inherent limitations in labor organizations. Many abuses are connected with them, and their efforts must always be partial; at the same time, they are indispensable. Altogether apart from a high educational value, they are necessary to enable the workers to combine their strength and to insure fair treatment, as the employer in any large establishment is so much stronger than the individual workman.

Profit sharing represents a desirable combination between employer and employee, and when carried out with a good intent on both sides, frequently produces excellent results. Profit sharing is especially well adapted to industry on a large scale, when the success of an undertaking depends in marked degree upon the peculiar skill and watchfulness on the part of the employee. Its field must, however, always be a limited one.[1]

Voluntary co-operation, both in production and consumption, has up to the present been able to conquer

[1] On this subject consult "Profit Sharing between Employer and Employee," by N. P. Gilman.

only a small share of the industrial field, but it has produced many beneficial effects, direct and indirect. The tendencies toward centralization of business have raised up new difficulties, which have impeded an extension of co-operation. It is naturally far more difficult for a large number of men to co-operate according to the voluntary system, than for a small number, and it is especially difficult if the number required in industrial establishments is one that fluctuates. At the same time, as the co-operative spirit, the spirit of mutual helpfulness, increases in intensity, we may anticipate that in a large number of cases the difficulties inherent in voluntary co-operation will in a large number of instances be overcome. Especially will a better education promote co-operation.

The farmers, who have already been helped by co-operation in the manufacture of butter and cheese in co-operative factories, and who have often advantageously combined their efforts for the purchase of goods, especially in the Patrons of Husbandry and other farmers' organizations, are able to use still further the advantages of co-operation; especially in the purchase and sale of commodities, also in the purchase of improved tools and stock, and in the introduction of scientific methods. Grape-growers in different parts of the country have entered into grape-growers' associations, in order to place their grapes on the market advantageously.

Fraternal societies, whose chief work has been mutual insurance, have accomplished a great deal, and under careful supervision by trained experts of government, as in New Zealand, are able to accomplish still more. No one who has not looked into the subject appreciates what they are doing in the United States and other countries already. It is scarcely an exaggeration to say that in parts of the South it is difficult to find a colored person who does not belong to some such society, and the relief which these societies afford explains the astonishingly small amount of pauperism which exists among the colored people; for it is astonishingly small when we remember that so short a time has passed since these people were slaves, and when we remember further how low, even now, is the condition of industrial development which they have reached. Unfortunately, the work of societies of this sort is greatly impaired by poor management. Generally speaking, there is no control over the insurance business of organizations of this kind by government in the United States, although our various commonwealths have extended their supervision over ordinary life insurance companies, which require it even less. Charity organization societies, with their friendly visitors and their careful control over relief given to the poor, to prevent fraud, have accomplished much, and deserve further encouragement. They are able to weed out a large proportion of all pauperism which exists, and would do so if properly assisted. The fact that, in cities where a large proportion of the people profess Christianity, it is so difficult to find the comparatively few friendly visitors needed, is a sad commentary upon the kind of Christianity taught in our churches.

Societies for the promotion of temperance have a well recognized field. Less well known are the beneficial effects of social or college settlements in the poorer parts of cities. These cultivate a spirit of neighborliness, beneficial alike to persons of means and culture living in the settlements, and to their less fortunate neighbors who need their leadership. It is hard to overestimate the good accomplished by a settlement like Hull House in Chicago. A very few persons, a mere handful, so to speak, have been able to influence beneficially an entire section of Chicago, numbering many thousands of human beings.[1]

Associated private effort becomes especially fruitful when it co-operates with public effort in the administration of law, and the building up of public institutions. This can be done by an enlightenment of public opinion, by inspection of institutions, by bringing about changes in legislation and administrative methods when these are needed, also by aiding the more ignorant and weaker portion of the community to secure their rights. The New York State Charities Aid Association [2] offers an example of a most useful society, which has secured the right of inspection of charitable institutions, prisons, etc.; which, by frequent visits, has improved very greatly the administration of public institutions designed for dependent and delinquent classes, and has recommended very beneficial changes in the laws. Among many other achievements this society has abolished the care of the insane by the counties, turning them over to the State, and has brought about an amelioration in the condition of that most unfortunate class, numbering some fifteen or twenty thousand persons.[3] The Bureau of Justice of

---

[1] A pamphlet on Hull House may be had by addressing Miss Jane Addams, 335 South Halsted Street, Chicago, Ill. Cf. also the chapter on that subject in Mr. W. T. Stead's work, "If Christ Came to Chicago."

[2] The secretary is Mr. Homer Folks, United Charities Building, Twenty-second Street and Fourth Avenue, New York City.

[3] Perhaps the Ohio system is still better than that which has been described. In Ohio the local Court of Common Pleas appoints a Board of County Visitors, consisting of three men and three women,

Chicago is an organization which offers the benefit of legal services to those who are ignorant of the law, or who are unable to secure their legal rights, and by comparatively small expenditure of time and money has accomplished noteworthy results.[1]

"Law and Order Leagues" are well known, and societies to improve legislation as a whole or in certain particulars have accomplished good results. Uniformity in legislation and simplification of legislation and legal processes are desirable. Under this head mention may be made of the Divorce Reform League.[2] Associated effort can accomplish much more than individual effort in the beneficial control of consumption. One of the methods is to boycott those who deserve such a punishment, — a dangerous proceeding which, unless carefully controlled, will work more harm than good, — and another is to issue "white lists" of those persons and firms who are to be commended for honest dealing, and especially for generous treatment of employees. But even associated effort has not, in this respect, been able to accomplish much. Attention must again be directed to the control of production rather than of consumption.

who have the right to visit all charitable and correctional institutions which spend public money in any way. Each board addresses its report to the court from which it receives its appointment, and also to the Board of State Charities. It is part of the duty of each judge to notify the board in his county when juveniles (under sixteen) are to be tried; and it is the duty of the board to be represented at the trial. The members of the board serve without pay.

[1] The annual reports of this society are most instructive. For these reports and other information the reader should apply to Joseph W. Errant, Esq., Agent and Attorney, Rooms 718 and 719, Garden City Block, Randolph Street and Fifth Avenue, Chicago, Ill.

[2] Rev. Samuel W. Dike, LL.D., secretary, Auburndale, Mass.

CHAPTER X.

POLITICAL REFORMS.

THE referendum and initiative, or imperative petition, as it is also called, and proportional representation, have already been mentioned as reforms advocated by socialists; but they are reforms which must meet the approval of those who desire far less radical changes. They receive and they deserve commendation from those who are to be classed among social reformers, as distinguished from socialists. They are of special importance in the United States, where legislative bodies so often betray their trust, and become subservient tools of great corporations and powerful private interests. The referendum and the initiative put legislation in the hands of the people, and give them as good legislation as they deserve. These measures do much to prevent corruption, because they make it possible to compel the submission of any proposed law to popular vote. The legislator who promises to give away valuable privileges can never be sure that, to use the phrase of the vulgar politician, "he will be able to deliver the goods."

The referendum and the initiative have, in Switzerland, been favorable to progressive conservatism, and nothing can be more desirable. Reforms have not proceeded so rapidly as many ardent reformers have desired, but, fortunately, progress has been continuous. When reforms are introduced by operation of the initiative and referendum, the people are ripe for them; or, if they do make a mistake, they are quick to correct it. The Swiss development has been superior to the constitutional development in the United States.¹

We, in our distrust of legislative bodies, have enlarged our constitutions unduly, and thus have restricted more and more the sphere of the legislature. At the same time, as our constitutions can be changed with difficulty, we have placed an increasing number of things entirely beyond our own control, and have thus weakened ourselves in the conflict with powerful private interests not similarly hampered. But this is not all. The result of the excessive development of constitutionalism has been to enlarge unduly the functions of the judiciary; and this has been encouraged by the fact that our judges have so generally been honest, upright, and able men. But it is not the function of the judges to represent the progressive element in society. They are rather a restraining force, and it is unfortunate for society to entrust to judges what are, in reality, legislative functions. The provisions of constitutions are more or less general, and it devolves upon the judges to say what they mean in concrete cases. The result is that the popular will is often thwarted. People, when voting upon a constitution, do not understand the full import of its provisions, and some of these provisions may have been inserted at the suggestion of special but powerful private interests, whose skilled attorneys have at once perceived their true import. If the masses wish an effective control over government, they must be able to decide upon concrete cases as they arrive. Government in accordance with general provisions to be interpreted by a few se-

¹ Cf. "State and Federal Government in Switzerland," by J. M. Vincent, Part I. chap. iv., and Part IV. chap. xiii.

lected individuals, is unfortunate for the development of popular rights, and a protection of public interests.[1]

The Swiss system enables the people to keep their hands upon the government at all times; and there is in Switzerland no great mass of constitutional law entirely beyond their reach. Under the referendum and the initiative, every law passed may be vetoed by the people, and any law may be proposed which a small fractional part of the population desires to see enacted. Another aspect of the question is of peculiar importance in the United States. One of the chief advantages of the referendum and initiative is that they would teach Americans to discuss measures more and men less. Our politics have an unfortunate tendency to become merely personal politics, and personal politics are apt to become petty and insignificant; in short, what American slang expressively designates as "peanut politics." When great measures become live questions good men will come to the front, whereas they now too often shrink from what seem to be merely personal contests for "spoils."

Proportional representation, on the other hand, by electing legislators and executive officers on general tickets, and giving to each one the right to cumulate his vote, so that in the district or State electing, let us say, ten congressmen, one could cast all his votes for a single congressman, makes it possible for any considerable minority of people to secure a representation in the law-making body. Legislative bodies under proportional representation

[1] It should hardly be necessary to caution the reader that this means the simplification, but not the abolition, of constitutions. The thought is that a more careful distinction should be made between constitutional and statute law, and that constitutional law should be restricted more nearly to the sphere assigned it by the founders of our republic.

thus become representative of all the people, and not of a fractional part of the people, as at present. Proportional representation is quite practicable, even in the largest country,[1] but there seem to be some difficulties in the way of carrying the initiative and referendum as far in a great country like the United States as in a small one like Switzerland. There is no reason, however, why, even in the largest countries, they should not be applied extensively. Certain classes of laws may be required to be submitted to the people, or, more accurately speaking, certain classes of bills, after passing the legislature, may be required to be submitted to the people; and, in case of other projects, submission may be required in case a considerable portion of the community demands it by officially attested petition.[2] The initiative can also be adapted to the conditions of a great country.

The Australian ballot has already proved beneficial in many American commonwealths, and this measure designed to purify the ballot must prove helpful to social reform.[3]

A "Corrupt Practices Act," like that which obtains in England, limiting expenses of candidates for office, and requiring complete accountability of political committees, with publication of accounts, may be heartily recommended.[4]

Civil service reform is of peculiar importance to those who desire social reform, but it has not been so urged

[1] Cf. J. R. Commons's "Social Reform and the Church."
[2] The referendum is now applied in a few instances in the United States. Frequently public debts cannot be incurred until they have been approved by popular vote.
[3] Cf. J. W. Sullivan's "Direct Legislation."
[4] Cf. Charles N. Gregory's "Corrupt Use of Money in Politics, and Laws for Its Prevention," published by the Historical and Political Science Association of the University of Wisconsin.

upon the wage-earning masses that they have appreciated its importance. Industrial reform has generally brought with it civil service reform, and it can scarcely fail to do so; but at the same time, the better the administration, the easier it would become to persuade people to accept social reforms which imply increase in the functions of government. Civil service reform has in the United States been considered only in its narrow aspects, and has thus failed to receive the support which naturally belongs to it. The use of examinations at the door of admission to the civil service can only be regarded as the first step in the improvement of administration. This must be followed by requiring special study and practical training for the various branches of the civil service. This is one of the conditions of peaceful progress. It is folly to suppose that the tasks demanded of men in public life can be met without the most careful training and long experience. Democracy does not mean that the first blundering fool one meets should be entrusted with the administration of a city involving annual expenditures of millions. But if it is to be successful, it does mean that the one who enters the public service should prepare himself therefor by protracted studies and by actual experience in subordinate offices. The conscientious man who would be a physician spares neither time nor expense to prepare himself to treat individual cases of disease; but the health of thousands upon thousands depends directly and indirectly upon the methods of municipal administration. The national government should have a civil academy, surpassing in equipment the military and naval academies by as much as civil administration is more important than the army and navy, in a country devoted to the arts of peace. Every State university should have, as its largest and best equipped department, the civil academy; and the few States of the Union without State universities should otherwise make provision for similar training.

The development of local self-government, bringing the government nearer to the people, is in line with the other social reforms mentioned, and renders the mechanism of government better adapted to the uses of the people. American cities are too dependent upon central legislative bodies; and, as a rule, one of them cannot take upon itself so simple a matter as the establishment of an electric lighting plant without first securing the consent of a central legislature. Decentralization of government and development of local self-government must be urged as one of the conditions of desirable social development.

CHAPTER XI.

CONCLUSION.

THE contrast between the program of social reform given in the present work, and that offered by the advocates of panaceas, is most marked. The reformer, who has his one remedy for all social evils, will have little patience with what he will regard as patchwork. He wishes us to go to the root of things and to reshape entirely some one great institution, claiming that then everything in the social world will be all that could be desired. At the same time, the advocate of a single reform, whether this be "free trade" or "single tax" or "land nationalization," has a position of vantage. He elaborates his reform in all its details, and concentrates attention upon that. Attention is divided, in the program of social reform presented in this work, among a multiplicity of reforms; and this may at first be thought a weakness, but careful reflection will show that it corresponds to the complexity of modern civilization.

Reforms must come from many different sources, and of thousands of agencies of genuine reform and progress not one can be spared. No one person will be in a position to take up all of the reforms which have been advocated and push them vigorously. One line of reform will interest one class of persons, and another line another class, and thus, working together more or less consciously, the progress of society will be secured.

What has been advocated is an ideal, and not something which can be speedily attained. Possibly this outline of reform contains in itself a strong argument against socialism, although not intended to do so. It shows, indeed, how long is the way we must travel before we can accomplish those desirable changes within the framework of existing society which even now suggest themselves.

One line of thought which has run through the entire treatment of practicable social reform is social solidarity. Men's interests are inextricably intertwined, and we shall never become truly prosperous so long as there is any class of the population materially and morally wretched. As a social body we can no more be in a sound condition while we have a submerged tenth, than a man can be whose arms or legs are suffering with a foul and corrupting disease. Whether we will or not, we must, in a manner, rejoice together and suffer together. The sooner the idea of social solidarity, which is not only a doctrine but also a real fact, is recognized in all its ramifications, the better it will be for us.

Perhaps an anxious reader feels concerned in regard to the claims of individuality, but it must be remembered that there is a wide distinction between individualism and individuality. Indeed, the two are opposed to each other. Man isolated and alone develops no individuality of value, but such individuality is developed only when he lives with and through his fellows. Giving up one's individualism means a growth in individuality. He who enters the marriage state, for example, gives up a portion of his individualism, but the life of the family promotes the growth of individuality. He who enters a church surrenders individualism and gains individuality.

He who lives in a highly developed society continually sacrifices individualism; but in and through society his individuality becomes vigorous.[1] Thus it is again true that he who saves his life shall lose it, and he who loses his life shall find it.

The way which we must travel is long and weary, and yet it is one which affords delight in the prospect of progress. Looking into the future we may contemplate a society with real, not merely nominal, freedom, to pursue the best; a society in which men shall work together for common purposes, and in which this wholesome co-operation shall take place largely through government, but through a government which has become less repressive and has developed its positive side. We have reason to believe that we shall yet see great national undertakings the property of the nation, and managed by the nation, through agents who appreciate the glory of true public service, and feel that it is God's work which they are doing, because church and state are as one. We may look forward to a society in which education, art, and literature shall be fostered by the nation, and in which federal government, commonwealth, local community, and individual citizens shall heartily cooperate for the advancement of civilization. We may anticipate a society in which the way to success shall be

---

[1] There are those who, strangely enough, seem to think that absence of government enterprise means individuality. We can find many towns in the United States where public enterprise is reduced to a minimum, and where life is dreary and uninteresting on account of the absence of individuality. On the other hand, if readers will reflect on cities and countries characterized by individuality, he will find that public undertakings are numerous and important in many of them; for example, let us take Boston as a city, and Germany as a country.

broadened, genuine merit appreciated, and social service rewarded. The coming of this society will mean the discouragement of great fortunes, the promotion of measures designed to increase the number enjoying a competence, and the reduction to its lowest terms of the chance element in the economic sphere, because that brings undeserved losses as well as unearned increment; and in removing the close connection which ought to exist between service and reward, weakens the springs of right conduct. This society will readjust taxation for social purposes, and will, by the taxation of bequests and inheritances and unearned incomes, more nearly equalize opportunities; and the best efforts of men will be more actively stimulated, because well directed effort will be more certain than now of reward. Individuals are thought of as working not merely in the service of government, but outside of government in material production, owning land and capital, yet with the individual element duly subordinated to the social, and without the power to coerce communities and reduce men by the thousands to degrading dependence. Without entertaining thoughts of a working-day of two or three hours, we may yet expect more leisure for the masses. On the other hand, with the perfection of the processes of material production, we may hope that an increasing proportion of men will be freed for the greater part of their lives from material production, and will have an opportunity to devote themselves to the higher pursuits of life. Men will, we may hope, act on their environment and improve it, and the improved environment will react on men favorably. We may anticipate an approximation of state and society as men improve, and we may hope that men outside of government will freely and voluntarily act with trained officers and experts in the service of government for the advancement of common interests. We may look forward to a society of men loving truth, continually progressing in goodness, and surrounded by an expanding beauty of subjugated nature.

APPENDIX.

APPENDIX I.

THE ERFURT SOCIAL DEMOCRATIC PROGRAM OF OCTOBER, 1891.[1]

THE economic development of industrial society tends inevitably to the ruin of small industries, which are based upon the workman's private ownership of the means of production. It separates him from these means of production, and converts him into a destitute member of the proletariat, whilst a comparatively small number of capitalists and great land-owners obtain a monopoly of the means of production.

Hand in hand with this growing monopoly goes the crushing out of existence of these shattered small industries by industries of colossal growth, the development of the tool into the machine, and a gigantic increase in the productiveness of human labor. But all the advantages of this revolution are monopolized by the capitalists and great land-owners. To the proletariat and to the rapidly sinking middle classes, the small tradesmen of the towns, and the peasant proprietors (*Bauern*), it brings an increasing uncertainty of existence, increasing misery, oppression, servitude, degradation, and exploitation (*Ausbeutung*).

---

[1] This is printed in the annual reports of the Proceedings of the Social Democratic Party of Germany, Verlag des *Vorwärts*, Berlin. The present translation is taken from the "Blue Book," giving the Report of the Royal Commission on Labor in Germany, published in London, 1893. For the sake of greater accuracy, however, a few changes have been made by the author.

Ever greater grows the mass of the proletariat, ever vaster the army of the unemployed, ever sharper the contrast between oppressors and oppressed, ever fiercer that war of classes between bourgeoisie and proletariat which divides modern society into two hostile camps, and is the common characteristic of every industrial country. The gulf between the propertied classes and the destitute is widened by the crises arising from capitalist production, which becomes daily more comprehensive and omnipotent, which makes universal uncertainty the normal condition of society, and which furnishes a proof that the forces of production have outgrown the existing social order, and that private ownership of the means of production has become incompatible with their full development and their proper application.

Private ownership of the means of production, formerly the means of securing his product to the producer, has now become the means of expropriating the peasant proprietors, the artisans, and the small tradesmen, and placing the non-producers, the capitalists, and large landowners in possession of the products of labor. Nothing but the conversion of capitalist private ownership of the means of production — the earth and its fruits, mines and quarries, raw material, tools, machines, means of exchange — into social ownership, and the substitution of socialist production, carried on by and for society in the place of the present production of commodities for exchange, can effect such a revolution that, instead of large industries and the steadily growing capacities of common production being, as hitherto, a source of misery and oppression to the classes whom they have despoiled, they may become a source of the highest well-being and of the most perfect and comprehensive harmony.

This social revolution involves the emancipation, not

APPENDIX I.

merely of the proletariat, but of the whole human race, which is suffering under existing conditions. But this emancipation can be achieved by the working class alone, because all other classes, in spite of their mutual strife of interests, take their stand upon the principle of private ownership of the means of production, and have a common interest in maintaining the existing social order.

The struggle of the working classes against capitalist exploitation must of necessity be a political struggle. The working classes can neither carry on their economic struggle nor develop their economic organization without political rights. They cannot effect the transfer of the means of production to the community without being first invested with political power.

It must be the aim of social democracy to give conscious unanimity to this struggle of the working classes, and to indicate the inevitable goal.

The interests of the working classes are identical in all lands governed by capitalist methods of production. The extension of the world's commerce and production for the world's markets make the position of the workman in any one country daily more dependent upon that of the workman in other countries. Therefore, the emancipation of labor is a task in which the workmen of all civilized lands have a share. Recognizing this, the Social Democrats of Germany feel and declare themselves at one with the workmen of every land, who are conscious of the destinies of their class.

The German Social Democrats are not, therefore, fighting for new class privileges and rights, but for the abolition of class government, and even of classes themselves, and for universal equality in rights and duties, without distinction of sex or rank. Holding these views, they are not merely fighting against the exploitation and oppression of the wage-earners in the existing social order, but against every kind of exploitation and oppression, whether directed against class, party, sex, or race.

Starting from these principles, the German Social Democrats demand, to begin with :[1] —

1. Universal, equal, and direct suffrage by ballot, in all elections, for all subjects of the Empire over twenty years of age, without distinction of sex. Proportional representation, and, until this system has been introduced, fresh division of electoral districts by law after each census. Two years duration of the legislature. Holding of elections on a legal day of rest. Payment of the representatives elected. Removal of all restrictions upon political rights, except in the case of persons under age.

2. Direct legislation by the people by means of the right of initiative and of veto. Self-government by the people in empire, state, province, and commune. Election of magistrates by the people, with the right of holding them responsible. Annual vote of the taxes.

3. Universal military education. Substitution of militia for a standing army. Decision by the popular representatives of questions of peace and war. Decision of all international disputes by arbitration.

4. Abolition of all laws which restrict or suppress free expression of opinion and the right of meeting or association.

5. Abolition of all laws which place the woman, whether in a private or a public capacity, at a disadvantage as compared with the man.

6. Declaration that religion is a private matter. Abolition of all expenditure from public funds upon ecclesiastical and religious objects. Ecclesiastical and religious bodies are to be regarded as private associations which order their affairs independently.

[1] That is, of the present State.

7. Secularization of education. Compulsory attendance at public national schools. Free education, free supply of educational apparatus, and free maintenance to children in schools, and to such pupils, male and female, in higher educational institutions, as are judged to be fitted for further education.

8. Free administration of the law and free legal assistance. Administration of the law by judges elected by the people. Appeal in criminal cases. Compensation to persons accused, imprisoned, or condemned unjustly. Abolition of capital punishment.

9. Free medical assistance, and free supply of remedies. Free burial of the dead.

10. Graduated income and property tax to meet all public expenses, which are to be met by taxation. Self-assessment. Succession duties, graduated according to the extent of the inheritance and the degree of relationship. Abolition of all indirect taxation, customs duties, and other economic measures, which sacrifice the interests of the community to the interests of a privileged minority.

For the protection of labor, the German Social Democrats also demand to begin with: —

1. An effective national and international system of protective legislation on the following principles: —

    a. The fixing of a normal working day, which shall not exceed eight hours.

    b. Prohibition of the employment of children under fourteen.

    c. Prohibition of night work, except in those branches of industry which, from their nature and for technical reasons or for reasons of public welfare, require night work.

    d. An unbroken rest of at least thirty-six (36) hours for every workman every week.

    e. Prohibition of the truck system.

2. Supervision of all industrial establishments, together with the investigations and regulation of the conditions of labor in the town and country by an Imperial labor department, district labor bureaus, and chambers of labor. A thorough system of industrial sanitary regulation.

3. Legal equality of agricultural laborers and domestic servants with industrial laborers; repeal of the laws concerning masters and servants.

4. Confirmation of the rights of association.

5. The taking over by the Imperial government of the whole system of workmen's insurance, though giving the workmen a certain share in its administration.

APPENDIX II.

BASIS OF THE FABIAN SOCIETY.

THE Fabian Society consists of socialists.

It therefore aims at the reorganization of society by the emancipation of land and industrial capital from individual and class ownership, and the vesting of them in the community for the general benefit. In this way only can the natural and acquired advantages of the country be equitably shared by the whole people.

The Society accordingly works for the extinction of private property in land, and of the consequent individual appropriation, in the form of rent, of the price paid for permission to use the earth, as well as for the advantages of superior soils and sites.

The Society, further, works for the transfer to the community of the administration of such industrial capital as can conveniently be managed socially. For, owing to the monopoly of the means of production in the past, industrial inventions and the transformation of surplus income into capital have mainly enriched the proprietary class, the worker being now dependent on that class for leave to earn a living.

If these measures be carried out, without compensation (though not without such relief to expropriated individuals as may seem fit to the community), rent and interest will be added to the reward of labor, the idle class now living on the labor of others will necessarily disappear, and practical equality of opportunity will be maintained by the spontaneous action of economic forces with much less interference with personal liberty than the present system entails.

For the attainment of these ends the Fabian Society looks to the spread of socialist opinions, and the social and political changes consequent thereon. It seeks to promote these by the general dissemination of knowledge as to the relation between the individual and society in its economic, ethical, and political aspects.

The work of the Fabian Society takes, at present, the following forms: —

1. Meetings for the discussion of questions connected with socialism.
2. The further investigation of economic problems, and the collection of facts contributing to their elucidation.
3. The issue of publications containing information on social questions, and arguments relating to socialism.
4. The promotion of socialist lectures and debates in other societies and clubs.
5. The representation of the society in public conferences and discussions on social questions.

The members are divided into local groups, are pledged to take part according to their abilities and opportunities in the general work of the Society, especially as regards their own localities, and although there is no compulsory subscription, are expected to contribute annually to the Society's funds. The amount of each member's subscription is known only to the executive committee.

The Society seeks recruits from all ranks, believing that not only those who suffer from the present system, but also many who are themselves enriched by it, recognize its evils and would welcome a remedy.

The Society meets for lectures and discussions on the first and third Fridays in the month, at eight P.M.

APPENDIX III.

PROGRAM OF THE SOCIAL-DEMOCRATIC FEDERATION.

(As revised at the Annual Conference held at Burnley, August 6th and 7th, 1893.)

OBJECT.

THE socialization of the means of production, distribution, and exchange, to be controlled by a democratic state in the interests of the entire community, and the complete emancipation of labor from the domination of capitalism and landlordism, with the establishment of social and economic equality between the sexes.

PROGRAM.

1. All officers or administrators to be elected by equal direct adult suffrage, and to be paid by the community.

2. Legislation by the people in such wise that no project of law shall become legally binding till accepted by the majority of the people.

3. The abolition of a standing army, and the establishment of a national citizen force; the people to decide on peace or war.

4. All education, higher no less than elementary, to be compulsory, secular, industrial, and gratuitous for all alike.

5. The administration of justice to be gratuitous for all members of society.

6. The land, with all the mines, railways, and other means of transit, to be declared and treated as collective or common property.

7. The means of production, distribution, and exchange to be declared and treated as collective or common property.

8. The production and distribution of wealth to be regulated by society in the common interests of all its members.

PALLIATIVES.

As measures called for to palliate the evils of our existing society, the Social-Democratic Federation urges for immediate adoption:—

The compulsory construction of healthy dwellings for the people, such dwellings to be let at rents to cover the cost of construction and maintenance alone.

Free secular and technical education, compulsory upon all classes, together with free maintenance for the children in all board schools.

Eight hours or less to be the normal working day fixed in all trades and industries, by legislative enactment, or not more than forty-eight hours per week, penalties to be inflicted for any infringement of this law.

Cumulative taxation upon all incomes exceeding £300 a year.

State appropriation of railways; municipal ownership and control of gas, electric light, and water supplies; the organization of tramway and omnibus services, and similar monopolies in the interests of the entire community.

The extension of the post-office savings bank, which shall absorb all private institutions that derive a profit from operations in money or credit.

Repudiation of the national debt.

Nationalization of the land, and organization of agricultural and industrial armies under state or municipal control on co-operative principles.

As means for the peaceable attainment of these objects the Social-Democratic Federation advocates: —

Payment of members of parliament and all local bodies and official expenses of election out of the public funds. Adult suffrage. Annual parliaments. Proportional representation. Second ballot. Abolition of the monarchy and the House of Lords. Disestablishment and disendowment of all state churches. Extension of the powers of county councils. The establishment of district councils. Legislative independence for all parts of the Empire.

APPENDIX IV.

MANIFESTO OF THE JOINT COMMITTEE OF SOCIALIST BODIES (OF ENGLAND).

THERE is a growing feeling at the present time that, in view of the increasing number of socialists in Great Britain, an effort should be made to show that, whatever differences may have arisen between them in the past, all who can fairly be called socialists are agreed in their main principles of thought and action.

This is the more hopeful, since, though much has been made of those differences by the opponents of socialism, it is safe to say that they have been rather of less than more importance than similar disputes of the early days of great movements, which have afterwards become solid and irresistible. There has, indeed, been constant cooperation in propagandist work between the individual members of different organizations, and occasional cooperation between the organizations in political emergencies; but more than this is now needed if we are to make a serious advance in the work of gathering together and directing the great body of thought and feeling which is setting towards socialism.

Meanwhile, the necessity for the development of a new social order is getting more obvious to all thinking people, and without the growing aspirations towards socialism the outlook of modern civilization would be hopeless.

The vigorous propaganda which has been carried on for the last twelve years, and the complete change in the attitude of the working classes and the public generally towards socialism, could not but attract the notice, and, perhaps, excite the anxiety, of the politicians of the possessing classes; but they have shown hitherto that they have lacked both the will and the power to do anything effective towards meeting the evils engendered by our present system. In spite of factory acts and factory inspectors, in spite of sanitary legislation and royal commissions, the condition of the working people is, relatively to the increased wealth of the country, worse than it was twenty years ago. Children are still growing up among such surroundings, and so insufficiently nourished, that health and strength are for them an impossibility; dangerous and unwholesome trades, inflicting hideous diseases on those who work at them, are still carried on by the capitalists with impunity; over-crowding, accompanied by increasing rents, is the rule rather than the exception in all our great cities.

At the same time, the great and growing depression in the most vital of industries, agriculture, tends to drive the people more and more from the country into the towns, while it so narrows the field from which healthy and vigorous industrial recruits have been drawn in the past, that the physical deterioration of our city population is more severely felt than ever before.

Moreover, the question of the unemployed is more pressing to-day than at any recent period. The incapacity of the capitalist class to handle the machinery of production without injury to the community has been demonstrated afresh by the crisis of 1890, itself following upon a very short period of inflation; since which time every department of trade and industry has suffered from lack of initiative, and want of confidence and ability among these "organizers of labor." As a result, the numbers of the unemployed have increased rapidly; the prospect of any improvement is still remote; and the stereotyped official assurance that there is no exceptional distress only emphasizes the fact that it is prosperity, not distress, which is exceptional. Indeed, the greatest "prosperity" possible under the present system could only lessen the mass of those without occupation, and bring them down to a number manageable by the employers. Meantime, small improvements, made in deference to the ill-formulated demands of the workers, though for a time they seem almost a social revolution to men ignorant of their own resources and of their capacity for enjoyment, will not really raise the condition of the whole people.

In short, the capitalist system, by which we mean the established plan of farming out our national industries in private property lots, and trusting to the greed of the owners, and the competition between them, to ensure their productive use, is the only arrangement possible in a society not organized enough to administer its own industry as a national concern. This shiftless method has, indeed, kept the shop open, so to speak, but at a frightful cost in human degradation, as might have been expected from its basis. All the investigations undertaken with a view to convicting socialists of exaggeration and one-sidedness in their attacks upon it, have shown that the facts are worse than any socialist dared to surmise, and that half a century of ameliorative regulation by means of factory legislation and the like has failed to weaken the force of former exposures of capitalism.

Among recent anti-socialist statisticians, Mr. Robert Giffen has been led by his own counter-blast to socialism into the exclamation, "That no one can contemplate the present condition of the masses without desiring something like a revolution for the better." And the facts as to London poverty, laid bare by Mr. Charles Booth, dispose of the possibility of leaving things as they are; although Mr. Booth, who is a conservative in politics, undertook his great inquiry expressly to confute what he then thought to be socialist over-statements. The horrible revelations concerning English home-life, made by the Society for the Prevention of Cruelty to Children, have effectually dispelled the illusion that the cruelty and selfishness of the factory and mine have not infected the household, or that society can safely abandon its children to irresponsible private ownership, any more than its land and capital.

Under these circumstances of a continued degradation of the really useful part of the population — a consequence as inherent in the present system of ownership as it was in the system of chattel slavery — the need for a new social order is obvious. Some constructive social theory is asked for, and none is offered except the feudal or Tory theory, which is incompatible with democracy; the Manchester or Whig theory, which has broken down in practice; and the Socialist theory. It is, therefore, opportune to remind the public once more of what socialism means to those who are working for the transformation of our present unsocialist state into a collectivist republic, and who are entirely free from the illusion that the amelioration or "moralization" of the conditions of capitalist private property can do away with the necessity for abolishing it. Even those readjustments of industry and administration which are socialist in form will not be permanently useful, unless the whole state is merged into an organized commonwealth. Municipalization, for instance, can only be accepted as socialism on the condition of its forming a part of national, and, at last, of international socialism, in which the workers of all nations, while adopting within the borders of their own countries those methods which are rendered necessary by their historic development, can federate upon a common basis of the collective ownership of the great means and instruments of the creation and distribution of wealth, and thus break down national animosities by the solidarity of human interest throughout the civilized world.

On this point all socialists agree. Our aim, one and all, is to obtain for the whole community complete ownership and control of the means of transport, the means of manufacture, the mines, and the land. Thus we look to put an end forever to the wage-system, to sweep away all distinctions of class, and eventually to establish national and international communism on a sound basis.

To this end it is imperative on all members of the socialist party to gather together their forces in order to formulate a definite policy, and force on its general acceptance.

But here we must repudiate both the doctrines and tactics of anarchism. As socialists we believe that those doctrines and the tactics necessarily resulting from them, though advocated as revolutionary by men who are honest and single-minded, are really reactionary both in theory and practice, and tend to check the advance of our cause. Indeed, so far from hampering the freedom of the individual, as anarchists hold it will, socialism will foster that full freedom which anarchism would inevitably destroy.

As to the means for the attainment of our end, in the first place we socialists look for our success to the increasing and energetic promulgation of our views amongst the whole people, and next, to the capture and transformation of the great social machinery. In any case the people have increasingly at hand the power of dominating and controlling the whole political, and through the political, the social forces of the empire.

The first step towards transformation and re-organization must necessarily be in the direction of the limitation of class robbery, and the consequent raising of the standard of life for the individual. In this direction certain measures have been brought within the scope of practical politics; and we name them as having been urged and supported originally and chiefly by socialists, and advocated by them, still, not, as above said, as solutions of social wrongs, but as tending to lessen the evils of the existing *régime;* so that individuals of the useful classes, having more leisure and less anxiety, may be able to turn their attention to the only real remedy for their position of inferiority — to wit, the supplanting of the present state by a society of equality of condition. When this great change is completely carried out, the genuine liberty of all will be secured by the free play of social forces, with much less coercive interference than the present system entails.

The following are some of the measures spoken of above : —

An Eight Hours Law.
Prohibition of Child Labor for Wages.
Free Maintenance of all Necessitous Children.
Equal Payment of Men and Women for Equal Work.
An Adequate Minimum Wage for all Adults Employed in the Government and Municipal Services, or in any Monopolies, such as Railways, enjoying State Privileges.
Suppression of all Sub-contracting and Sweating.
Universal Suffrage for all Adults, Men, and Women alike.
Public Payment for all Public Service.

The inevitable economic development points to the direct absorption by the state, as an organized democracy, of monopolies which have been granted to, or constituted by, companies, and their immediate conversion into public services. But the railway system is, of all the monopolies, that which could be most easily and conveniently so converted. It is certain that no attempt to reorganize industry on the land can be successful so long as the railways are in private hands, and excessive rates of carriage are charged. Recent events have hastened on the socialist solution of this particular question, and the disinclination of boards of directors to adopt improvements which would cheapen freight, prove that in this, as in other cases, English capitalists, far from being enlightened by competition, are blinded by it even to their own interests.

In other directions the growth of combination, as with banks, shipping companies, and huge limited liability concerns, organized both for production and distribution, show that the time is ripe for socialist organization. The economic development in this direction is already so far advanced that the socialization of production and distribution on the economic side of things can easily and at once begin, when the people have made up their minds to overthrow privilege and monopoly. In order to effect the change from capitalism to co-operation, from unconscious revolt to conscious re-organization, it is necessary that we socialists should constitute ourselves into a distinct political party with definite aims, marching steadily along our own highway, without reference to the convenience of political factions.

We have thus stated the main principles and the broad strategy on which, as we believe, all socialists may combine to act with vigor. The opportunity for deliberate and determined action is now always with us, and local autonomy in all local matters will still leave the fullest outlet for national and international socialism. We, therefore, confidently appeal to all socialists to sink their individual crotchets in a business-like endeavor to realize in our own day that complete communization of industry for which the economic forms are ready, and the minds of the people are almost prepared.

    ALFRED BEASLEY, TOUZEAU PARRIS,
    SAMUEL BULLOCK, HARRY QUELCH,
    J. E. DOBSON, H. B. ROGERS,
    W. S. DEMATTOS, GEO. BERNARD SHAW,
    W. H. GRANT, WILLIE UTLEY,
    H. M. HYNDMAN, SIDNEY WEBB,
    WILLIAM MORRIS, ERNEST E. WILLIAMS,
       SYDNEY OLIVIER,

The Joint Committee of the Social-Democratic Federation, the Fabian Society, and the Hammersmith Socialist Society.

Signed on behalf of the undermentioned bodies :—

H. W. LEE, *Secretary Social-Democratic Federation*, 337, Strand, W. C.

EDWARD R. PEASE, *Secretary Fabian Society*, 276, Strand, W. C.

EMERY WALKER, *Secretary Hammersmith Socialist Society*, Kelmscott House, Hammersmith.

APPENDIX V.

SOCIALIST LABOR PARTY OF THE UNITED STATES.

Platform.

THE Socialist Labor Party of the United States, in convention assembled, reasserts the inalienable right of all men to life, liberty, and the pursuit of happiness.

With the founders of the American republic we hold that the purpose of government is to secure every citizen in the enjoyment of this right; but in the light of our social conditions we hold, furthermore, that no such right can be exercised under a system of inequality, essentially destructive of life, of liberty, and of happiness.

With the founders of this republic we hold that the true theory of politics is that the machinery of government must be owned and controlled by the whole people; but in the light of our industrial development we hold, furthermore, that the true theory of economics is that the machinery of production must likewise belong to the people in common.

To the obvious fact that our despotic system of economics is the direct opposite of our democratic system of politics, can plainly be traced the existence of a privileged class, the corruption of government by that class, the alienation of public property, public franchises, and public functions to that class, and the abject dependence of the mightiest of nations upon that class.

Again, through the perversion of democracy to the ends of plutocracy, labor is robbed of the wealth which it alone produces, is denied the means of self-employment, and, by compulsory idleness in wage slavery, is even deprived of the necessaries of life.

Human power and natural forces are thus wasted, that the plutocracy may rule.

Ignorance and misery, with all their concomitant evils, are perpetuated, that the people may be kept in bondage.

Science and invention are diverted from their humane purpose to the enslavement of women and children.

Against such a system the Socialist Labor Party once more enters its protest. Once more it reiterates its fundamental declaration that private property in the natural sources of production and in the instruments of labor is the obvious cause of all economic servitude and political dependence; and

Whereas, the time is fast coming when, in the natural course of social evolution, this system, through the destructive action of its failures and crises on the one hand, and the constructive tendencies of its trusts and other capitalistic combinations on the other hand, shall have worked out its own downfall; therefore be it

Resolved, that we call upon the people to organize with a view to the substitution of the Co-operative Commonwealth for the present state of planless production, industrial war, and social disorder, a commonwealth in which every worker shall have the free exercise and full benefit of his faculties, multiplied by all the modern factors of civilization.

We call upon them to unite with us in a mighty effort to gain by all practicable means the political power.

In the meantime, and with a view to immediate improvement in the condition of labor, we present the following "Demands."

Social Demands.

1. Reduction of the hours of labor in proportion to the progress of production.

2. The United States shall obtain possession of the railroads, canals, telegraphs, telephones, and all other means of public transportation and communication; but no employee shall be discharged for political reasons.

3. The municipalities to obtain possession of the local railroads, ferries, water-works, gas-works, electric plants, and all industries requiring municipal franchises; but no employee shall be discharged for political reasons.

4. The public lands to be declared inalienable. Revocation of all land grants to corporations or individuals, the conditions of which have not been complied with.

5. Legal incorporation by the States of local trade unions which have no national organization.

6. The United States to have the exclusive right to issue money.

7. Congressional legislation providing for the scientific management of forests and waterways, and prohibiting the waste of the natural resources of the country.

8. Inventions to be free to all; the inventors to be remunerated by the nation.

9. Progressive income tax and tax on inheritances; the smaller incomes to be exempt.

10. School education of all children under 14 years of age to be compulsory, gratuitous, and accessible to all by public assistance in meals, clothing, books, etc., where necessary.

11. Repeal of all pauper, tramp, conspiracy, and sumptuary laws. Unabridged right of combination.

12. Official statistics concerning the condition of labor. Prohibition of the employment of children of school age, and the employment of female labor in occupations detrimental to health or morality. Abolition of the convict labor contract system.

13. Employment of the unemployed by the public authorities (county, city, State and nation).

14. All wages to be paid in lawful money of the United States. Equalization of women's wages with those of men where equal service is performed.

15. Laws for the protection of life and limb in all occupations, and an efficient employers' liability law.

Political Demands.

1. The people to have the right to propose laws and to vote upon all measures of importance, according to the referendum principle.

2. Abolition of the veto power of the Executive (national, State and municipal), wherever it exists.

3. Municipal self-government.

4. Direct vote and secret ballots in all elections. Universal and equal right of suffrage without regard to color, creed, or sex. Election days to be legal holidays. The principle of proportional representation to be introduced.

5. All public officers to be subject to recall by their respective constituencies.

6. Uniform civil and criminal law throughout the United States. Administration of justice to be free of charge. Abolition of capital punishment.

APPENDIX VI.

NATIONALIST DECLARATION OF PRINCIPLES.

THE principle of the brotherhood of humanity is one of the eternal truths that govern the world's progress on lines which distinguish human nature from brute nature.

The principle of competition is simply the application of the brutal law of the survival of the strongest and most cunning.

Therefore, so long as competition continues to be the ruling factor in our industrial system, the highest development of the individual cannot be reached, the loftiest aims of humanity cannot be realized.

No truth can avail unless practically applied. Therefore, those who seek the welfare of man must endeavor to suppress the system founded on the brute principle of competition, and put in its place another based on the nobler principle of association.

But, in striving to apply this nobler and wiser principle to the complex conditions of modern life, we advocate no sudden or ill-considered changes; we make no war upon individuals; we do not censure those who have accumulated immense fortunes simply by carrying to a logical end the false principle on which business is now based.

The combinations, trusts, and syndicates of which the people at present complain demonstrate the practicability of our basic principle of association. We merely seek to push this principle a little further, and have all industries operated in the interest of all by the nation — the people organized — the organic unity of the whole people.

The present industrial system proves itself wrong by the immense wrongs it produces; it proves itself absurd by the immense waste of energy and material which is admitted to be its concomitant. Against this system we raise our protest: for the abolition of the slavery it has wrought and would perpetuate, we pledge our best efforts.

APPENDIX VII.

SOCIETY OF CHRISTIAN SOCIALISTS.[1]

Declaration of Principles.

Adopted in Boston, April 15, 1889.

To exalt the principle that all rights and powers are gifts of God, not for the receiver's use only, but for the benefit of all; to magnify the oneness of the human family, and to lift mankind to the highest plane of privilege, we band ourselves together under the name of Christian Socialists.

I. We hold that God is the source and guide of all human progress, and we believe that all social, political, and industrial relations should be based on the Fatherhood of God and the Brotherhood of Man, in the spirit and according to the teachings of Jesus Christ.

II. We hold that the present commercial and industrial system is not thus based, but rests rather on economic individualism, the results of which are: —

---

[1] While this society no longer exists as a formal organization, this Declaration of Principles may be taken as a fairly accurate expression of the general drift of opinion of those persons in the United States *who call themselves* Christian socialists. The former secretary of this society, the Rev. W. D. P. Bliss of Roslindale, Mass., still publishes *The Dawn*, which was its organ, and still advocates Christian socialism. Mr. Bliss writes, "Its principles are still spreading." The expression, "Who call themselves Christian socialists," is used, because men of all shades of opinion *are called by others* Christian socialists.

APPENDIX VII.

1. That the natural resources of the earth and the mechanical inventions of man are made to accrue disproportionately to the advantage of the few instead of the many.
2. That production is without general plan, and commercial and industrial crises are thereby precipitated.
3. That the control of business is rapidly concentrating in the hands of a dangerous plutocracy, and the destinies of the masses of wage-earners are becoming increasingly dependent on the will and resources of a narrowing number of wage-payers.
4. That large occasion is thus given for the moral evils of mammonism, recklessness, overcrowding, intemperance, prostitution, crime.

III. We hold that united Christianity must protest against a system so based, and productive of such results, and must demand a reconstructed social order, which, adopting some method of production and distribution that starts from organized society as a body, and seeks to benefit society equitably in every one of its members, shall be based on the Christian principle that "We are members one of another."

IV. While recognizing the present dangerous tendency of business towards combinations and trusts, we yet believe that the economic circumstances which call them into being will necessarily result in the development of such a social order, which, with the equally necessary development of individual character, will be at once true socialism and true Christianity.

V. Our objects, therefore, as Christian Socialists, are : —

1. To show that the aim of socialism is embraced in the aim of Christianity.

2. To awaken members of Christian churches to the fact that the teachings of Jesus Christ lead directly to some specific form or forms of socialism; that, therefore, the Church has a definite duty upon this matter, and must, in simple obedience to Christ, apply itself to the realization of the social principles of Christianity.

VI. We invite all who can subscribe to this declaration to active co-operation with us, and we urge the formation of similar fellowships in other places throughout the land.

APPENDIX VIII.

PLATFORM OF CENTRAL LABOR UNION OF CLEVELAND, OHIO.[1]

National Issues.

1. ABOLITION of national banks, and substituting legal tender treasury notes for them. Issue of all money direct by the government. Establishment of postal deposit and savings banks.

2. Prohibition of alien ownership of land and of gambling in stocks, etc.

3. Adoption of a constitutional amendment requiring the election of President and Vice-President by the direct vote of the people. Also providing for election of United States Senators by direct vote of the people.

4. Government ownership of all railroads, telegraphs, and telephone lines, and means of communication and transportation.

5. Thorough reform of the judiciary laws.

6. Abolition of all indirect taxes.

7. Abolition of contract system in public works.

8. Rigid enforcement of eight-hour law in all public departments. Equal pay for equal service for men and women.

---

[1] This platform is selected from many which suggest themselves, as one indicating, as well as any other, the tendencies of thought of American labor organizations. This central labor union issues one of the most ably conducted labor newspapers in the country, the Cleveland *Citizen,* which is at the same time the official organ of the Ohio State Trades and Labor Assembly.

9. Adoption of the initiative and of the referendum, i.e., that all laws passed by the legislative bodies be referred to the electors for ratification or rejection at the ensuing elections.

State Issues.

1. Abolition of capital punishment.
2. Sanitary inspection of mines, factories and dwellings, and all conditions of labor.
3. Taxation of land values, irrespective of improvements.
4. Abolition of contract prison labor.
5. Prohibition of child labor under sixteen years.
6. Payment of wages in lawful money, and abolition of truck pay.

Municipal Issues.

1. Municipal service wholly divorced from partisan politics. Tenure of office during good behavior, and promotion for meritorious service.
2. Municipal ownership of gas and electric light plants, telephones, and all street railroads; all municipal franchises to be owned and operated by the municipality in the interest of the people.
3. Eight-hour service for all municipal employees.
4. All municipal work to be performed directly by the municipality, without intervention of contractors.
5. Payment of wages weekly, and equal pay to women for equal work performed with men.
6. Revision and simplification of the municipal code.
7. Thorough revision and equalization of salaries of public officials.

APPENDIX IX.

GROWTH OF THE SOCIAL DEMOCRATIC PARTY OF GERMANY SINCE THE FOUNDING OF THE GERMAN EMPIRE, AS SHOWN IN THE IMPERIAL ELECTION RETURNS. WITH A CHART SHOWING THE VOTES RECEIVED BY THE FOUR LARGEST POLITICAL PARTIES.

ELECTION IN	TOTAL NUMBER OF SOCIAL DEMOCRATIC VOTES.	PERCENTAGE OF VOTES OF SOCIAL DEMOCRATIC PARTY.	MEMBERS ELECTED.	VOTES CAST FOR EACH MEMBER.
1871	124,655	3.	2	62,327
1874	351,952	6.8	9	39,106
1877	493,288	9.1	12	41,107
1878	437,158	7.6	9	48,573
1881	311,961	6.1	12	25,997
1884	549,990	9.7	24	22,916
1887	763,128	10.1	11	69,375
1890	1,427,298	19.7	35 [1]	40,780
1893	1,876,738	23.3	44	40,608 [2]

[1] In the by-election in the 22d district of Saxony, held in 1892, the 36th member was elected.

[2] The above table is taken from Braun's "Die Parteien des Deutschen Reichstages," Stuttgart, 1893.

Growth of the Social Democratic Party in the leading cities of Germany.

PLACE.	1878.	1890.	1893.
Hamburg	29,629	67,303	70,553
Breslau	13,065	21,555	26,205
Munich	5,259	28,218	29,907
Dresden	17,303	25,079	29,455
Leipzig	5,822	12,921	11,784
Cologne	2,189	10,646	12,093
Magdeburg	6,235	17,261	16,633
Frankfurt am Main	4,080	12,663	13,482
Königsberg	1,108	12,370	10,964
Hanover	6,588	15,789	19,538
Stuttgart	4,136	10,446	13,340
Bremen	6,304	14,843	14,572
Düsseldorf	486	8,228	9,367
Nüremberg	10,162	17,045	18,015
Danzig	114	3,525	4,265
Strassburg	141	4,773	6,206
Chemnitz	9,809	24,641	23,296
Elberfeld-Barmen	11,325	18,473	19,005
Altona	11,662	19,533	20,448
Stettin	914	7,759	9,586
Aix-la-Chapelle	909	1,744	3,029
Krefeld	467	3,030	3,730
Brunswick	7,876	13,621	15,470
Halle	1,046	12,808	12,991
Lübeck	1,588	6,393	7,339

Growth of Social Democracy in Berlin.

YEAR.	VOTES CAST.	MEMBERS ELECTED.
1871	2,058	0
1874	11,279	0
1877	31,522	2
1878	56,147	1
1881	30,178	0
1884	68,535	2
1887	93,335	2
1890	126,317	2
1893	151,122	5

APPENDIX IX. 389

Districts, while in a "minor state of siege" under the "Socialist Law," voted as follows: —

ELECTORAL DISTRICT.	1878.	1890.	1893.
Niederbarnim	2,775	13,362	17,044
Charlottenburg	4,763	19,169	31,424
Potsdam-Spandau	—	3,977	10,140
Harburg	1,763	6,860	9,055
Ottensen-Pinneberg	5,452	10,820	13,097
Lauenburg	347	2,072	3,287
Leipzig (district)	11,253	30,127	33,349
Offenbach am Main	5,557	10,343	11,063
Spremberg	1,242	5,610	6,542

Growth of Social Democracy in the agricultural districts.

PROVINCE.	1878.	1890.	1893.
Brandenburg	15,009	83,331	128,606
Pomerania	1,069	20,631	37,308
Mecklenburg	2,070	28,235	32,220
Bavaria	22,532	101,100	125,952
Alsace-Lorraine	141	19,157	44,885 [1]

NOTE.

In the general election to the State Legislature of Saxony, in 1891, 36,000 votes were cast by social democrats, over one-third of the total number cast, 97,000. (Vide: Wolf's Sozialismus, p. 203.)

Current Publications of Social Democratic Party:

    31 daily newspapers.
    41 weeklies and semi-weeklies.
    1 scientific review.
    1 family magazine.
    2 humorous publications.
    55 trade journals.[2]

[1] The above tables are taken from "Protokoll . . . der Sozialdemokratischen Partei Deutschlands," Berlin, 1893; also, in British Foreign Reports of Royal Commission on Labor, for Germany, London, 1893.

[2] Vide: *The People*, Dec. 3, 1893.

APPENDIX X.

SOCIALISM IN FRANCE.[1]

A.

General Statement.

THE organization of the socialist party in France was really begun in 1871, after the Commune. Blanqui was then its chief, but it had very few adherents. Elections in France show that the socialists have now at least 900,000 adherents, representing different schools. The entire socialistic party may be divided into five groups or subdivisions. They are the following: —

1. *Possibilists.* This group is divided into two subgroups, *a.* the Broussists, under the leadership of Paul Brousse; *b.* the Allemanistes, whose chief is Jean Allemane.

2. *Collectivists*, or *Marxists;* partisans of the theory of Karl Marx, also called Guesdists, from the name of their French chief, Jules Guesde.

3. *Blanquists*, so named from their leader, Blanqui. The adherents of this group are revolutionary socialists; they are communists.

4. *Independents.* At the head of this group of inde-

[1] The author has not been able to get as complete statistics of the progress of socialism in France as he desired. But he presents herewith three carefully prepared statements sent him by correspondents.

pendent socialists are found Millerand, Jaurès,[1] and Fournière.

5. *Socialistic Radicals*, such as M. Goblet.

The Schools.

The different groups of the socialistic party have all the same general aims, but they are divided among themselves with respect to the means to be employed; that is to say, the tactics to be followed to attain their aims. The foundation of the doctrines of the different schools is the principle of the suppression of the wages-system by the socialization of the means of production. Nevertheless, while the collectivists wish to centralize the social organization in the hands of the State, the Blanquists, Allemanists, and Possibilists have a very marked preference for decentralization and administration by free communes. The Broussists are distinguished somewhat from the others with respect to this point, namely, that they are less revolutionary, and are willing to form alliances with the established government as a means to accomplish their purposes.

The Broussists have more adherents in Paris than the other schools, and the Allemanists are notably in the minority there. In the provinces, on the other hand, the Collectivists are dominant. An exception, however, ought to be made of the Department des Ardennes, where all the socialists are Allemanists, Jean Baptist Clément, who was the apostle of socialism and the organizer of the socialistic forces in this region, belonging to this school.

Socialism in Parliament.

The socialistic party has no representatives in the

[1] **Professor of Literature in the University of Toulouse.**

APPENDIX X.

Senate. In the Chamber of Deputies there are about sixty socialistic deputies, among whom the following are the most important in each group: —

Collectivists: MM. Guesde, Chauvin, Pierre Vaux.

Blanquists: MM. Vaillant, Chauvières, Walter (recently Mayor of St. Denis), Ernest Roche.

Possibilists (Broussists) : MM. Prudent-Dervilliers, Lavy.

Possibilists (Allemanists): MM. Fabérot, Groussier, Coutant, Dejeante, Avez, Toussaint.

Independents: MM. Millerand, Jaurès, Viviani, Clovis-Hugues, Senbat, Thierry, Cazes, Goujat, Mirman.

Socialism in the Municipal Council of Paris.

The socialists are represented in the Municipal Council of Paris as follows :

Four Possibilists (Allemanists), namely, MM. Faillet, Weber, Chausse, and Berthaut; five Possibilists (Broussists), namely, MM. Brousse, Réties, Picau, Blondeau, and Caumeau; and eight Independents, namely, MM. Landrin, Fournière, Moreau, Girou, Grébauval, Breuillé. Daniel, and Brard, making seventeen in all. Adding to these seventeen votes those of the nineteen radicals who frequently vote with the socialists, and who are called socialistic radicals, we have a group of thirty-six members representing the socialistic party in the municipal assembly.

List of Socialist Deputies.

Exactly fifty-three deputies represent the socialists. They are as follows: —

From the Department of the Seine (including Paris) : MM. Millerand, Hovelacque, E. Roche, Goblet, René Viviani, A. Petrot, Dr. Frebeault, Groussier, Fabérot, Paschal

APPENDIX X. 393

Grousset, Chauvière, Marcel Sembat, G. Rouanet, Lavy, Clovis-Hugues, Prudent-Dervilliers, Dejeante, Vaillant, Walter, Alexandre Avez, Emile Chauvin, Coutant.

From the other departments : MM. Antibe Boyer, Baudin, Pajot, Raymond Leygue, Bepmale, Salis, Jouffray, Jules Guesde, Dr. Defontaine, Basly, Lamendin, Hubbard, Jaurès, Couturier, Compayré, Rousse, Abel, Cluseret, Labussière, Thivrier, Sauvanet, Vaux, Desfarges, Gendre, Jourde, Cousin, Vigne-d'Octon, Charpentier, Mirmans, Goujat, Dr. Masson.

Several radicals, who do not call themselves socialists, vote, nevertheless, with the socialists in most cases, and make up the sixty votes to which reference has been made.

The Programs.

Very nearly the same demands are found in the programs of all the socialist schools. Citizen Vaillant[1] said in one of his latest election circulars that the necessary point of departure was the conquest by the socialists of the political power, which would lead to the revolution bringing liberty to all, to the annihilation of the capitalistic *régime*, to the emancipation of the working class, to *de facto* equality, to the well being of the man and the citizen in the solidarity of the social republic. M. Vaillant demanded that parliamentarism be replaced by direct government of the people by the people, the abolition of militarism and the creation of a national militia, amnesty, the abolition of appropriations to churches, the resumption of church property, progressive taxation, the municipalization and nationalization of the services of credit, of the supply of provisions, food, work, etc.

If to these demands in the program we add those for

[1] This Vaillant must not be confounded with the recently executed anarchist.

the abolition of court fees, for elective and removable magistrates, jury trials in all cases, the obligation of all representatives to follow the instructions of their constituents, free instruction in all schools, complete separation of the civil service and elective offices, taxation upon capital and income, pensions for old age and invalidism, we shall have very nearly all the demands which are formulated in the election programs of the socialists.

Christian Socialism.

In conclusion, it is well to say a word about the Christian Socialist movement, at the head of which were found Mgr. Freppel and M. de Mun, and which they initiated. This movement gave rise to the encyclical of Pope Leo XIII. (*rerum novarum*), which began by a refutation of socialism itself. If we call attention to Christian socialism in this place it is simply to mention it.

B.

The Socialistic Vote, 1889-1893.

In 1889, eight socialistic candidates stood for the legislature in eight departments. In 1893, 141 candidates stood in fifty-nine departments. The socialists received 73,124 votes in 1889, and in 1893 they received 473,241, or six and a half times as many as in 1889.

It is to be observed that only those votes are counted which were cast for socialists. The socialistic radicals, such as M. Goblet and Pelletin, are not included among the fifty socialist deputies which form the socialist group in the Chamber; and the votes which they and their friends received in the last election are not counted among the 473,241 votes mentioned. It is, nevertheless, certain that at the coming elections the majority of the voters who in 1893 voted for the socialistic radicals,

APPENDIX X. 395

will cast their votes for pure socialists, such as Jules Guesde and Professor Jaurès.

C.

Memorandum Concerning French Socialist Publications, and a Brief Characterization of French Socialism.[1]

The socialist newspapers of France may be divided into two distinct classes, according as they are more especially political or educational, although both kinds, of course, advocate independent political action.

Among the first may be ranked the two widely circulated dailies published in Paris, *L'Intransigeant* and *La Petite République.*

L'Intransigeant, whose chief editor is Henri Rochefort, has a daily circulation of about 140,000. It does not expound — to any extent, at least — economic doctrine. It is essentially a *journal de combat* (a fighting paper); a demolisher of the *bourgeoisie*. Taking for granted that the socialists know exactly what they want and that what they want is good, it supports their candidates and attacks

[1] The correspondent who furnished this statement seems to have overlooked certain recent tendencies in French socialism which are more conservative, and to which attention has already been called. Nevertheless, it is probably true that French socialism is, even now, more radical than that of England or Germany: and for this, representatives of the various vested interests in France must bear a large share of the blame. Those who, as political economists and as writers generally, represent the interests of wealth are as extreme as the socialists, only in the opposite direction. There is no great modern country in which there is so little economic liberalism; no country in which there is so little inclination on the part of wealth to make timely concessions of moment. Fortunately, of late, there are some evidences of a change for the better. In connection with the lawschools of France, there has sprung up a more liberal class of economists, and in the Protestant Church, tendencies more favorable to social reform are becoming pronounced, while Catholics like M. de Mun deserve praise for zeal in economic reform.

their enemies. Rochefort goes not to the root, but into the *persons of things*. If an opponent of socialism comes out with a "strong" argument, *L'Intransigeant* does not take the trouble of considering the points made; it simply shows that the opponent in question is a "rascal" hired, bribed, or in some way bound by venal interests, to speak as he does. And it must be granted that one hundred times in a hundred *L'Intransigeant* happens to be right.

La Petite République was founded and is edited by M. Millerand, an eminent lawyer of Paris and a member of the Assembly. The primary purpose of its founder was to unite in political action the various socialist groups (eight in number), between which there was some difference of opinion as to tactics, but none whatever concerning fundamental principles and final aims. Circumstances favored Millerand's undertaking, and his harmonizing task is now accomplished. His paper is also a success. The leaders of each group write in turn the leading editorial article. *La Petite République*, as a *journal de combat*, is hardly less aggressive than *L'Intransigeant*, but it frequently contains economic articles of an educational character.

The socialist newspapers more especially educational are, in their order of importance: 1. *Le Socialiste*, published weekly, edited by Jules Guesde and Paul Lafargue, of the Marxist group, and chiefly circulated in the provinces; 2. *Le Parti Socialiste*, organ of the Blanquists, published weekly and chiefly circulated in Paris; 3. *Le Parti Ouvrier*, bi-weekly, edited by Jean Allemane, who leads one of the two groups formerly known as "Opportunists" (Possibilists), but now styled the "Labor Party." There are also various trade papers, all of which are socialistic.

Neither does *La Revue Socialiste*, nor any other socialistic publication, occupy in France a position similar to that of the *Neue Zeit* in Germany.

The present leaders of socialist thought in France hold that the theory of collectivism is now complete. They waste no time in trying to improve it; they merely strive to popularize it by presenting it to the masses in the clearest and simplest language; and in this they succeed admirably.

The only peculiarity of French socialism — or rather of the French socialists as a body — is the tendency to be more intensely revolutionary than the socialism (or socialists) of any other country. The lines of the class struggle are nowhere — not even in Germany — more strongly marked than in France, although nowhere are so many "intellectuals" identified with the proletarian class movement. With a profound conviction, rooted in the knowledge of history, that the capitalist class will grant nothing of fundamental value so long as it rules, and that it will fight for the preservation of its privileges so soon as it finds itself a minority at the ballot box, every French socialist looks to the coming day of battle as the most natural and inevitable of all phenomena.

Holding these views, they have no written platform. They don't need any. The single word "collectivism," (meaning thereby the complete socialization of all the means of production and distribution), is their motto universally understood, and therefore sufficiently expressive of their object in entering the political field with a view to the necessary conquest of the public powers. As to temporary, or transient, measures of relief — such as the eight hours normal work-day, a minimum salary, and others of an essentially trade-union character — they demand them as they go, by special resolutions in their trade congresses and through their representatives in the Chamber of Deputies, in departmental boards, or in municipal councils. These representatives meet from time to time, — usually once a month, — render to their constituents at public meetings of the party an account of their acts, and push such measures as are demanded at those special meetings.[1]

[1] It will be noted that these statements are not in entire agreement as to election statistics. The explanation is to be found in different modes of calculating results, which are easily enough understood when one is familiar with the actual situation.

APPENDIX XI.

BIBLIOGRAPHY.

GENERAL SOCIALISM.

AABERG, A.
Ferdinand Lassalle: biographie. Leipzig, Polytech. Buchh., 1883.

APEL, CURT.
Christenthum, sozialdemokratie und wahrer freisinn. Freiburg, 1891.

ADLER, G.
Die grundlagen der Karl Marx'schen kritik der bestehenden volkswirthschaft. Tübingen, Laupp, 1887.

One of the best critiques of Marxist socialism.

Rodbertus, der begründer des wissenschaftlichen socialismus. Leipzig, Duncker, 1883.

ADVIELLE, VICTOR.
Histoire de Gracchus Babeuf et du Babouvisme; 2 vol. Paris, chez l'auteur, 1867.

AIMEL, H.
La question sociale et le collectivisme. Paris, Libr. Graly, 1890.

ALEXEJERO, LEO.
Durch socialismus und anarchie zum menschenthum. Paris, Baillière et Messager, 1883.

ALLIX, JULES.
Socialisme pratique. Paris, Le Chevalier, 1869.

ALVAREZ, CIRILO.
Individualistas, socialistas, y comunistas, 1873.

AMMON, OTTO.
Der darwinismus gegen die socialdemokratie. Hamburg, 1891.

ANGE, *Baron d'*.
La nouvelle république sociale; étude pratique du socialisme. Paris, Chaudron, 1887.

ARGYRIADES, P.
Essai sur le socialisme scientifique. Paris, Admin. de la Question Sociale, 1891.
La femme et le socialisme. Paris, 1893.
Le poète socialiste, Eugène Pottier. Paris, chez l'auteur, 1889.

ARMAND, C.
Questions sociales. Paris, Claye, 1873.

ASCHINASI, M.
Ferdinando Lassalle. Milano, Ambrósoli.

AUERBACH, ALB.
Der kaufmann und die socialdemokratie. Berlin, Berger, 1891.

AULNIS DE BOUROUILL, D'.
Het hedendaagsche socialisme toegelicht en beoordeeld. Amsterdam, van Kampen, 1886.

AVELING, EDWARD.
Die darwin'sche theorie. Stuttgart, Dietz, 1892.
Student's Marx. London, Sonnenschein, 1891.

AVOGADRO, EMILIO.
Saggio intorno al socialismo e alle dottrine e tendenze socialistiche. S. Pier d'Arena, 1879.

AZZALI, LUIGI.
Organizzazione collettivista. Milan, Ambrosoli.
Principii socialisti. Milano, 1879.

BABEUF, GRACCHUS.
Vide: Advielle; Buonarroti: Manifesto of the Equals.

BAGGIO, CH.
Entretiens socialistes. Paris, chez l'auteur à Carvin, 1886.
Petit catéchisme socialiste. Paris, chez l'auteur à Carvin, 1889.

BAMBERGER, LUDWIG.
Deutschland und socialismus. Leipzig, Brockhaus, 1878.
A politician's attack on socialism; popular rather than scientific.

BAMBERGER, LUDWIG.
Die kulturgeschichtliche bedeutung des socialistengesetzes. Leipzig, Brockhaus, 1878.

BARBECK, HUGO.
Die sociale frage, und das programm Bebel's. Nürnberg, Heerdegen-Barbeck, 1890.

BARTH, THEODOR.
Der socialistische zukunftsstaat. Berlin, Simion, 1890.

BAX, ERNEST BELFORT.
Ethics of socialism. London, Sonnenschein, 1889.
The author is a defender of materialist socialism and presents socialism in one of its least attractive forms.
Outlooks from the new

standpoint. London, Sonnenschein, 1891.
Religion of socialism. London, Sonnenschein, 1887.

BEBEL, AUGUST.
Charles Fourier. Stuttgart, Dietz, 1892.
Der deutsche bauernkrieg mit berücksichtigung der hauptsächlichsten sozialen bewegungen des mittelalters. Berlin, Verlag des "Vorwärts," Berliner Volksblatt, 1890.
Die frau und der sozialismus. Stuttgart, Dietz, 1891.
Woman in the past, present, and future. New York, Lovell, 1886. Also, London, Mod. Press, 1885.
Die parlamentarische thätigkeit des deutschen reichstages . . . und die sozialdemokratie. Berlin, Verlag des " Vorwärts," 1890.
Die ziele der arbeiterbewegung. Berlin, Verlag des "Vorwärts," 1883.

BELLAMY, EDWARD.
Vide: Socialistic fiction. Criticism of "Looking Backward." Vide: Fränkel; Laicus: Lestrade, Michaelis.

BÉNARD, TH.
Le socialisme d'hier et celui d'aujourd'hui. Paris, Guillaumin, 1870.

BERFRIED, EDGAR.
Der anti-socialdemokrat. Mittelwalde, Hoffman, 1890.

BERG, ALEX.
Judenthum und socialdemokratie. Berlin, Dewald, 1891.

BERNSTEIN, ED.
Ferdinand Lassalle as a social reformer. London, Sonnenschein.
Gesellschaftliches und privateigenthum. Ein beitrag zur erläuterung des sozialistischen programms Berlin. Verlag des "Vorwärts," 1891.

BERTRAND, L.
La crise économique en Belgique et M. Eudore Firmez. 1885.
Qu'est-ce que le socialisme ? Bruxelles, 1887.

BESANT, ANNIE.
Modern socialism. London, Freethought Publ. Co., 1890.

BIONDI, U.
Individualismo o socialismo ? Castello, Lapi, 1887.

BIRKMYRE, ADAM.
Practicable socialism. Glasgow, Bryce, 1885.

BLANC, LOUIS.
Histoire de dix ans, 1830–1840. 5 vol. Paris, Paguerre, 1841–44.

BLANC, LOUIS.
Histoire de la révolution française. 12 vol. Paris, Langlois, 1847-62.
Organisation du travail. Paris, Paguerre, 1840.

One of the most important works in the history of earlier French socialism.

BLISS, W. D. P.
What is socialism? Pph. Boston, Dawn Publ. Co., 1894.

BLOCK, MAURICE.
Le quintessence du socialisme de la chaire, 1894.
Le socialisme moderne. Paris, Hachette, 1891.
Théoriciens du socialisme en Allemagne. Paris, Guillaumin, 1872.

A strong but not altogether fair antagonist.

BLUM, HANS.
Die lügen unserer socialdemokratie. Wismar, Hinstorffs, 1891.

BOCCARDO, G.
Il socialismo e l'Italia. Padova, Salmin, 1879.

BÖHM-BAWERK, EUGEN V.
Capital and interest: tr. by W. Smart. London, Macmillan, 1890.

Able criticism and refutation of the Marx theory of value is given in Bk. 6.

BÖHMERT, V.
Der socialismus und die arbeiterfrage. Zürich, Schmidt, 1872.

BOILLEY, P.
Socialisme, capitalisme et suffrage universel. Paris, Libr. de la Revue Socialiste, 1887.

BOLOGNE, L.
Le triomphe du socialisme. 4 vols. Paris, Libr. du Progrès, 1881.

BONTHOUX, ADOLPHE.
Le collectivisme, organisation du travail. Paris, Imprimerie nouvelle lyonnaise, 1888.

BOOTH, ARTHUR, J.
Robert Owen, founder of socialism in England. London, Trübner, 1869.

Booth, while not an adherent, is sympathetic and fair-minded.

Saint-Simon and Saint-Simonism. London, Trübner, 1871.

BOUCHER, ARMAND.
Darwinisme et socialisme. Agen, Michel, 1891.

BOUCTOT, J. G.
Histoire du communisme et du socialisme. Paris, Ghio, 1890.

BOURDEAU, M. J.
Le socialisme allemand et le nihilisme russe. Paris, Alcan, 1892.

BRAC DE LA PERRIÈRE, J.
Le socialisme. Paris, Baltenweck, 1880.

BRAMWELL, LORD.
Economics versus socialism. London, Lib. and Prop. Def. League, 1888.
Strongly anti-socialistic.

BRANDES, G. M. C.
Ferdinand Lassalle : en critisk fremstilling. Kopenhagen, Gyldendal, 1882.

BREYNAT, JULES.
Les socialistes modernes. Paris, Garnier, 1849.

BRISSAC, HENRI.
Résumé populaire du socialisme. Paris, au Progrès.
La société collectiviste. Paris, Libr. de la Revue Socialiste, 1892.

BROWN, THOMAS EDWIN.
Studies in modern socialism and labor problems. New York, Appleton, 1886.
The author is a clergyman who has given considerable attention to the subject, and endeavors to be fair, while at the same time critical.

BRUNELLIÈRE.
La question ouvrière devant le socialisme. Paris, Libr. de la Revue Socialiste, 1892.

BÜCHER, K.
Die entstehung der volkswirthschaft. Tübingen, Laupp, 1893.

BUONARROTI, FILIPPO.
Conspiration pour l'égalité dite de Babeuf. 2 vol. Bruxelles, Libr. romantique, 1828.
History of Babeuf's conspiracy for equality. Tr. by Bronterre. London, Hetherington, 1836.

CALBERLA, G. M.
Carl Marx, "Das kapital," und der heutige socialismus. Dresden, Schönfeld, 1877.

CARLYLE, THOMAS.
Socialism and unsocialism. 2 vol. New York, Humboldt, 1891.

CARPENTER, E.
England's ideal. London, Sonnenschein, 1889.
Civilization, its cause and cure. London, Sonnenschein, 1889.

CATHREIN, V.
Socialism. 1892.
Anti-socialistic from Roman Catholic standpoint.
Der socialismus. Freiburg, Herder, 1891.

CHIRAC, A.
La prochaine révolution: code socialiste. Paris, Arnould, 1889.

CIURRI, C.
Socialismo e progresso. Roma, Tip. econ. dell' impresa generale di pubblicità, 1890.

CLARKE, WILLIAM.
Fabian society. (New Eng. Mag., March, 1894.)

Influence of socialism upon English politics. (Pol. Sci. Quar., June, 1888.)

COGNETTI DE MARTIIS.
Socialismo antico. Torino, Bocca, 1889.

Il socialismo negli Stati Uniti d'America. Torino, 1887.

COLAJANNI, N.
Socialismo e sociologia criminale. C a t a n i a, Tropaea, 1885.

COLINS.
Socialisme rationnel. 3 vol. Paris, Bestel, 1851.

Vide: Land Reform.

Colins was a follower of Marx. His views on the nationalization of land have been adopted by many modern land reformers.

COMMONS, J. R.
Distribution of wealth. New York and London, Macmillan, 1893.

Able treatment of some of the economic principles involved in socialism, with valuable statistics on the concentration of wealth.

CONSIDERANT, VICTOR.
Destinée sociale. 2 vol. Paris, Libr. phalanst. 1851.
Ablest exposition of principles of Fourierism.

CONTZEN, HEINRICH.
Agricultur und socialismus. Berlin, Luckhardt, 1871.

Die sociale frage, ihre geschichte und ihre bedeutung in der gegenwart. Berlin, Luckhardt, 1872.

COOK, JOSEPH.
Socialism. Boston, Houghton, Mifflin, & Co., 1880.

COPELAND, J.
Socialism: or, Wrongs and remedies of our social condition. London, Hamilton, 1879.

CORVEY, J.
Die deutsche socialdemokratic unter dem Ausnahmegesetz. Hagen, Pifel, 1884.

COURTOIS, ALPHONSE, *fils.*
Histoire critique des systèmes socialistes. (Jour. d' Écon., Dec., 1884.)

DALMASSO.
Il socialismo esaminato sulla bilancia dell' opinione pubblica. Mondovi, 1879.

DAWSON, W. H.
Bismarck and state socialism. London, Sonnenschein, 1890.

German socialism and Ferdinand Lassalle. London, Sonnenschein, 1888.

DELAPORTE, J.
Les collectivistes du socialisme rationnel ne sont pas communistes. Paris, Libr. de la Science Sociale, 1878.

DELHERT, PH.
Social evolution. London, Eden, 1891.

DELOLME, J. L.
Le socialisme par excellence. Paris, Bonhoure, 1879.

DE PAEPE, CÉSAR.
Collectivisme et services publico. Paris, Libr. de la Revue Socialiste, 1892.

DENAYROUZE, L.
Le socialisme de la science. Paris, Guillaumin, 1881.

DEVILLE, GABRIEL.
Philosophie du socialisme. Paris, Libr. de la Revue Socialiste, 1892.

DIEHL, KARL.
Proudhon: seine lehre und sein leben. (Sammlung nat. ökon. abhandl. d. staatswiss., seminars zu Halle. Bd. 5–6. 1888–90.)
This critique is characterized by German thoroughness and fairness.

DIETZEL, H.
Karl Rodbertus: darstellung seines lebens und seiner lehre. Jena, Fischer, 1886–88.
Bd. 1. Darstellung seines lebens.

DIETZEL, H.
Bd. 2. Darstellung seiner socialphilosophie.
One of the most important critical works on Rodbertus.

DIETZGEN, JOS.
Die religion der socialdemokratie. Leipzig, Genossensch. Buchdr., 1875.
Die zukunft der socialdemokratie. Berlin, Verlag des Vorwärts, 1891.

DODD, A. B.
Republic of the future, or Socialism a reality. New York, Cassell, 1888.

DONISTHORPE, WORDSWORTH.
Individualism. New York and London, Macmillan, 1890.
Criticism of socialistic views, from the standpoint of extreme individualism.

DRAMARD, L.
Transformisme et socialisme. Paris, au bureau du Prolétaire, 1887.

DRUMONT, E.
La fin d'un monde. Étude psychologique et sociale. Paris, Savine, 1888.

DÜHRING, E.
Kritische geschichte der national ökonomie und des socialismus. Leipzig, Fues, 1877.

DÜRNBERGER, ADOLF.
Der einfluss socialistischer postulate auf das privatrecht. Wien, Konegen, 1893.

DUVERGER, A.
Le parti socialiste belge; son histoire et son programme. Lyons, Albert, 1880.

EICHTHAL, EUGÈNE D'.
Socialisme, communisme et collectivisme. Paris, Guillaumin, 1892.

ELY, RICHARD T.
French and German socialism. New York, Harper, 1883; London, Kegan Paul, 1886.

Labor movement in America. New York, Crowell, 1886.

Gives an account of socialism in America.

EMELE, S.
Die sociale frage, die socialdemokratie und die sogenannten kathedersocialisten in Deutschland. Sigmaringen, Tappen, 1883.

Der socialismus, Rodbertus-Jagetzow, das Manchesterthum und der staatssocialismus. Sigmaringen, Tappen, 1885.

ENGELS, FRIEDRICH.
Entwickelung des sozialismus von der utopie zur wissenschaft. Berlin, Verlag des "Vorwärts," 1891.

Socialism, utopian and scientific. London, Sonnenschein, 1892.

ENGELS, FRIEDRICH.
Die lage der arbeitenden klasse in England. Leipzig, Wigand, 1848.

Condition of the working class in England in 1844. Tr. by Florence Kelley. New York, Lovell, 1887.

Ursprung der familie, des privateigenthums und des staates. Stuttgart, Dietz, 1891.

EYNERN, ERNST V.
Wider die sozialdemokratie und verwandtes. Leipzig, Wigand, 1874.

FABIAN SOCIETY.
Fabian Tracts. Nos. 1–49. London, Fabian Society Publ., 1893–1894.

What to read: a list of books for social reformers. (Tract 29.) London, Fabian Society Publ.

Fabian Essays in Socialism. London, Fabian Society, 1890.

Contents: — Shaw, Webb, Clarke, and Olivier, on the Basis of socialism; Wallas; Property under socialism; Besant, Industry under socialism; Shaw, Transition to social democracy; Bland, The Outlook.

FAIRMANN, FRANK.
Principles of socialism made plain. London, Reeves, 1885.

FABIAN SOCIETY.
Herbert Spencer on Socialism; a reply to the article entitled, "The coming slavery." London, Modern Press, 1884.

FALK, KURT.
Die bestrebungen der sozialdemokratie. Stuttgart, Dietz, 1892.

FELIX, L.
Kritik des socialismus. Leipzig, Duncker, 1893.

FLEISCHMAN, OTTO.
Wider die sozialdemokratie. Kaiserslautern, Tascher, 1891.

FINDEL, J. G.
Der innere zufall der sozialdemokratie. Leipzig, Findel, 1880.

FORNI, EUGENIO.
L'internazionale e lo stato. Napoli, Hoepli, 1878.

FOUILLÉ, ALFRED.
La propriété sociale et la démocratie. Paris, Hachette, 1884.

FOURIER, CHARLES.
Œuvres choisies. Édition Gide. Paris, Guillaumin, 1890.
Œuvres complètes. 6 vol. Paris, Libr. sociétaire, 1841-1848.
The most influential of his works were: —

Théorie des quatre mouvements et des destinées générales, 1840.
Théorie de l'unité universelle, 1843.
Vide : Biography: Bebel, Flint, Gatti de Gamond, Pellarin, Warschauer.

FOURNET, BORIN.
La société moderne et la question sociale, 1893.

FRÄNKEL, HEINRICH.
Gegen Bellamy. Würzburg, Stuber, 1891.

FRÖBEL, JUL.
Die irrthümer des socialismus. Leipzig, Wigand, 1871.

GATTI DE GAMOND.
Fourier et son système. 2 vol. Paris, Capello, 1841-1842.
One of the best treatments of Fourierism.

GAUTIER, ÉMILE.
Le darwinisme social. Paris, Derveaux, 1880.

GEMELLI, CARLO.
Lezioni sul comunismo e socialismo antico e moderno. Bologna, 1876.

GILMAN, NICOLAS PAINE.
Socialism and the American spirit. Boston, Houghton, Mifflin, & Co., 1893.
Directed chiefly against Nationalism.

GLADDEN, WASHINGTON.
Socialism and unsocialism, 1887. (Forum iii. 122.)
Strength and weakness of socialism. (Cent. xxxi. 737.)
Three (social) Dangers. 1884. (Cent. xxviii. 620.)

GODIN, ANDRÉ.
Mutualité sociale. Paris, Guillaumin, 1880.
La république du travail. Paris, Guillaumin, 1889.
Social solutions. Tr. by Marie Howland. New York, Lovell, 1887.
Familistère in Guise, France, founded by the author.

Vide: Socialistic Experiments: Guise.

GOUBAREFF, DEMETRIUS.
Le socialisme à notre époque. Beaulieu-sur-Mer, 1886.

GRAHAM, WILLIAM.
Socialism, new and old. New York, Appleton, 1891.
The social problem. London, Kegan Paul, 1886.

GREAT BRITAIN. — ROYAL COMMISSION ON LABOUR.
Foreign reports, edited by Geoffrey Drage, Secretary. London, Eyre & Spottiswoode, 1893.

GREAT BRITAIN. — ROYAL COMMISSION ON LABOUR.
Belgium; Colonies and the Indian Empire (Australasia); France; Germany; Holland; Italy; Switzerland; United States.

In treating of the condition of the laboring classes in the different countries, statements are also given of the socialistic activity in each.

GREELEY, HORACE.
Greeley and other pioneers of American socialism, by Charles Sotheran. New York, Humboldt Publ. Co., 1892.

GRÖNLUND, LAURENCE.
Ça ira! or, Danton in the French Revolution. Boston, Lee & Shepard, 1888.
Our destiny: influence of nationalism on morals and religion. Boston, Lee & Shepard, 1891.
Co-operative commonwealth : an exposition of modern socialism. Boston, Lee & Shepard, 1884. New York, Lovell, 1887.

GUYOT, YVES.
Les principes de '89 et le socialisme. Paris, Delagrave, 1893.
La tyrannie socialiste. Paris, Delagrave, 1893.

GUYOT, YVES.
   Tyranny of socialism, ed. by Levy. London, Sonnenschein, 1894.
   Strongly anti-socialistic.

HALL, B. T.
   Socialism and sailors. (Tract 46.) London, Fabian Society, 1893.

HALLEUX, L.
   Le socialisme considéré au point de vue de droit naturel. Bruges, Beyaert-Storie, 1887.

HAMON, H. D.
   Catéchisme populaire contre les socialistes. Paris, Lecoffre, 1847.

HANSEN, GEORG.
   Der deutsche arbeiter und die socialdemokratie. Berlin, Puttkammer, 1891.

HEITZ, E.
   Die socialpolitische bewegung in Deutschland, 1863-1890. Stuttgart, Kohlhammer, 1891.

HELD, ADOLF.
   Sozialismus, sozialdemokratie und sozialpolitik. Leipzig, Duncker, 1878.
   Zwei bücher zur socialen geschichte Englands. Leipzig, Duncker, 1881.

HERTZKA, THEODOR.
   Die gesetze der socialen entwickelung. Leipzig, Duncker, 1886.

HERTZKA, THEODOR.
   Socialdemokratie und socialliberalismus. Dresden, Pierson, 1891.

HILL, DAVID JAYNE.
   Principles and fallacies of socialism. New York, Lovell, 1885.

HITCHCOCK, ROSWELL D.
   Socialism. New York, Randolph, 1887.

HOBBEL, J.
   Socialistisch onverstand. Amsterdam, Sikken, 1883.

HOLENIA, EDM.
   Der socialismus und seine stellung zur staatsgewalt. social politische studie. Wels, Haas, 1890.

HOLMES, G. K.
   Concentration of wealth. (Pol. Sci. Quar., Dec., 1893.)
   Has an important bearing on fundamental principles involved in a discussion of socialism.

HUBBARD, N. G.
   Saint-Simon, sa vie et ses travaux. Paris, Guillaumin, 1857.

HUNDHAUSEN, THEODOR.
   Wir sind nicht sozialdemokraten. Berlin, Brieger, 1891.

HYNDMAN, HENRY MAYERS.
   Commercial crises of the nineteenth century. London, Sonnenschein.

HYNDMAN, HENRY MAYERS.
England for all. Pph. London, Soc. Dem. Fed., 1883.
Historical basis of socialism in England. London, Kegan Paul, 1883.
Radicals and socialism. 1885.
Socialism and slavery. London, Modern Press.
Socialism made plain. Pph. London, Soc. Dem. Fed.

HYNDMAN, H. M., and MORRIS, W.
Summary of principles of socialism. [1884.] London, Soc. Dem. Fed., 1892.

JÄGER, EUG.
Geschichte der socialen bewegung und der socialismus in Frankreich. 2 vol. Berlin, Puttkammer, 1890.
Der moderne socialismus. Berlin, van Muyden, 1883.

JAMES, H. A.
Communism in America. New York, Holt, 1879.

JANET, PAUL.
Les origines du socialisme contemporain. Paris, Ballière, 1883.

JANNET, C.
L'internationale et la question sociale. Paris, Durand, 1871.
Le socialisme d'état et la réforme sociale. Paris, Plon Nourrit.

JAY, A. O.
The social problem, its possible solution. 1893.

JEANNIN, JULES.
Égoïsm et misère. Paris, Allemane, 1893.

JHOURNEY, ALBERT.
Ésotérisme et socialisme. 1893.

JONES, LLOYD.
Life of Robert Owen. London, Sonnenschein, 1892.

JOURDAN, ALFRED.
Du rôle de l'état dans l'ordre économique, ou Économie politique et socialisme. Paris, Rousseau, 1882.

JOYNES, J. L.
Socialist catechism. London, Soc. Dem. Fed., 1884.

KAUFMANN, MORITZ.
Socialism. London, Kegan Paul, 1874.
Socialism and communism. London, S. P. C. K., 1883.

KAUTSKY, KARL.
Das Erfurter programm. Stuttgart, Dietz, 1892.
Karl Marx's ökonomische lehren gemeinverständlich dargestellt und erläutert. Stuttgart, Dietz, 1887.
Der parlamentarismus, die volksgesetzgebung und die sozialdemokratie. Stuttgart, Dietz, 1894.

KEGEL, MAX.
Ferdinand Lassalle: eine biographie. Stuttgart, Dietz, 1889.

KEMPNER, M.
Common-sense socialism. London, Sonnenschein, 1887.

KIRKUP, THOMAS.
History of socialism. London and Edinburgh, Black, 1892.
Inquiry into socialism. London, Longmans, 1887.

KLEIN, E.
Das paradies der socialdemokratie so wie es wirklich sein wird. Freiburg, Herder, 1891.

KLEINWACHTER, FRIEDRICH.
Die grundlagen und ziele des sogenannten wissenschaftlichen socialismus. Innsbruck, Wagner, 1885.

KÖHLER, OSWALD.
Der sozialdemokratische staat. Nürnberg, Wörlein, 1892.

KOHUT, A.
Ferdinand Lassalle: sein leben und wirken. Leipzig, Wigand, 1889.

KUNOWSKI, LEOPOLD V.
Wird die socialdemokratie siegen? Ein blick in die zukunft dieser bewegung. Bielefeld, Velhagen u. Klasing, 1891.

LABOR COMMISSION.
Epitome of the evidence and report. London, Sonnenschein, 1894. (In press.)
    An abridged account of the present socialistic activity in the different European countries, taken from the reports of the Royal Commission on Labour. *Vide :* Great Britain.

LAFARGUE, PAUL.
The evolution of property. London, Sonnenschein, 1891.
Le matérialisme économique de K. Marx (Cours d'économie sociale.) Paris. Oriol, 1884.
Le socialisme utopique. Paris, Libr. de la Revue Socialiste, 1892.
    Son-in-law and follower of Karl Marx.

LAICUS, PHIL.
Etwas später (Continuation of Bellamy's "Looking backward"). Mainz, Kirchheim, 1891.

LASPEYRES, ÉTIENNE.
Die kathedersocialisten und die statistischen congresse. Berlin, Lüderitz, 1875.

LASSALLE, FERDINAND.
Ausgewählte reden und schriften. Leipzig, Pfau, 1891.

LASSALLE, FERDINAND.
Bastiat-Schulze von Delitzsch, oder Capital und arbeit. Berlin, Schlingman, 1864.
Briefe an Rodbertus-Jagetzow. Berlin, Puttkammer, 1878.
Reden und schriften. Mit einer biographischen einleitung, herausgegeben von Ed. Bernstein. 3 vols. Berlin, Verlag des "Vorwärts," Berliner Volksblatt, 1891.

Carefully edited, and altogether the best edition of Lassalle's works.

Working man's programme. London, Soc. Dem. Fed., 1884.

Vide: Aaberg, Aschinasi, Bernstein, Brandes, Kegel, Kohut.

LAUR, F.
Essais de socialisme expérimental. Paris, Dentu, 1886.

LAVERGNE, L. DE.
L'évolution sociale. Paris, Fischbacher, 1893.

LAVELEYE, ÉMILE DE.
Le socialisme contemporain. Paris, Félix Alcan, 1893.
Socialism of to-day. Tr. by G. H. Orpen. London, Field & Tuer, 1885.

LECLER, ADHÉMARD.
La quintessence du collectivisme. Paris, Carbillet, 1881.

LEPETIT, E.
Del socialismo: studi giuridici e politici. Milano, Hœpli, 1891.

LE PLAY.
La réforme sociale. Tours, Mame, 1887.

LEROY-BEAULIEU, PIERRE PAUL.
Collectivisme: examen critique du nouveau socialisme. Paris, Guillaumin, 1885.

Partisan and anti-socialistic.

Papacy, socialism, and democracy; with the Papal encyclical. London, Chapman & Hall, 1892.

LESTRADE, COMBES DE.
Seul de son siècle, en l'an 2000. Paris, Guillaumin, 1891.

LEVY, J. H.
Outcome of individualism. London, King, 1892.

LIEBKNECHT, W.
Die politische stellung der sozialdemokratie. Berlin, Verlag des "Vorwärts," Berliner Volksblatt, 1890.
Zur grund- und bodenfrage. Pph. Leipzig, 1876.

MACKAY, THOMAS, editor.
Plea for liberty: argument against socialism. New York, Appleton, 1891.

Contents : — Spencer: From freedom to bondage; Robertson: Impracticability of socialism; Donisthorpe: Limits of liberty; Howell: Liberty for labour; Fairchild: State socialism in the Antipodes; Vincent: Discontent of the working-classes; Mackay: Investment; Alford: Free education; Raffalovich: Housing of the working-classes; Millar: Evils of state trading; O'Brien: Free libraries; Gordon: State and electrical distribution; Herbert: True line of deliverance.

MALATO, CHARLES.
Révolution chrétienne et révolution sociale. Paris, Lib. de la Revue Socialiste. 1892.

MALDO, ROMERO.
Problemos sociales. Madrid, Quignones, 1886.

MALLOCK, WILLIAM HURRELL.
Labour and the popular welfare. London, Black, 1893.
Social equality. London, Bentley, 1882.

Mallock considers social *inequality* indispensable to the development and maintenance of civilization.

MALON, BENOÎT.
Exposé des écoles socialistes françaises. Suivi d'un aperçu sur le collectivisme international. Paris, Le Chevalier, 1872.
Histoire du socialisme. Paris, Derveaux, 1885.
Précis historique, théorique, et pratique du socialisme. Paris, Alcan, 1892.
Le socialisme intégral.
Pt. 1. Histoire des théories et tendance générales. Paris, Alcan, 1892.
Pt. 2. Des reformes possibles et des moyens pratiques. Paris, Alcan, 1891.

MANIFESTO OF ENGLISH SOCIALISTS. London, Twentieth Cent. Press.

MANIFESTO OF THE EQUALS, the programme of the Babouvists, drawn up by Maréchal, is to be found in Reybaud's Études sur les réformateurs. Vol. 2. Paris, 1864.

MARIELD JEAN.
Études de socialism pratique. Paris, Best, 1889.

MARINIS, ENRICO DE.
Il collectivismo nel programma della democrazia italiana. Forli, Burdondini, 1892.

MARLO, KARL.
System der weltökonomie; untersuchungen über die organisation der arbeit. Kassel, Appel, 1842–1852.
System of world economy, or investigations concerning the organization of labor. 1849.

MARTENS, HEINRICH.
Socialdemokratie und socialpolitik in den skandinavischen reichen. (Schmoller's Jahrb. 1891.)

MARTIN, CH.
Liberté ou communisme. Paris, Ghio, 1878.

MARTINET, C.
Le socialisme en Danemark. Paris, 1893.

MARX, KARL.
Das elend der philosophie; antwort auf Proudhon's "Philosophie des elends." Stuttgart, Dietz, 1892.
(Translation of the following).
Misère de la philosophie; réponse à la philosophie de la misère. Proudhon, Paris, 1847.
Original edition out of print.
Das Kapital. Bd. 1. Der productionsprocess des kapitals. Hamburg, Meissner, 1867. 4 Aufl. hrsg. von Engels. Hamburg, Meissner, 1890. Bd. 2. Der circulationsprocess des kapitals. Hrsg. von Engels, Hamburg, Meissner, 1885.
Vol. 3 already announced.
Capital: critical analysis of capitalist production, from the German by Moore and Aveling. 2 vol. London, Sonnenschein, 1878. [Translation edited by Engels.]
Lohnarbeit und kapital. Mit einer einleitung von Engels. Berlin, Verlag des "Vorwärts," 1891.
Wage-labor and capital. London, Soc. Dem. Fed., 1892.
Vide: Adler, Aveling, Kautsky, Lafargue.

MARX, KARL, AND ENGELS, FRIEDRICH.
Das communistische manifest. 1848. Berlin, Verlag des "Vorwärts," Berliner Volksblatt, 1891.
Manifesto of the communist party, 1848. London, Reeves, 1888.
Modern socialism was largely shaped by this document.

MASSART, J., AND VANDEERELDE, ÉMILE.
Parasitisme organique et parasitisme social. 1893.

MASSERON, ISID.
Danger et nécessité du socialisme. Paris, Baillière, 1883.

MAXWELL, DAVID.
Stepping-stones to socialism. London, Hull Press, 1891.

MAZEL, A.
Solidarisme, individualisme, et socialisme. Paris, Bonhoure, 1882.

MAZZINI, JOSEPH.
Socialistes français. Bruxelles, Tarride, 1852.

Thoughts upon democracy in Europe. London, Alexander & Shepherd.

Review of the various aims of socialists and communists.

MEHRING, FRANZ.
Die deutsche socialdemokratie: ihre geschichte und ihre lehre. Bremen, Schünemann, 1879.

Anti-socialistic. Since writing this work he has joined the social democratic party.

Richter's "Bilder aus der gegenwart." Nürnberg, Wörlein, 1892.

MENGER, ANTON.
Das bürgerliche recht und die besitzlosen volksklassen. Tübingen, Laupp, 1890.

MENGER, ANTON.
Das recht auf den vollen arbeitsertrag. Stuttgart, Cotta, 1891.

MERMEIX.
La france socialiste. Paris, Fetcherin, 1886.

MEYER, RUDOLF.
Die bedrohliche entwickelung des socialismus und die lehre Lassalle's. Berlin, Schindler, 1873.

Der emancipationskampf des vierten standes. 2 vol., 1874–1875. Berlin, Bahr, 1882.

Der kapitalismus fin de siècle. Vienna, Verl. Buchh. "Austria," 1894.

Der socialismus in Dänemark. Berlin, Schindler, 1874.

Die wirkung der massregelungen der socialdemokratie. Berlin, Schindler, 1874.

MICHAELIS, RICH.
Looking further forward: an answer to Bellamy's "Looking backward." Chicago, Rand, 1890.

MILL, JOHN STUART.
Socialism, ed. by Bliss. New York, Humboldt Publ. Co., 1891.

MOLINARI, G. DE.
Le mouvement socialiste avant le révolution du 1870. Paris, Garnier, 1872.

MORRIS, WILLIAM.
Art and socialism. Pph. London, Reeves, 1884.

Monopoly. Pph. London, Hammersmith Soc. Society, 1893.

Signs of change. London, Reeves, 1889.

Socialism, its growth and outcome. London, 1893.

True and false society. London, Reeves, 1885.

Useful work and useless toil. London, Hammersmith Soc. Society, 1893.

MORRIS, WILLIAM.
William Morris, poet, artist, socialist, ed. by Lee. New York, Humboldt Publ. Co., 1891.

MÜLLER, HANS.
Der klassenkampf in der deutschen sozialdemokratie. Zürich, Schabelitz, 1892.

This little work emanates from a representative of the so-called "Opposition," a radical faction of the social-democracy in Germany. The author attacks the present management of the party, which he alleges has lost its proletarian and revolutionary character and become conservative.

MÜLLER, MORITZ.
Ueber den atheismus unter den socialdemokraten. Leipzig, Kessling, 1892.

MUSER, OSCAR.
Socialistengesetz und rechtspflege. Karlsruhe, 1889.

NACQUET, ALFRED.
Collectivism and socialism. London, Sonnenschein, 1891.

Socialisme, collectivisme et socialisme libéral. Paris, Dentu, 1890.

NATIONALISM, Principles of. *Vide:* Bellamy, "Looking backward;" New Nation; Nationalist.

NEWTON, R. HEBER.
Social studies. New York, Putnam, 1887.

OBERWINDER, HEINRICH.
Socialismus und sozial-politik. Berlin, Elwir, 1886.

OSGOOD, HERBERT L.
Scientific socialism. Rodbertus (Pol. Sci. Quar. i. 560), 1886.

OWEN, ROBERT.
Autobiography. London, Effingham Wilson, 1857.

Book of the new moral world, containing the rational system of society. London, Effingham Wilson, 1836.

OWEN, ROBERT.
Development of the origin and effects of moral evil. Manchester, Heywood, 1838.
Lectures on the rational system of society. London, Home Colonization Office, 1841.
Revolution in the mind and practice of the human race. London, Effingham Wilson, 1849.
Vide: Booth; Jones; Sargant; Seligman.

PEARSON, KARL.
Ethics of free thought. London, Denny, 1888.
Moral basis of socialism. London, Reeves, 1887.
Socialism in theory and practice. London, Reeves, 1887.

PELLARIN, CHARLES.
Fourier, sa vie et sa théorie. Paris, Libr. phalanst., 1849.

PELLEGRINI, PIETRO.
Borgo a Mozzano, Vanniani, 1891.
Diritto sociale.

PETERSEN, N. L.
Rapport sur le mouvement socialiste en Danemark. Brussels, Maheu.

PETZLER, J. ALOIS.
Die sociale baukunst. Gründe und mittel für den umsturz und wieder-aufbau der gesellschaftlichen verhältnisse. 2 vol. Berlin, Verlag des "Vorwärts," Berliner Volksblatt, 1891.

PEYRON, ÉLIE.
Les questions sociales. Paris, Riviere, 1885.

PÖHLMANN.
Geschichte des antiken communismus und socialismus. Munich, 1893.

POTEL, A.
Le socialisme en Allemagne. Paris, Thorin, 1890.

POTTER, BEATRICE (Mrs. Sidney Webb).
Co-operation and trade unionism. Pph. Manchester, Co-op. Union Publ., 1892.
Co-operative movement in Great Britain. London, Sonnenschein, 1891.
Treats admirably of the relation of co-operation and trades unionism to socialism.

POTTIER, EUGÈNE.
Vide: Argyriades.

PROUDHON, PIERRE JOSEPH.
Œuvres complètes. 33 vol. Paris, Lacroix, 1868–1876.
Of Proudhon's works, the most influential were:—
Qu'est-ce-que la propriété? 1848; Système des contradictions économiques. 1846; La révolution sociale, démonstrée par le coup d'état, 1852.

PROUDHON, PIERRE JOSEPH.
Philosophy of misery. New York, Humboldt Publ. Co., 1893.
System of economical contradictions. Tr. by Tucker. Boston, Tucker, 1888.
The doctrines of Proudhon may be regarded as the beginning of modern anarchy.
What is property? Tr. by Tucker. Boston, Tucker, 1876.

PROUDHON P. J.
Vide: Diehl.

PUTNAM, J. PICKERING.
Architecture under Socialism. Pph., Boston, 1890.

QUACK, H. P. G.
De socialisten: personen en stelsels. 4 vol. (Vol. 4. not yet published.) Amsterdam, van Kampen, 1887.
The most extensive work on socialism yet issued.

QUIGNONES, U. R.
Que hay? Verdades psicologicas segun los principios de la ciencia moderna. Sabadell, Ribeya, 1885.

RABBENO, UGO.
Il movimento socialiste in Italia, 1892.

RAE, JOHN.
Contemporary socialism. London, Sonnenschein, 1891.
With additional chapters on Anarchism, State socialism, and Russian nihilism.

RAYDT, TH.
Die socialdemokratie, und ihre bekämpfung. Hannover, Kniep, 1893.

REYBAUD, LOUIS.
Études sur les réformateurs: (Saint-Simon; Fourier; Owen). 2 vol. Paris, Guillaumin, 1844.

RITCHIE, D. G.
Darwinism and politics. London, Sonnenschein, 1891.
In opposition to the *Laissez faire* principle in government.

ROBERTSON, J. M.
Fallacy of saving. London, Sonnenschein, 1892.

RODBERTUS, KARL.
Aus dem literarischen nachlass. 8 vol. Berlin, Puttkammer, 1878–85.
Bd. 1. Briefe von Lassalle an Rodbertus, 1878: Bd. 2. Das kapital, 1884: Bd. 3, Zur beleuchtung der socialen frage, Th. 2., 1885.
Zur beleuchtung der socialen frage. Berlin, Puttkammer, 1890.
Zur erkenntniss unserer staatswirthschaftlichen zustände. Neubrandenburg, Barnewitz, 1842.
Der normal arbeitstag. Berlin, Hickethier, 1871.

RODBERTUS, KARL.
Vide: Adler; Dietzel; Osgood; Wagner

ROLES, J. P.
    Social danger, or Two years of socialism in Europe and America. Chicago, Belford, Clarke & Co., 1886.

ROUCHOT.
    Histoire du communisme et du socialisme. Paris, 1889.

RUGE, A.
    Briefwechsel und tagebuchblätter, 1825-1880. Berlin, Weidmann, 1886.
    Ueber Cabet, Fourier, Blanc, Marx, Bakunin, Engels, Stirner, Weitling.

RUSKIN, JOHN.
    Communism. Ed. by Bliss. New York, Humboldt Publ. Co., 1891.

SAINT-SIMON, H.
    Œuvres. 7 vol. Paris, E. Dentu, 1866.
    Œuvres choisies. 3 vol. Paris, Castel, 1861.

SAINT-SIMON, H., AND ENFANTIN, PROSPER.
    Œuvres de H. Saint-Simon ed d'Enfantin publiées par les membres du conseil. 47 vol. Paris, Dentu, 1865-1878.

SAINT-SIMON.
    Vide: Booth; Flint; Hubbard; Warschauer.

SARTORIUS VON WALTERSHAUSEN.
    Der moderne socialismus in den Vereinigten Staaten von Amerika. Berlin, Bahr, 1890.

SARGANT, W. L.
    Owen and his social philosophy. London, Smith, Elder & Co., 1860.
    Social innovators and their schemes. London, Smith, Elder & Co., 1858.
    St.-Simon, Fourier, Blanc, Proudhon, Girardin.

SAY, LEON.
    Le socialisme d'état. Angleterre, Allemagne, Italie. Paris, Levy, 1890.
    Pronounced opponent of socialism.

SCHÄFFLE, A. E. F.
    Capitalismus und socialismus. Tübingen, Laupp, 1878.
    Impossibilities of social-democracy. London, Sonnenchein, 1892.
    Quintessenz des socialismus. Gotha, Perthes, 1879.
    Quintessence of socialism. New York, Humboldt Publ. Co., 1890.

SCHALL, ED.
    Die sozialdemokratie auf dem lande, ihre abwehr und sicherste ausbreitung. Oebisfelde, Radwitz, 1893.

SCHEEL, H. V.
Die theorie der sozialen frage. Jena, Mauke, 1878.

SCHMIDT, EDUARD OSKAR.
Darwinismus und social-demokratie. Bonn, Strauss, 1878.
Science and socialism. 1879. (Pop. Sci. Mo. xiv. 577.)

SCHMOLLER, H.
Ueber einige grundfragen des rechts und der volkswirthschaft. Jena, 1875.
Reply to Treitschke's attack, in the work mentioned below, on so-called professorial socialism.

SELIGMAN, E. R. A.
Owen and the Christian socialists. Pph. New York, Ginn, 1886.
Contains a full bibliography of Owen and the Christian Socialists.

SEMLER, HEINRICH.
Geschichte des socialismus und communismus in Nord-Amerika. Leipzig, Brockhaus, 1880.

SICILIANI, PIETRO.
Socialismo, darwinismo e sociologia moderna. Bologna, N. Zanichelli, 1885.

SIEGWART, KARL.
Der communisten-staat. Berlin, Denicke, 1878.

SMITH, GOLDWIN.
False hopes, or Fallacies socialistic and semi-socialistic. London, Cassell, 1886.

SMITH, H. L.
Economic aspects of state socialism. London, Simpkin, 1887.
Socialism, labor, and capital. London, Routledge, 1890.
Socialism in Australian Colonies.
Vide: Great Britain.— Royal Commission on Labour.
Socialism in America.
Vide: Cognetti de Martiis; Ely; James; Sartorius von Waltershausen; Semler.
Also: Socialistic Experiments. Ely; Hinds; Nordhoff; Noyes.
Socialism in Belgium.
Vide: Bertrand; Duverger; Wollmann; Great Britain.— Royal Commission on Labour.
Socialism in Denmark.
Vide: Meyer; Petersen; Martinet.
Socialism in England.
Vide: Fabian Society Publications; Held; Hyndmann.
Socialism in France.
Vide: Ely; Jäger; Mermeix; Great Britain.— Royal Commission on Labour.

Socialism in Germany.
Vide: Bamberger; Corvey; Ely; Emele; Hansen; Heitz; Kautsky; Liebknecht; Mehring; Meyer; Muser; Potel; Raydt; Schall; Great Britain. — Royal Commission on Labour.
Also: Sozialdemokratische partei Deutschlands.

Socialism in Holland.
Vide: Great Britain. — Royal Commission on Labour.

Socialism in Italy.
Vide: Boccardo; Rabbeno. Great Britain. — Royal Commission on Labour.

SOTHERAN, CHARLES.
Greeley and other pioneers of American socialism. New York, Humboldt Publ. Co., 1892.

Sozialdemokratische Partei Deutschlands.
Protokolle der Parteitage. Berlin, Verlag des "Vorwärts," Berliner Volksblatt.
Dresden, 1871; Coburg, 1874; Wyden, 1880; Copenhagen, 1883; St. Gallen, 1887; Halle, 1890; Erfurt, 1891; Berlin, 1892; Cologne, 1893.

Sozialdemokratische (Der).
"Zukunftsstaat," Berlin, Verlag des "Vorwärts," Berliner Volksblatt, 1893.

Debate on social democracy held in the German Reichstag, Jan. 31 — Feb. 7, 1893. It is significant that this debate was reprinted without note or comment and circulated by the social democratic party.

SPENCER, HERBERT.
Economics, ed. by Owen. New York, Humboldt Publ. Co., 1891.
Man *versus* the state. London, Williams & Norgate, 1884.
Also contains: New toryism; Coming slavery; Sins of legislators; Great political superstition.

STAMMHAMMER, JOSEF.
Bibliographie des socialismus und communismus. Jena, Fischer, 1893.
The most complete bibliography of socialism yet published.

STARKWEATHER, A. J., and WILSON, S. R.
Socialism. New York, Lovell, 1884.

STEGEMANN, RICH.
Die idee des socialismus. Berlin, Nitschke u. Löchner, 1888.

STEGMANN, C., UND HUGO, V.
Handbuch des socialismus. Zürich, Schabelitz, 1894.

STEGMANN, C., UND HUGO, V.
An encyclopædia of socialism, giving information in regard to the socialist movement in all countries.

STEIN, LORENZ V.
Der socialismus und communismus des heutigen Frankreichs. 2 vol. Leipzig, Wigand, 1848.
Geschichte der socialen bewegung in Frankreichs, 1830–1848. Leipzig, Wigand, 1850.

STEPHENS, J. F. J.
Liberty, equality, and fraternity. New York, Holt & Williams, 1873.
In general, takes issue with Mill's idea of liberty.

SUDRE, ALFRED.
Histoire du communisme, ou Refutation d'utopies socialistes. Paris, Guillaumin, 1856.

SYBEL, HEINRICH V.
Die lehren des heutigen socialismus und communismus. Bohn, Cohen u. Sohn, 1872.

TAINE, HIPPOLYTE ADOLPHE.
Socialism as government. 1884. (Contemp. xlvi. 507.)

THIERS, LOUIS ADOLPH.
Du communisme. Paris, Paulin et L'heureux, 1849.
The rights of property a refutation of communism and socialism. London, 1848.

THONISSEN, J. J.
Le socialisme, depuis l'antiquité jusqu'à la constitution française, 1852. Paris, Sagnier et Bray, 1852.

THUN, ALPHONS.
Geschichte der revolutionären bewegungen in Russland. Leipzig, Duncker, 1883.

TREITSCHKE, H. G. V.
Der socialismus und seine gönner. Berlin, Reimer, 1875.
Replied to by Schmoller.

TRUMPLEMANN, AUG.
Was hat der landmann von der socialdemokratie zu erwarten? Leipzig, Werther, 1891.

TUFFERD, FRÉD.
Un programme social. Paris, Bouriand, 1887.

TURATTI, F.
Socialismo et scienza. 1885.

UNGER, S.
Fortschritt und socialismus. Berlin, Puttkammer, 1886.

VERDAD, P.
Le faux et le vrai socialisme. Nantes, Libr. de la Relig. Univ., 1892.

VOLLMAR, GEORG V.
Ueber die nächsten aufgaben der deutschen socialdemokratie. Munich, Ernst, 1891.

VOLLMAR, GEORGE V.
This author represents the most conservative wing of the German social democrats.

WACHENHAUSEN, OTTO.
Grundsätze der nationalökonomie sowie des staatssocialismus und der socialdemokratie. Leipzig, Wigand, 1886.

WAGNER, ADOLPH.
Einiges von und über Rodbertus-Jagetzow. (Tübingen, Zeitschrift, 1878.)

Grundlegung der politischen ökonomie. Leipzig and Heidelberg, Winter, 1892.

Treats of the fundamental principles of socialism in a most liberal, fair-minded manner.

Das neue sozialdemokratische programm. Berlin, Rehtwisch, 1893.

WALCKER, CARL.
Die ursachen und die heilmittel der socialdemokratischen umsturzbestrebungen. Berlin, Heymann, 1879.

WARSCHAUER, OTTO.
Geschichte des socialismus und neueren communismus. Leipzig, Foch, 1893.

Bd. 1. Saint-Simon und Saint-Simonismus; Bd. 2. Fourier, seine theorie und seine schule.

WEBB, SIDNEY.
Difficulties of individualism. Pph. London, 1892.

London programme. London, Sonnenschein, 1891.

Socialism in England. London, Sonnenschein, 1893.

WERNER, JUL.
Socialrevolution oder socialreform? Halle, Schwetschke, 1891.

WILDE, OSCAR.
Soul of man under socialism. Pph.

Also contains: Morris, Socialist ideal: Art; Owen, Coming solidarity.

WINTERER, L.
Le socialisme international. Paris, Lecoffre, 1890.

WOLF, JULIUS.
Sozialismus und kapitalistische gesellschaftsordnung. Stuttgart, Cotta, 1892.

Attempts to disprove the law of evolution, which is the main feature of Marx's socialism.

WOLLMANN, MORIZ.
Die arbeiterbewegung in Belgien. (Die Gegenwart, 1886.)

Der socialismus in Belgien. (Die Gegenwart, Bd. 31, 1887.)

WOOLSEY, T. D.
Communism and socialism in their history and theory. New York, Scribner, 1880.

WYZEWA, T. de.
Le mouvement socialiste en Europe. Paris, Perrinet, 1892.

ZANETTI, F.
Il socialismo, sue cause e suoi effetti. Turin, Salesiana, 1893.

ZELLER, J.
Zur erkenntniss unserer staatswissenschaftlichen zustände. Berlin, Bahr, 1885.

ZIEGLER, TH.
Naturwissenschaft und die socialdemokratische theorie. 1894.

Die sociale frage, eine sittliche frage. Stuttgart, Göschen, 1891.

ANARCHISM.

ADLER, G.
Anarchismus. Jena, 1889.

BAKUNIN, MICHEL.
God and the state. Tr. by Tucker. Boston, 1883.
Il socialismo e Mazzini: lettera. Ancona, 1886.
La théologie politique de Mazzini et l'internationale. Comm. de la propaganda socialiste, 1871.
Michel Bakunin und der radicalismus. 1877. (Deut. Rund., xi. 293, 314.)
Sketch of nihilists, including Bakunin. 1880. (Nineteenth Cent., vii. 1.)

BOULARD, EDOUARD.
Théorie et pratique du collectivisme intégral révolutionnaire. Paris, Lecourtois, 1892.

BUCCELLATI, A.
Il nihilismo e la ragione del diritto penale. Milano, Rebeschini, 1883.

CABOSSEL.
Solution de la question sociale par le communisme anarchiste. Paris, Reiff, 1883.

CHICAGO ANARCHISTS.
Altgeld. Reasons for pardoning Fielden, Neebe, and Schwab. Chicago, 1893.
Illinois Supreme Court. [Decision in anarchist case.] 1887.
Lewis. Facts [on] eight condemned leaders. Pph., 1887.
Lum. History of trial. 1886.
Speeches in court. London, Reeves, 1891.
Vide: Parsons.

APPENDIX XI.

CLAUS, F. O.
Die wahren anarchisten im preussischen staate. Stuttgart, Lutz, 1891.

COURTOIS, ALPHONSE, *fils*.
Anarchisme théorique et collectivisme pratique. Paris, Guillaumin, 1885.

GODWIN, WILLIAM.
Inquiry concerning political justice and its influence on morals and happiness. 2 vol. London, Robinson, 1798.

Political justice. [On property.] Ed. by Salt. London, Sonnenschein, 1891.

Earliest philosophical anarchist.

GRAVE, JEAN.
La société mourante et l'anarchie. Paris, Tresse, 1893.

HAMON, E.
Les hommes et les théories de l'anarchie. Paris, Bibl. de l'Art Social, 1893.

JAMES, C. L.
Anarchy. Pph. Eau Claire, Wis., James, 1886.

KRAPOTKIN, *Prince* P. A.
Appeal to the young. London, Soc. Dem. Fed., 1890.

Coming anarchy. 1887. (Nineteenth Cent., xxii. 149.)

KRAPOTKIN, *Prince* P. A.
Commune of Paris: Wage system; Anarchist morality; War. London, Reeves.

La morale anarchiste. Paris, Grave, 1891.

Law and authority. London, Internat.Publ.Co., 1886.

Paroles d'un révolté. Paris, Marpon, 1885.

Place of anarchism in socialistic revolution. London, Internat. Publ. Co., 1886.

Scientific bases of anarchy. 1887. (Nineteenth Cent.,) xxi. 238.

LAISANT, A.
L'anarchie bourgeoise. Paris, Marpon, 1887.

LE VAGRE, JULIAN.
La organisation de la propagande révolutionnaire. Pph., Paris, 1885.

LUM, DYER D.
Economics of anarchy. New York, Twentieth Cent. Publ. Co., 1892.

MOST, JOHANN.
Die anarchie. New York, 1888.

Die freie gesellschaft. New York, 1884.

Kapital und arbeit. Chemnitz, Genoss-buchdr., 1873.

Most, Johann.
Der kleinbürger und die sozialdemokratie. Berlin, Verlag des "Vorwärts," Berliner Volksblatt.
Die lösung der socialen frage. Berlin, 1876.
Revolutionäre kriegswissenschaft. New York.
Social monster. New York, 1890.
Die sozialen bewegungen im alten Rom und der cäsarismus. Berlin, Verlag des "Vorwärts," Berliner Volksblatt, 1889.

Malato, C.
La philosophie de l'anarchie. Paris, Libr. Cosmopolite, 1889.

Musoin, P.
Propaganda in miscarea sociala. Bukarest, Lupta, 1892.

Osgood, Herbert L.
Scientific anarchism. (Pol. Sci. Quar., March, 1889.)

Parsons, Albert R.
Anarchism, its philosophy and scientific basis. Chicago, 1887.

Pessine, E.
L'anarchie. Naples, Ugenio Geronimo, 1891.

Preval, Jehan.
Anarchisme et nihilisme. Paris, Savine, 1892.

Proudhon, P. J.
Vide: General socialism: Proudhon.

Quarangiii, C. T. de.
Russian Panslavist programme. (Contemp. Rev., Aug., 1881.)

Rawson, Edward Kirk.
Anarchic socialism. 1884. (New Eng., xliii. 113.)
Rationale of Russian socialism. 1884. (And. Rev., ii. 246.)

Reclus, J. J. E.
Anarchy, by an anarchist. 1884. (Contemp., xxxix. 232.)
Evolution and revolution. London, Reeves, 1891.

Seelye, Julius Hawley.
Dynamite as a factor in civilization. 1884. (North Amer., cxxxvii. 1.)

Shaw, G. Bernard.
Impossibilities of anarchism. (Tract 45.) London, Fabian society, 1893.
Socialism and anarchism: Antagonistic opposites. Pph. New York., Soc. Labor Party, 1886.

Testut, Oscar.
Le livre bleu de l'International. Paris, Lachaud, 1871.

TUCKER, BENJAMIN R.
Instead of a book: exposition of philosophical anarchism. New York, Tucker, 1893.

VAN ORNUM, W. H.
Why government at all? Chicago, Kerr, 1892.

YARROS, VICTOR.
Anarchism: its aims and methods. Pph. New York, Tucker.

ZACHER.
Die rothe Internationale. Berlin, Hertz, 1884.
The Red International. London, Sonnenschein, 1886.

CHRISTIAN SOCIALISM.

ABELOUS, L.
Le christianisme et le problème social. Alais, Martin, 1872.

ABRAHAM, W. H.
Studies of a socialistic parson. London, Simpkin, 1892.

ASSOCIATION (L'), PROTESTANTE, pour l'étude pratique des questions sociales.
Travaux du congrès du Havre, 1893. Paris, Fischbacher, 1894.
Gives a good idea of the work being done by the Christian socialists of the Protestant denominations in France.

BARRY, ALFRED.
Christianity and socialism. London, Cassell, 1890.
Christianity is to seek to balance socialism by emphasizing the sacredness of individuality.

BEHRENDS, A. J. F.
Socialism and Christianity. New York, Baker & Taylor, 1886.

BÉNÉDICT.
Le catholicisme social. Paris, Libr. de la Rev. Soc. 1886.

BIERBOWER, A.
Socialism of Christ. Chicago, Sergel, 1891.

BLISS, W. D. P.
What is Christian socialism? Pph. Boston, 1894.

BLISSARD, W.
Socialism of Christianity. London, Stock, 1891.

BRAKE, G.
Der christliche socialismus des pfarrers Todt. Oldenburg, Schmidt, 1879.

BRENTANO, LUJO.
Die christlichsoziale bewegung in England. Pph. Leipzig, Duncker, 1883.

BRÜLL, ANDR.
Die encyclica über die arbeiterfrage. (*In* Christl. soc. Blätter, 1891.)
Soziale reformbestrebungen — katholisch soziale. (*In* Handw. d. Staatswissen.)

CABRINI, A.
Il socialismo religioso e le rivendicazioni del proletariato. Piacenza, Marchesotti, 1891.

CHEROUNY, HENRY W.
Socialism and Christianity. New York, Cherouny, 1882.

CHOUTEAU, OLIVIER.
Programme de socialisme catholique. Dôle, Breune, 1894.

COURTEPÉE, P. F.
Socialisme catholique. Nantes, Libr. de la Relig. Laïque, 1892.

DAVIDSON, J. MORRISON.
Gospel of the poor. London, Reeves, 1894.
Evangelisch-sociale zeitfragen, Ser. 1–10 Hefte. Leipzig, Grunow, 1891.

FURRER, K.
Darwinismus und socialismus im lichte der christliche weltanschauung. Zürich, Müller, 1889.

GIBBONS, *Cardinal.*
Letter to the Knights of Labor. (London Tablet. 1887.)

GIRDLESTONE, E. D.
Christian socialism *versus* Present day unsocialism. London, Reeves, 1887.
Society classified. London, Reeves, 1886.
Thirty-nine articles of belief for Christian socialists. Bristol, Arrowsmith, 1886.

GÖHRE, PAUL.
Drei monate fabrikarbeiter. Leipzig, 1891.
Socialism can and must be Christianized.
Three months a factory hand. Tr. by A. B. Carr. London, Sonnenschein, 1894. (In press.)

GREIFFENRATH.
Bischof von Ketteler und die deutsche sozial reform. Frankfurt, Fösser, 1893.

HEADLAM, S. D.
Christian socialism. Pph. London, Fabian Soc., 1892.

HOHOFF, WILHELM.
Protestantismus und socialismus ; historisch - politische studien. Paderborn, 1883.

HUGHES, HUGH PRICE.
Social Christianity. New York, Funk & Wagnall, 1889.
Philanthropy of God. New York. Funk & Wagnall, 1889.

JOY, HENRI.
Le socialisme chrétien. Paris, Hachette, 1892.

KANNENGIESER, A.
Le socialisme et la rôle politique du clergé en Allemagne. Paris, Soye, 1891.

KAUFMANN, MORITZ.
Charles Kingsley, Christian socialist and reformer. London, Methuen, 1892.
Theory of Christian socialism. London, Kegan Paul, 1888.

KETTELER, W. E. F. v.
Die arbeiterbewegung und das christenthum. Mainz, Kirchheim, 1890.
Liberalismus, socialismus und christenthum. Pph. Mainz, Kirchheim, 1871.

KINGSLEY, CHARLES.
Vide: Kaufmann.

KOBER, JOHANNES.
Karl Mez (1808-1877) : ein vorkämpfer für christlichen socialismus. Basel, Splittler, 1892.

LEO XIII., *Pope.*
Lettre encyclique de la condition des ouvriers. Texte latin et traduction française officielle. Paris, Poussielgue. 1891.

MARSON, C. L.
Socialism of the Fathers. (*In* West. Rev., Feb., 1894.)

MAURICE, F. D.
What Christian socialism has to do with the question at present agitating the Church. London, 1850.
Social morality. London, Macmillan, 1869.

MEDLEY, D. J.
Socialism as a moral movement. Oxford, Blackwell, 1884.

MEZ, KARL.
Vide: Kober.

NAUMANN, FR.
Das sociale programm der evangelischen kirche. Leipzig, Deichert, 1891.

NITTI, F. S.
Il socialismo cattolico : studi sul socialismo contemporaneo. Torino, Roux, 1891.
Treats of the attitude of the Catholic Church toward the social question, and of the leading Catholic socialists throughout Europe.
Catholic socialism. Tr. by Killea. London, Sonnenschein, 1894. (In press.)

OETTINGEN, ALEX. V.
Was heisst christlich-social ? Leipzig, Duncker, 1886.

PERIN.
Le socialisme chrétien. Pph., Paris, Lecoffre, 1879.

RYLANCE, J. H.
Lectures on social questions. New York, Whittaker, 1880.

SCHMIDT, C. W. A.
Social results of early Christianity. London, Ibister, 1885.

SCUDDER, VIDA D.
Spiritual socialism, Pph. Boston, Dawn Publ. Co., 1893.

SPRAGUE, PHILO W.
Christian socialism: what and why? New York, Dutton, 1891.

STÖCKER, ADOLF.
Christlich-sozial: reden und aufsätze. Berlin, Buchh. d. Berliner Stadtmission, 1890.

TAFEL, R. L.
Socialism and reform in the light of the new church. London, Spiers, 1891.

TODT, RUDOLF.
Der radikale deutsche socialismus und die christliche gesellschaft. Wittenberg, Herosé, 1878.

TODT, RUDOLF.
Vide: Brake.

TUCKWELL, W.
Christian socialism. London, Simpkin, 1891.

WACH, AD.
Die christliche-sociale arbeiterpartei. Leipzig, Tauchnitz, 1878.

WESTCOTT, B. F.
Socialism: read before Hull Congress. London, Reeves, 1890.
Social aspects of Christianity. London, Macmillan, 1887.

SOCIALISTIC FICTION.

ADDERLEY, JAMES.
Stephen Remarx. London, Arnold, 1893.
Socialistic novel, similar in style and aim to Alton Locke and Yeast.

BELLAMY, EDWARD.
Looking backward. (2000–1887.) Boston, Houghton, Mifflin & Co., 1890.

BESANT, WALTER.
All sorts and conditions of men. London, Chatto., 1887.

BILDERBUCH für grosse und kleine kinder. Illus. Stuttgart, Dietz, 1893.
This work has special significance as the first illustrated children's book designed to inculcate social democracy.

BREAD-WINNERS. New York, Harpers, 1884.
Written in opposition to labor organizations. Anti-socialistic in its nature.

CHIRAC, AUGUSTE.
Si: étude sociale d'après demain. Paris, Savine, 1893.

DISRAELI, BENJAMIN.
Sybil, or Two nations. London, Longmans.

DRAGE, GEOFFREY.
Cyril, a novel. London, Allen, 1892.

GISSING, G.
Demos: a story of English socialism. 3 vol. Paris, Klincksieck, 1886.

GREGOROVIUS.
Himmel auf erden: 1901–1912. Pph. Leipzig, Grunow, 1892.

HAWTHORNE, NATHANIEL.
Blithedale Romance. [Brook Farm.] Boston, Houghton, Mifflin & Co.

HOWELLS, WILLIAM DEAN.
Hazard of new fortunes. 2 vol. New York, Harpers, 1890.
Traveller from Altruria. New York, Harpers, 1893.
World of chance. New York, Harpers, 1892.

KINGSLEY, CHARLES.
Alton Locke. London, Macmillan, 1882.
Yeast. London, Macmillan, 1890.

KRETZER, MAX.
Die betrogenen. 2 vol. Berlin, Xogge, 1882.

MACKAY, J. H.
Die anarchisten: kulturgemälde aus dem ende des 19. jahrhunderts. Zürich, 1891.
The anarchists: picture of civilization at the close of the nineteenth century. Tr. by Schumm. New York, Humboldt Publ. Co., 1893.

MALLOCK, W. H.
Old order changes. London, Bentley, 1887.

MONEY-MAKERS: a social parable. New York, Appleton, 1885.
In reply to the Breadwinners.

MORRIS, WILLIAM.
Dream of John Ball. London, Reeves, 1889.
News from nowhere. London, Reeves, 1892.

RICHTER, EUGENE.
Pictures of the socialistic future. Tr. by Wright. London, Sonnenschein, 1894.
Replied to in Mehring's Bilder aus der gegenwart.
Vide: General Socialism.

SHAW, G. BERNARD.
Quintessence of Ibsenism. London, Scott, 1891.
Widowers' houses: comedy. London, Henry, 1893.

STORY OF MY DICTATORSHIP. London, 1894.
Discussion of the land question.

TCHERNYCHEWSKY, N. G.
Que faire ? Roman. Paris, Ghio, 1876.

TOLSTOÏ, LEO.
Works. New York, Crowell. Vols. 1-11. London, Walter Scott, 1888-1889.
All of Tolstoï's works have a trend in the direction of Christian socialism; in particular, My Confession, Sevastopol, What to Do.
Also: Le travail. Paris, Marpon, 1890.

WOODS, KATE PEARSON.
Metzerott, shoemaker. Boston and New York, Crowell, 1889.

SOCIALISTIC SONGS AND POEMS.

CARPENTER, E.
Chants of labor, with music. London, Sonnenschein, 1892.

Song book for socialists. London, Reeves.

GLASIER, J. B.
Socialistic songs. Glasgow, 1893.

HOCHFLUT.
Socialistische zeitgedichte. Leipzig, Volksbuchh., 1891.

JOYNES, J. L.
Songs of a revolutionary epoch. London, Reeves, 1888.

KEGEL, MAX.
Socialdemokratisches liederbuch. Stuttgart, Dietz, 1891.

MONTICELLI, CARLO.
Canzoniere socialista. San Remo, Dernetrio, 1888.

MORRIS, WILLIAM.
Chants for socialists. London, Reeves, 1885.

Poems by the way. London, Reeves, 1891.

POTTIER, EUGÈNE DE.
Chants révolutionnaires. Paris, Dentu, 1887.

SOCIALISTIC UTOPIAS.

BACON, FRANCIS.
New Atlantis. London, Ward, 1885.

BRASCH, MORITZ.
Socialistische phantasiestaaten. Leipzig, Huth, 1885.

CABET, ÉTIENNE.
Voyage en Icarie. Paris, au Bureau du Populaire, 1848.

CABET, ÉTIENNE.
Utopian romance, containing the principles of Cabet's theory of communism, on which the settlement in *Icaria* was founded.

Vide: Malon; Écoles des socialistes françaises; Nordhoff; Shaw.

GEHRKE, A.
Communistische idealstaaten. Bremen, Schünemann, 1878.

HARRINGTON, JAMES.
Commonwealth of Oceana [1656]. London, Routledge, 1887.

HERTZKA, THEODOR.
Freiland: ein sociales zukunftsbild. Leipzig, Duncker, 1890.
Freeland. London, Chatto, 1891.
Ostafrikanaan. Leipzig, Schaumburg-Fleischer, 1891.

IDEAL COMMONWEALTHS.
Ed. by Morley. London, Routledge, 1885.
Contents: — Plutarch's Lycurgus; More's Utopia; Bacon's New Atlantis; Campanella's City of the Sun; Hall's Mundus alter et idem.

KAUFMANN, MORITZ.
Utopias. London, Kegan Paul, 1879.

KLEINWÄCHTER, F.
Die staatsromane: beitrag zur lehre vom communismus und socialismus. Wien, Breitenstein, 1891.
Discusses all utopias from Plato to Cabet.

MORE, THOMAS.
Utopia [1516]. Tr. by St. John. London, Scott Lib., 1886.

PETZLER, J.
Life in Utopia. London, Author's Co-op. Soc., 1890.

PLATO.
Republic. London, Macmillan, 1892.

SECRETAN, C.
Mon utopie. [Gillette.] Paris, Alcan, 1892.

SOCIALISTIC EXPERIMENTS.

ELY, RICHARD T.
Labor movement in America. New York, Crowell, 1886.

HINDS, W. A.
American communities. Oneida, Amer. Socialist, 1878.
Economy; Zoar; Bethel; Aurora; Amana; Icaria; Shakers: Oneida; Wallingford; Brotherhood of the New Life.

NORDHOFF, C.
Communistic societies of the United States. New York, Harper, 1875.

NOYES, J. H.
History of American socialisms. Philadelphia, Lippincott, 1870.

AMANA.
Gruber. Inspirations-historie. 1884.

AMANA.
Shaw. Life in Amana colony. (Chat., Feb., 1888.)
ICARIA.
Beluze, Jean Pierre.
Lettres icariennes. Paris, chez l'auteur, 1859-1864.
Hepner.
Die Ikarier in Nord-Amerika. New York, 1886.
Lux, H.
Étienne Cabet und der ikarische kommunismus. Stuttgart, Dietz.
Merson, Ernst.
Le communisme. Réfutation de l'utopie icarienne. Paris, Garnie, 1848.
Shaw, Albert.
Icaria: chapter in the history of communism. New York, Putnam, 1884.
ONEIDA COMMUNITY.
Noyes, J. H.
Home talks. Oneida, 1875.
History of American socialisms (Oneida Community). Philadelphia, Lippincott 1870.
SHAKERS.
Evans, F. W.
Autobiography. London, 1878.

SHAKERS.
Evans, F. W.
Ann Lee, biography. London, 1858.
Shaker communism. London, 1871.
Robinson.
Shakers. 1893.
PARAGUAY.
Dezamy, Theodore.
Le jésuitisme vaincu et anéanti par le socialisme. Paris, Plon, 1845.
Gothein, E.
Der christlichsociale staat der Jesuiten in Paraguay. (Staats und socialwissen. forschungen, Bd. IV. 4 Heft, 1883.)
GUISE.
Godin.
La richesse au service du people: la familistère de Guise. Paris, Libr. de la Bibl. Démocr., 1874.
Gronlund, Laurence.
Godin's "Social Palace." (Arena, May, 1890.) Neale, E. V.
Associated homes; lecture on the Familistère at Guise, and a biographical notice of Godin. London, Macmillan, 1880.
Vide: General Socialism: Godin.

PARIS COMMUNE.
  Becker, Beruh.
    Geschichte und theorie der Pariser revolutionären Commune, 1871. Leipzig, Wigand, 1879.
  Blos, Wilhelm.
    Zur geschichte der Commune von Paris. Braunschweig, 1876.
  Lepage, A.
    Histoire de la Commune. 1871.

PARIS COMMUNE.
  Lepage, A.
    Description by an eye-witness.
  Lissagaray.
    Histoire de la Commune de 1871. Bruxelles, 1876.
    History of the Commune. Tr. by Aveling. London, Reeves. 1886.
  Morin, Georges.
    Histoire critique de la Commune. Paris, Libr. internat. 1871.

SOCIAL REFORM.
GENERAL.

AUSTRALASIAN COLONIES.
  Vide: Coghlan; Great Britain. — Royal Commission on Labour: Colonies and the Indian Empire. Land Reform: Epps. Legislative reform: New South Wales.
BARNETT, S. and H.
  Practicable socialism. London, Longmans, 1889.
BEMIS, E. W.
  Relation of the church to social problems. Pph. Boston, Dawn Publ. Co., 1893.
BUSHILL, T. W.
  Profit-sharing and the labor question, by a profit-sharing employer. London, Methuen, 1893.

  Advocates semi-compulsory thrift for the laborer.

COGHLAN, T. A., *Government Statistician.*
  Statistical account of the seven colonies of Australasia. Sydney, Gov't. Publ., 1892.
  Wealth and progress of New South Wales. Sydney, Gov't. Publ., 1893.
  Statistical register to 1892. Sydney, Gov't. Publ., 1894.

ELY, RICHARD T.
  Social aspects of Christianity. New York, Crowell, 1889.

ELY, R. T., and FINLEY, J. H.
Taxation in American states and cities. New York, Crowell, 1888.

FRY, T. C.
Social policy for the Church. London, 1894.

GEDDES, PATRICK, and THOMSON, J. A.
Evolution of sex. New York, Scribner & Welford; London, Walter Scott, 1889.

Important in the treatment of the question of population.

GILMAN, NICOLAS PAINE.
Profit-sharing between employer and employee. Boston, Houghton, Mifflin & Co., 1890.

GLADDEN, WASHINGTON.
Applied Christianity. Boston, Houghton, Mifflin & Co., 1886.

Tools and the man. Boston, Houghton, Mifflin & Co., 1893.

JACOBSON, AUGUSTUS.
Higher ground. Chicago, McClurg, 1888.

Advocates taxation of inheritances and manual training.

JEVONS, W. STANLEY.
Methods of social reform. London and New York, Macmillan, 1883.

KIDD, BENJAMIN.
Social evolution. New York and London, Macmillan, 1894.

Emphasizes religion as a social force.

LANGE, F. A.
Die arbeiterfrage in ihrer bedeutung für gegenwart und zukunft beleuchtet. Winterthur, Bleuler, 1879.

LOOMIS, S. L.
Modern cities and their religious problems. New York, 1887.

OETTINGEN, ALEX. V.
Die moralstatistik und die christliche sittenlehre. Erlangen, Deichert, 1874.

SAMTER, ADOLPH.
Das eigenthum in seiner socialen bedeutung. Jena, Fischer, 1879.

Emphasizes the social side of private property.

SCHÄFFLE, A. E. F.
Theory and policy of labor protection. London, Sonnenschein, 1893.

Treats of practicable social reforms.

SOETBEER, HEINRICH.
Die stellung der sozialisten zur Malthusschen bevölkerungslehre. Berlin, Puttkammer, 1886.

SPRAGUE, F. M.
Socialism from Genesis to Revelation. New York, Dutton, 1892.
Treats largely of the application of socialism to modern problems.

STÖPEL, FRANZ.
Sociale reform. Leipzig, Wigand, 1884–1885.

STRONG, JOSIAH.
New era. New York, Baker & Taylor, 1891.
Our country. New York, Baker & Taylor, 1891.

SUMNER, W. G.
What social classes owe each other. New York, Harpers, 1884.

WARD, LESTER F.
Psychic factors of civilization. Boston, Ginn, 1893.
In his chapter on Sociocracy, he advocates a societary form of government, which, by extending the powers of the state, will remedy the present evils of the competitive system.

LEGISLATIVE REFORM.

FABIAN SOCIETY.
Municipal program (Tracts 30–37). London, Fabian Society, 1893.
1. Unearned increment; 2. London's heritage in the City Guilds; 3. Municipalization of the gas supply; 4. Municipal tramways; 5. London's water tribute; 6. Municipalization of the London docks; 7. Scandal of London markets; 8. Labor policy for public authorities.

Eight hours by law: the practical solution (Tract 49). London, Fabian Soc., 1894.

Plan of campaign for labor (Tract 49). London, Fabian Soc., 1894.

GLADDEN, WASHINGTON.
Cosmopolis city club. New York, Century Co., 1894.
Discusses problems of municipal reform.

GREGORY, C. N.
Corrupt use of money in politics, and laws for its prevention (Univ. of Wis. Publ. of Hist. and Pol. Science Assoc., 1893).

HOLE, JAMES.
National railways; argument for state purchase. London, Cassell, 1893.
Author is the Secretary of the Association of the Chambers of Commerce of Great Britain.

JEVONS, W. STANLEY.
State in relation to labor. London, Macmillan, 1882.

LUBBOCK, JOHN.
Representation. London, (Imper. Parl. ser.).

MASSACHUSETTS LEGISLATURE.
Report on the Norwegian system of liquor selling. Boston, 1894. (House Document, 192.)

NEW SOUTH WALES.
Railway Commission. Report on the government railways and tramways for 1893. Sydney, 1893.

PROPORTIONAL REPRESENTATION REVIEW. Quarterly. Chicago, 1893 to date.
Organ of the American Proportional Representation League, devoted to the reformation of the method of electing representatives.

RAE, JOHN.
The eight hours' day and foreign competition. (Contemp. Rev., Feb., 1894.)

RITCHIE, D. G.
Principles of state interference. London, Sonnenschein, 1891.

RITCHIE, D. G.
Discusses the political philosophy of Spencer, Mill, and Green.

ROBERTSON, J. M.
Eight hours' question. London, Sonnenschein, 1893.

SULLIVAN, J. W.
Direct legislation by the citizenship through the initiative and referendum. New York, True Nationalist Publ. Co., 1893.

VINCENT, J. MARTIN.
State and federal government in Switzerland. Baltimore, J. Hopkins Press, 1891.
For referendum and initiative *see* Chaps. 4, 13; for government monopoly, Chap. 9.

WEBB, SIDNEY.
Eight hours' day. London, Scott, 1891.
Moral of the elections. (Contemp. Rev., Aug., 1892.)

WIGMORE, J. H.
Australian ballot system. Boston, 1889.

WOLFF, HENRY W.
People's banks: a record of social and economic success. London, Longmans, 1893.

LAND REFORM.

COLINS.
L'économie politique: source des révolutions et des utopies prétendues socialistes. 3 vol. Paris, Bestel, 1856, Bruxelles, Manceaux, 1891.
Science sociale. 6 vol. Paris, Bestel, 1857. 12 vol. Bruxelles, Lamertin, 1884.

CONVERSE, J. B.
Bible and land. Morristown, Tenn., Converse, 1889.
An attempt to present the subject of land taxation from the standpoint of the Bible.

COX, HAROLD.
Land nationalization. London, Methuen, 1892.

DAWSON, W. H.
Unearned increment. London, Sonnenschein, 1890.

EICHTAL, EUGÈNE D'.
Nationalization du sol, et collectivisme agraire. Paris, Bur. des annal. économ., 1891.

ENGLISH LAND RESTORATION LEAGUE.
[Publications.] London, Off. of Land Restor. League.

EPPS, WILLIAM.
Land systems of Australasia. London, Sonnenschein, 1894.

FLÜRSCHEIM, MICHAEL.
Der einzige rettungsweg. Leipsic and Dresden. Pierson, 1890.
The best German treatment of the principles of Henry George.

GEORGE, HENRY.
Progress and poverty. New York, Appleton, 1880.
Social problems. London, Kegan Paul, 1884.
Condition of labour. London, Sonnenschein, 1891.

GRONLUND, LAURENCE.
Insufficiency of Henry George's theory. New York, 1886.
Socialism vs. Tax reform: answer to Henry George. New York, N. Y. Labor News Co., 1886.

LAND AND LABOUR.
Monthly. London.
Organ of the land nationalization Society.

MALLOCK, W. H.
Property and progress. London, Murray, 1884.

ROSE, HENRY.
Henry George, a biographical, anecdotal, and critical sketch. London, 1884.

STOLP, HERM.
Der reform des eigenthumrechts als grundlage der socialreform. Berlin, Issleib, 1884.

THACKERAY, S. W.
Land and the community. New York, Appleton, 1889.

WALKER, FRANCIS A.
Land and its rent. Boston, Little, Brown & Co., 1883.

WALKER, FRANCIS A.
Contains a noteworthy argument against the theories of Henry George.

WALLACE, ALFRED RUSSEL.
Land nationalisation. London, Sonnenschein, 1892. Why and How of land nationalisation. 1883. (Mac. 48: 357, 485.)

REFORM METHODS IN THE TREATMENT OF POVERTY.

ADDAMS, JANE, and others.
Philanthropy and social progress. New York, Crowell, 1893.

BERTHOLD, G.
Die deutschen arbeiter-colonien. (Jahr. f. Gesetz, 10, Heft. 2.)

BOOTH, CHARLES.
Life and labour of the people in London. 4 vol. London and New York, Macmillan, 1892–1893.
Pauperism and the endowment of old age. London, Macmillan, 1892.

BOOTH, WILLIAM.
In darkest England and the way out. New York, Funk & Wagnall, 1891.

BURNS, JOHN.
The unemployed. (Tract 47.) London, Fabian Society, 1893.

CHARITIES REVIEW.
New York, 1891 to date.

COIT, STANTON.
Neighborhood guilds; an instrument of social reform. London, Sonnenschein, 1891.

MILLS, HERBERT V.
Poverty and the state, or Work for the unemployed. London, Kegan Paul, 1886.

REYNOLDS, M. T.
Housing of the poor in great cities. New York, Amer. Econ. Ass. Publ., 1893.

SPENDER, J. A., and ACLAND, ARTHUR.
The state and pensions in old age. London, Sonnenschein, 1892.

WAGNER, ADOLPH.
Mittel und wege zur errettung des deutschen volkes, aus seiner verarmung. Breslau, Max, 1892.

WARNER, AMOS G.
Some experiments in behalf of the unemployed. (Quar. Jour. Econ., Oct., 1890.)

WILLINK, H. G.
Dutch home labour-colonies: their origin and development. London, Kegan Paul, 1890.

SOCIALISTIC AND ANARCHISTIC PUBLICATIONS.

ALMANACH DE LA QUESTION SOCIALE, ET DE LA LIBRE PENSÉE. Paris, 1891 to date.
    Annuaire du socialisme international par Argyriades.

DER ANARCHIST. Anarchistisch-communistiches organ. Weekly. New York.

BROTHERHOOD. Monthly. London.

CHICAGOER ARBEITER ZEITUNG. [Anarchist.] Daily, except Sunday. Chicago.

CHURCH REFORMER. Edited by Stewart D. Headlam. Monthly. London.
    Official Organ of Guild of St. Matthew (Eng.).

THE DAWN. Edited by W. D. P. Bliss. [Christian-socialist.] Monthly. Boston.

ECONOMIC REVIEW. Quarterly. London, 1891 to date.
    Organ of (Eng.) Christian Social Union.

L'ÉTUDIANT SOCIALISTE. Annual. Organ de la Fédération des Étudiants socialistes belges. Brussels.

FABIAN NEWS. [Socialist.] Monthly. London.
    Organ of Fabian Society.

DIE FACKEL. [Socialist.] Sunday issue of Chicagoer Arbeiter Zeitung. Chicago.

DIE FREIHEIT. Edited by Johann Most. [Anarchist.] Weekly. New York, 1879 to date.

GOODWILL. Edited by J. Adderley. [Christian-socialist.] Monthly. London, 1894.

L'INTRANSIGEANT. Edited by Henri Rochefort. [Socialist.] Daily. Paris.

JUSTICE. [Socialist.] Weekly. London, 1884 to date.
    Organ of (Eng.) Social Democratic Federation.

LIBERTY. Edited by B. R. Tucker. [Anarchist.] Weekly. New York.

DIE NEUE ZEIT. Revue des geistigen und öffentlichen lebens. Weekly. Stuttgart, 1883 to date.

NEW YORKER VOLKSZEITUNG. Daily. 1879 to date.
Leading German publication of American socialistic labor party.

THE NATIONALIST. Monthly. Boston, 1889-91.

THE NEW NATION. Weekly. Boston, Jan. 31, 1891, to Feb. 3, 1894.

THE PEOPLE. [Socialist.] Weekly. New York.
Leading (Eng.) organ - of American socialistic party.

LA PETITE RÉPUBLIQUE. Edited by A. Millerand. [Socialist.] Daily. Paris.

LE PEUPLE. Brussels.
Leading socialist newspaper in Belgium.

LA PHILOSOPHIE DE L'AVENIR, par F. Borde. Bimonthly. Paris, 1876 to date.
Revue du socialisme rationel.

LA REVUE SOCIALISTE. Monthly. Paris, 1885 to date.

LE SOCIALISTE, par J. Guesde et P. Lafargue. [Socialist.] Weekly. Paris.

SÜD-DEUTSCHER POSTILLON. Semi-monthly. Illus. Munich, 1882 to date.

SÜD-DEUTSCHER POSTILLON.
This publication and Der Wahre Jacob compare favorably with other German comic papers of to-day.

TERRE ET LIBERTÉ. [Anarchist.] Weekly. Paris.

TWENTIETH CENTURY. Weekly radical magazine. New York, 1889 to date.
Originally anarchistic in its views, it has become socialistic. The publication covers somewhat the same field as the New Nation, which has recently ceased to appear.

DER VORBOTE. [Anarchist.] Weekly. Chicago.

"VORWÄRTS," BERLINER VOLKSBLATT: Chef-Redakteur, Wilhelm Liebknecht. Daily. Berlin, 1876 to date.
Official organ of the social democratic party of Germany.

VORWÄRTS. [Socialist.] Weekly. New York, 1893 to date.
Central organ of the socialist labor party of North America.

LA VRAIE RÉPUBLIQUE. [Socialist.] Weekly. Paris.

DER WAHRE JACOB. Semi-monthly, comic socialistic paper. Stuttgart, 1878 to date.

INDEX.

A

Accident legislation needed, 318.
Activity of government not always socialistic, 26.
Abilities, exceptional, would not be appreciated under socialism, 237.
Adler, Georg, "Die Gründlagen der Karl-Marx'schen Kritik," 109.
Advertising, waste by, under competitive system, 122.
Agriculture not adapted to socialism, 219–221.
All-inclusiveness of socialism, 114.
American Federation of Labor, platform, 69–71.
Anarchy and socialism, 92, 372.
Aristotle cited, 138.
Attitude to be taken in approaching question of social reform, 260.
Austria, socialist movement in, 65, 66.
Aveling, Dr. Edward, on Karl Marx, 98.

B

Barry, Rev. Alfred, "Christianity and Socialism," 105.
Bebel, August, 35; works of, 99.
Belgium, socialist movement in, 64, 65.
Bellamy, Edward, 116, 147; definition of nationalism, 23; on dependent classes, 148; originator of nationalist movement in United States, 69; plan of distributing labor forces unsatisfactory, 248; "Looking Backward," 104.
Bibliography, 399–442.
Blanc, Louis, 57.
Booth, William, "In Darkest England," 253.
Brace, Charles Loring, work of, 260.
Brisbane, Albert, as a socialist, 36.
Brotherhood of man, not realized under competitive system, 147.
Browning, Elizabeth Barrett, 254.

C

Capital, effects of recent changes in management of, on distribution, 52, 53.
Caritative principle in distribution, 194.
Catholic writings on socialism, 106.
Chamberlain, Joseph, on improvement in the last half century, 258.
Character of leading socialists, 38.

Christianity and socialism, 42; social teachings of, 231.
Christian socialism, 89, 383; literature of, 104, 106, 427-430.
Church, the, as an educational institution, 326.
Civil service reform, need of, 346, 348.
Clarke, William, definition of socialism, 24; on moral earnestness of socialist, 145; *note.*
Classes to which socialists belong, 179.
College settlements, work of, 341, 342; *note.*
Combination supplanting competition, 226.
Communistic settlements, failure of, no test of socialism, 182; opposed by Fabian Society, 184.
Compensation, question of, 83.
Competition encourages inventions, 224; effect upon educational and charitable institutions, 228; evils of, 222; wastes of, 115-123, 269, 315; supplanted by combination, 225.
Compulsory education under socialism, 164.
Concentration of wealth in United States, 273, 275.
Conscience of public aroused by socialistic discussion, 166.
Constitutionalism, excessive development of, in United States, 345.
Co-operation, 339; and socialism, 92.
Copyrights, 294.
Cotton, effect of over-production of, 133.
Corruption of politics by monopolies, 282, 284.

Criminals, attitude toward Henry George, 40, 41; general political tendencies of, 40.
Crises abolished by socialism, 127; mitigated by proper management of governmental industries, 270.
Curtis, George William, part in socialist movement, 56.

D

Definition of socialism, 19; Bellamy's, 23; William Clarke's, 24; in Fabian Society's program, 24; Thos. Kirkup's, 28; Lafargue's, 25; Schäffle's, 20; by Social Democratic Federation of England, 25; A. Wagner's, 5, 21; Wallas's, 24; Westcott's, 4.
Demand and supply, difficulty of maintaining an equilibrium between, 245.
Disagreeable work under socialism, 131, 185, 187.
Dissatisfaction, concentration of, under socialism, 199.
Dishonest definitions of socialism, 7.
Distribution, difficulty of a just, under socialism, 233; in the family, 236; improved by socialization of monopolies, 271-275; strength of socialism as a scheme for, 140, 144; under socialism, 13.
Distributive justice, chief purpose of socialism, 14; what is it? 15; Baboeuf on, 15; St. Simonians on, 16; Louis Blanc on, 16.
Division of property not proposed by socialists, 37.
Dwellings, improved, 328.

INDEX. 445

E

Economic tyranny of present system, 207.
Educational institutions, effect of competition on, 222.
Education, importance of, at present time, 323.
Eight-hour day and socialism, 163.
Ely, R. T., "French and German Socialism," 107; "Labor Movement in America," 107.
Employers, choice of, under socialism, 211.
Employment offices, evils of private, 331; public, 331; in Ohio, 331, and *note*.
Employment, right to, 332; recognition of right to, in Cincinnati, 332, *note*.
Engels, Friedrich, 22, 34; works, 99.
England, programs of socialism in, 59, 60, 365-375.
Environment, importance of, 151, 153; and art, 138.
Erfurt program, 100; on evolution of socialism, 78; of 1891, 357.
Evolution of socialism, 176, 374; theory of socialism, 74, 81; Marx on, 74; Engels on, 74; Erfurt program on, 78; Fabian Society on, 80.
Experience of countries that have socialized natural monopolies, 288.

F

Fabian Society, 24; basis of, 363; essays quoted, 32; on evolution of socialism, 80; opposed to organization of communistic settlements, 184; work and writings, 102, 103, *notes*.

Factory legislation, boards of conciliation and arbitration. 318.
Family, distribution in, 236; effect of socialism on, 43, 47-49; effects of modern industrial organization on, 43-47.
Foreign commerce, difficulty of carrying on, under socialism, 218.
France, growth of socialism in, 61-64, 390-398; socialistic writers in, 101.
Fraternal societies, work of, 340.

G

Gas supply, wastes of, under competition, 120-121; a natural monopoly, 265.
Germany, progress of socialism in, 57, 58; see Erfurt program.
Göhre, Paul, effect of modern industrial organization on the family, 44-47.
Government, extension of functions not necessarily socialistic, 26; improved by socialistic agitation, 170; under socialism, 154-156.
Graham, William, "Socialism, New and Old," 107.
Great men, public *versus* private service as a means of producing, 155, *note*.
Greeley, Horace, his part in socialistic movement, 56.
Gronlund, Laurence, "Co-operative Commonwealth," 102.
Guesde, Jules, cited, 34, *note*.

H

Harrison, Frederic, on London municipal government, 171.

Heredity as a social force, 151, and *note*.
Holland, socialism in, 65.
Hospitals, effect of competition among, 223.
Hyndman, H. M., "Historical Basis of Socialism in England," 102.

I

Idle classes under socialism, 186.
Increase of productive power through inventions, 138, 139.
Individual effort should co-operate with public, 239.
Individual property not wholly abolished under socialism, 10.
Individuality *versus* individualism, 351.
Inequalities in needs not provided for under socialism, 234.
Inheritance tax, 310–313.
Industrial revolution, origin of socialism in, 50, 51.
Initiative and referendum, 344.
Instruments of production, but not all wealth, to be common property under socialism, 11.
Insurance, government, in Germany, 330; in New Zealand, 331; importance of, 330; under socialism, 164.
Inventions and discoveries, effect of, on industrial classes under competitive system, 128; utilization of, under socialism, 131; partially a social product, 295.
Interests of individuals and society not always identical under competition, 133.
Italy, socialist movement in, 66, 67.

K

Kirkup, Thos., definition of socialism, 23; works of, 104.

L

Labor, provisions of Erfurter program regarding, 361.
Labor forces, difficulty of a desirable distribution of, under socialism, 247, 249.
Labor value theory not essential to socialism, 177.
Lafargue, definition of socialism, 25; "Evolution of Property," 101.
Land not a natural monopoly, 300; policy of Savannah, Ga., 301; of New Zealand, 304; public ownership of, helpful in the solution of social problems; nationalization of, and socialism, 94.
Lassalle, Ferdinand, revives socialist movement, 57; works of, 101.
Laveleye, Emile de, "Socialism of To-day," 107.
Law and order leagues, 343.
Leaders, difficulty of securing good, under socialism, 235.
Legislation necessary to raise ethical plane of private business, 316.
Libraries, public, importance of, 325; in Massachusetts, 325; in New York, 326.
Loan shops, public, need of, 333; in France, Germany, and Switzerland, 333.
Loans, public, to individuals in New Zealand, 333.
London, socialism in, 59, 60.
Lloyd, H. D., quoted, 209.

M

Machinery, effects of, on production, 139.
Mallock, works of, 108.
Manifesto of the Joint Committee of Socialist Bodies (Eng.), 368.
Marx, Karl, 22; Aveling on, 98; founder of non-ethical socialism, 74, 259; writings of, 96–98.
Materialism and socialism, 175.
Menger, Anton, 22, *note*; 242, and *note*; works of, 100.
Meyer, Dr. Rudolf, works, 108.
Milk business, wastes of, under competitive system, 121.
Mill, J. S., 34, *note*; on classes in society, 136, and *note*.
Monetary reform, need of, 334.
Money under socialism, 247.
Monopoly, artificial, 293; *versus* business on a large scale, 216; classification of, 262; fiscal, 298; inevitableness of, not proved, 217; Socialization of, would abolish dependent monopolies, 279; alternative to, 291; effect on farmers, 281; on free speech, 282; on labor question, 280; on purification of politics, 282–285; simplify legislation, 287.
Moral results of competitive system, 81.
Morris, Wm., on socialism and art, 159.
Motives to economic activity under socialism, 221.

N

Nationalism, 87, 88, *note*.
Nationalists, declaration of principles, 380; in United States, 69.
Nationalization of land and socialism, 94.
Natural aristocracy needed in modern society, 240.
Natural monopolies, 215; characteristics of, 263; proof of existence of, 263–267.
New Zealand, taxation in, 304.

O

Objects to be accomplished by social reform, 256.
Optimism of socialists as to future, 188-194; as to rapidity of changes, 192; as to wealth creation, 189-191.

P

Payment for socialized monopolies, 289.
Paraguay, socialism in, 184.
Paternalism and socialism, 91.
Patents, 296; abuses in present laws relating to, 297.
Pessimism of socialists as to past and present, 194–196.
Philanthropy, private, should co-operate with public effort, 338.
Planlessness of competitive production, 124–127.
Platform of Central Labor Union, Cleveland, O., 385.
Population, law of, and socialism, 242.
Portugal, socialistic movement in, 67.
Possibility of reform, 257.
Postal service superior to service of express companies, 200.
Private property in income retained under socialism, 16; social side of, 196.

Problem of the twentieth man, 316.
Production, strength of socialism as a scheme for, 138.
Productive forces, utilization of, by socialization of monopoly, 268.
Program of the Social-Democratic Federation, 365.
Progress toward social reform hindered by designing men, 205.
Professional men, effect of socialistic distribution on, 141, 142.
Proportional representation, 346.
Public *versus* private expenditures, 142-144.

R

Rae, "Contemporary Socialism," 107.
Railways, failures of, 270, *note;* natural monopolies, 266; wastes of, under competitive system, 117-119.
Referendum and initiative, 344.
Regulation of private property, 309; of inheritance, 310-313.
Restriction of production under competitive system, 133-135, 150.
Rodbertus-Jagetzow, '22; works of, 100.
Russia, socialistic movement in, 67.

S

Salaries, effect of socialism on, 238, and *note.*
Sanitary inspection, 319.
Savannah, Ga., land policy in, 302.

Scandinavian countries, socialist movement in, 65.
Services of capitalists to society, 194.
Schäffle, works of, 108.
Shaftesbury, Earl of, on moral improvement of the working people, 327, *note;* work of, 257.
Simplification of government by socialism, 162.
Sismondi on religion of criminals, 40.
Single tax and socialism, 94.
Social Democratic Federation of England, 103.
Social Democratic Party of Germany, growth of, 58, 387.
Social esteem as a motive to human exertion, 227-230.
Socialistic Labor Party of the United States, 68; platform, 376.
Social reform and socialism, 95.
Social side of economic life emphasized by socialistic discussion, 167.
Social side of man slow to develop, 231.
Social teachings of Christianity, 221.
Society of Christian Socialists, 382.
Spain, socialist movement in, 67.
Sprague, F. M., 105.
Stages of socialism, 55.
State, attitude of socialists toward, 29-33; centralized, not desired by socialists, 30; Socialists would reduce functions of, to a minimum, 33-35.
State socialism, nature of, 85.
Stephens, Sir James Fitzjames, 108.

Stewardship idea of private property, 307–309.
Stewart, Ethelbert, on the effect of modern industry on the family, 43, 44.
Sunday legislation, need of, 320.
Sweat-shops, legislation regarding, 320, and *note*.
Switzerland, socialist movement in, 66.

T

Tariff reform, comparative importance of, 334.
Taxation under socialism, 163.
Telegraph business a natural monopoly, 265.
Thrift, promotion of, through postal savings banks, 329.
Tyranny of majorities under socialism, 212, 214.

U

Unemployed, problem of, under socialism, 12.
United States, socialist movement in, 68–71.

V

Votes of government employees, 286.

W

Wages, probable effect of socialism on, 237–239.
Wagner, Dr. Adolph, definition of socialism, 5, 21; works of, 109.
Wallas, Graham, definition of socialism, 24.
Wastes of competitive system, 115–123; railways, 117–119; telegraph, 119; gas-works, 120; milk business, 121.
Wealth, concentration of, in United States, 273; diagram of, 274.
Wealth creation, optimism of socialists concerning, 189–192.
Westcott, Dr., definition of socialism, 4; on socialism and art, 160.
Wolf, Julius, 109.
Women and children, legislation concerning, 321.
Woods, Miss Katharine Pearson, 104.

LABOR MOVEMENT IN AMERICA.

By RICHARD T. ELY, Ph.D., LL.D., author of "Problems of To-Day," "Social Aspects of Christianity," "Socialism and Social Reform," etc. 12mo. Price, $1.50.

"*The best work on the subject.*" — *North-Western Presbyterian.*

"The review of the labor organizations in this country from the year 1800 to 1886 is a masterly presentation, and will justify even a poor man buying the book." — *The Beacon.*

"Every intelligent reader in the country will find the book most useful." — *St. Louis Republican.*

"No one who wishes to understand the problems of labor and capital can afford to be without Professor Ely's work." — *Rochester Chronicle.*

"Professor Ely's volume deserves the careful study of manufacturers and employers of labor especially. It deals with well-authenticated facts more than theories — a remarkable and timely book." — *Boston Traveller.*

"Heartily commended to the careful attention of all concerned in the labor question, whether employers or employed." — *Cleveland Plaindealer.*

SOCIAL ASPECTS OF CHRISTIANITY.

By RICHARD T. ELY, Ph.D., LL.D., author of "Labor Movement in America," "Problems of To-Day," "Socialism and Social Reform," etc. A new and revised edition, with additional chapter, entitled "The Social Crisis and the Church's Opportunity." 12mo. 90 cts.

Professor Ely has no respect for shams. He shows what Christian socialism is, and how wide the gulf is between the professed Christianity of many churches and the Christianity of the gospel.

The book has been in use for some time by a number of advanced Sunday-school classes engaged in the study of the deeper questions of religion and life.

"Full of practicality, helpful suggestiveness, and pregnant with ideas on the social problems of to-day. No better book could be put into the hands of a beginner in this department. There is no book in its capacity so calculated by its focal compass, direct appeal, correct judgments, and impartial statements, to convey to the mind of the reader the righteousness of the plea for the study and practice of sociology, and the adaptability of the gospel of Jesus Christ to meet its highest demands, and lead it to its best attainment." — *Christian Nation.*

"Professor Ely has well earned the right to speak his whole mind, and it behooves all right-minded people to know what he says." — *Public Opinion.*

"Many a Christian professor would gain important, and perhaps novel, suggestions from his pages about the true uses of wealth, opportunities, etc." — *Congregationalist.*

"To the conscientious Christian man they will be profitable; to the Christian preacher they are most suggestive." — *Churchman.*

For sale by all booksellers, or sent postpaid by the publishers upon receipt of price.

THOMAS Y. CROWELL & CO., PUBLISHERS,

NEW YORK: 46 E. 14th St.   BOSTON: 100 Purchase St.

PROBLEMS OF TO-DAY.

A discussion of protective tariffs, taxation, and monopolies, by RICHARD T. ELY, Ph.D., LL.D., author of "Labor Movement in America," "Taxation in American States and Cities," etc. Revised and enlarged edition. 12mo. $1.50.

This work appeals to all classes and conditions of men, "Republicans," "Democrats," "Independents," Legislators, Private Citizens, Merchant Princes, Mechanics, and Day Laborers. All are alike interested in the question of a protective tariff, the nature of monopolies, the welfare of labor, the national surplus, the morality of subsidies, etc.

"Written in an impartial spirit." — *Commercial Bulletin.*
"Strong and vigorous." — *Age of Steel.*
"Consummate skill and the most cogent reasoning." — *Detroit Free Press.*
"What he writes is always worth reading." — *Baltimore Sun.*
"Which every citizen who has the best interests of the country at heart should read." — *Western Christian Advocate.*

TAXATION IN AMERICAN STATES AND CITIES.

By RICHARD T. ELY, Ph.D., LL.D., author of "Labor Movement in America," etc. 12mo. $1.75.

Professor Ely has written the first broad and critical treatise upon the manifold systems of taxation that obtain in our chief cities and States. It is a work of immense research, and presents in a masterly manner the whole complex subject of taxation, as well as the inconsistencies which prevail in parts of this country. The volume is made especially valuable by numerous and carefully compiled tables showing the various methods of levying taxes, and the comparative results in every State of the Union; and while it will not fail to interest every tax-payer, it will appeal especially to tax-assessors, lawyers, legislators, and all engaged in public affairs.

"Full of interesting facts." — *Rochester Morning Herald.*
"We have found Professor Ely's volume one of surprising interest." — *Literary World.*
"His reasonings are well fortified throughout, and no student of political economy can afford to disregard them. . . . It must have a strong and useful influence." — *Congregationalist.*
"We have not for a long time read a book containing more really valuable information. . . . Should be in the hands of every thoughtful man." — *Boston Daily Traveller.*
"All good citizens ought to get this admirable work, and study it from the first to the last page." — *Real Estate Record and Guide.*

For sale by all booksellers, or sent postpaid by the publishers upon receipt of price.

THOMAS Y. CROWELL & CO., PUBLISHERS,
NEW YORK: 46 E. 14th St.   BOSTON: 100 Purchase St.

THE ENGLISHMAN AT HOME:
His Responsibilities and Privileges.

By EDWARD PORRITT, formerly London Editor of the Manchester Examiner.

The author's aim has been to make the book not only of use and interest to students of civics and of English history and contemporary politics, but also of value to American visitors to England, and to readers of English news in the American press. His accuracy and carefulness of statement may be subjected to the most critical test. The style is good and entertaining. The book cannot fail to be a welcome addition to every library. One vol. Cloth, 12mo, xiv.+379 pp. Appendices, index. $1.75.

"No adequate book has been easily procurable which briefly and simply has told how the Englishman is governed, and what are his responsibilities and privileges. Mr. Porritt has endeavored to supply this sort of book, and has succeeded admirably. He has told about everything an American needs to know, and has told it according to a method which leaves hardly anything to be desired." — *New York Times.*

"A valuable book, and one that ought to be read by all who seek to be well informed." — *Chicago Times.*

"A highly welcome volume." — *Philadelphia Press.*

"Of rare interest and great value." — *Boston Advertiser.*

"A better account of the working institutions of England than is elsewhere accessible to American readers." — *Boston Herald.*

"A very useful and instructive book." — *The Beacon.*

PHILANTHROPY AND SOCIAL PROGRESS.

Seven Essays delivered before the School of Applied Ethics at Plymouth, Mass., by Miss Jane Addams, Father J. O. S. Huntington, Robert A. Woods, Prof. Franklin A. Giddings, and Bernard Bosanquet, with an introduction by Prof. H. C. Adams of Michigan University. Cloth, 12mo. xi.+268 pp. $1.50.

"Specialization in modern life has decreased the dependencies of men and classes to such a degree that interdependence is a thing which is *felt*, rather than an idea to be *reasoned about*. Society is coming to be, in fact, organic; and the claim of a perfect organism, that all parts should find harmony of life in the recognition of a common aim, shows itself in the attitude which large numbers of persons are assuming before the vexed problems of the day. And I doubt not that many who find this book attractive will do so because it expresses in vigorous and decided language a feeling of which most of us are at least dimly conscious. *It is a privilege to introduce such a book to the reading public.*" — FROM THE INTRODUCTION.

"These essays contain the expressions of no mere theorists, but are the calm statements of practical philanthropists, who outline their experiences and successes in a way to carry power and conviction." — *Boston Home Journal.*

"The readers of these lectures will be informed, startled, piqued, aroused, and put to thinking." — *Altruistic Review.*

"The book is, in fact, a sort of text-book in philanthropy, and no one should think of engaging in charitable work or lending aid to any charitable cause, without first becoming thoroughly familiar with its contents." — *The Beacon.*

"The topics are live ones, and discussed with genuine earnestness and spirit." — *Minneapolis Tribune.*

"The whole book is a noble contribution to a cause which must prevail." — *The Churchman.*

"One of the most valuable volumes from the standpoint of the student of social economics." — *Boston Traveller.*

For sale by all booksellers, or sent postpaid by the publishers on receipt of price.

THOMAS Y. CROWELL & CO., PUBLISHERS,
NEW YORK: 46 East 14th St.   BOSTON: 100 Purchase St.

THE INDEPENDENT TREASURY SYSTEM OF THE UNITED STATES.

By DAVID KINLEY, of the University of Wisconsin. Cloth, 12mo. viii.+325 pp. Appendix, index. $1.50.

An historical and critical examination of this important institution. A work which will prove valuable to bankers and financiers generally, as well as to scholars. This is the initial volume of a series to be entitled, " *Library of Economics and Politics*," under the editorial control of Prof. Richard T. Ely, Ph.D., LL.D., Professor of Political Economy and Director of the School of Economics, Political Science, and History at the University of Wisconsin. It is designed to include in the series only such volumes as deal with timely topics in a fresh, interesting, and instructive manner; and the standard of excellence maintained will, it is hoped, give to this series a leading rank in this country and abroad.

" His treatment of the influences of the independent treasury upon the finances of the country is admitted by the best authorities in the country to be eminently sound."—*Wisconsin State Journal.*

" A thoughtful treatise, and of unquestionable value." — *Public Opinion.*
" A solid scholarly work * * * of great interest." — *Review of Reviews.*
" A valuable and delightfully readable history." — *Boston Traveller.*
" A valuable and dispassionate discussion." — *Philadelphia Ledger.*
" A thorough-going, impartial, and sensible treatise." — *Congregationalist.*
" A book of decided interest." — *The Dial.*
" In his treatment of the whole subject from first to last * * * he maintains the judicial spirit." — *Commercial Gazette.*

REPUDIATION OF STATE DEBTS IN THE UNITED STATES.

By WILLIAM A. SCOTT, Ph.D., Assistant Professor of Political Economy in the University of Wisconsin. (Volume II. in the Library of Economics and Politics.) 12mo, cloth. vii.+325 pp. Appendices, index. $1.50.

" Will prove an instrument of education in the social and economic necessities of our people." — *Philadelphia Ledger.*
" Dr. Scott's book should find its way to the library of every thoughtful business man in this country." — *New York Herald.*
" His temperate, calm, and unprejudiced tone will appeal to every candid reader." — *Toledo Blade.*
" Indispensable to every public library and every collection of books of reference." — *Christian Intelligence.*
" Of unusual value to students of finance, for the reason that it contains a great deal of information regarding those unfortunate epidemics in the history of some of our States, which it is extremely difficult to obtain elsewhere." — *Boston Journal.*
" One of the most important contributions of the day to financial history." — *Herald and Presbyter.*
" The manual is one of great value, and is done carefully and with discreet impartiality." — *The Independent.*

For sale by all booksellers, or sent postpaid by the publishers upon receipt of price.

THOMAS Y. CROWELL & CO., PUBLISHERS.
NEW YORK: 46 East 14th St.   BOSTON: 100 Purchase St.

AMERICAN CHARITIES. A Study in Philanthropy and Economics.

By AMOS G. WARNER, Ph.D., Professor of Economics in the Leland Stanford Jr. University. (Vol. IV. in Crowell's Library of Economics and Politics.) 12mo, cloth, $1.75.

Most students of pauperism have erred in trying to find one chief cause for such conditions: one claims that it is over population; another, that it is rent; still another, that it is low wages. Professor Warner recognizes a whole nexus of causes: heredity, environment, social conditions, intoxicants, selfishness, sickness, all almost inextricably interwoven. He traces the origin of philanthropy in the past, and shows how widespread, even among heathen nations, was the idea of assisting the unfortunate. He next takes up the various theories of the cause of poverty, and criticizes them, showing the extent of their justification. He then analyzes the various methods of relief, and shows, by carefully prepared tables, what influences tend toward deepening degradation, and what, on the other side, tend to elevate and improve. There is no phase of poor relief, or of pauperism, that he does not throw light upon.

His tone is optimistic and wholesome. It would be hard to pick flaws in his arguments, supported as they are by concrete examples selected from a wide range of reading and experience.

The book fills a needed place, and will be *indispensable for all students* of the fine art of charity. It ought to work a revolution, and do a vast deal toward overcoming the pall of despair that settles thick over our great cities. Its practical suggestions would save millions of dollars now wasted in this country by reason of preventable crime, wretchedness, and disease. In this respect alone it is an epoch-making book, and may be justly regarded as the most important treatise that has been published on the subject in this century. *As a text-book* it cannot fail to be welcomed by every teacher in political economy and social science. Clear, logical, cogent, complete, and good-tempered, it is a model manual on a subject that is taking its place as one of the most important of modern times. The numerous calls for this book from professors of political economy all over the land indicate that it will be largely used in our colleges and universities.

Among other institutions the book will be used by the Leland Stanford Jr. University, the University of Wisconsin, the University of Indiana, and the University of Cincinnati.

For sale by all booksellers, or sent postpaid by the publishers upon receipt of price.

THOMAS Y. CROWELL & CO., PUBLISHERS,
NEW YORK: 46 E. 14th St.   BOSTON: 100 Purchase St.

LIBRARY OF ECONOMICS and POLITICS.

MESSRS. T. Y. CROWELL & CO. take pleasure in announcing that they have completed arrangements for a series of volumes dealing with timely topics in a fresh, interesting, and instructive manner. The series is entitled "Library of Economics and Politics," and is under the editorial control of Prof. **Richard T. Ely, Ph.D., LL.D.**, Professor of Political Economy, and Director of the School of Economics, Political Science and History at the University of Wisconsin.

It is proposed to issue volumes at irregular intervals, and to supply only the best literature. A standard of excellence will be maintained which it is hoped will give to this series a leading rank in this country and abroad.

The following volumes are now ready: —

"THE INDEPENDENT TREASURY SYSTEM OF THE UNITED STATES."

An historical and critical examination of this important institution; a work which is most valuable to bankers and financiers generally, as well as to scholars. The author of this volume is **Prof. David Kinley, Ph.D.**, Professor of Economics in the University of Illinois. 12mo, $1.50.

"REPUDIATION OF STATE DEBTS IN THE UNITED STATES."

By **William A. Scott, Ph.D.**, Associate Professor of Political Economy in the University of Wisconsin. This is a work which deals with one of the most important phases of American finance. Perhaps there is no field of financial investigation in the United States which has been so neglected. The work is of practical importance to all those who are concerned with investments, as well as to scholars interested in our financial history and institutions. 12mo, $1.50.

"SOCIALISM AND SOCIAL REFORM."

By **Prof. Richard T. Ely**, Editor of the Series. The work is divided into four parts: Part One treating of the Nature of Socialism; Part Two, of the Strength of Socialism; Part Three, of the Weakness of Socialism; and Part Four, the Golden Mean, or Practicable Social Reform.

Numerous appendices and an exhaustive bibliography add to the value of the work. The author's views are presented in a clear, candid, and fearless manner, and furnish one of the best discussions of this subject. 12mo, $1.50.

"AMERICAN CHARITIES: A STUDY IN PHILANTHROPY AND ECONOMICS."

By **Amos G. Warner, Ph.D.**, Professor of Economics in the Leland-Stanford Jr. University, and late Superintendent of Charities for the District of Columbia. This work will be the first exhaustive treatment of the subject. It is a careful presentation of theory and of practical experience, making it an indispensable handbook for all those who are theoretically and practically interested in charities. 12mo, $1.75.

"HULL HOUSE MAPS AND PAPERS,"

Is the fifth volume in the series, and will furnish an account of the methods of work at this celebrated social settlement in Chicago.

It will also include a series of carefully prepared papers by specialists on topics of vital interest to students in sociology.

One of the most valuable features of this book will be a series of colored maps or charts showing the nationality and wages of all families in a considerable section of Chicago, based upon a most careful investigation.

Albert Shaw, Ph.D., American Editor of the *Review of Reviews*, is engaged in the preparation of a work suitable for the series, the title of which will be announced subsequently. The publishers, however, venture to assure the public that the work by Dr. Shaw will be one of the most popular and useful volumes in the series.

THOMAS Y. CROWELL & CO., NEW YORK and BOSTON.

www.ingramcontent.com/pod-product-compliance
Lightning Source LLC
Chambersburg PA
CBHW022107300426
44117CB00007B/620